WALTER GREENWOOD'S
LOVE ON THE DOLE:
NOVEL, PLAY, FILM

D1338998

LIVERPOOL ENGLISH TEXTS AND STUDIES 71

WALTER GREENWOOD'S
LOVE ON THE DOLE:
NOVEL, PLAY, FILM

CHRIS HOPKINS

LIVERPOOL UNIVERSITY PRESS

First published 2018 by
Liverpool University Press
4 Cambridge Street
Liverpool
L69 7ZU

British Library Cataloguing-in-Publication data

A British Library CIP record is available

ISBN 978-1-78694-114-5 cased
ISBN 978-1-78694-179-4 paperback

Typeset by Carnegie Book Production, Lancaster
Printed and bound by TJ International Ltd, Padstow, Cornwall, PL28 8RW

To Lisa and Sam Hopkins, as usual.

But also in memory of my parents:

*Marjorie June Hopkins (née Thake), 1927–1987,
and Christopher Douglas Hopkins, 1924–2007.*

Contents

Acknowledgements

I have many helpful people and institutions to acknowledge and thank. First of all, I must thank Anthony Cond of Liverpool University Press, who commissioned me to write a book on *Love on the Dole*. I am sorry it has taken so long to complete (a decade, in fact), but I hope it has been worth the wait – your patience (even among academic publishers) has been extraordinary. Secondly, I should thank Ian Johnston, archivist at Salford University, for all his help over a long period with my work at the Walter Greenwood Collection: I became a regular visitor and it was largely the richness of these holdings that made the book more complex than I originally envisaged. Then I must thank all the professors and readers in the Humanities Research Centre's English Research Planning Group, who twice agreed that I could be allocated research leave to progress the book (and in Matt Steggle's case also took over as Head of the HRC while I was away writing). Thank you also to colleagues (Professors Steven Earnshaw, Lisa Hopkins, Matthew Steggle, and Dr Mary Grover) who kindly read a draft and made many helpful suggestions for improvement, which I mainly followed. Many thanks to my film colleague Dr Sheldon Hall for reading my work on film and helping me to develop a degree of understanding in that fascinating field. I am grateful too to the reviewers appointed by Liverpool University Press to report on the original plan and on a near final draft: I have incorporated most of your suggested improvements, though in a few instances lack of space means that I will need to follow up interesting suggestions as separate future projects. Thank you to four colleagues in History: Dr Alison Twells and Dr Nicola Verdon suggested where to look for a history of the 'perm', Professor Kevin McDermott sought information on the elusive Russian translation of *Love on the Dole*, and Professor Tony Taylor kindly visited archives on the Isle of Man and reported back. Thank you to the organisers (Dr

Mary Grover and Dr Kate Macdonald) of the 'Masculine Middlebrow' conference at the Institute of English Studies, Senate House, University of London for letting me give my paper 'After *Love on the Dole*: Walter Greenwood as Middlebrow Writer' in 2009, and thank you too to Dr Erica Brown at Hallam and Professor Faye Hammill at Strathclyde for much fruitful discussion of matters middlebrow under the aegis of the AHRC-funded Middlebrow Network: http://www.middlebrow-network.com/. Thank you to colleagues at Salford University's English department, who invited me to give a paper on Greenwood's 1944 novel *Something in My Heart* in 2011, and to Ben Harker (now at the University of Manchester) for subsequently suggesting I submit an article on Greenwood to *Keywords – A Journal of Cultural Materialism*. Thank you also to colleagues in Hull University's English Department who invited me to talk about 'Hanky Park (P)Re-visited: Walter Greenwood and Arthur Wragg's Prequel and Sequel to *Love on the Dole* (1933): *The Cleft Stick* (1937)' in 2016. Thank you to colleagues at Sheffield Hallam who gave me opportunities to run ideas past them as papers, including 'Word and Image in Walter Greenwood and Arthur Wragg's *The Cleft Stick* (1937)' (Development and Society Research Conference, 2014) and 'Walter Greenwood's *Love on the Dole* (1933, 1935, 1941): From Novel to Play to Film' (at the Sheffield Hallam Film, Theatre and Television Research Network in 2016). Thank you to Professor Tony Collins, a sports historian at De Montfort University, both for his work on Walter Greenwood's first film story, *Where's George?* (1935), and for sending me copies of the associated primary sources he had discovered. Many thanks to members of the Sheffield-based *Reading 1900–1950* Reading Group, who kindly devoted June to July 2016 to reading most of Greenwood's fiction, including a number of novels that had, I think, rarely been read in recent times, and who shared their views of how well his writing worked for contemporary readers (some reviews are at https://reading19001950.wordpress.com/tag/walter-greenwood/). Thank you to the Reading Sheffield community group (http://www.readingsheffield.co.uk/) for seeking (and finding) traces of *Love on the Dole* in their work on personal reading histories and the history of Sheffield Libraries. Thank you too to Jenny Howard at Liverpool University Press who oversaw the final production process, and to Dr Richard Wood for his meticulous work on the index. And thank you to all those Humanities colleagues who have listened to me talking about Walter Greenwood for most of a decade – I hope they will now be reassured that there really was a book behind the obsession.

A number of cultural institutions and their archivists and other experts have been wonderfully responsive and have helped fill many gaps in Walter Greenwood's story. I am very grateful to Trisha Hayes at the BBC Written archives at Caversham, to Jonny Davies at the BFI Reuben Library, to Catherine Anderson at the British Board of Film Classification and to Robin Bray at ITV Programme Sales for their assistance. Thanks also to Jane Salter, Civil Registrar of the Isle of Man, for helping me to obtain a certified copy of Greenwood's death certificate, and to the Army Personnel Centre (Support Division, Historical Disclosures) for a copy of his Army Service Record. As always, colleagues in the Document Supply service at Adsetts Library at Sheffield Hallam have been hugely helpful in obtaining obscure books and articles (and, as it turned out, a completely forgotten Greenwood short story). Many thanks too to Simon Baker (at the Institute of Historical Research, University of London) and to the incomparable film critic Geoff Brown for helpful and invigorating email discussion about the date of the final caption to the film of *Love on the Dole*. I was very pleased to be commissioned by Mariantha Makra to write an introductory essay for the BFI re-release on DVD/Blu-Ray of John Baxter's film of *Love on the Dole* in 2016, which helped me develop my thinking about the movie. Thank you to Tony Flynn at Salford Online (http://salfordonline.com/) for talking to me about Hanky Park, as well as for his books on Salford's history, and to Mike Sweeney at BBC Radio Manchester for his interest in *Love on the Dole*. And thank you to the Octagon Theatre in Bolton and the cast for their excellent production of the play of *Love on the Dole* in 2010, directed by David Thacker. It was the first time I had seen the play and it fully lived up to my expectations. As it happened, I went to a matinee and had the pleasure of sharing the experience with an audience of a certain average age, a number of whom, interval conversations suggested, had read the novel, seen the play before, and also knew the film: an ideal audience from my point of view.

Though the papers preserved in hard copy archives are irreplaceable and priceless, and have contributed enormously to this study, I should also observe that databases/digital archives (especially of newspapers) and the internet have made certain kinds of search and discovery possible that once would not have been viable. In addition to the UK and US newspaper and other databases subscribed to by Sheffield Hallam University Library, the free and open access newspaper databases hosted by the National Library of Australia and the National Library of New Zealand are particular models of excellence. So too, for extraordinary access to regional newspapers, is the British Library National Newspaper Archive, which became available towards the end of my work on this book. The BFI and the British Council Films websites have also been invaluable (http://www.bfi.org.uk/; http://film.britishcouncil.org/british-council-film-collection). Many other 'official' websites were also very useful, such as the Australian War memorial site (https://www.awm.gov.au/findingaids/special/Souvenirs/ww2ctp.xml) and the BBC Genome Project (http://genome.ch.bbc.co.uk/). Equally I should mention as more than useful for preserving important knowledge 'fan-sites' such as, for example, the Saturday Night Theatre tribute site (http://www.saturday-night-theatre.co.uk/) and the Television Heaven website (http://www.televisionheaven.co.uk/love_on_the_dole.htm). Finally, I am grateful to Dr Judy Gielgud and the BBC Written Archive for permission to quote from an internal BBC memo by Val Gielgud, and to James Brooks and the V&A Archives for permission to quote from an unpublished letter (V&A, Archive of Art and Design, AAD/2004/8) from Arthur Wragg to Sir Stafford Cripps (and many thanks to the V&A Archivist Alexia Kirk for her assistance). I have made every effort to trace a current copyright holder for Greenwood's published and unpublished writings, but without success: if anyone has information please contact me. I hope that the book will help further the study of Walter Greenwood's work, reputation, impact, and achievement, that it will stimulate interest in working-class writing, and that it will draw attention to the continuing relevance to modern Britain of the cultural histories of the 1930s, 1940s, and 1950s.

Chris Hopkins
Sheffield Hallam University

Introduction

Love on the Dole:
Significance, Context, History

I. The Significance of *Love on the Dole*

It would be interesting a hundred years hence to hear what students of twentieth-century England have to say about such a book as *Love on the Dole*.[1]

Love on the Dole is the story of the Hardcastle family and their neighbours in a specific and poor part of Salford. Mr Hardcastle is a miner and Mrs Hardcastle a housewife; their son Harry works first at a pawnshop and is then an apprentice engineer, while their daughter Sally works at a textile mill. Neighbours include the qualified engineer Larry Meath and a group of older women who both help and exploit for their own gain the other inhabitants of Hanky Park. The characters represent a working-class economy that is always fragile, and which is then further fractured by the consequences of the Depression after 1929.

Love on the Dole has a significant and substantial place in British cultural history, not least because it quickly became, and has remained, an iconic 1930s text, *the* text to turn to to illustrate or analyse the conditions of British working-class life and the terrible impact of the Depression on the lives of individuals as well as whole towns and cities. A. J. P. Taylor refers to the novel precisely in these kind of terms in

---

1 Review by Mrs D. L. Murray, also known as Leonora Eyles, in the *Times Literary Supplement*, 29 June 1933.

his widely read 1965 book *English History 1914–1945*: 'Unemployment became ... a way of life, commemorated in *Love on the Dole* by Walter Greenwood, one of the few genuinely "proletarian" novels written in English.'[2] In a 1982 essay Ramon Lopez Ortega observed that the novel had acquired 'the status of a trustworthy documentary of the decade' and that 'historians like A.J.P Taylor and Arthur Marwick in fact used it as such'.[3] Indeed, as this book will argue, the importance and influence of Greenwood's text has not been over-estimated, but on the contrary considerably under-estimated through various acts of cultural forgetfulness and neglect.

Strictly speaking, the title used above – *Love on the Dole* – and the label 'the text' are both concealing something that has contributed to the work's persistence in cultural memory. It is, of course, not a single text but at least a triple one: novel, play and film (it also had a considerable radio footprint). Not only did these three versions enlarge the story's readership and widen the social classes making up its audience, but they also play a part in why it is remembered, and perhaps in why you are reading this book, for this triple-medium *Love on the Dole* is widely studied both inside and outside the UK in university history, literature, film, and (where they still exist) extra-mural departments, and has had a sustained degree of wider readership/viewership too. Some brief reference to the work's reception in the 1930s and since – something which subsequent chapters will develop in more detail – helps make clearer some of the ways in which it achieved such status.

Love on the Dole became the best-known novel of working-class life published during the 1930s. It was praised in newspaper reviews across the spectrum of political affiliations. 'We passionately desire this novel to be read', said the *Manchester Guardian*.[4] Later *The Times* quoted Sir Herbert Samuel's plea that the entire House of Commons should ensure they had seen the stage version to enhance their understanding of what unemployment figures actually meant:

> I wonder whether hon. Members have seen a play which is now being performed in London, called, 'Love on the Dole.' If not, I would urge them

---

2 (Harmondsworth: Penguin, 1970 edition), p. 436. Originally written for the *Oxford History of England* in 1965.

3 'The Language of the Working-Class Novel', in *The Socialist Novel in Britain*, ed. Gustav Klaus (Brighton: Harvester, 1982), pp. 122–44, p. 128.

4 30 June 1933.

to see it. That play paints in very poignant fashion the position of those 400,000 families who are in the state which I have just described.[5]

A journalist records that 'a copy of Hansard was posted up outside the [Garrick] theatre', constituting 'an unprecedented advertisement'.[6] It seems likely that Ramsay MacDonald himself had read the novel, for it is recorded as being among sixty of his books that he donated to the 'Million Books for the Unemployed Scheme' in January 1934.[7]

The novel sold well too, with thirteen imprints, reprintings and a cheap edition between first publication in 1933 and the beginning of the war in 1940. One local newspaper (the Sheffield-based *Daily Independent*) even turned the whole novel into a (slightly abridged) serial for its readers, expecting them to be gripped by daily installments which ran from 18 April 1935 to their conclusion on 21 June 1935.[8] The West Riding County Council's 11th Annual Library Report named Greenwood's novel as one of the most borrowed fiction works.[9] It was also translated into a number of languages (French, Hebrew, and Czech – the latter with a photomontage dust wrapper by the designer Toyen) during the 1930s (and also into Russian, probably in the 1940s), and there was a US edition published by Doubleday, Doran and company in 1934.[10] The stage version, co-written with Ronald Gow, had its first night at the Manchester Repertory Theatre

---

5 Hansard, Parliamentary Debates, House of Commons, 5th Series, Vol 298, Col 1665, 4/3/1935 – cited by Andy Croft in *Red Letter Days: British Fiction in the 1930s* (London: Lawrence and Wishart, 1990), p. 108 and footnote 8, p. 119.

6 Reported in the (Sheffield) *Daily Independent* 12 March 1934 by 'Big Ben' in the 'Talk of London' column, p. 6.

7 Reported in the (Sheffield) *Daily Independent* 13 January 1934, p. 6.

8 The series is available via the British Library National Newspaper Archive.

9 Reported in the (Sheffield) *Daily Independent* 28 October 1935, p. 3.

10 Information from Paul. W. Salmon's essay on Walter Greenwood in George M. Johnson (ed.), *Dictionary of Literary Biography Vol. 191: British Novelists Between the Wars* (Detroit, Michigan: Gale Research, 1998), pp. 132 and 134; and on the Russian translation from Isaiah Berlin's *Personal Impressions* (London: Hogarth Press 1980; Kindle edition, location 4237), where he reports that while working in the USSR in 1945–46 he was asked about 'modern writers' such as Walter Greenwood and records that *Love on the Dole* was widely known, having been published in a 'large edition' (however, he had not himself read the novel nor heard of its author). The Czech edition of 1937, with its photomontage showing a worker dominated by two large black buildings, is included in the online resources of the Chicago Institute of Art: <http://www.artic.edu/aic/resources/resource/3102?search_id=1&index=0>.

in February 1934 before moving to the Garrick Theatre in London. Some 391 London performances followed, making the reputation of the actress Wendy Hiller, who played Sally Hardcastle, as well bringing the whole cast to an admiring public attention (I have a Garrick programme dated by its owner 31 January 1935 and carefully inscribed 'A very important play very well acted').[11] A national tour then began in 1935, which was so successful that it soon became a two-company tour, with a 'Blue' and 'Red' company performing simultaneously in different towns and cities. The actors' professional newspaper, *The Stage*, had an invaluable weekly 'on tour' column that shows the geographical reach of these two companies. During 1936 alone their venues (normally for a week of performances) included places such as Barrow, Birmingham, Brighton, Brixton, Cambridge, Cardiff, Douglas (Isle of Man), Eastbourne, East Ham, Edinburgh, Finsbury Park, Folkestone, Gateshead, Hackney, Keighley, Leeds, Lewisham, Liverpool, Luton, Manchester, New Cross, Penge, Plymouth, Poplar, Rotherham, Scarborough, Sunderland, Swansea, Walthamstow, and Woolwich. Some theatres were visited twice, suggesting sustained good audience numbers – thus Brighton hosted the play in May and then again in August, and Brixton also had two performances, one in March and in May. Something that has been overlooked in discussions (including Constantine's seminal article), which often assume a middle-class theatre audience, is that quite a few performances were not in 'straight' theatres but in 'variety' theatres, usually the home of more popular entertainments, which probably broadened the social class of the audience (for example, there were performances at the Finsbury Park Empire, the Hackney Empire, the Liverpool Empire, the Manchester Hippodrome, and, in February 1937, the Salford Hippodrome – which the play is said to have visited four times by June 1939, when it was still reported as 'attracting crowds').[12] Indeed, a neglected account by

11 Author's collection.
12 The list of venues given here is not exhaustive, but all the evidence can be found in the issues of *The Stage* in its 'On Tour' feature; information referred to here is from the 1936 issues for 9/1, 27/2, 5/3, 16/4, 11/5, 25/5, 11/6, 18/6, 16/7, 13/8, 20/8, and 10/9. Accessed via the *Entertainment Industry Magazine Archive* (online: ProQuest <http://www.proquest.com/products-services/eima.html> accessed 15 May 2016). The four visits of the play to Salford are referred to in *The Stage*, 29 June 1939, p. 2. The titles 'Empire' or 'Hippodrome' generally indicated venues offering a range of popular entertainments, often including 'variety' acts, such as singers, comic and serious, acrobats and comedians, though such theatres might also put on

Ronald Gow of early productions suggests that audiences at many venues (he refers to 'Salford, Sheffield, Birmingham, Wigan and all the other Northern cotton and pottery towns') were not used to 'straight' theatre, or even to live performance at all:

> Many of our audiences were persons seeing a real flesh and blood play for the first time in their lives. I confess I have never seen nor heard audiences more unsophisticated. They laughed at the wrong places … . But gradually … our audiences realised that it was themselves they were seeing upon the stage, and that *Love on the Dole* was a slice of life – their own life. As one local critic put it, the cinema had so accustomed these provincial people to stories of trivial or superficial people that [it] came to them as something of a shock when they discovered that a real and vital problem could be presented on the stage.[13]

Of course, Gow has his own arguments to make through his interpretation of audience response (for example, the allegedly inferior fare offered by cinema as opposed to theatre), but the account does suggest a broader audience for the play – and also records that Greenwood and Gow were pleased with this particular kind of success. Gow also reports that the seriousness of the play was widely recognised: 'in many places clergymen had preached sermons on the play, among them the Rev. Pat McCormack of St. Martin's-in-the-Fields and the Bishop of Edinburgh' (in 1939 the *Daily Herald* published an article about love, marriage, and poverty headed 'Ex-preacher condemns the Church for permitting the crushing miseries of *Love on the Dole*', still secure in an assumption that readers would be able to decode this shorthand).[14]

Contemporary sources estimated that more than 1 million people saw the play during 1935 alone in Britain.[15] Greenwood himself claimed in

successful plays from time to time. See an informative illustrated article on British 'Hippodromes' by Peter Longman (originally published in the *Theatres Trust Newsletter*, September 2002: <http://www.arthurlloyd.co.uk/Archive/Jan2003/Hippodromes.htm>, accessed 24 October 2017. The *Arthur Lloyd Music Hall and Theatre History* website also has an Article about the Finsbury Park Empire that suggests the similar range of theatrical entertainments offered by 'Hippodromes' and Empires': <http://www.arthurlloyd.co.uk/FinsburyPark.htm>, accessed 24 October 2017.

13 *New York Times* 23 February 1936, p. XI.

14 1 July 1939, p. 3.

15 Stephen Constantine gives an account of contemporary estimates of the possible audience numbers for the play in his '*Love on the Dole* and its Reception in the 1930s'. *Literature and History*, 8, Autumn 1982, pp. 233–47.

1940 that 3 million people had now seen the play, including the king and queen.[16] There was a Broadway production in 1936 (and at least one Federal Theatre production), and a production in Paris the following year with the title *Rêves Sans Provisions*.[17] The play also had considerable impact in Australia, with a number of productions between 1935 and 1943 and a revival in 1946. In contrast to the British stage history, in which the play was firmly part of the mainstream commercial theatre after its Manchester Repertory Theatre premiere, the first Australian production was given in 1935 by the Workers' Art Club (and reviewed in the *Workers' Weekly*), followed by a production in 1938 by the Newcastle New Theatre League and then by Workers Art Guild productions in 1940, when the first professional production in Australia was also given by the Minerva Theatre Company in Sydney.[18] There seems to have been a similar pattern of seeing the play as in the province of the Left in New Zealand, with performances of the play presented by the Workers Educational Association at a 'Winter school' in 1937 and readings or performances given by the left-sympathetic 'Thespians' in Wellington in 1936 and by the definitely left (New Zealand) Unity

16 In a letter to *The Manchester Guardian* 26 February 1940 (brought to my attention by footnote 1 in Carole Levine's 'Propaganda for Democracy: the Curious Case of *Love on the Dole, Journal of British Studies*, 45, October 2006, p. 846. The letter's main purpose was to complain that the censorship and prohibition of the film version of *Love on the Dole* in 1935 undermined the claim that the war against Germany was being fought to safeguard free speech (indeed, Greenwood likened the British Board of Film Censors to the Nazi propaganda minister Dr Goebbels) – see Levine, 'Propaganda', p. 848.

17 The text, translated by Charlotte Neveu, was published complete, together with a review of the production, in a special issue of the periodical *La Petite Illustration* (no. 418). YouTube has a number of production photographs posted by Benoit Gautier: <https://www.youtube.com/watch?v=aLPnop_RPVM>; The Broadway production was widely reviewed – see Walter Greenwood Collection, Salford University Library (http://www.salford.ac.uk/__data/assets/xml_file/0007/530476/ Greenwood.xml), items WGC 3/1 (henceforth referred to simply as WGC plus relevant catalogue number for referenced items). The poster for the Federal Theatre production was included on the Federal Theatre Materials site: <http://digilib. gmu.edu/dspace/handle/1920/3478/discover>, accessed 10 June 2012.

18 Australian productions in various cities can be traced through the National Library of Australia's online newspaper collection via the Trove search engine <http://trove.nla.gov.au/>, accessed 24 October 2017. See, for example, *The Workers' Weekly* 29 October 1935, p. 4 and 2 December 1938, p. 2, *The Newcastle Morning Herald and Mining Advocate* 14 December 1938, p. 12 and the *Tribune*, 6 February 1940, p. 4.

Theatre in 1943. Indeed, in an example of covert censorship, it is said that a planned Victoria University student production in 1942 had to be abandoned after all the copies of the play 'mysteriously vanished from the libraries'.[19] However, as we shall see, this initial context for the play did not prevent the film being very well and widely received in both Australia and New Zealand. Ben Harker makes the point that in Britain at least 'Love on the Dole's combination of realistic conventions, dispersed political readings and commercial success made it unlikely adaptation material for early 1930s leftist theatre groups such as the Communist-dominated Workers' Theatre Movement, which favoured highly stylised agitprop modes to carry the message', while 'these very properties raised the possibility of the novel's more mainstream stage adaptation'.[20] However, even in Britain the leftist Unity Theatre did in a small way acknowledge something of the impact of the play in their 1938 satirical pantomime *Babes in the Wood*, which included a song 'Love on the Dole' that is clearly based closely on the proposition of Greenwood's text that unemployment strips life of the value it should have. Decca released a record of the song in 1939. The lyrics are repeated three times, first by a male voice then a female and then by both voices as a duo, agreeing that 'Love on the dole is a luxury we can't afford / on the Unemployment Assistance Board ... We have no room of our own and we can't do the things other lovers do ... . There's no such thing as love on the dole.'[21] The poet A. S. Vaughan-Thomas in the generally left–liberal literary journal *Wales* also paid tribute to Greenwood in his poem 'Love on the Dole', which similarly took the proposition of his texts and developed it in concise form, in this case seeing prostitution as the essential outcome of unemployment and capitalism:

19 *Alexandra Herald and Otago Gazette*, 19 May 1937, p. 5; *Evening Post* (Wellington) 28 July 1936, p. 15; Rachel Barrowman, *A Popular Vision: The Arts and the Left in New Zealand 1930–1950* (Wellington: Victoria University Press, 1991), pp. 244, 209, 203 (the quotation is from the student magazine *Spike* – see Barrowman's chapter 6 endnote 113).

20 Ben Harker, 'Adapting to the Conjuncture – Walter Greenwood, History and *Love on the Dole*', *Keywords – a Journal of Cultural Materialism*, 7, 2009, pp. 55–72, p. 58.

21 The British Library holds a score (Music Collections VOC/1938/FASE) and the Decca 1939 recording (DR3201/F6933) is also available on a CD, *The Rise of Communism* (Opal CD 9856, nd, track 16). The song lyrics are by Geoffrey Parsons, the music by Berkeley Fase, and the singers are Vicki Miller and Bill Rowbotham.

Poverty-stream slides the gold dirt of its waters,
(Sliming the crumbling banks falling from grassy yards)
While she, who would have borne my sons and daughters
Parades her city-glamour to the Guards.[22]

However, apart from the interesting Antipodean variation, the play, like the novel, was in the main a commercial and/or popular success in the UK and the US, being critically well received from a wide range of political and social perspectives.

Given the success of the play, Greenwood was keen to press ahead with a film version (he had had a recent film success as story-writer for the 1935 George Formby film *No Limit*). He came to an agreement with Gaumont Studios. However, when the play-script was submitted to the British Board of Film Censors their objections made production impossible. The Censor's report showed a remarkable nervousness about allowing this already popular success to appear in what was considered an even more persuasive, emotive, and mass medium, saying that it showed 'too much of the tragic and sordid side of poverty'.[23] However, with the outbreak of war, and via a specific intervention by a senior member of staff at the Ministry of Information, feelings about the effect and meaning of the film in this new context changed. Greenwood co-wrote a new script for British National Studios and the 1941 *Love on the Dole* was sympathetically directed by John Baxter, with a well-regarded score by Richard Adinsell (composer of *The Warsaw Concerto* for the film *Dangerous Moonlight*, also released in 1941). Again, this new version of *Love on the Dole* was received with critical commendation. The story as filmed now acquired new meanings that linked the eradication of this kind of poverty with a promised new world after the war: 'our working men and women have responded magnificently to any and every call made upon them. Their reward must be a new Britain.'

All this is a remarkably *national* history for a text (or three texts) portraying Salford during the Depression ('its success is quite remarkable for what is a noticeably local play', notes Claire Warden[24]) – indeed, it became a national and even international phenomenon and the novel changed Greenwood's fortunes, making him into a celebrity and a professional writer. But almost equally significant is the post-1930s

---

22 *Wales*, no. 8/9, August 1939, p. 239.
23 Cited by Croft, *Red Letter Days*, p. 119.
24 'Ugliness and Beauty: the Politics of Landscape in Walter Greenwood's *Love on the Dole*', *New Theatre Quarterly*, 29, 1, February 2013, p. 40.

history of the novel. In the 1940s the film version associated it with a past to which Britain must never return. This, among other factors, may have helped not only to keep the novel in print during the war, when there was great interest in the shape of post-war Britain, among servicemen and servicewomen as well as civilians, but also to ensure its post-war life. The post-war welfare state (let alone a potential *post-welfare* state) has not entirely succeeded in banishing periods of high unemployment, nor the impact of class on life chances, nor poverty, so that the text's politics have remained relevant. Nostalgia may, though, also have played some part (as it also may have done in the 1970 stage musical adaptation called *Hanky Park*), with some pleasure perhaps being taken in the novel having a sense of working-class community, despite the text's own doubts about the depth of real solidarity. Cape kept the novel in print during the 1950s and 1960s, and Penguin brought out their first edition in 1969 and kept it in print until the 1990s. There have been other editions too, in the UK and USA (including by Landsborough Publications, Consul Books, and, most recently, Vintage books). As the 1930s became a period for study in expanding university departments during the 1960s and after, the fact that *Love on the Dole* had been kept in print by a general readership became an important factor in its further longevity. Historians, literary critics, and film critics who wanted to include material on the important topic of pre-welfare state Britain did not necessarily have a large choice of texts to draw upon, while for film historians in particular the film was very relevant to study not only of film censorship but also of the role of cinema in Britain in the Second World War. For university literature teachers there was relatively little choice: despite an interest in working-class writing in the 1930s and the corresponding publication of contemporaries of Greenwood's such as Walter Brierley, Leslie Halward, and many others, only Greenwood has remained reliably and continuously in print. This does, though, accurately reflect his original influence: he was the most successful working-class writer of the 1930s. For historians and film critics there was other material available, but the attractions of Greenwood's original narrative power, as well as the issues raised by the text's impact on the public consciousness and its interactions with mechanisms of government and social control, made it an interesting and highly teachable text. It thus became, as suggested above, *the* novel/play/film about working-class life in the north of England during the 1930s. Equally, outside the academy, both play and novel maintained a life of their own, the play remaining popular enough with schools and amateur drama groups to justify both

Samuel French keeping the acting edition in print for many years and a Heinemann 'secondary education division' paperback edition, which was still in print up to 1987.

At present, *Love on the Dole* retains its status as the representative working-class text of the 1930s: Andrew Marr in his popular BBC television history, *The Making of Modern Britain* (2009), used the novel and the film and some quotations from contemporary reviews to concisely represent interwar unemployment.[25] It is a text widely taught in literature, history, and film departments in the UK and elsewhere. A good number of articles have been published on *Love on the Dole* since the 1980s,[26] and it is referred to widely in literary and film surveys of the period, as well as in history books.[27] The most compelling reason for writing this casebook is simply that Walter Greenwood's *Love on the Dole* (1933) is itself an important work, about which neither critical monograph nor textbook has thus far been written, as Roger Webster noted as far back as 1984: 'The English academic establishment has been conspicuously reluctant to embrace the author or his work; there is no major critical study to date.'[28] This book-length study will put that right by relating the text to its contexts in literary and social history and to Greenwood's own life and career – his own biography, his other writings, and the extensive and rich resources constituted by the collection of his literary papers that he left to the University of Salford on his death in 1974. Early in his writing career – a career which took him quite suddenly from unemployment and poverty in Salford to celebrity – Greenwood hired a clippings agency to scour local, national, and US

25 Episode 5, 'Little Britain', first broadcast 25 November 2009. However, none of this material appeared in the book version (London: Macmillan, 2010). Marr's treatment of the novel and film as identical texts from the 1930s is criticised by Lawrence Napper in passing in his essay '*No Limit*: British Class and Comedy of the 1930s', in *British Comedy Cinema*, ed. I. Q. Hunter and Larraine Porter (Abingdon: Routledge, 2012), pp. 39–40.

26 Including Stephen Constantine's essay of 1982 cited above, Roger Webster's '*Love on the Dole* and the Aesthetic of Contradiction', in *The British Working-Class Novel in the Twentieth Century*, ed. Jeremy Hawthorn (London: Edward Arnold, 1984), pp. 49–61, Carole Snee's 'Working-class Literature or Proletarian Writing?' in *Culture and Crisis in Britain in the Thirties*, ed. Jon Clark, Margot Heinemann, David Margolies and Carole Snee (London: Lawrence and Wishart, 1979), pp. 165–91, and my own 'Dialect and Dialectic: Region and Nation in Walter Greenwood's *Love on the Dole*', 1994, pp. 2–12.

27 See Bibliography.

28 'The Aesthetic of Contradiction', p. 49.

newspapers for reviews and other stories about his works and his life: the clippings-books held in the University of Salford's Walter Greenwood archive provides the basis for a particularly detailed study of the reception of his writing in the 1930s and 1940s (as Stephen Constantine was the first to realise). Based in this rich primary material, this book therefore offers the fullest existing account of Greenwood's life and career in the 1930s and 1940s, as well as substantial critical discussion of the novel, the play, and the film. The triple media in which Greenwood's text appeared was one of the things that greatly expanded its reach – a best-selling novel was adapted into a widely seen play and then (after a significant pause) into a widely discussed film.[29] There certainly were other interesting working-class authors in the period, but none reached as wide an audience as Greenwood, nor had his level of celebrity. Some historians have registered this reach, including Stephen Constantine in his seminal work on Greenwood and, more recently, Richard Overy in his book about the 1930s, *The Morbid Age* (2010), as well as the numerous historians who refer to the representative testimony of *Love on the Dole* for Depression Britain. As we have seen, the play reached a wider audience than even the novel and some contemporaries often referred primarily to the play when they mentioned the title *Love on the Dole*. However, among literary critics there has been far more work on the novel – with only three essays specifically on the play, though one of these is especially original. The film has received extensive discussion by film historians, with discussion of it in key critical works such as Jeffrey Richards' *The Age of the Dream Palace – Cinema and Society in 1930s Britain* (1984) and Robert Murphy's *Realism and Tinsel: Cinema and Society in Britain 1939–1949* (1989) and *British Cinema and the Second World War* (2000), though there is surprisingly little sustained critical attention to it as a film text, rather than to its historical significance. While Greenwood was very open to adaptation across genres and media, there could certainly be more interchange between the three disciplines – History, Literature, Film – which mainly read *Love on the Dole*. Stephen Constantine showed the way as a historian by paying a writer and a text serious attention as a significant historical phenomenon, but there is room for literary critics to historicise Greenwood's work much more fully – and that is one thing this case study will seek to do. Film critics and film historians have done a great deal to bring out the movie's

---

29 A BBC radio adaptation was broadcast in 1945 and a musical version called *Hanky Park* produced in 1970: though less influential, these will also be discussed.

significance, but they have not generally read the literary criticism on the novel or play or tried to make connections or contrasts between the possible meanings or receptions of the different versions of *Love on the Dole*. Thus, though Ben Harker's very good essay about the play version has detailed discussion of the consequences of adaptation decisions made between the novel and the play (or, strictly speaking, plays, since there were two distinct adaptations), there has been no previous discussion of adaptation decisions made between either novel and film or play and film, or, more complicatedly, but as is in fact the case, between novel, play(s), *and* film. This case study will try to put that right by being the first critical work to consider in one place the novel, play, and film texts and the relationships between them (and their contexts). The book thus necessarily has inter-disciplinary aspects: it draws on local and national history to try to understand the possible range of meanings of Greenwood's work as a novel and a play, and, though I am a literary critic by training, I have tried to read the film in something of the mode of a film critic and film historian in order to make fruitful connections between the work of historians and literary and film critics on the history of the 1930s and 1940s in Britain. All the chapters have interdisciplinary aspects, but particular modes of approach lead in specific chapters: this first introductory chapter draws on literary criticism and history, Chapter 1 is literary critical, Chapter 2 is partly theatre history/criticism and partly film history/criticism, and Chapter 3 is largely literary biography and cultural history.

I have been particularly keen not only to historicise the contexts of the work but also to focus on understanding the responses of readers/audiences/viewers of the texts within those historical frameworks. Readership/spectatorship is of course a complex matter (and one often relatively neglected in the Anglo-American literary critical tradition, which has tended to place more emphasis on the author and the text), but it seems a crucial focus for understanding a work that, in all three of its texts, has been variously seen as highly persuasive and yet also often politically cautious and/or controversial and/or ambiguous. Moreover, the extent to which *Love on the Dole* was discussed in newspaper reviews allows a detailed exploration of how some individual readers interpreted the novel, the play, and the film. One of the chief issues in studying how readers/viewers responded to a text is that 'the reader'/'the viewer' or 'readers'/'viewers' are hardly unitary concepts. In saying anything about how a reader or viewer might respond to a text we are referring to the reader in several different possible ways. There is what literary criticism sometimes refers to as 'the reader in the text': that is, the reader constructed or implied by the textual strategies of the text; or there are actual individual readers, with social, political, and gendered assumptions and identities of their own and consequently their own various ways of making sense of the text and its textual strategies. On the whole, I have assumed in my discussions of the texts that these readerly identities may intersect, overlap, and conflict:

- so that readers are positioned by textual strategies that give a certain commonality of experience, though these strategies may often offer the possibility of more than one or ambiguous responses;
- so that textual strategies may be resisted, modified, or rejected by readers;
- so that readers at a particular time read within particular frameworks available to them, which they invoke in variable ways depending on their individual conceptions of their identities within society.

This approach is akin to that suggested by the narratologist James Phelan in his book *Living to Tell About It – a Rhetoric and Ethic of Character Narration*:

> For the purposes of interpreting narratives, the conception assumes that texts are designed by authors in order to affect readers in particular ways, that those designs are conveyed through the language, techniques, structures, forms, and dialogic relations of texts as well as the conventions and genres readers use to understand them, and that reader responses are a function, guide, and test of how designs are created through textual and intertextual phenomena ... . [This] entails the possibility of shared readings among different flesh-and-blood-readers. The author designs the textual phenomena for a hypothetical audience (what I call the authorial audience) ... and the individual rhetorical reader seeks to become part of that audience ... . Rhetorical reading acknowledges that individual readers will find some authorial audiences easier to enter into than others, and it stops short of ever declaring any one reading as definitive and fixed for all time.[30]

This book is attempting, then, to be a piece of original research and a useful textbook – I see no reason why these aims should be incompatible, why student and other kinds of reader should not share a book that brings together archive work on primary sources, reference to the existing secondary literature, a fresh approach to a text, and an attempt to give a full account of all three versions of Greenwood's best-remembered work. New material in the book includes some originating in archive work

30 (London and Ithaca, New York: Cornell University Press, 2005), pp. 18–19.

13

(hard copy and digital) or readings of Greenwood's other work– particularly the light cast on *Love on the Dole* by the press exchange between Greenwood and the Salford social worker Mrs Sydney Frankenberg,[31] the relationship between MetroVick and Marlowe's, the critically unnoticed short-story sequel Greenwood wrote to the novel in 1938, the undiscussed relationships between *The Cleft Stick* (1937) and *Love on the Dole*, the comparison of the British Board of Film Censors' report on the proposed screenplay with the Lord Chamberlain's censorship report on the proposed play version, the recognition of Greenwood's 1944 novel, *Something in My Heart*, as another kind of sequel to *Love on the Dole*, the extent of his film production activity, his two forgotten film scripts for *Six Men of Dorset* (1944) and *A City Speaks* (1947), the censorship and reception of the film of *Love on the Dole* in Australia and New Zealand, and the fact that the film *Eureka Stockade* (1949) also revisits the character of Larry Meath and the struggle for political representation. Additionally, the book gives a concise account of the remainder of Greenwood's writing career and shows how he responded to social changes to which he had contributed and how he engaged in dialogue with *Love on the Dole* in his own later work. Other material arises from discussion of recent historical research that, while not itself necessarily mentioning Greenwood's work, seems productively applicable, yet has largely not been referred to in critical debates about him: this includes research on the history of midwives and 'handywomen', on hair-dressing, on spiritualism, on censorship, and on the histories of policing and betting.

The book is organised into an introductory chapter, three further chapters and a conclusion. The Introduction gives a concise overview of the cultural importance of Greenwood's text and its social, historical, and political context. Chapter 1 gives a detailed critical analysis of the novel of *Love on the Dole*, with a focus on the construction of the reader within specific historical contexts. Chapter 2 carries out a similar task for the play and film versions. Chapter 3 gives a literary biography of Walter Greenwood and an account of his other published work with most emphasis on the period up to 1945 (which has generally been disregarded in discussions of *Love on the Dole* and its contexts), and a briefer sense of how his writing up until his death in 1974 may also be

---

31 Matthew Gaughan was the first critic to note the interest of this exchange between Greenwood and Frankenburg (in his essay 'Palatable Socialism or "The Real Thing"? Walter Greenwood's *Love on the Dole*', *Literature and History*, 17, 2, 2008), but I think there is more to discuss.

related to his first successful work. These accounts draw on the existing critical literature on Greenwood, so that readers will have a good sense of how *Love on the Dole* has been interpreted. The overall aim is to produce a deeply historicised and interdisciplinary approach to *Love on the Dole* in each of its versions so that old and new readers may have the evidence to make their own interpretations of Walter Greenwood's *Love on the Dole* and to analyse our uses of his influential text and our cultural memory of the 1930s and 1940s.

II. 'There Was a Time':[32]
Love on the Dole and the 1930s in Great Britain

Unemployment was a key feature of the 1930s:

> Britain's worst years for unemployment were those after the financial and political crisis of 1931. From 1931 until 1935, the number of those officially classed as unemployed never fell below two million, while in the winter of 1932–3 unemployment reached its highest point when almost three million workers, a quarter of the insured working population, were out of work.[33]

However, historians have pointed out that the Slump did not represent the entire national experience of economic and social conditions:

> Recovery, despaired of in 1931, was in the air by 1933, obvious by 1935. The National Government got little thanks for it, partly because it did not deserve it ... partly because recovery like the depression, was uneven, so that the misery of the depressed areas drew attention away from the return of prosperity elsewhere ... . Two things stand out in the economy of the thirties: increasing consumption and the development of the home market and the consumer and service industries ... . While prices were low, those persons who were in regular employment – after all, the great majority – had a greater margin than before between their income ... and their basic needs ... . They had more to spend on consumer goods and, perhaps, for a better house which they might even 'own'.[34]

The Greenwood of the novel and play is a 1930s figure precisely because his work spoke about the centrality of the Slump in the early part of

---

32 The title of Greenwood's autobiography (1966), taken from the opening line of Wordsworth's 'Intimations of Immortality'.

33 John Stevenson, *British Society 1914–45*, Penguin Social History of Britain (Harmondsworth: Penguin, 1984), p. 266.

34 Charles Loch Mowat, *Britain Between the Wars 1918–1940* (London: Methuen, 1955, 1968), pp. 432, 451 and 458.

the decade, but, nevertheless, the effect of his work may arise partly from the uneven and regional nature of slump and boom. Indeed, his literary career might not have happened at all without two preconditions: his own periods without work ('unemployment actually gave working-class writers *time* to write'[35]) and a new literary – and publishing – interest in unemployment and working-class writing arising from social concerns about the condition of Britain. As Christopher Hilliard observes, 'Working-class writing has a long pedigree in Britain, but the 1930s were especially important in that tradition, as established publishers and left-wing intellectuals encouraged manual workers' literary efforts.'[36] Equally, perhaps part of the widespread impact of *Love on the Dole* – its success with readers and audiences – arose from the gap between the society it depicts and the more modern-seeming consumer society that many ordinary people across the working and middle classes outside Distressed Areas – consumers of novels, plays, radio, gramophone records, cinema, and holidays, among other things – were coming to see as normal. Gary Day, when discussing *Love on the Dole* in his book *Class*, suggests, indeed, that the 'the identities and pleasures of [the] characters are centred upon the emerging consumer society'.[37] I am not sure though that the word 'centred' is quite right when applied to the characters – it seems more likely that it is the implied reader who registers that most of the inhabitants of Hanky Park have only the barest contact with the possibilities of the new consumer society, though they often crave them. The overall period from 1914 to 1945 saw a steady change in the patterns of leisure, consumption, and social life, with far-reaching effects on identity across the nation. In the 1930s there was, for some, continued growth in these aspects of life, while for others there was clearly something of a suspension, with the loss of any surplus beyond that needed to meet necessities (if that). *Love on the Dole* suggests that in many ways there is a lack of a 'common culture' across Britain, with Hanky Park in a number of respects still subsisting in a nineteenth-century style of deprivation. This may influence a very specific and major omission in the novel's coverage of 'history' – the lack (first pointed out by Constantine) of any reference at all to the General Strike of 1927, though the novel is set

---

35 Matthew Gaughan, summarising a point made by Andy Croft in *Red Letter Days* in his article 'Palatable Socialism or "the Real Thing"'.

36 In his *To Exercise Our Talents: the Democratization of Writing in Britain* (Cambridge, Massachusetts/London: Harvard University Press, 2006), p. 5.

37 In the New Critical Idiom Series (London: Routledge, 2001), p. 176.

between 1924 and 1931. In addition to Constantine's suggestion that any mention of the General Strike would under-cut middle-class (and some 'respectable' working-class?) sympathies, it might be that Greenwood also wants to give a sense of a static society unable to change itself and left out of the majority national life.[38] It may be that part of the text's dynamic was an appeal on behalf of Hanky Park for access to what were now more widely perceived as the everyday benefits of that new and more 'homogenous society'. Equally, it should be said that aspects of the new consumer society certainly did reach even into places like Hanky Park, as detailed work on leisure in Salford and Manchester by the historian Andrew Davies suggests, and the early 1930s may represent a pause of that growth in the distressed areas rather than a complete exclusion from social developments in the rest of Britain over the longer period.[39] It seems likely that the conditions under which people in distressed areas accessed – or among the worst-off did not access – these new kinds of modern leisure both sharply differentiated them *and* gave them some common culture with more prosperous communities: it is a paradox to which we will return.

One important social development was paid holidays – something to which *Love on the Dole* makes a perhaps surprising number of references (the word is used twenty times). Legislation – as well as some voluntary action by employers – made paid holidays a much more common experience than before the war: 'in the early 1920s only one and a half million people had paid holidays, by 1939 over eleven million' (however, only 3 million had paid holidays in 1938 – it was the 1938 Holidays With Pay Act which led directly to the 1939 figure).[40] The chapter title 'Holidays with Pay' in Greenwood's autobiography refers ironically to the continuing rarity for many people of such a thing, since it covers the period in the 1930s when he was working in the countryside rather

38 'Love on the Dole and its Reception in the 1930s'.

39 See his essay 'Leisure in the "classic slum" 1900–1939', in *Workers' Worlds: Cultures and Communities in Manchester and Salford, 1880–1939*, ed. Davies, Andrew and Steven Fielding (Manchester: Manchester University Press, 1992), pp. 102–32, and, in the same collection, David Fowler's 'Teenage Consumers? Young Wage-earners and Leisure in Manchester, 1919–1939', pp. 133–55, as well as Andrew Davies's book-length study *Leisure, Gender and Poverty: Working-Class Culture in Salford and Manchester, 1900–1939* (Buckingham: Open University Press, 1992).

40 Quotation is from Stevenson, *British Society 1914–45*, p. 393: the remainder of this discussion of consumer society is also indebted to his account; further specific information here comes from Mowat, *Britain Between the Wars 1918–1940*, p. 501.

than in Salford. The new annual holiday rhythm is, of course, in sharp contrast with the once-in-a-lifetime holiday experience of Mrs and Mrs Hardcastle and Harry and Helen in *Love on the Dole*. Andrew Thorpe points out that a 'parallel and perhaps more widespread development' to the paid holiday was 'the rise of the "day out"': this was facilitated by trains, commercial motor coaches, private cars (for some, including Sam Grundy), motor cycles, and bicycles, and fed into the popularity of rambling and hiking (the last activity a novelty to which Larry introduces Sally in Greenwood's text).[41] Sports, including football, cricket, and horse racing, were well-established as organised leisure activities by 1914, but the 1930s saw the introduction of greyhound racing and national football pools, adding an eagerly appreciated gambling interest to football's already popular status as a spectator sport.[42]

The importance of betting is made very clear in *Love on the Dole* through the important part played by Sam Grundy in the story as well as the near universal engagement with gambling of the Hanky Park community. Greenwood interestingly suggested in a piece of writing on the unemployed from 1940 that the growth of the football pools was intimately linked to the depression itself, and a sign that 'real' productive industry was being replaced with something so insubstantial that it did not even have to invest in 'real' estate:

> And now, behind the crumbling major industries there rises, like a grim jest, that new industry which ranks conspicuously in the list of national importance, the derisively successful industry of the Football Pools which has achieved its position of financial importance without the aid of the money spent on the horse and dog race tracks.[43]

New forms of media were also an important part of the new consumer society, promoting the kinds of product that, for example, Coty Cosmetics Ltd was now making for mass rather than elite 'luxury' consumption.[44]

---

41 *Britain in the 1930s: the Deceptive Decade* (Oxford: Blackwell, 1991), p. 107. Stevenson discusses the relative popularity of cars, motor-cycles, cycling and walking in further detail, *British Society 1914–45*, pp. 390–93.

42 Stevenson, *British Society 1914–45*, p. 385. See also p. 384.

43 *How the Other Man Lives* (London: Labour Book Service,1940), p. 40.

44 Stevenson, *British Society 1914–45*, p. 407. See also Coty's continuing commitment to the image of 'mass luxury': the 'heritage' section on its website sees the company's origins in its founder Francoise Coty's realisation that perfume could become 'an international mass-market luxury' (<http://www.coty.com/>, accessed 23 June 2008).

In one way, this world of 'glamour' and consumption seems a world away from Hanky Park, where disposable income is very restricted. However, there are many signs in *Love on the Dole* that the mental, if not the material, worlds of characters such as Sally and Helen (and Harry?) are affected by some of the dreams that cinema and other forms mediated. The novel's interest in, and use of, popular romance modes (even if ironically) has been noted, particularly by Ian Haywood:

> the narrative presents an anti-type of conventional fictional romance, in which erotic desire confronts the obstacles of property relations. There are two elements of Greenwood's ironic reworking of the romance plot, shared between the two main characters Harry and Sally Hardcastle. Both are *Bildungsroman* heroes *manqué* – their development is attenuated; their destinies primarily dependent on the iron laws of slump and boom, not individualized choice.[45]

As we shall see, this is a key point: the characters must be seen by the reader as rendered incapable by economic forces from making their own choices. The participation in and separation of its characters from the world of possibility helps give Hanky Park its partly old-fashioned and partly modern atmosphere. The fact that Harry and the other unemployed 'lads' cannot afford the cinema is surely a sign of how poor they have become, how excluded they are from the mainstream of modern ordinary life. Thorpe suggests a profound impact for cinema as a *democratising* agent in English culture: 'Cinema was democratising in its effects: as well as providing a common experience to all classes, it also provided, in film stars, a new focus for deference and admiration much more exciting than the aristocracy.'[46] The portrayal of Sally Hardcastle in at least the play and film of *Love on the Dole* may draw, as we shall see, on this new sense of the star as a focus for popular admiration.

III. 'Wharram *Ah* gonna do?': The Dole, the National Government, and the Means Test

Such, then, was the very mixed state of crisis and boom in the texture of social life in 1930s England. We need now to turn from the social history of the 1930s to the closely related political history of the decade. As we shall see, against the more general background of Hanky Park

---

45 *Working-class Fiction from Chartism to Trainspotting* (London: Edward Arnold, 1997), p. 49.
46 *Britain in the 1930s*, p. 107.

life and unemployment, three particular aspects of this political history are central to the narrative of *Love on the Dole*:

> Wharram *Ah* gonna do? By the Christ, it was tekkin' us all our time t'manage on me wages … . But when Ah think o' the seven of 'um at home, an her ma livin' wi'us, all on what they'll gimme on the dole … . Yaaa! An' the bloody liars at election said everthing'd be apple pie if National Government went back. Well, where are we? (p. 186)

> 'Ha! Means Test, eh? They can't knock *me* off. Blimey it's tekkin' us all our time t'manage as it is … . Yaach, they won't touch the likes of us. They daren't. There'd be a bloody revolution. (p. 197)

The Dole, the National Government, the Means Test are three key phrases – representing key political crises – the impact of which we need to understand if we are to understand the reception of *Love on the Dole*.

The decade began with a Labour government. With Ramsay MacDonald as leader the government had a narrow margin over the Tories and could be defeated on any issue where the Liberals might vote against them.[47] It was doubly unfortunate that MacDonald's government came to power as economic crisis began to bite: 'during its two years in office, the official unemployment level rose from 1.1 million to 2.8 million and the government was unable even to stem the rising tide.'[48] Thorpe suggests that the government's failure to contemplate dealing with the depression through more radical economic measures came from the core beliefs about the relationship of socialism to capitalism held by MacDonald and his chancellor of the exchequer, Philip Snowden:

> Believing that socialism could only come from the *success* of capitalism, MacDonald and Snowden had no distinctive policy to deal with capitalism in crisis. The only solutions they had were orthodox ones – reducing taxation and public expenditure, and allowing industry to become more competitive by cutting its costs and, hence, wages.[49]

Though the Labour government did make some attempts at intervention these had little ambition or impact. This conservatism, in combination with a similar reluctance in succeeding governments up until the outbreak of war in 1939, may in the long run have helped fuel an even more widespread belief across many elements of the political spectrum in the need to plan for a better future society. This was especially the case

47 Figures are given in Mowat, *Britain Between the Wars 1918–1940*, p. 351.
48 Thorpe, *Britain in the 1930s*, p. 23.
49 *Britain in the 1930s*, p. 23.

once war was declared – which began to be shaped often as a 'people's war' dedicated to the ultimate development of a much better post-war society.

Meanwhile, the government had to make some decisions about the Unemployment Insurance Fund, since it was under exceptional strain owing to the rising numbers of unemployed drawing on it. The Fund had to work within its budget and had a borrowing limit of £40 million, which it had already reached by 1929. The government increased the Treasury contribution in July 1929 and then passed a bill in November which increased the number of people eligible for what were termed 'transitional benefits' (that is, benefits payable to those who had not been in employment for a long enough period to pay in enough insurance contributions to qualify for benefits on the terms originally envisaged by the scheme). This bill again increased the Treasury contribution. As Thorpe points out, there were a number of underpinning beliefs determining benefits policy, with considerable shared ground across the mainstream of all three parties: 'First was the conviction that state expenditure should be kept within bounds … [and that] benefits should preserve the old principle of "less eligibility" – they should always be lower than wages, so as not to push up wage levels or discourage people from working.'[50]

These assumptions were put under great strain from 1929 onwards and played a major part in the downfall of the Labour government in August 1931. The English benefits system in the 1930s was complex: the 'system' was in fact made up of several interlinked sets of provision, some of considerable antiquity, and it also underwent a continuing process of adaptation to the realities of the economy, political crises, and the political beliefs of different administrations in the period. There are a number of technical terms used in the period and specifically in Greenwood's novel, including 'Transitional benefit', 'Unemployment Assistance Board' (UAB), 'Public Assistance Committee' (PAC), and 'the Means Test'.[51] If the precise distinctions between some of these terms are bewildering for us, some were certainly also bewildering for many at the time, as the quotations above from *Love on the Dole* and the relevant scene in the film suggest. While the novel is set at a particular time that includes the period from the fall of the Labour government

50 *Britain in the 1930s*, p. 76.
51 Stevenson give the best account of these terms in *British Society 1914–45*, pp. 297–300.

in August 1931 to the formation of the National Government in August, the consequent introduction of the Means Test in September, and the October elections that confirmed the National Government in office, it is also clear why the text remained topical throughout the 1930s, as the issues it raised continued during 1935 and, in public perception at least, right up until the outbreak of war.

Among the chief of these issues was the Means Test. One of the key aspects of the public impact of the Means Test was that it blurred the line between unemployment benefits and a kind of provision that felt to those on the receiving end as if it came from the Poor Law tradition. The Unemployed Insurance Fund and then (after 1935) the Unemployment Assistance Board, in principle, paid benefits to insured workers who were out of work, and was thus *neither* charity *nor* poor law relief – a provision traditionally designed for those at the very bottom of the social scale, with no hope nor means of helping themselves. However, in 1931, legislation was enacted to allow transitional benefits to be paid, but subject to a strict Means Test. This was intended as an outward sign of rigour, as an economy measure, and in continuance of assumptions about the need to deter the 'work-shy'. Stevenson gives a very clear account of the impact of this detested measure:

> Assessment of 'means' involved relieving officers visiting people's homes, prying into their circumstances, suggesting they sell items of furniture, or reducing relief because of savings, or incomes from sons, daughters or pensioners living within the household ... . The means test became one of the most despised aspects of the inter-war years and long after the Second World War a source of bitterness and ill-feeling ... for many, the transfer to a body tainted with the relief of 'pauperism' provided a lasting humiliation.[52]

As the title signals, the humiliation of the Means Test hangs over the whole of the other best-remembered piece of 'dole literature', Walter Brierley's *Means Test Man* (1935). The Means Test could involve a family having to sell alleged 'luxuries' (like wireless sets as well as other items of furniture beyond the bare necessities), thus seeming to punish the results of hard work, saving and self-improvement in preceding better times. It also deterred families from continuing to live together in one house, as sons and daughters at work (including young working adults) were made financially responsible for unemployed parents, and vice-versa. All these humiliations had to be gone through in order to gain a benefit which

---

52 *British Society 1914–45*, pp. 276–77.

had, anyway, been much reduced in 1931 and seemed to many – both among the unemployed and among observers – inadequate to sustain life even at subsistence levels.

The Means Test was, as Larry Meath in *Love on the Dole* points out, intimately connected to the National Government:

> National Government Ach! Ha, well, they told us what they'd do if they went back; wage cuts and the rest. But everybody was too busy with their daft Irish Sweepstakes and all the rest of it ... . Augh! Watch them waken up when they get it in the neck with this Means Test. (pp. 186–87)

The National Government's origins go back to the crisis that overtook the Labour government in August 1931. A financial crisis had been building since February, when the Conservatives had censured in a vote the government's allegedly imprudent spending and borrowing carried out in order to keep the Unemployment Insurance Fund afloat. In July the government's financial management looked much worse after the collapse of banks in Austria and Germany, and gold began to be withdrawn from the Bank of England (to the tune of £2.5 million a day in July). There was a resulting 'lack of confidence in British finance', according to both Labour's own chancellor, Snowden, and the Conservative shadow chancellor, Neville Chamberlain.[53] The government-commissioned May Report gave a severe diagnosis and recommended correspondingly strict economy measures, taxation, and reduction of public expenditure: 'of the economies £66½ millions were to be found in reductions in unemployment expenditures, including a 20 per cent reduction in benefits'.[54]

During July and August the cabinet worked along these lines to try to produce a 'balanced budget' that would restore confidence: given their parliamentary position, they needed to produce a plan that the opposition parties would broadly support. There were a number of

---

53 In Mowat's view Chamberlain and Snowden took the normally curious route of prearranging an announcement to this effect – presumably a sign of Snowden's concern about the crisis as well as further confirmation of his essentially orthodox and conservative views of economic management. In general, my account of the crisis follows Mowat's superb narrative and analysis. See *Britain Between the Wars 1918–1940*, p. 381 and the whole of Chapter 7, 'The Turning Point: 1929–1931'. There is, of course, a large historical literature on the political events of 1931 – see Mowat and Thorpe's bibliographies for suggestions for further reading, as well as Thorpe's own book devoted entirely to the 1931 election, *The British General Election of 1931* (Oxford: Clarendon Press, 1991).

54 Mowat, *Britain Between the Wars 1918–1940*, pp. 381–82.

agonised cabinet meetings, but finally, at such a meeting on Sunday, 23 August, the cabinet was split by their own willingness or not to support a 10 per cent reduction of unemployment benefit. Eleven cabinet members felt able to support the measure, including the prime minister MacDonald and the chancellor Snowden; ten members (including 'men who could not be ignored'[55]) felt that it was impossible for a Labour government to enact such a thing.

This deadlock led directly to the formation of the National Government. MacDonald asked the cabinet to resign, as the only possibility under these circumstances. He then went to the palace to see the king on the following morning, as his cabinet supposed to offer that government's resignation. Actually, what emerged during the course of two meetings with the king, the second of which included the opposition leaders Stanley Baldwin and Herbert Samuel, was the resignation of the Labour cabinet, but *not* of the Labour prime minister. MacDonald agreed, at the king's request, to help address the crisis by forming a National Government with himself as prime minister, but which also included the Conservative and Liberal leaders and a cross-party cabinet. In fact, the cabinet was made up of five Conservatives, three Liberals and four Labour Party members, counting the three party leaders. The new government was thus dominated by opposition members, and the Labour members were themselves from the right of the party and likely to support orthodox financial and economic policies. Moreover, when the new government sought a mandate from the country in the general election of October 1931, during which it received overwhelming electoral support, 470 of the 544 MPs elected as 'National' MPs were from the Conservative Party.[56] A National Government, first under MacDonald (until he lost his seat in the election of 1935) and then under the Conservatives Baldwin and Neville Chamberlain, led the country until a wartime coalition was formed by Churchill in May 1940. In this sense then, as Thorpe, observes, 'the 1930s were dominated politically by the National Government, which were themselves dominated by Conservatives'.[57]

Immediately the National Government was formed it put in place the

---

55 Mowat, *Britain Between the Wars 1918–1940*, p. 392. Mowat usefully lists the two camps – among those who could not support the measures were A. V. Alexander, whose words about the need to ensure that Britain never again returned to the social conditions of the 1930s prefaced the film of *Love on the Dole*.

56 Thorpe, *Britain in the 1930s*, p. 12.

57 *Britain in the 1930s*, p. 7.

economy measures rejected in August, including cuts to unemployment benefits, the introduction of the Means Test, and reductions in pay for public servants of all sorts. Though the National Government did take some unorthodox actions, especially in abandoning the Gold Standard in September 1931, its performance has mainly been remembered as lacking initiative: 'The history of the National government was one long diminuendo', says Mowat.[58] There were some further economic and social actions by government. Among these the chief was the recognition of 'Depressed Areas' (later euphemistically renamed 'Special Areas'), worth noting partly because this terminology itself contributes to the memory of unemployment as the central experience of the 1930s. The act of naming itself gave public and policy recognition to the unprecedented impact of unemployment in particular areas. Not all the areas that suffered from depression were included in the Special Areas Act – despite *Love on the Dole* and the collapse of textiles, Lancashire itself was not designated as a Special Area ('how long will it be before the Lancashire factory chimneys are ivy-grown and the mills roofless and a shelter for thriving trees?' wrote Greenwood).[59] Lloyd George critically compared the limited ambitions of the Act to the scale of New Deal legislation in the US.[60] Overall, and despite an upturn in the economy after 1931 and the economic benefits of rearmament after 1936, the basic economic situation of most depressed areas in Britain remained in many ways static until 1939, when the final consequences of foreign policy transformed the economy to a wartime one. Greenwood's *Love on the Dole* therefore retained its resonance with the public throughout the 1930s: it also, as we shall see, expanded these resonances during the war itself.

58 *Britain Between the Wars 1918–1940*, p. 413.
59 Quotation from the chapter on 'The Cotton Operative' in *How the Other Man Lives*, p. 222.
60 Mowat, *Britain Between the Wars 1918–1940*, p. 465.

CHAPTER ONE

Love on the Dole: the Novel

Introduction: Readers and Histories

In this first of the chapters devoted to the three main versions of *Love on the Dole* I will focus particularly on how *Love on the Dole* might be seen to have shaped the responses of its readers and viewers. This seems a promisingly central line of enquiry because *Love on the Dole* became an important text in British culture and history through its ability to move its audiences (in several senses) towards a particular, and perhaps new, view of their relationship to the people of Hanky Park, a people literally of one Salford district, but also imaginable as representative of other social, geographical, and imaginative regions of Britain in the 1930s. This is a line of enquiry that Stephen Constantine clearly initiated in many ways in his influential article of 1982, but I hope to add to his historical insights about intended readership with some literary critical approaches to readership. In fact, the ability of *Love on the Dole* to tap into a national vision suggests that what might look at first like a formalist approach to the texts on my part (how do they construct their implied readers/viewers?) is also really a strongly historicist approach as well (how did the texts draw on situations, contexts, codes, and assumptions available to audiences at the time?). In this first chapter I shall pursue these two linked sets of questions carefully through the novel version of *Love on the Dole*. In the following chapter I will pursue the same issues through the play and film texts: the discussion of the three versions will naturally enough have comparative elements, which is important because, surprisingly enough, there has so far been no sustained critical attempt to compare all three versions of the work.[1]

---

1 The play has been very productively compared to the novel in an article by Harker in 'Adapting to the Conjuncture', pp. 55–72 – but there is little detailed work on how the film differs from the novel or play versions.

I. The Opening Chapter and the Epigraphs

Love on the Dole is the story of an ordinary working-class family, the Hardcastles, and of their neighbours, who all live in a part of Salford called Hanky Park. The story takes place over the seven-year period of Harry Hardcastle's apprenticeship, which ends in 1931 – just as the Slump, unemployment and government responses bite deep. A life which was just about sustainable during ordinary times is shown to become increasingly desperate as the story goes on. I will discuss first the beginning of the novel and then each of the major characters and groups of characters as a way of working through the issues raised by the novel.

Greenwood's novel opens, epigraphs apart, with a place-name which came to stand for much of what the book is about: Hanky Park. An overview of Hanky Park is precisely the concern of the very short (under 800 words) but important opening chapter, whose introductory function is to a degree distinct from that of any other chapter. The imagined position of the narrator of this chapter, at any rate, is strongly implied by the first sentence: 'THEY call this part "Hanky Park"' (p. 11). 'They' are presumably the anonymous collectivity who live in Hanky Park, to be distinguished from both the narrator and the reader – who together constitute the implied 'we' who are looking down from an outside position onto the cityscape to which the chapter is a guide. This is an aerial and distanced view of 'that district opposite the parish church of Pendleton', which – somewhat like the cinematic zoom-shot that the film version actually did deploy – then moves in from roofs to streets to the detail of front doorsteps (though without lingering on any individuals, only on exemplary instances of the inhabitants of the landscape: 'Women, girls and children are to be seen kneeling on all fours in the streets …' [p. 11]). However, the technique is not, in fact, as visual or cinematic or documentary as it might be – the items in the landscape are not on the whole left to speak immediately and for themselves, but are immersed in a highly verbal commentary with a strongly historical and anthropological focus:

> In the early nineteenth century Hanky Park was part of the grounds of a wealthy lady's mansion; at least, so say the old maps in the Salford Town Hall … . Some women there are whose lives are dedicated to an everlasting battle with the invincible forces of soot and grime … . (p. 11)

This knowledge on the narrator's part, drawing on research and observation, seems important, because it establishes both his nearness to, his knowledge of, Hanky Park and his social, educational, and geographical distance. Implied reader and narrator are, then, constructed as seeing over Hanky Park as outsiders, viewing from a superior position, able to come and go, unlike its inhabitants, and apparently able to reach a clear overview about everything which could possibly happen in Hanky Park.

This aligning of narrator and reader is reinforced by several other features of the text. The anthropological account of the cleaning and whitening of the pavement in front of the houses using a rubbing-stone is specifically placed as a regional custom:

> Families from south of the Trent who take up residence here are astonished at the fashion and say that from whence they came nothing like this is ever seen. The custom persists. The 'sand-bone men' who purvey the lumps of sandstone ... can be seen pushing their handcarts and heard calling their trade in rusty, hoarse, sing-song voices: 'San'bo- Donkey brand brown sto – bo-one,' which translated, means: 'I will exchange either brown or white rubbing stone for rags, bones or bottles.' (p. 12)

The language that records the astonishment of incomers to Hanky Park from south of Nottinghamshire at the habit of 'white-stoning' is notably formal, with its delayed main verb and repeated choice of Latinate or slightly archaic vocabulary and ponderous word-order ('astonished' itself, 'take up residence', 'the fashion' and 'from whence they came'). In fact, the claim to a higher register verges on the parodic, with the implication of snootiness or class-affectation on the part of these outsiders, a suggestion that they assume a language and thus hold themselves apart from such a northern, working-class habit. Despite this possible suggestion of ridicule (which perhaps diverts accusations of snobbery) of the (relative) southerners, the effect on the whole is to align the implied reader with the outsiders – both are observing for the first time this strange custom, which needs to be explained and, indeed, 'translated'. The word 'translated' draws attention to another aspect of the text, its construction of an explicit contrast between the language of Hanky Park (a 'dialect') and the language the narrator apparently shares with the reader, presumably Standard English. In fact the gloss – a feature we shall meet again in the novel – offers more than a translation, since it explains the whole nature of the transaction which the phrase 'Donkey Brand Brown Stone' makes immediately clear to the people of Hanky Park (and to most people in Lancashire at the time).[2] The linguistic assumption written into this introduction is, therefore, that the reader is imagined as an educated southerner or, at any rate, as distanced by either class or region or education or all three from this world into which the novel is taking him or her.

If there is a strong anthropological and historical flavour to the opening chapter, the language of external description is also markedly literary, which may additionally bind the reader's and narrator's positions together. Thus this opening chapter is notable for carefully composed if largely unremarkable literary or rhetorical effects, including combinations of rhythmically balanced clauses and expansions, unpretentious metaphors, and a distinctly learned vocabulary intervening at some point in most sentences. The following quotation is characteristic and illustrates most of these devices:

> On either side of this are other streets, mazes, jungles of tiny houses cramped and huddled together, two rooms above and two below, in some cases only one room alow and aloft; public houses by the score where forgetfulness lurks in a mug; pawnshops by the dozen where you can raise the wind to buy forgetfulness; churches, chapels and unpretentious mission halls where God is praised; nude, black patches of land, 'crofts', as they are called, water-logged, sterile, bleak and chill. (p. 11)

It may be that an implied reader of this text is partly having their status *as an educated reader*, as someone in possession of cultural capital, reinforced by these familiar markers of mainstream literary descriptiveness. The description does not concentrate on the literal, on letting the detail of actuality itself point to or stand for something of larger significance (as a more modern 1930s documentary technique might have done), but draws on a traditional kind of interpretation *by* an omniscient narrator *for* the reader. In short, and despite the main and pessimistic theme of life in Hanky Park as 'an everlasting battle with the invincible forces of soot and grime' (p. 11), there may be an element of reassurance in this opening through its very construction

---

2 *OED* does not have an entry for Donkey Stone and nor does its entry for rubbing stone quite define the usage Greenwood means. Donkey Brand rubbing stone was first made by Reads of Manchester – it came in white, cream and brown and was used for 'stoning' or whitening the pavement. See the Tameside website about the closure of Eli Whalley's Lion Brand stone works: <http://www.tameside.gov.uk/blueplaque/eliwhalley>, accessed 21 July 2010. Greenwood's book *Lancashire* (County Book Series [London: Hale, 1951]) also discusses the custom (p. 15), though he feels it died out after 1939.

of the reader's point of view, since it strongly reinforces or creates a certain safe distance between the narrator and reader, and the subject(s) of Hanky Park to which/to whom the narrator is created as a safe guide. The people of Hanky Park may be pitiable and eternally there, but they are assuredly not wholly like me, the reader. Their whole lives can apparently be summarised from the outside by the chapter's final sentence: 'Places where men and women are born, live, love and die and pay preposterous rents for the privilege of calling the grimy houses "home"' (p. 13).

This effect, whereby the limited viewpoint of those in the novel is contrasted from the outset with the relative freedom of perspective of those implied to be reading the novel, may be reinforced even before the text proper begins by the novel's epigraphs, which, despite their impact on the reader's initial engagement with the book, have been rarely discussed. There are no fewer than six epigraphs, one on the title-page and five on the page following the Contents page. The title-page epigraph is the only one taken from poetry, being a one-and-a-half-line quotation from the American writer James Russell Lowell's 'A Glance Behind the Curtain' (1890), which reflects upon and narrates Oliver Cromwell's decision not to flee from England to the New World but to oppose the king and thus, through individual will and a sense of destiny, to change the future of England from its present monarchical tyranny: 'The Time is ripe, and rotten ripe, for change;/Then let it come ...'. Clearly, there is an application to Greenwood's novel and this is its first call to its reader to take their part in bringing about change to the current condition of England.[3]

The following five epigraphs are from a range of sources, all non-fiction, all first-person testimony, and each, too, has a bearing on Greenwood's narrative. The bearing, though, is not always the most obvious one (only two refer directly to Britain and none quotes from available material about unemployment in the early 1930s). The first epigraph is from a once well-known travel book, *Those United States* (first published in 1912 and brought out in a new edition in 1926[4]) by the then both popular

---

3 The poem was first published in James Russell Lowell's *The Writings, Vol 1. Poems, Miscellaneous Poems* (London: Macmillan, 1890); the epigraph quotes ll. 230–231 of the poem.

4 First published by Martin Secker in the UK and simultaneously by Harper and Brothers in the US (as *Your United States*). Secker reprinted the book in their Adelphi Modern Library Series in 1926.

and critically well-regarded novelist Arnold Bennett. The relevance to
Love on the Dole stems from Bennett's comment on housing conditions
in apartment blocks in the US at the time of his visit in 1911:

> I would have liked to live this life, for a space, in any one of half a million
> restricted flats, with not quite enough space, not quite enough air, not quite
> enough dollars and a vastly too much continual strain on the nerves. I would
> have liked to have come to close quarters with it and got its subtle and sinister
> toxin incurably into my system.

The implied similarity of conditions between American apartments
and Hanky Park comes from their shared lack of what is needed for
an adequate life. The second epigraph comes from Siegfried Sassoon's
Memoirs of an Infantry Officer (1930) and seems more straightforwardly
connected to the novel in its realisation by a member of a more privileged
class of the fact that life 'for the majority of the population is an
unlovely struggle against unfair odds, culminating in a cheap funeral'.
Again, there is the theme of the revelation of an aspect of English
life to someone who is, but maybe should not be, an outsider – with
perhaps also the implication that this insight from 1917 is still entirely
true sixteen years later, in 1933, in a post-Great-War nation allegedly fit
for heroes. The third epigraph, from a D. H. Lawrence letter, seems the
most political in that it uses the word 'revolutionary', but this may be
tempered by the characteristic Lawrencian reference to 'life' rather than
more directly to class-politics. In fact, this idea of an authentic kind of
life currently denied in European so-called 'life' runs through all five of
the epigraphs and is a key idea for the novel (and one that Greenwood
often refers to elsewhere too[5]). The fourth epigraph states the idea again,
though the source here suggests a more revolutionary politics as well as
a sense of apocalypse: 'I feel that you are suffering because the years are
passing irretrievably without one's "living" … What we are witnessing
first is a whole old world sinking.' The quotation is from one of the
well-known letters of Rosa Luxembourg to Sophie Liebknecht, second
wife of Karl Liebknecht. Both Rosa Luxembourg and Karl Liebknecht
were imprisoned between 1916 and 1918 as members of the anti-War
German Sparticist Party. Here the state of imprisonment, as well as the
proposition that the old world order is failing, can be linked to the novel.

---

5 For examples of Greenwood's use of the 'life which is not a life' theme, see,
  for example, Ch. 2, opening quotation from *Lancashire*, or on the same page
  the quotation from *The Secret Kingdom* (London: Jonathan Cape, 1938; Leeds:
  Morley-Baker, 1970), p. 10.

The last epigraph comes from a related First World War context, being taken from Annie Eisenmenger's *Blockade! The Diary of an Austrian Middle Class Woman 1914–24* (the Penguin edition of *Love on the Dole* had an unfortunate error at this point, citing *The Diary of an <u>Australian</u> Middle Class Woman 1914–24* [my emphasis], and thus confusing the context). The reduction of life in Hanky Park to a mere struggle for physical survival is presaged: 'I must thrust all spiritual and cultural interests into the background, and … hunt for shillings in order to keep body and soul together.'

The effect of these varied yet thematically linked epigraphs seems quite complex. They all reinforce the topics to be expected in the novel (restriction, entrapment, reduction, and the suggestion that a wartime-like crisis is now a permanent state in Hanky Park), but may also suggest to those who can read these quotations and recognise their range of cultural reference that they are themselves somewhat cosmopolitan readers, with access to the life of letters (or as Greenwood might later put it, the internal 'Secret Kingdom'[6]). In effect these suggestions increase the number of implied readers who are positioned as cultural haves rather than have-nots – something that may be important for the whole political project of *Love on the Dole*, as we shall see later.

There may also, though, be aspects of the epigraphs that are not entirely reassuring for some kinds of possible reader. Many critics think that Greenwood is wary in the novel of upsetting middle-class or uncommitted readers, but quoting Rosa Luxembourg seems slightly problematic from this point of view in that she was remembered as a Communist martyr (she was executed after the Spartacist rising in Weimar Germany in January 1919). This might push some potential readers out of their political comfort zone. Equally, the next quotation, from Eisenmenger, may both reassure and disturb: on the one hand it comes back to a middle-class point of view, but on the other it suggests that historical events can reduce the middle classes to 'a proletariat', implying that social identities are not necessarily a matter of personal merit or choice, or under individual control. In short, even in the novel's epigraphs there may be signs that Greenwood's construction of his reader is more complex than has sometimes been assumed, and that if he seeks to avoid offence and recruit middle-class opinion (as well, perhaps, as educated working-class opinion), he may also be able to take such imagined readers into territories beyond those they might willingly

6 See Chapter 2 above.

or easily choose. One needs also to note Ben Harker's point in one of the few discussions taking any note of the epigraphs – that they were omitted from the second edition. However, I note that the epigraphs were restored in the new mass market Guild Books edition of January 1942, so Greenwood must have continued to think them of importance.[7]

Greenwood's construction of an imagined reader suggests some possible insights into anxieties or assumptions on his part about who might read the book and how they might react to the story of Hanky Park and life on the dole there. It seems important to ask the underlying question of *why* the novel starts with this introductory, distancing chapter and its strong emphasis on the positions of narrator, reader, and the subjects of Hanky Park. The most obvious answer to this question is that Greenwood is assuming a complete gulf between the reader and the novel's setting: the kind of person likely to be reading *Love on the Dole* will have no real experience of such a life and will therefore need an introduction to bridge that gap. Certainly, this is part of the chapter's function. However, the apparent certainty which the opening chapter builds up through its view from above, and the evident distance between narrator–reader and the subjects of Hanky Park, is actually only a temporary one. The conclusion of the opening chapter seems to say that there is nothing more to say about these people than this reductive and despairing summary of a cyclical life that has continued without much change since the nineteenth century and which shows little chance of change. But this dissolves into a much more inward view of life in Hanky Park as the reader progresses into Chapter 2, 'Getting Up', and opens up a view of this lifecycle as it is being lived out in the present and into the future, rather than as a narrative with an inevitable end.

II. Harry Hardcastle and a Narrative of Progress

Though Chapter 2 in some ways echoes and continues the narrative rhythm of the first chapter in that it begins with an external scene before moving into a household in Hanky Park, the reader immediately

---

7 'Adapting to the Conjuncture', p. 57. Harker suggests that 'Recognising that the finished text did not live up to these revolutionary inscriptions, Greenwood cut them.' It is also possible that he feared some might push too hard at the limits of what some of the readers he wished to reach might tolerate. The wartime restoration of all the epigraphs in the Guild edition (p. 9) might suggest a returning radical confidence during 'the people's war'.

has a more individuated representation of life there. Thus we focus on particular people, on a specific time, and a particular place in the life of Hanky Park (at first on Mr Hulkington's the grocer's and then on the Hardcastle household). There is still a narrator who inserts commentaries that do not stem from the people themselves, but the reader is now positioned much closer to the characters' own speeches, actions, and thoughts. In fact, there are noticeable differences in how we gain knowledge of the characters: we hear Blind Joe's dialect speech, but have no more inner access to his thoughts; for Mrs Hardcastle, we get only her appearance, physical actions, and a small amount of speech; for Sally we get, for the moment, very little speech and no revelation of thought, but instead a noticeably explicit narrative intrusion in the shape of a long paragraph of commentary on her physical appearance, including the deployment of a number of literary figures: 'Eighteen, a gorgeous creature whose native beauty her shabbiness could not hide. Eyes dark, lustrous, haunting; abundant black hair tumbling in waves; a full, ripe, pouting mouth and a low, round bosom' (p. 15).

The language here seems, as is often the case for Sally, to come from the world of popular romance, and clearly for both Mrs Hardcastle and her daughter there is a concentration on their physical appearances, as if for women that is the only significant mode of being (or so the masculine-centred gaze or narration here assumes). It is only when we get to Harry that there is any real attempt to represent thought, with his inner perspective dominating the remaining three pages of the chapter. His portrayal does begin, as for the other characters, with a physical description of his awakening and some speech, but this soon modulates into a narrative report of his thought on coming to consciousness on this rainy Monday morning:

> Harry muttered something ... his sullen expression mirroring the surly dissatisfaction he felt towards the day's prospects ... . Bleak visions both of the school classroom and of Price and Jones's pawnshop where he worked as half-time clerk rose to his mind ... . Then he remembered ... . He'd done with schooling ... . Price and Jones though! *that* above all things. Couldn't they understand that he'd had a surfeit of desks there? That the pawnshop was a worse prison than school? ... Damned in a fair handwriting. (pp. 16–17)

This is a version of Greenwood's own escape from school, as told in his 'Langy Road' essay and later in his memoirs (see Chapter 3). The reported internal viewpoint, after the more external narrative viewpoint thus far in the chapter, draws the reader strongly into Harry's perspective, as might also his picking up of the themes of imprisonment and lack of authentic life prefigured in the epigraphs. Ideas of liberty and especially masculine independence quickly come to the fore in the depiction of Harry's mind. Thus the novel's Chapter 3, titled 'Looking for it', sees not only a more optimistic-seeming dawn come to Hanky Park but also Harry leaving home early (and before his father returns home from his night shift at the pit) in order to put a plan, about which he has consulted no-one, into action:

> 'They ain't getting me clerking.' He muttered.
>   He found himself listening to the beat of the men's feet again; an entrancing tune, inspiring, eloquent of the great engineering works where this army of men were employed. Reverently he murmured its name: 'Marlowe's'. Marlowe's, a household word throughout the universe of commerce; textiles, coal, engineering, shipping and home trade; a finger in the pile of them all. (p. 19)

Harry fervently assigns Marlowe's a sacred role as he ritually and 'reverently' intones its name. Its aura comes partly from the impressive extent of its power – it is known everywhere, both by consumers and throughout the whole economic system, which, significantly, makes up a 'universe'. But it also clearly symbolises for Harry a cluster of linked qualities: community, masculinity, and modernity. He is desperate to join in with the collective male experience that Marlowe's focuses, the very anonymity paradoxically seeming to him to add power to the masculine identity that membership guarantees: 'There, in those vast works, the thousands of human pygmies moved in the close confines of their allotted sphere, each performing his particular task, an infinitesimal part of a pre-ordained whole, a necessary cog in the great organisation' (pp. 19–20).

To serve in Marlowe's is, for Harry at this point of the narrative, to be free: free particularly to be an adult male, a state of being that he represents to himself by mundane and romantic means. Thus he notes that the men going into work 'reek' of 'oily clothes' and 'tobacco smoke' and 'buzz' with 'conversation to do, mostly, with weekend sport', but they are also in Harry's mind 'gods of the machine', 'infinitely and ineffably superior' to 'mere pushers of pens' (pp. 20–21). The machine is, indeed, very important here, and at times the description has a futurist dynamism (with the following image perhaps influencing the cover design of the first edition): 'Three huge chimneys challenged the lowering sky ... a double row of six smaller chimneys thrust up their steel muzzles like cannon trained on air raiders. Tongues of flame shot up, fiery sprites' (p. 20).

And the machine is, again, explicitly associated with the religious and mystical; even the apprentices talk 'in terms of magic': 'entrancing names such as "machine shop", "foundry", "riveting shop" slipped from their tongues with spellbinding ease' (p. 21). Thus Harry's personal narrative of self-development into manhood is entirely transposed onto his version of a larger narrative of industrial modernity in which working-class men are the heroes. No wonder, then, that Harry sees Marlowe's as the sacred site for a rite of passage and fears that he may not pass the test of manhood: 'his courage ebbed' (p. 21).

Harry needs a helper, a man already initiated, to make his rite of passage. However, he instantly rejects the most evidently masculine man at Marlowe's, though he is close at hand:

> There was Ned Narkey, a huge fellow with the physique of a Mongolian wrestler. But he wouldn't, couldn't ask Ned. There was something about the beefy hulking brute that repelled one; though Harry admired his strength ... . Ned could lift a girder that four ordinary men couldn't move. But he wasn't a nice fellow; there was a foul side to his tongue, and there were tattoos on his arms of naked females ... . (p. 22)

Ned is popular with the other boys and something of a local figure, having won a medal in the First World War and having had his picture in the newspaper, but Harry rejects asking him for help partly because he may get a humiliating response (especially if Ned is not yet 'recovered from his weekend carousal') and partly because he dislikes seeing Ned speak to his sister Sally. Instead Harry will seek help from a more approachable intermediary:

> Larry Meath! Harry's heart leaped and his eyes glowed with eagerness. *He'd* understand; he was that kind. His quality of studiousness and reserve elevated him to a plane beyond that of ordinary folk; he seemed out of place in his lodgings in North Street. He wasn't for drinking, gambling, swearing or brawling ... . (p. 22)

Despite Harry's own desire to enter as quickly as possible into the ranks of adult masculinity, Ned is clearly represented here as exemplifying an undesirable kind of masculinity – a hyper-masculinity that instantly makes Harry uncomfortable, partly because he may be found lacking by Ned, partly because it seems to him excessive, disorderly, and transgressive. Ned is associated with intemperance of several kinds: he drinks and swears, is violent, bad-tempered, and crudely sexual. Indeed, even his surname 'Narkey' (meaning 'bad-tempered') reinforces this angry quality, since it is a meaningful name in the Dickensian tradition.[8]

Larry, on the other hand, is constructed as an evident contrast to the 'brute' Ned, with numerous references to his intelligence, patience, and kindness. Larry seems, in Harry's mind, to possess sufficient masculinity to be part of Marlowe's, but is also temperate in every way, an example of controlled power and knowledge. He is, then, Harry's ideal intermediary with the world of work. However, it is not only for Harry that Larry works as an intermediary: it seems to be his characteristic role. Thus, when Harry thinks in a nearby paragraph about Larry's general reputation, it is this role as universal intermediary that quickly emerges:

> People were always going to No.21 with their troubles: 'Ah've had a summons for me rent, Larry. *Could* y'go for me?' ... or if somebody had an official form to fill in they, demoralised by the questions set forth and distressed at the thought of having to take up pen and ink would come, nervous and stare-eyed to ask his assistance, going home, beaming and relieved, with the completed paper clasped in their hands. (p. 23)

It is, of course, immediately important to ask the question: intermediary between what and what, and who and whom? For Harry, Larry is intermediary between the (in Harry's scale of values) childish/effeminate world of 'clerking' and the masculine world of work. For the nameless, representative characters in Harry's more general account, Larry can pass between their world and that of the entirely adult world of the rent-collector and the official form: in short, between their fearful sense of their own innumeracy and inarticulacy and the world of numbers, words, and – underpinning both – laws, rules, and authority. These two somewhat differing views of Larry's direction of travel may suggest a number of ironies: what Harry is so desperate to escape is also a possible source of power; what may seem an 'effeminate' sphere may also partly constitute the power of Larry as an unofficial man of 'influence' (p. 23), as well as informing in a less enlightening way the power of both the local and national government and of those not unconnected grandees who rule their petty princedoms in Hanky Park – 'Sam Grundy,

---

8 The word itself is usually spelled without an 'e' – see *OED* entries for 'narky' and 'nark'.

the gross street corner bookmaker, Alderman Ezekiah Grumpole, the money-lender proprietor of the Samaritan Clothing Club, Price the pawnbroker, each an institution' (p. 24).

Indeed, if Larry is through his boundary-crossing powers a possible helper for Harry, Harry is also aware that he can be a tricky helper: 'He paused ... alarmed, a sudden remembrance occurring to him that Larry's kindliness might take an unexpected turn. Yes! Remember when Jack Lindsay asked Larry to introduce him to Marlowe's? Larry warned him against it: told him that it was a waste of time serving an apprenticeship to engineering' (p. 23). In fact, Larry's role of intermediary is a vital one in the novel, but also gives him an in-between identity as someone who does not quite belong in the streets of Hanky Park. But his mediation goes beyond the world of the novel, for he also has a vital role as a mediator for the implied reader – between Hanky Park and their implied superior social worlds, in which his association with literacy and education plays a major part. I shall return to this mediation between reader and novel shortly, when discussing Larry in his own right. As it turns out, though, Harry does not in the end require Larry's help in crossing the border, for, significantly, the mass movement of workers as the whistle blows sweeps him over into the adult realm without any action on his part: 'Swept forward by the irresistible current ... he found himself in the machine shop' (p. 24).

Larry, however, does notice Harry in passing and his thoughts help to reinforce the various other hints made to the reader that Harry's own perceptions of the wonders of Marlowe's may not tell the only story about industrial modernity and progress:

> Larry, slowly stuffing his newspaper into his pocket regarded the boy sympathetically, thoughtfully. A thin, down-at-heel child dressed in a worse-for-wear knickerbocker suit ... . Another recruit to this twelve thousand strong army of men who all, at one time had come, eagerly, to some such place as this on a similar errand. Larry too. All had been young Harrys then. They now were old, disenchanted Harrys; families dependent on their irregular and insufficient wages; no respite to the damnable, eternal struggling. (p. 24)

Harry is to report for work at Marlowe's tomorrow. However, the narrative follows him back to his job at Mr Price the pawnbroker's for one more day, establishing what appear to be sharp contrasts between the worlds of today and tomorrow. If Marlowe's is where men work, then the pawnshop, the presence of Price and Harry apart, is deeply part of the feminine sphere in Hanky Park. This morning, as every other, there is, waiting for opening time, 'a backyard full of women', 'a crush of unwashed women', 'a rowdy, pushing, shoving, squeezing crowd of women' (p. 30): 'Harry gazed at the women as a soon-to-be-released prisoner might stare at the stones of his prison cell' (p. 31). In many respects the whole narrative so far has been centred on masculine experience and, given the close identification built up between Harry and the reader, there seems to be an assumption that the implied reader is being cast as masculine too. This reading position is certainly strongly continued here too, with a clear distaste on Harry's part for the 'feminine', associated by him with crowds, disorder, dirt, and anonymity – apparently the very opposite of the ennobling modern collectivity he has so proudly joined in with (or anyway *imagined*) at Marlowe's early that morning.

Indeed, this distaste for and identification of women both as trapped themselves and as forces of incarceration starts off in Harry's perception, but is soon elided into what reads more like a narrator's voice:

> By the time he was on the other side of the counter again the place was full. In the staring gas light, the women throwing back their shawls from their dishevelled hair revealed faces which, though dissimilar in features, had a similarity of expression common, typical, of all the married women around and about: their badge of marriage, as it were. (pp. 30–31)

There are various ways in which readers can process this elision of voices; it could read as an articulation of the underlying rationale behind Harry's more visceral reactions to these women – implying, of course, that Harry is unable to make his thoughts clear without this Standard English and the literary narrator's assistance. However, as the passage goes on it seems to leave Harry's perceptions some way behind and, indeed, to articulate understandings that cannot readily be attributed to him at all, not even second-hand. Thus narration of what is in Harry's mind begins to turn into a separate and somewhat aerial/literary narrator's overview of women's lives, reminiscent of the narration from above in Chapter 1 of the novel:

> The vivacity of their virgin days was with their virgin days gone ... Marriage scored on their faces a kind of preoccupied, faded, lack-lustre air as though they were constantly being plagued by some problem. As they were. How to get a shilling ... [and] make it do the work of two ... .
>
> Simple natures all, prey to romantic notions whose potent toxin was become part of the fabric of their brains.

As virgins they had cherished a solitary dream, the expectation of the climax of their wedding day. Wedding day, when, clad in the appropriate – afterwards utterly useless – finery, they appeared for the moment the cynosure of a crowd of envious females.

For a moment only.

The finery was discarded for less conspicuous apparel which devoured their identity; they became one of a multitude of insignificant women by a mere change of costume ... . Patronage of Price and Jones, and all that it signified and implied was an aspect of marriage unanticipated in their dreams. (p. 31)

The apparent acceptance of (complicity in?) a romance genre in the earlier narrative description of Sally is here replaced by a critical view of romance as the central delusion of the female population of Hanky Park (John Kirk suggests that in the novel 'working-class women ... signify the very depths to which working-class life can sink').[9] The fulfilment of the romantic dream appears here to be a moment of publicly recognised individuation by female peers as much as the pairing with a romantically and sexually desirable male partner (though that is implied to an extent by the several references to virginity). But that state of individual identity lasts for only a moment, and just as it is brought into being partly by clothing, so clothing too 'devoured identity'. This clothing theme and metaphor for the nature of their lives is, of course, entirely appropriate for the setting of the scene in the pawnbrokers, for both the wearing of drab everyday clothes and the unending circulation of clothing for very little return is at the core of their business there. Indeed, the implication that they all wear essentially the same uniform and share the same condition is really only confirmed by the description of a range of types of garment, many of which replay the theme that such pleasures as they have are fleeting and borrowed: 'boots, shoes, clogs, girls' cheap, gaudy dance frocks, men's Sunday suits, mixed bundles of bedding, table linen and underclothing'. It is 'a tale told by an idiot, never to be concluded until the characters had no further use for pawning or redeeming' (p. 32).

The reader is returned from this highly literary articulation of the sole narrative of women's lives in Hanky Park to a piece of dialect speech that a reader might take to signal a moment of particular inarticulacy on Harry's part: 'Well, Ah'm glad t' be leavin' all this ... . Eeee, glad t' be going'. Phoo, not half!' (p. 32). It may be that this statement is to

9 *Twentieth Century Writing and the British Working Class* (Cardiff: University of Wales Press, 2003), p. 39.

be read as encompassing Harry's unconscious appreciation of everything spelt out above about the systematic disappointment of women's lives in Hanky Park. From this indistinguishable feminine mass-experience, Harry can turn away: 'Lathes, milling machines, engineering, 2510 and evenings and Saturday afternoons free! FREE! ... Listen to Marlowe's!' (p. 42). His own enlistment in the mass-experience of masculinity is, it appears, a very different thing: he is distinguished by his own 'individual' clocking-in number on his brass check: 2510.[10]

However, various ironies may soon develop for the attentive reader: the lifecycle of the women at the pawnshop is surely proleptic – a flash-forward to Harry's own participation in this economy in a mere seven years. At first, the reader may seem to be wholly caught up in Harry's perspective, carried along by his dreams of masculinity and his rejection of the entrapping feminine sphere. But, as Larry's thoughts about Harry as 'another recruit' may have suggested, he will in time find out that the masculine and feminine spheres in Hanky Park are inter-dependent and closely related: his escape through modern, industrial masculinity is as illusory as the escape offered by romance and is, in fact, merely another mode of romance. Indeed, the next chapter's title and interests reinforce through evident ironies the sharp limitations of Harry's understanding of how adult masculinity – outside his boyish and romanticised vision of it – might actually relate to the feminine world which he thinks he has left behind him: 'Girls make Him Sick.'

If up to this point the implied reader has been able to participate fairly innocently in Harry's dream of industrial masculinity, Chapter 5 marks a change, a developing gap, between what Harry knows and what the reader knows. Harry, meeting the female cotton-mill workers on their way home for their midday meal, is embarrassed because, having taken off his overalls, he is left wearing his 'schoolboy clothes'. But he has a more specific embarrassment too, for he meets Helen Hawkins, an adolescent mill-girl who had in the recent past afforded a sympathetic ear to the 'black despair' he had felt at the prospect of continuing at Price's:

> Things were changed now ... . He felt that her acceptance of his confidences had placed him under a puzzling kind of obligation ... that gave her the

10 Greenwood implies that 2510 was his own clock-in number when he worked at the Ford works at Trafford Park as a clerk, in his 'Author's Preface' to *The Cleft Stick* (London: Selwyn & Blount, 1937), p. 8: 'I declined ... to cease being Walter Greenwood when the time-clock rang and turned me into Number 2510 or whatever number I was.'

privilege to take a proprietary interest in his affairs. He felt uneasy. He sensed a restraining influence, a lack of freedom to associate himself with the boys. (p. 43)

Helen is now an unwelcome link to his feminised past – and doubly so because she represents a challenge to his view that departure from Price's is a progressive step. In a rash moment, he had been caught up by her different romantic vision of individual social progress and told her that 'he was to seek work in a proper office' (p. 43). We briefly switch to her point of view and see how bitterly disappointed she is, largely because Harry is cast by her as an escape route from her own family life, which is far more squalid and miserable than that of the 'respectable' Hardcastle household: 'what a bathos ... to imagine Harry dressed in overalls instead of as she had always pictured him, clean, tidy, going to an office where gentlemen worked' (p. 45). They part on bad terms as Helen remarks, 'But look at fellows y'll mix with, Harry ... . Swearers like Ned Narkey'. Readers might suspect that Harry's distaste for 'girls' may turn out to be part of the adolescent phase which is so nicely caught by early chapters in the novel (Harry meeting Helen here is filled with 'a creeping self-reproach ... that conflicting emotion named being at 'sixes and sevens' with oneself' [p. 43]). But they may also note that Helen's distaste for Ned Narkey has, in fact, already been voiced by Harry himself as he waited outside Marlowe's sacred precincts.

The next two chapters that complete 'Part One' of *Love on the Dole* portray Harry in his achieved dream of being a Marlowe's apprentice: the pouring of hot metal by 'men with ... bare sinewy arms' is a 'magnificent, inspiring sight' (p. 49). There are some warning signs, though, as when the politely disturbing Larry suggests that these days neither skill nor masculinity are that necessary to engineering:

'Don't you remember the women during the war?'
'What women?' Harry asked, troubled ...
'The women who took the places of the engineers ... the women picked up straightaway what Marlowe's and the others say it takes seven years' apprenticeship to learn.' (p. 47)

As Part Two of the novel opens Harry's satisfaction continues, but he begins also to mark for the reader an increasing awareness of time passing, as the narrative rhythm speeds up:

These new experiences ... brought with them a calm serenity which gradually assumed an air of permanency ... (p. 69)

He had been superseded by younger boys! This was the price that had to be paid for promotion ... (p. 73)

He saw groups of young men lounging at corners ... . Why were they lounging there? (p. 76)

Soon, Harry realises that he is less well-off than when he was first signed as an apprentice, since he no longer has tips from the men and older boys for running errands. Notably, it is at this point that he again appreciates the worth of female company, seeking out Helen as the only solution to his growing anxiety ('only she could assuage this fear of the future' [p. 78]). He cannot afford a suit and his only hope of spare cash is if one of his bets with Sam Grundy were to be a winner. As it happens, after three years of weekly expenditure one of Harry's 'thripenny triples' does hit the jackpot, to the incredulity of the envious ('twenty-two quid for thrippence? Yaah. Some hopes' [p. 110]) and to the longer-term benefit of Sam Grundy, who proves in public that his motto is indeed true: 'Sky's limit' (p. 115).

This stroke of good fortune, however, merely suspends temporarily the rhythm of which the reader is now so conscious, as Harry and Helen enter what seems to them a parallel universe, which the title of Chapter 8, 'Magic Casements', indicates through its allusion to Keats' 'Ode to a Nightingale', a text further recalled in some of the chapter's description of Harry and Helen's brief escape from Hanky Park: 'This unusual mode of life was full of witchery ... lost in fairyland they wandered, arm in arm' (p. 121). Indeed, the chapter is heavy with language that is romantic in both a high literary and more popular genre mode: 'The road the lovers were to traverse home wound ... through sable coppices and between high thorn hedges heavy with honey-suckle and blossom' (p. 125). But the ironic nature of this escape from place and time is already clear to the reader: the chapter gives full but conscious access to the subjective experience of the romantic narrative that has been so coolly critiqued in the pawnshop scene previously discussed. Now Harry is prey to these notions too, for it is clear to them both that marriage will be a kind of perpetual version of this holiday – will be if only Harry can get a qualified engineer's job as soon as he has served his apprenticeship. Harry may not be able to take an objective view of the influence of romance on his life, but the reader is now well able to see that it is not at all a genre that operates only in the feminine sphere: betting, holidays, marriage are all part of what Collette Colligan has acutely called the 'politics of hope':

Reviewers and critics who have commented on the overwhelming pessimism of the novel have overlooked the kinds of hope it describes – probably because the fortune-teller's vision, the bookie's promise, and the romantic dream around which Greenwood's characters build their lives are regarded as socially irresponsible or politically complaisant. Greenwood's novel is not naive about how such kinds of hopes serve as cheap palliatives for the disenfranchised working classes and do little to change existing economic conditions; however, it also realises that these hopes help sustain the working classes through hardship. In other words, it offers a doubled perspective on compensatory hope: it describes how cheap entertainment and wishful thinking can pander to illusion, but also offset nihilistic despair.[11]

This apparently unique experience of an idyllic holiday by the sea is indeed firmly put into its context as simultaneously an escape from Hanky Park and part of the whole system that reproduces Hanky Park through the playing out of natural and individual desires. Thus, at the beginning of the chapter, Harry's parents recall that they too, just once, had a holiday, and in the next chapter, the first of Part Three, we are also told the story of Joe Simmons, which strips away any romantic gloss. He and his wife both regret their present state ('Nowt t' wear an' ne'er a blasted penny to call me own'), which had a similar origin: 'A week's holiday at the seaside, fifteen pounds and the girl of his pre-nuptial fancy – now his wife – had been the basis of Joe's venture into matrimony' (p. 131). Part Three shifts the narrative in several ways: it marks the end of Harry's naiver dreams and also a shift of focus towards the adult Sally and Larry – and it delivers what Harry has long suspected and feared: that his life-story will not progress as he had hoped. He is laid off from Marlowe's: 'they now were fully qualified engineers. They also were qualified to draw the dole' (p. 154).

III. Larry: 'a cut above the ordinary engineer' (p. 23)

Larry Meath might seem to illustrate the social gradations of class in Hanky Park (something discussed in relation to Greenwood himself in Chapter 3). The first description of him in the novel follows the description of Ned Narkey quoted above, and runs like this: 'Nearer

---

11 "'Hope on, hope ever. One of these fine days my ship will come in:" The Politics of Hope in Walter Greenwood's *Love on the Dole* (1933)', *Postgraduate English: A Journal and Forum for Postgraduates in English in the UK and Europe*, 3, March 2001: available online at <http://www.dur.ac.uk/postgraduate.english/waltergr. htm>, accessed 10 September 2011.

the gates Harry glimpsed Larry Meath reading a newspaper' (p. 22). This is a perfectly ordinary activity, but actually Larry is the only man waiting for the whistle to blow at Marlowe's who is depicted as reading a paper, and his association with literacy is reinforced by several further references to reading in the remainder of the paragraph, for which Harry is the focal point: 'if you went to the library to look at the illustrated papers or to watch the old geysers playing dominoes, you sometimes saw Larry ... absorbed in some book or other that looked dry as the desert' (p. 22). While other inhabitants of Hanky Park, or boys and old men anyway, play games to pass the time or look at the pictures in the illustrated papers, Larry reads the kind of book that is clearly seen as a closed one for Harry and other library users (who do not at this point seem to include any men or women of working age). If our sense so far of the implied reader(s) of the novel has any force, then the mere fact that Larry is distinguished by being a reader may provide a sympathetic link between him and the novel's readers, since both are showing how through that invaluable tool they have the means to acquire a wider view of the world through the word (as well as a consequent cultural status).

Indeed, Larry's possession of literacy is reinforced quite frequently in the novel, as is Hanky Park's lack of understanding of the point of literacy except on what is portrayed as a more basic and utilitarian level (to Sally's observation in the novel that Larry knows the names of all the birds [p. 96] the film adds Mrs Hardcastle's comment that she supposes that is what education is – knowing things which are of no use). Thus, Larry refers to his enjoyment of 'books, music, brief holidays' (p. 150) when he contemplates having to forego these luxurious necessities if he and Sally marry on his present wages. However, his status as a reader is actually noticed more frequently by others than referred to by himself. Sally on her one visit to his lodgings (he is absent) notes that though his room is identical in plan to the equivalent room at the Hardcastle household, it is transformed by one item of 'furniture': 'Books arranged on shelves either side of the fireplace. A comforting sight; so extraordinary a furnishing of a North Street front room. Their presence enhanced, lent an intangible part of themselves to the meagre rickety furniture provided by the landlady' (p. 190).

Mrs Bull regrets that no-one will take notice of the political advice of an 'eddicated and well-read feller like Larry Meath' (p. 164), while the perception that his reading matter is 'dry as dust' is evoked again by Sally (p. 139) – though here she refers to the political pamphlets he is giving out, rather than to his books. It is notable that his books are always referred to generically only, as if 'books' is on its own a sufficiently detailed categorisation. This generality is in contrast to the rich set of carefully attributed epigraphs which precede the novel text itself and even to the discussion of music in the shape of Bach, Beethoven, and the Hallé orchestra on the Labour Club ramble (though these specific musical allusions may be motivated mainly by the humour at Sally's expense). It may be that what is being registered here is indeed how closed these books are to these witnesses – Sally admires Larry, but is presented as seeing his books much more as physical markers of his class status – as furniture indeed, rather than as an entreé into his intellectual and cultural world. Given the importance of Larry as a reader and the links this may create with the reader of *Love on the Dole*, it does seem curious that we are given no further insight into what he reads – and even he simply refers to his need for 'books, music' (though in association with him we *might* be more inclined to read that very general reference as indicating the infinite worlds they lead to). The overriding effect may show how cut off from reading Hanky Park is, except where it at least offers more immediate rewards, or prospect of reward – the novel does make numerous references to more popular uses of numeracy and literacy. Thus there are the frequent mentions of racing papers and more occasional references to popular romance, which is mainly associated with Sally, Harry, and Helen (who realises with profound misery that even the 'opiates' of 'cheap novelettes or the spectacle of films' [p. 65] cannot block out her squalid home life). There are also accounts of highly utilitarian uses of literacy, such as the short text that directs Mr Price's whole life and on which his literal 'price code' is based (p. 40):

S   H   U   N   P   O   V   E   R   T   Y   X

1   2   3   4   5   6   7   8   9   10   11   12

This is 'the simple code of which he was author': a code that, ironically, uses a moral exhortation underpinned by an idea of free moral choice as a numerical key to an exchange that feeds on and exploits inescapable poverty. The simple equivalence here between a moral and economic code may well encapsulate an upper-/middle-class view of poverty as caused by poor moral/economic choices on the part of the lower working-classes – a key proposition that the novel overall contests. These popular and commercial uses of literacy are often explicitly or implicitly mocked by the novel, and this further locates Larry as an in-between figure, neither a part of the mass experience of Hanky Park nor part of the local social elite, whose culture is utterly philistine and whose little learning is deployed solely for exploitation.

Instead, Larry partakes of literacy both for its own sake and as a way of fighting back on behalf of the community – for he often uses his skills in reading and writing for communal and political ends. We see him, for example, using chalked diagrams on walls both to explain Marxist economics (p. 183) and to encourage political activism, such as joining the demonstration against the benefit cuts (p. 193). The two aspects of his literacy may have slightly varying effects in terms of the possible relationship with the reader – the love of books may lead to sympathy, but the chalking of political messages and explanation of Marx may be less endearing for some readers at least (Nicola Wilson sees Larry's books as clearly signifying his 'political engagement', but perhaps another possible reason for not giving more detail about what exactly he reads is that it leaves a useful ambiguity about whether he is reading literary books or more political texts).[12] Certainly, though, his literacy is a key contribution to his role as intermediary. Just as the narrative voice of Chapter 1 and the voice that glosses dialect elsewhere in the text acts as an intermediary, so too in a more general way does Larry, explaining things to Hanky Park residents for sure within the novel (though they often do not hear), but also explaining Hanky Park to those from outside. Indeed, if there is something of a problem with the glosses (they are plainly interventions in the world of the novel by a mediating narrator on behalf of the reader), this intermediary status may also produce some problems for and *about* Larry, as many critics have observed.[13]

His often-noted set-piece political speech exemplifies most strikingly of all some of the ways in which he is not of Hanky Park in quite the way that (nearly) all his neighbours are:

> And to find the cost of this present system you have only to look at our own lives and the lives of our parents and their parents. Labour never ending, constant struggles to pay the rent and to buy sufficient food and clothing; no time for anything that is bright and beautiful ... . And the houses in which we are compelled to live are as though they have been designed by fiends in hell for our especial punishment. When work is regular we are just able to live from week to week: there is no surplus. But for ever, there hangs over

---

12 *Home in British Working-Class Fiction* (Farnham: Ashgate, 2015), p. 78.
13 See, for example, Stephen A. Ross, 'Authenticity Betrayed: the "Idiot Folk" of *Love on the Dole*', *Cultural Critique*, 56, December 2004, pp. 189–209.

us that dread threat of unemployment ... . This existence is what is fobbed
off on to us as Life ... . In every industrial city of the land you will find
places such as this, where such people as us who do the work of the world
are forced to spend their days. *That* is the price we will continue to pay until
you people awaken to the fact that Society has the means, the skill, and the
knowledge to afford us the opportunity to become Men and Women in the
fullest sense of those terms. (p. 86)

This is not, of course, the everyday language of common men and
women in Hanky Park – and, indeed, it is in a notably high register
that Larry himself uses rarely in the novel. Thus wherever the passage
can use a more literary or rhetorical construction or more elevated
choice of vocabulary it does so: 'constant struggles', 'sufficient food',
'are as though they have been designed by fiends in hell for our
especial punishment'. Quite abstract ideas are also evoked, with little
explanation: 'the cost of this present system', 'there is no surplus',
'existence ... fobbed off on to us as Life', 'the knowledge to afford us
the opportunity to become Men and Women in the fullest sense of
those terms'. These relative abstractions derive from the language of
economics combined with the kind of Lawrencian distinction between
subsistence and full life already evoked in the actual Lawrence epigraph
and its interplay with the other epigraphs. Particularly telling too is the
final distinction Larry makes between himself and others in Hanky
Park; despite his initial 'We', he concludes that all will go on as it is
'until you people waken to the fact' (the film censor Colonel Hanna,
in his plot summary of the play, captures the situation and the problem
baldly if unwittingly: 'he speaks at street corners in an endeavour to
make the working classes think').[14] Larry can see what most others in
Hanky Park cannot, or will not.

How is the reader to deal with this important speech? It may further
reinforce Larry's outsider–insider status (thus aligning him firmly with
the authorial narrator of Chapter 1): he does know how the system
works, but he does not communicate it in terms familiar to those inside
the system (in seeing Hanky Park *as* a system Larry is demonstrating
that he is precisely not fully part of it). This reading may lead to various
assumptions. It could suggest an element of blame towards the 'people'
for their lack of insight, and/or it could suggest a kind of double-bind
for Larry or one like him: anyone who can see through the system
removes themselves to a marked degree from the system and from the

14 BBFC 'Scenario Notes', 1936, p. 42.

terms that those trapped within it can easily comprehend. Or it could suggest that Larry himself lacks certain kinds of insight – he cannot see that his language here is counter-productive, patronising, and removed from concrete experience. Maybe this is ineffective political rhetoric, an example of a man misusing his education and energy, since no-one will listen – a prophet is never recognised in his own country.

However, these possibilities may be controlled to a degree by the strong steer about how to read the speech given by the way it is inset within Sally's perceptions. Thus Larry's speech is prefaced by an exchange between Sally and Ned Narkey:

> 'Y'aint th'only tart around here,' sneeringly: 'P'raps y'd rather listen t' him and his blather'. He stamped off fuming, promising himself that this high-handed attitude towards her would teach her a lesson and that she would come back to him of her own accord to ask his pardon.
>
> She shrugged her shoulders … . Imagine having her name coupled with Larry's, even though only in the imagination of a jealous mind … . She found that she was vastly pleased …
>
> Larry's presence, somehow, seemed to demand your best behaviour. You became so very conscious of the loose way of your speech when you heard him speaking. (pp. 85–86)

Just as for Harry outside Marlowe's, the contrast between the 'rough' Narkey and the 'gentle' Larry suggests to Sally a distinction between more and less attractive and respectable modes of masculinity. Moreover, this is closely linked to the use of language and to language as a class marker. There is a sharp contrast between Ned's dialect speech and the high-register standard English of Larry's political speech. Indeed, Sally becomes positively conscious of language through this contrast and, while clearly admiring Larry's speech and the 'superiority' it signifies for her, she may fear that actually her own speech is closer to that of Ned. However, one of the novel's mediating devices confuses this issue somewhat, since it tends to render most characters' thoughts substantially through standard English – in effect always glossing their speech as it narrates their thinking. Thus Sally's own thoughts are here delivered through a formal and standard English: 'you became so very conscious of the loose way of your speech'. So, too – in an example where the novel's techniques work less well – are Ned's thoughts: 'promising himself that this high-handed attitude towards her would teach her a lesson' (I always feel I have to re-read to check here that these are Ned's thoughts being reported rather than Sally's).

Overall, though, it seems clear that the dominant reading the text is suggesting is that Larry's (political) speech is both a sign of his admirable, superior learning and an indicator of his estrangement from the common experience of Hanky Park. I began this section by suggesting that Larry might in the novel represent aspects of the internal gradations of class within a place like Hanky Park. Certainly, many of what are regarded as his eccentricities by others of the place's inhabitants can be seen in this way. He is, uniquely, a skilled engineer who is not married, has no children, and who therefore has some surplus income (and hence those books, gramophone records and player, and holidays). Moreover, he has worked out that marriage and children on too little income are part of the system that renders most inhabitants of Hanky Park the same – which reproduces their poverty. However, what could be seen as a status difference (highly skilled, single, employed engineer as against an unemployed family man) seems to be elided here into an individual difference: there is no one else like Larry in Hanky Park, it appears.

How did he get his education and his articulacy? The obvious answer is through self-education and/or the kinds of self-help group that certainly existed in various forms in working-class culture. Greenwood, in his 1935 *Spectator* article 'Poverty and Freedom', writes of how 'there was, of course, the consolation of the public library and of the evening study classes provided by political organisations. Here one could seek historical explanation of one's own predicament.'[15] However, the reader of *Love on the Dole* gets remarkably little insight into this collective autodidactic strand of working-class culture in Hanky Park. Larry does allude lightly to it – he tells Sally a little about this aspect of Salford society just after she has heard his political speech: 'Why not join us at the Labour Club? ... It isn't all politics there ... though you can't altogether escape them ... . There's the Sunday rambles into Derbyshire; they should interest you; and they're a jolly crowd of young folks who go ... . They're a sociable lot of people, you know' (p. 87).

But none of the members of the Labour Club, ramblers or otherwise, make it into the novel as actual characters – they are marginal figures, referred to, not seen. Perhaps they are implied to be not from Hanky Park itself but from better-off parts of Salford – they have cultural knowledge that Sally lacks and can afford hiking shorts and walking boots. Even by mixing with them Larry may again be showing his exceptional social status rather than showing that he is but one of many working-class

15 *Spectator* 22 November 1935 – WGC/3/1, p. 53.

self-improvers or intellectuals. While his lack of a family may be in itself partly a politically informed choice, one might note also that he has no relatives at all – no parents, for example, to look after (Carole Snee quite rightly points out that this odd lack of family network is widespread in the novel's fictional world, including for the Hardcastles: 'There are no uncles and aunts or grandparents close by – a strange phenomenon in an established working-class community'[16]). When studying the novel, my students have often suggested that Larry must have moved to Hanky Park from another part of Britain, making him a geographical as well as social outsider. But there is no evidence given in the text for such a very reasonable explanation: Larry, I conclude, is overall a man without parallel and without origins as far as the novel is concerned, rather than a more realistically justified example of internal class gradation within Hanky Park, despite the biographical and historical parallels, and indeed the internal thematic evidence, suggesting the presence and importance of such hierarchies. It is perhaps no wonder, then, that the 1941 film version came to the same conclusion as my students and cast the Welsh actor Clifford Evans as Larry. David Berry, in his book *Wales & Cinema: the First Hundred Years*, suggests that nothing is made of Evans' evident Welsh identity in the film: 'Meath is described as Welsh in studio publicity but no attempt is made to point up his origins.'[17] I think this is not quite right: the film does not explicitly fill in the novel's apparent gap with an explanation of Larry's origins, but merely by casting Evans with his Welsh accent as Larry it implicitly supplies an explanation. Larry in the film *is* an outsider – and brings to the apathy of Hanky Park some of the political radicalism and collective feeling that was in the 1930s so strongly associated with Wales (indeed, cinema audiences in 1941 might have recalled Clifford Evans playing the part of a Welsh miner in another sympathetic portrayal of British working-class people in the 1940 film *The Proud Valley*).[18]

16 In her essay 'Working-Class Literature or Proletarian Writing?', p. 176.
17 (Cardiff: University of Wales Press, 1994), p. 225 (see also pp. 177–78 for some further comment on Clifford Evans and *Love on the Dole*).
18 For discussion of images of Wales in the period, see the opening discussion in chapter 5 'Depressed Pastorals? Documenting Wales in the 1930s' in my book *English Fiction in the 1930s: Language, Genre, History* (London: Continuum, 2006). For discussion of *The Proud Valley* (directed by Pen Tennyson and starring Paul Robeson), see Jeffrey Richards' *The Age of the Dream Palace* (London: Routledge, 1984; New York: I. B. Tauris, 2010), pp. 308–09 and Berry, *Wales & Cinema*, pp. 166–71.

The novel, though, does not provide any such explanation, and the reader is bound to draw some conclusions from Larry's singularity. It might be that this factor is politically neutralising, making Larry a much less politically-effective figure than a Larry who springs from that community, who is not utterly exceptional, and who could both understand the situation *and* influence the other members of the community. His singularity might also make him much less politically threatening for some readers: Larry can describe the problems, but not directly change them – he will not lead a revolution of his less articulate fellow workers. Carole Snee makes very much this point about Larry in her thought-provoking essay of 1979, 'Working-Class Literature or Proletarian Writing?':

> Greenwood presents him as a person whose 'essential self' ... has escaped the coarsening effects of working-class life so evident in the other occupants of Hanky Park ... . Larry 'proves' that the working-class militant is exceptional, and above all is an isolated *individual*. Thus he in no way challenges the dominant ideology, but confirms that socialism is only a belief propounded by maverick individuals. He is so exceptional that the implicit suggestion is that no one could or should aspire to be like him. His socialism is rejected by all those around him, and ... his 'natural' character distances him from the rest of the community.[19]

However, there is more than one way of having political influence and this reading may miss a range of possible ways in which readers might engage with this character who is both politically activist and apparently politically ineffective. It seems to me that the implied reader is so strongly invited to identify with Larry (in parallel with their identification with the mediating narrator) that he becomes a focus for their own relationship with the people of Hanky Park and thus with what is represented as an inarticulate, politically unconscious mass. Clearly this has strongly conservative aspects (the automatic association of intelligence, literacy, standard English, education, self-knowledge, and self-determination), but I am not certain that the whole effect is necessarily to produce a politically inactive reader in a position of complacent, comfortable, or defeated neutrality. If Larry – and his identifying reader – is not an ideal working-class community activist, neither is s/he exactly a conventional aper or reproducer of bourgeois values, despite Snee's general argument that *Love on the Dole* never challenges the 'form of the bourgeois

---

19 'Working-Class Literature or Proletarian Writing?', p. 173.

novel, nor its underlying ideology'.[20] When Snee observes that 'he is so exceptional that the implicit suggestion is that no one could or should aspire to be like him', she is very much confining political effect to the world of the novel itself: it seems possible that (some) readers might indeed aspire to be like Larry in some respects, to see themselves as perhaps often ignored, but also more articulate intermediaries for those who could not make their voices heard directly.

And it may be a mistake on Snee and others' parts to assume that Larry did simply slot into many readers' minds as an obvious and easy-to-accept conventional hero: 'Take away his socialist beliefs and he could be the hero in any women's magazine story.'[21] It is true that Greenwood does have a strong interest in romance (as discussed in Chapter 3, this may strengthen in later novels), but the casual injunction to 'take away his socialist beliefs' may obscure just how unlikely and unconventional the socialist romance hero is (how many women's magazine stories in the 1930s did have socialist heroes, I wonder?). Equally importantly, the literate, educated working-class socialist novel hero, even if he does have some bourgeois tendencies, may not have been that obvious a combination: a novel that constructed a socialist working-class hero who could be identified with and admired by working-class and middle-class readers would be an extraordinary and perhaps politically potent achievement in itself.

Indeed, Snee specifically comments on how readers might receive the novel, but does so in terms that are a little abstracted and based on a curiously exclusive (and positively Leavisite) assumption:

> The novel's special impact both in the 1930s and after is difficult to understand, for its retained power as a symbol far outweighs its impact as a text when read. Its status is partly due to the fact that it was the first novel of its kind by a working-class writer in the twentieth century, or at least the first to reach a wide audience and receive critical acclaim. The more difficult question to answer is, why did it become an immediate success? In trying to answer that question one is faced with the problem of the difference between a critical reading of the text, and the non-literary reading of the majority of readers.[22]

I do not, of course, accept that there is only one possible or 'proper' reader's response to the novel (it is not at all a universally accepted *fact*

---

20 'Working-Class Literature or Proletarian Writing?', p. 171.
21 'Working-Class Literature or Proletarian Writing?', p. 173.
22 'Working-Class Literature or Proletarian Writing?', p. 170.

that it lacks impact on the reader, and that the text itself is capable of only one reading), or that the reading of 'the majority of readers' is inherently undiscriminating. The terms in which Snee opposes her two kinds of reader are odd: we would expect a 'critical reading of the text' to be put against a 'non-critical reading', but in fact her second term is 'non-literary reading', which is surely something different. This confusion is added to when she later argues that the novel was accepted into the (bourgeois) canon precisely because it could be readily seen as 'Literature':[23] 'it has been able to receive both popular acclaim and literary recognition because it exists firmly within the tradition of "Literature", despite its subject matter.' By this latter, if inconsistent point, I am more persuaded: part of the power of the novel for many possible readers may well come from the numerous markers of its literary status. As I have suggested in earlier discussion of the novel's epigraphs and other features, Larry and the intermediary narrator use literariness and ideas about reading to help readers enter into what might otherwise be an anxious political area, precisely without alienating them. Perhaps the novel has, unlike Larry, but through him, found a political language that does work for its audience without alienating either the more politically committed or the politically wary or nervous? The very positive reception of the novel (and later the play and film) by such a wide range of newspaper reviewers with very different political allegiances might support the novel's capacity to recruit a wide range of readers to its exploration of why life in Hanky Park is not Life 'in its fullest sense'. In short, the novel's concrete political success in reaching and persuading large numbers and types of readers (as opposed to a more abstract political success in fulfilling a conventional socialist political programme) may come from a kind of tactfulness towards the potential reader that is deliberate, rather than a result of unconscious immersion in bourgeois ideology.

Snee perhaps mistakes how a novel can act by limiting its effects to the world of the novel and underestimating the reader's role:

> It is a deeply pessimistic novel ... because within the novel Greenwood himself denies the possibility of change, or of any solution to the social problems he identifies. The novel is a cry of outrage, but the rage is impotent, for his own ideological position is essentially that of the liberal reformer. He reacts with horror at the injustices of society, but cannot really conceive of any alternative to that society.[24]

23 'Working-Class Literature or Proletarian Writing?', p. 171.
24 'Working-Class Literature or Proletarian Writing?', p. 171.

John Kirk argues for a similar political inefficacy in the novel:

> [It] stands alongside those nineteenth-century novels of reform in terms
> of both form and overall structure of feeling. The desire to generate a
> sympathetic response towards the working-class predominates, and this is
> orientated towards an inferred and attendant middle-class readership with
> whom agency lies.[25]

However, the novel's power does indeed surely rely on its ability to
recruit the reader (potentially working, middle, and upper class) to the
view that there must and could be an alternative to Hanky Park – a
possibility in itself realised by the reader's own implied wider view of
the world – and indeed that people like themselves can help bring
about change, presumably through democratic pressure on the largely
non-interventionist central government of the 1930s. It is true that the
novel does not portray 'the possibility of the working class changing
its own conditions of existence',[26] but I am not sure that the novel
regards Hanky Park as representing the whole of British working-class
experience (it is rather the experience of a portion that is especially cut
off and left behind); and, anyway, that is not its political programme,
which is instead to unite a broad range of readers in a shared conviction
that Hanky Park is intolerable and that its people can be helped through
outside intervention.

One point on which I have touched may illustrate again that the
novel is willing to take some risks with its readership: if it does work
hard to avoid appealing only to the converted and to avoid putting
off the unconverted, it is also willing to try to expand the political
consciousness of some possible readers. As we have seen, Larry's main
political speech has been seen as a problem for the novel, and for Larry
himself. Certainly, he does not always seem to communicate well with
his fellow workers 'within the novel', but there is another audience that
these speeches and explanations may address: these political debates
may be as much for the reader's education as for Hanky Park's (an idea
also inherent in Ben Harker's argument that 'the reader of the novel is
required "to take up a position towards the action", actively producing
a dialogue between Meath's teaching and the narrative's events'[27]). Thus
the well-turned and sharply reasoned phrases in Larry's main political

25 *Twentieth Century Writing and the British Working Class*, p. 39.
26 Snee, 'Working-Class Literature or Proletarian Writing?', p. 171.
27 'Adapting to the Conjuncture', p. 60.

speech might speak very effectively to the possible readers of the novel, inviting recognition or contrast, or possibly a mixture, with their own lives: 'No time for anything that is bright and beautiful ... . When work is regular we are just able to live from week to week: there is no surplus. But for ever, there hangs over us that dread threat of unemployment' (p. 86). Equally, Larry's careful Marxist explanation of how capital and labour works might suggest to some readers relatively unfamiliar with this discourse that this is not just the language of wild, un-British, 'bolshevik' rhetoric, but something worth considering both aesthetically and politically:

> We are the ones who plough the soil and grow food; we make the clothes and the houses and motor-cars and the ships and the trains; and we man the ships and drive the trains. In short, it's our labour power that makes all and every one of these commodities. (p. 183)

This is not to dispute that Larry's politics are carefully modulated in the novel, but it is to disagree with those critics who see *Love on the Dole* as disappointingly neutral or conservative in political effect. Larry's socialist politics are not completely muted in the novel, but they are represented as gradualist rather than as anything like revolutionary. Indeed, at several points it becomes clear that, despite his use of marxist economics, Larry is firmly a Labour Party activist rather than a Communist. This is certainly the case in the climax of his story – the protest march on Salford Town Hall against the Means Test, remembered in Salford as the Battle of Bexley Square and narrated mainly in the chapter called 'Historical Narrative'.[28] Here, the novel distinguishes systematically between Larry and other leaders who use a more revolutionary rhetoric:

> A youngish man, wearing an open-neck shirt was lifted shoulder-high: 'Comrades,' he shouted, spiritedly, and proceeded to an inflammatory speech which communicated restless animation to his audience ... . (p. 197)

> The great pale sea of faces were turned to an improvised rostrum where a stocky wire-haired fellow speaking in a strong Scots accent, passionately weighed against the government and urged all to resist, by force if necessary, the threat to their standard of life ... he jabbed the air in the direction of the plain-clothes police, their size rendering them conspicuous ... . He

---

28 Commemorated since 2011 by a red plaque – see <http://www.blueplaqueplaces. co.uk/battle-of-bexley-square-red-plaque-in-salford-30214#.VUTQhv7wtiA>, accessed 2 May 2015.

condemned them as 'traitors to their class', as 'enemies of the workers', 'servants of the boss class'. (p. 198)

A finely featured young man with long hair took his place on the rostrum instantly winning the acclamation of the crowd by heaping invective upon all with whom he disassociated himself in the social scale. (p. 199)

It is noticeable that Larry, who until this point in the novel has always been seen as a partial outsider to Hanky Park, is now seen as a relative insider compared with these speakers from elsewhere (and he does for once have allies among the organisers and some authority over the crowd, despite his disagreement with the 'finely featured young man' referred to as 'the organiser' [p. 200]). But still the question of whether Larry will be listened to by his neighbours persists. The outsider identities of the other speakers are swiftly established through the use of what could reasonably be called stereotypes (the Scots communist with his ready-made phrases, the intellectual with his long hair and urge to disassociate himself from his own class). They are clearly meant to be seen as demagogues: their rhetoric is either about themselves and/or catches up the situation into a revolutionary narrative, reflecting back to the agitated crowd of unemployed men whose dole has been stopped the idea that immediate and violent action will doubtless yield results. This works on Harry, who becomes very much part of the crowd – 'resentment had disappeared for the nonce in face of the imagined possibilities engendered by the speech-making' (p. 199). Larry takes a different view, drawing attention to a very different reading of the immediate situation and likely consequences:

Larry began with a repudiation of the previous speaker; urged his audience to appreciate the preparations, in the way of attendant police, which had been made in anticipation of any disorderliness; reminded the crowd that the cause of their protest was of their own making; recalled the scares and the people's response at the general election. (p. 198)

He tries to tell the people what he thinks is most likely to happen if the police are given any opportunity to make it a physical fight. This seems a reasonable if pessimistic point: injury and imprisonment may be more immediate results than either the withdrawal of the Means Test regulations or the beginning of the revolution. However, blaming the people for their plight owing to their being duped by the National Government's election promises and scare-tactics does seem both under-hand and unlikely to persuade people angered by being utterly abandoned by the state, and takes us back to his set-piece speech in which he has also blamed the people of Hanky Park for their lack of agency. Moreover, Larry's illness also distracts him from events: 'He wished all this over so that he might return home to bed' (p. 198).

It is not surprising, then, that Carole Snee sees the scene as heavily reinforcing the failure of the novel to present Larry as an effective political leader or to make its own political points clear:

> The only other overtly political event in the novel is also marred by the structure of the romance fiction which Greenwood superimposes on his naturalistic fiction. ... Its precise meaning and function, both within the fictional world, and to the real world is difficult to locate ... the political implications of the scene are undermined because of the personal romantic drama ... and the march of the unemployed begins to function simply as a setting for the personal drama which is about to reach its climax.[29]

There is much truth in this accusation that Larry's illness dilutes the political impact of his death after the march, that it diverts attention away from its political significance and back to the romance plot of his relationship with Sally. But, evasive as these moves are in many ways, there are certainly some very 'precise meanings and functions' for these fictional tactics that can readily be seen as part of Greenwood's construction of his readership – and, particularly in this case, some anxieties about how readers might respond to this climactic scene. Larry's attempts to rein in the marchers is surely a vital move in allowing many readers who have thus far identified with him to continue to class this labour leader as 'respectable' and a democratic gradualist rather than, in their eyes, a revolutionary. Indeed, *The Times* review of the film version in 1941 specifically noted Larry as being an 'agitator who believes in constitutional methods'[30] (though, of course, it is very possible that other readers might at this stage accuse Larry of 'kow-towing to the boss-class', as the 'organiser' does at this point in the play version[31]). It is notable that this climactic scene was several times remarked on in the 1930s (if usually by conservative commentators) not as lacking political edge but as the

29 'Working-Class Literature or Proletarian Writing?', p. 175.
30 'Love on the Dole', 30 May 1941, p. 6. Accessed via the *Times Digital Archive* 25 July 2012.
31 In the French Acting Edition, the organiser is called 'O'Leary', which may imply a different background to that of the implied undergraduate of the novel and also of the Jonathan Cape edition of the play, where he is simply called 'Young Man'. Both characters, however, use this same line in Act III, Scene i (London: French, 1936, p. 55; London: Cape, 1935, p. 99).

most extreme moment of the story and the least politically acceptable. Thus, the British Board of Film Censors' report on the proposed 1935 film, noting that in the play version this took place mainly off stage, was very anxious about the need to show the scene more directly in a film version: 'The scenes of mobs fighting the police are not shown in the stage-play, but only described. They might easily be prohibitive.'[32]

In May 1940, when the *Manchester City News* reported that a film version was again being considered, the scene was also specifically mentioned:

> *Love on the Dole* is to be filmed after all. Manchester novelist Mr Walter Greenwood, British National Films, and the British Board of Film Censors have come to terms, and the Board is to give the film a certificate if the street fight between the unemployed and the police does not appear.[33]

In fact, as we shall see, and suggesting a significant shift in sensibilities, the film was to include a quite graphic scene of the marchers and the police clashing, and even constructed some complex action for a medium-budget film of mounted police charging the demonstrators. There are, however, also some interventions to support Larry's analysis of the likely outcome of such a struggle.

The point that needs to be made about this is a specifically historicising one: that, in the handling of this scene, the novel – and the other two versions as well – are not just falling into bourgeois defeatism in a general and abstract way but are instead showing a very particular awareness of the text's probable political effects on a broadly imagined readership. One or two of the reviews of the play in particular illustrate how strong was the need on the part of some viewers to retain their sense that its characters were 'respectable', still part of the 'deserving working-class', if they were to sympathise with them. Thus the reviewer for the *Stage* wrote that: 'Mr and Mrs Hardcastle are entirely decent persons. Mr Hardcastle has fought in the war, and his medals hang on the kitchen wall. Julien Mitchell (an actor) makes the fine ex-soldier a truly tragic figure ... and Larry Meath is [also] a worthy young fellow.'[34] The emphasis on Mr Hardcastle's war service is notable – something which in fact neither novel text nor play script as printed refer to at all (but the

32 Richards, *The Age of the Dream Palace*, p. 119, citing British Board of Film Censors' Report 1936/42.
33 WGC/3/14: *Manchester City News*, 25 May 1940.
34 WGC/3/1: the *Stage*, 7 February 1935.

medals *are* listed in the minutely detailed 'Property Plot' at the end of the French acting edition: 'small dark-coloured picture-frame, containing 3 war-medals on red plush, on wall down R.').[35] Clearly, this emphasis rapidly reminds readers of this review of the promises after the war of 'a land fit for heroes' and that men like Hardcastle deserve something very different from Hanky Park; and Larry, though he is a political activist, is also drawn into this sphere of the decent and deserving working man.

The context for this is, of course, a very real anxiety on the part of government and the upper and middle classes about the effects of chronic unemployment on the British working classes, perhaps combined a little uncertainly with a narrative about the essential 'decency' of the 'respectable' working people and the cohesiveness of British society. Thus Stephen Constantine notes in his book *Unemployment in Britain Between the Wars* both the existence of an anxiety about serious dissent and also its failure to materialise:

> [Some] including politicians in office, trembled at the thought of Bolshevik agitators stirring up trouble among the misguided unemployed. This fantasy inspired the plot for Sapper's novel *The Black Gang* (1922) and it lay behind regular police reports to the cabinet on political activities among the unemployed.
>
> [But] it is clear that extremist political action attracted only a handful of the unemployed; demonstrators asked for more liberal relief not for social revolution.[36]

Indeed, a Carnegie UK Trust enquiry felt that political apathy was in itself an undesirable result of unemployment:

> It has, perhaps, been assumed too readily by some that, because men are unemployed, their natural state of want and discontent must express itself in some revolutionary attitude. It cannot be reiterated too often that unemployment is not an active state; its keynote is boredom ... [and] this boredom was invariably accompanied by a disbelief which gave rise to cynicism ... . These young men ... were not likely to believe that their own active participation in affairs would permanently affect an order of things that had already ... shown itself to be so powerful and so devastating.[37]

35 See Samuel French edition, pp. 72–75.

36 *Unemployment in Britain Between the Wars*, Seminar Studies in History (Harlow: Longmans, 1980), pp. 42–43. Sapper's novel seems a little too early to be good evidence for the 1930s, however.

37 Quoted in Constantine, *Unemployment in Britain Between the Wars*, p. 97, Document 16 – extract from *Disinherited Youth*, Carnegie UK Trust (London: Constable, 1943), pp. 78–79.

It could be said that one of the differences between Larry and the characters represented as 'agitators' is an underlying dispute as to whether this march against the Means Test is about 'more liberal relief' or 'social revolution', with their speeches vying for the ear of the marchers and for possession of the march as either social democratic or revolutionary in tone and intention. It is notable that, despite the chapter's title, 'Historical Narrative', which claims the march and its consequences as a real event – as indeed it was – there is certainly one suppressed context in Greenwood's narrative, which is the role of the NUWM (National Unemployed Workers Movement) in its organisation. Though there are references to 'the organiser', the novel gives quite a strong impression that the march is largely spontaneous, a response to the shock of those on the dole to the application of the Means Test. An alternative and very full account of his memories of the 'Battle of Bexley Square' by Eddie Frow (the model for the 'finely featured young man', who was in fact arrested during the march) quotes some of Greenwood's description, but also makes it very clear that the march was organised by the NUWM, among many other differences from the novel's representation of events. The NUWM is picked out by Constantine as being a sharp exception, at least in some respects, to his sense that a relative minority of unemployed men were politically engaged:

> [The NUWM] organised a large number of local demonstrations and six impressive national hunger marches against unemployment and rates of benefit. Many of these protests ended in violent clashes between the demonstrators and the police. Government, police and press usually took an alarmist view of its work, exaggerating its influence, its communist connections and its revolutionary implications.[38]

Greenwood's probable reasons for failing to mention the NUWM by name are clear from this: it might well have scared off some readers and undermined his careful presentation of Larry as a moderate.

Larry, then, is a key feature of the novel's engagement with its readers – acting as intermediary, shaping carefully their response to its politics, and helping it to achieve a balance point between showing an educated, literate, politically active labour leader articulating his ideas and still engaging the sympathies of a broad implied readership, whose investment in 'respectability' (the values of literacy, democratic gradualism, moral agency, and a corresponding fear of their contraries) is imagined as deep. It is significant that after his death Larry is finally

---

38 *Unemployment in Britain Between the Wars*, p. 42.

bidden a kind of ironic farewell through the careless rejection of his books, which are also not properly valued in Hanky Park: 'One of the furniture broker's men ... came to the door ... carrying a pile of Larry's books slung about with a length of cord. He pushed past Sally, then dropped the books on the pavement' (p. 217). Sadly, in the film version Larry's possessions in this scene do not include any books, but Sally is shown as having a handful of books – perhaps some of Larry's? – when she leaves her parents' home to live with Sam Grundy.

IV. Sally: 'a face and form such as any society dame would have given three-quarters of her fortune to possess' (p. 15)

I noted in my discussion of Chapter 2 of the novel that at Sally's very first appearance it is, indeed, her appearance that seems to be emphasised, and through this her striking 'natural' capacity to bring the world of romance into the grim reality of Hanky Park. The portion of the quotation that I have used above for the section heading partly constructs her uncommon attractiveness, but notably also puts a monetary value on this quality, perhaps prefiguring the hard bargain she makes with the monetary-exchange system at the end of the novel. In fact, this hard-headed commercial confirmation by an imagined social superior of her unusual beauty in terms of exchange stands out in a paragraph where much of the imagery draws on romance evocations of the natural ('colour tinted her pallid cheeks such as the wind whipped up when it blew from the north or east' [p. 15]). And perhaps this too prefigures the way in which romance – a strong interest for both the text and many of its characters – is in the novel also often seen as part of the economy of Hanky Park, rather than as only an imaginary escape into a different realm.

Certainly Sally, like Larry, does seem to be a rarity in Hanky Park, someone whose presence there is slightly out of place, and this seems a good place to start to explore how her character might work for the reader and how it might influence the possible meanings of the novel. But where Larry's distinctiveness is based on language, situation, ideas, and aspirations, Sally's distinctiveness is, at first anyway, firmly narrated as being based in her beauty and sexual attractiveness (later her inchoate aspirations are added in: 'she felt that she wanted something urgently, but what it was she wanted she did not know' [p. 83]). The omniscient narrator notes her 'full, ripe, pouting mouth and a low round bosom' (p. 15), while the following scene where Harry and Sally dress, though no doubt giving an important documentary sense of the impoverished living conditions of the Hardcastle family and the lack of privacy, might nevertheless also have erotic possibilities for 1930s readers: 'She pulled on her knickers and half-turned ... . She stood in front of the candle slipping her clothes over her head, an enormous shadow of herself reflected on wall and ceiling' (the scene is omitted from the play, but the film certainly takes up this possibility, and while apparently adding respectability to the shared bedroom with a curtain dividing it in two, makes something of the shadows on the curtain as Sally dresses).[39]

Indeed, the way in which Sally is represented (while still very much seen through the 'male gaze') does seem to differ from the ways in which many other female characters are represented in the novel. Her mother Mrs Hardcastle, 'an old woman of forty' (whose first name is only rarely used) feels defeated by life in Hanky Park, and this seems to be the commonest female experience, as is represented in Harry's/ the narrator's reflection on the lifecycle of women, as well as by more direct means. Thus Helen, whose relationship with Harry is surely there partly as a mundane counterpart to the more extraordinary relationship of Sally and Larry, seems likely to reproduce Mrs Hardcastle's lifecycle. Despite the ironies that undermine Harry's imagination of women's lives as utterly different from men's in their lack of individuation and agency, this model does still seem to hold good for the way in which many women characters are presented. Snee comments slightly sweepingly of Sally's 'difference': 'her beauty is to be marvelled at ... the other women represent "woman as slut"'.[40] Though Sally is unique, there are nevertheless some important distinctions and gradations made among the other women portrayed. Thus Helen is from a household looked down on by the Hardcastles and where there is indeed a confirmation of the hint in Chapter 2 of the problems lack of privacy brings through the all-too noticeable sexual behaviour of her drunken parents, who plainly fall below the contemporary 'respectability' line. Nicola Wilson notes the antithesis in the novel between 'the "rough" and "respectable"; between cleanliness and dirt, sex within and outside of marriage, the private and the public'.[41] Towards the end of the novel Mr Hardcastle is very ready to call the pregnant Helen 'a slut', but Mrs Hardcastle and Sally seem to accept the consequences of Helen and Harry's pre-marital sex

---

39 Nicola Wilson notes the hint in the novel of fears of incest in overcrowded housing in her *Home in British Working-Class Fiction*, p. 98.
40 'Working-Class Literature or Proletarian Writing?', p. 174.
41 *Home in British Working-Class Fiction*, p. 99.

as being unremarkable: they simply help as best they can, though they are not represented as making any direct comment. Sally's tolerance and defiance of the conventional sexual morality of the time becomes much more explicit in the play version where she comforts Helen:

> HELEN. Ah know what y're going to say. Y're going to call me names an' say as it's my fault ...
>
> SALLY. Well, ah weren't going to congratulate y' Helen, but Ah'm not going to call y' names. Got a bit mixed in y' dates, didn't y'?[42]

In the play Sally then gives Helen a ten-shilling note for a marriage licence – in the novel Helen simply tells Harry that she has borrowed this money from a girl in the mill (p. 223). As Constantine pointed out, the novel is very interested in respectability and the unrespectable, and, I might add, in sexual behaviours as markers of a borderline.[43] Harry, we may recall, is wary of Ned's display of 'excessive' masculinity, and also repelled by the crude and entirely unromantic sexual references of Tom Hare. In the Hardcastle household the status of respectability, and indeed the word itself, is invoked on a number of occasions. Thus Mr Hardcastle expresses his view that Harry has fallen in status through his connection with Helen as well as his own behaviour: "'Yah, y' damn fool, don't y' think there's enough trouble here wi'out you bringin' more? ... Well, no slut like that's gonna come t' live here, d'y' hear?'" (p. 221). Later, when Sally returns home having come to her 'agreement' with Sam Grundy, Mr Hardcastle again strongly invokes the language of respectability: "'So y'd go whorin' an' mek respectable folk like me and y' ma the talk of the neighbourhood, eh? Damn y'! Y'aint fit to be me dowter'" (p. 246; both versions of the play refer to the Hardcastles' concern with respectability in an opening set description: 'It is important to remember that this is not slum property, but the house of a respectable working man, whose incorrigible snobbery would be aroused if you suggested that North Street was a slum'[44]). The word 'respectable' is picked up again in connection with Sally towards the end of the novel by Mrs Hardcastle ("'We've allus bin respectable. An' now neighbours're all talking'" [p. 253]) and by Mrs Scodger ("'the carryings on o' some folks

---

42 Cape edition, Act 3, Scene, 1, p. 103. Presumably the mention of dates refers to the 'rhythm method' of contraception – which in itself seems very daring for a play of this time. See further discussion of contraception later in the chapter.

43 'Love on the Dole and its Reception in the 1930s', p. 239.

44 Cape edition, 1936, p. 13; French acting edition, 1936, p. 9.

wot could be named ain't fit for the ears o' respectable folk'" [p. 252]). However, as we shall see, there are voices raised in opposition to respectability, including that of Mrs Bull.

Nevertheless, Mr and Mrs Hardcastle's desire to hang on to respectability is certainly not treated with contempt in the novel, though it is exposed to some other perspectives.[45] It is made very clear that part of Mr Hardcastle's vehemence and aggression comes from his knowledge that he is barely keeping his own grip on respectability and, indeed, that he knows that such a status is no longer exactly a matter of personal or 'moral' choices. Thus Harry, defending Helen, makes the point that actually he and his father are both equal under current conditions. Neither does the thing that a respectable working man should do and which underpins their position as head of the household – bringing in a weekly wage sufficient to keep the household together: "'Ah'm not th' only one out o' work i' this house, remember. Yah, y' treat me like as though Ah was a kid, just-a-cause Ah've got nowt an' Ah'm out o'work'" (pp. 221–22).

If Helen and Harry have 'fallen' sexually and thus socially, Mr Hardcastle and Harry have both also fallen economically and in terms that are devastating to their senses of themselves as working men. Harry and Mr Hardcastle are equally 'unmanned' by their joblessness, and it is only Helen of the three involved who still has employment and such self-determination as that brings: it is she who can at least borrow the funds from a work-mate to buy a marriage licence and restore, to an extent, their respectability. Judging by the lack of moral reaction from Mrs Hardcastle and Sally (even more so in the play version), it seems reasonable to suppose that pregnancy before marriage is not that uncommon in Hanky Park and that under 'normal' economic conditions the couple involved would simply get married, as Harry and Helen eventually do. For Mr Hardcastle, though, condemnation is the only remaining part of respectability he can afford.

His arguments with Sally replay much of the dynamic of his argument with Harry about Helen, but one might say that Sally has more exceptionally crossed a boundary – and indeed one that removes her from Hanky Park. Nevertheless, the same logic is applied – that Mr Hardcastle is not in a substantially different position to Sally when

---

45 The text on the inside flap of the dust-jacket for the UK edition of *The Cleft Stick* also invokes respectability, commenting that the stories 'show facets of the life of the people of the North who are condemned to live on the knife-edge poverty and a wry sort of respectability'.

it comes to the independence that underpins the idea of respectability. After a dialect rehearsal in Mr Hardcastle's mind of her words of recrimination, there is a standard English narration of his thoughts:

> What had he done for his children? ... What had he been *able* to do other than what had been done? ... These last few months since he had been knocked off the dole he had been living on Sally's earnings. Living on a woman, his daughter, whom he had just dismissed for living on a man! She had gone now, taken her income with her. What was he to do to meet the home's obligations? (p. 248)

The moral for the reader is clear: life in Hanky Park makes it impossible for virtuous aspirations – Sally's desire to marry Larry, Harry's desire to marry Helen and live something like his parents (rather than hers), Mr Hardcastle's wish to meet his proper obligations to his family – to thrive or be sustained.

Unemployment, and even more so the cutting of benefits and the specific family-disintegrating effects of the Means Test, reduce the differences between the Hardcastles and those they would, if they could, distinguish themselves from. Snee's comment that, *apart* from Sally, all the rest of the female characters are 'woman as slut' is, of course, not exactly true at the end in terms of sexual morality: from Mr Hardcastle's point of view Sally has joined the unrespectable. That, of course, is part of her tragedy and part of the tragedy of the present system against which the novel seeks to bring readers to protest. However, there do remain some clear distinctions between Sally and those to whom the Hardcastles feel themselves superior. It seems important to invoke the curious range of meaning for the word 'slut', which figures as the negative term in the novel's discourse of respectability. The word's most literal senses have to do with women who are physically dirty, and who keep themselves and their houses in a 'slatternly' state. Indeed, this was one of a number of topics dealt with in the novel that offended the Salford social worker Charis Frankenberg: 'We ... cannot surely pass without comment a novel in which every time Salford women are mentioned in the mass they are described as on their doorsteps with 'unwashed faces and matted hair ... idly watching their filthy, half-naked children playing in the gutter.'[46] This primary meaning then becomes associated

---

46 *Daily Dispatch* 26 September 1933 (the quotation from the novel is on p. 157); Greenwood replies that it is a 'notorious slum to which the paragraph refers'. See WGC/3/2, p. 9.

with sexual 'looseness'.[47] Now, it is true that for most of the female characters in the novel a connection is made between bad housekeeping and 'unregulated' sexual behaviour, bringing the two senses of the word together in a conventional way. But this is certainly not true for Sally, whose final defiance of conventional sexual codes could in a way be said to be the opposite of bad housekeeping or a descent into slovenliness. In an appalling sense, given her lack of viable choice, it is good housekeeping to make the best of what assets and possibilities she has left to her, via access to Sam Grundy: '"Ah knows what money means, now. An' he's got it and an' by God Ah'll mek him pay"' (p. 245). The film censor Miss Shortt articulated this in her plot summary of the story: 'She is strictly business-like and takes no risks till she has a fixed settlement.'[48]

Sally is seen in contrast with a number of other female characters and their fates. Thus Helen (with Harry) does her best to reproduce a 'normal' Hanky Park working-class lifestyle along the lines just about sustained by the Hardcastles in (slightly) better times, and Helen's behaviour is wholly motivated by her desire to rise above her background and to escape what she fears is the taint of her upbringing. Once Harry has the job as bus driver that Sally obtains for him, they will surely achieve this goal. But the novel is careful to draw attention to other female characters who have much worse outcomes in the 'normal' environment for women of Hanky Park. Thus there is the salutary case of Kate Malloy, whom Sally pities from early on in the novel:

> A thin, pale faced girl, Kate's facial expression reminded one of a hunted animal; always there was a light of furtive nervousness in her eyes. She rarely spoke to anyone at the mill save Sally, for whom she nursed a dog-like devotion … . Since she had no parents and lived in lodgings … . Sally never could find it in her heart to rebuke her. (p. 144)

Kate, too, is an outsider – presumably either of Irish descent or herself an Irish immigrant to Hanky Park.[49] Her lack of family or social support

---

47 See *OED*, which distinguishes these as senses 1 and 2 – but some of the examples of use suggest the two meanings frequently run into each other.

48 BBFC Scenario Notes, 1936, p. 42a. Though Miss Shortt's conclusions are often quoted, her plot summary (effectively her own reduction of the play text to something like a 'scenario') and the separate one that Colonel Hanna wrote have not been explored.

49 Her ethnicity is a slight exception (though not in itself enough to alter the general proposition) to Matthew Gaughan's point that: 'Rather than representing an ethnically heterogeneous community made up of the English (Protestant), Irish

makes her easy prey for Ned Narkey – precisely through the operation of an entirely self-deluding romance in her mind. He treats her without any respect, leaving her to wait for him outside the pub, and she submits to her powerless position through romantic fantasy: "'But Ah can't go, Sal. Ah promised Ah'd wait. – An' Ah don't want him to – oh, Ah want t' see him. You'd be the same about a feller if y'thought owt about him like Ah do'" (p. 144). Sally simply replies, "'You make me sick.'" Sally is open to romance, but not helpless prey to it: she is notably an active agent, rather than a passive victim when it comes to seeking a partner. Thus, she does not deny Ned's account of a time when she was to some extent interested in him:

'[My hands] wusn't dirty when I'd got plenty of jack an' Ah wus payin' for y't' go dancin', wus they?'
'I ne'er asked y' t' pay. Ah'd ha' paid my whack an' you know it.' (p. 145)

It is consistent that she, to her mother's thrilled shock, is also very much an active agent in the relationship with Larry, asking him to marry her: "'then let's get married'" (p. 151 – in the play Sally points out this own role reversal explicitly to her mother). In assuming that she 'possesses' herself, Sally is distinct from other women in Hanky Park: she is represented as a 'modern woman', perhaps, against the background of the more nineteenth-century-seeming victims and exhausted married women who surround her. Her ramble with Larry gives even Mrs Hardcastle some rare access to 'vicarious enjoyment': 'she had built up a wonderful romance out of the situation. It was delectable food to that starved side of her nature whose existence she would not even admit to herself' (p. 95). In short, for much of the novel, it seems that Sally may be able to realise a genuine romance even in this actuality (in the play version she points out to Larry that "'Ah'm not a film-star'", but this may nevertheless imply a certain star quality while also reinforcing her ordinariness).[50]

She does show awareness that romance may be delusion, and fears at one point that her love for Larry may be just the mechanism that will translate them all too soon into exact replacements for Mr and Mrs Hardcastle: 'dreariness of No.17 North Street. A stupendous suspicion pounced upon her' (p. 142). And the novel also shows that there are

(Catholic), and Jewish working classes, Greenwood creates a community made up entirely of the English working class' ('Palatable Socialism or "the Real Thing"?'.
50 Cape edition, p. 22.

even worse roles for women. As well as Kate Malloy, who faces an abused future as Ned Narkey's wife, there is Mrs Cranford, for whom the burden of repeated child-birth makes life intolerable – as we shall see, her account of her own life, as well as Mrs Bull's commentary on it, is notably placed against the 'choice' that Sally makes at the end of the novel. In the main, though, the distinctiveness given to Sally by her self-confident agency is kept to the forefront of the reader's attention. One aspect of this which seems not to have been much noted is her openness about sexuality – which is quite clear in the novel and in some ways even more pronounced in the play. Thus it is she rather than Larry, for example, who openly challenges Ned Narkey about his sexual irresponsibility and who, and at his victim's dreadful insistence, makes him marry Kate. For 1933 this is a surprisingly explicit dialogue between a female romantic lead (which is surely one of Sally's roles in the novel) and a brutal sexual predator:

> 'Allus y'fit for's to tek best out of a girl like Kate what'll let y'do what y'like, then blame it on somebody else.'
> 'What about that bloody swine as y' let muck about wi' you? How many times has 'e had wot 'e wants? ...'
> 'Leave him out of it ... He's doing more for me than you'll do for her. He will marry me.' (p. 167)

Her 'choice' of Sam Grundy at the close of the novel both continues, in a sense, this agency and simultaneously shows that no free agency is possible in Hanky Park, that there are only 'choices' between different kinds of violation.

Nevertheless Sally's agency and determination up until that point and a certain comic exuberance are important ("'Wrap 'em round y'neck of a night and then y'll know where to find 'em'" she says to Harry *a propos* of his socks in the novel [p. 16] – an aspect of her dialogue which is further strengthened in the play: "'If y' feel as grateful in ten year's time, y' can pay me back'", the play's Sally says to Helen about the ten shillings for the marriage licence[51]). This comic aspect and her independence combined may play a part in influencing the reader's response to Sally and to the novel's ending. I have discussed at several points the care the novel takes to avoid offending some potential readers' political sensibilities (while also ensuring that it does make its own points about the poverty of Hanky Park and implied possible social solutions),

---

51 Cape edition, pp. 105–06.

but it seems important, too, to think about moral and sexual sensibilities given that *Love on the Dole* does push at some boundaries here too. Respectability in these terms might be a concern for readers of the novel as much as for characters within it. It seems both obvious and slightly unexpected that the novel does not invite readers to make any moral condemnation of Sally for her 'assent' to Sam Grundy's proposition – that is, her assent to one of a very limited choice of options. Ben Harker suggests a reading of Sally's 'choice' as follows:

> Greenwood might not represent the exploiting class in action, but Meath's teachings indelibly fix into the text the idea that all workers are reduced to commodities under capitalist relations of production and have no choice but to sell their labour to the highest bidder. Though Greenwood pulls back from making the link explicitly, the novel's ending is powerful in part because Sally breaches conventional morality and pushes that lesson to its grotesque limit, skilfully managing the commodification of her body and using her new influence to secure work for her brother and father … . Sally's insight into her own commodity status is geared instead towards individual survival: she withdraws her labour from the mill and takes it in-house, splitting herself between the business woman who manages her only commodity and the worker who does the work. This moral outrage – the labour of prostitution –enables her to secure a social promotion unavailable by any other means.[52]

This is an insightful reading: thus Sally's breaking of the moral code leads not to *her* condemnation but to that of the system which makes this the best of the choices open to her. The 'moral outrage' is directed not at Sally but at the social system. One notes how skilfully this transforms what might be melodrama into a political critique and how it has the potential to transform a reader's sense of what constitutes morality and respectability (indeed, *The Times* review of the London production of the play in 1935 made exactly the point that the end of the play might sound like melodrama, but was not: 'the story as it is told is by no means melodrama … . Presented with the facts, each spectator may for himself select their social or political causes').[53]

However, I think there is some further commentary to add about the novel's own arguments for the 'rationality' of Sally's choice and about how this is made acceptable for readers. I noted earlier that there were a few voices in the novel that queried the Hardcastles' and their neighbours' conventional sense of the 'respectable'. Chief of these voices is Mrs Bull's

---

52 'Adapting to the Conjuncture', p. 58.
53 'Garrick Theatre', 31 January 1935, p. 12.

(though supported in passing by Mrs Cranford's) and another is that of Sally herself, who makes explicit her reasoning. After Larry's death Sally's situation is desperate in every way: 'Bleakness; daily slaving at the mill … . Brother a pauper … . Parents dependent on her … and never more to see Larry' (p. 242) – and she needs to pay for Larry's cremation, since he did not believe in burial clubs. She quickly seems to conclude that, life having nothing decent to offer, she will choose the one thing (apart from continuing in Hanky Park) that is open to her:

> Sam Grundy … . He had everything to offer; she had nothing to offer. He had money … the fast conveyance in the search for forgetfulness; money that would give the quietus to gnawing memory … . Compunction pinched her as she imagined what Larry might say to this characterless capitulation to impulse … . Larry? Ha! Dead, and so was Sally Hardcastle. (p. 242)

Certainly, there is desperation and loss of hope here, and Sally asks herself if she is betraying Larry and losing her own true self; but there is also a continuity between this unorthodox route to a kind of independence and Sally's earlier capacity to be an agent. She should, were she in a melodrama, be a pitiable, friendless outcast at this stage of the narrative – but in fact she has a strong ally in Mrs Bull, who not only supports her decision but has actually suggested it several chapters before: '"five quid … Ah wonder, now … Wot about Sam Grundy, eh Sal? He ain't a bad feller at heart, y'know"' (p. 216). Sally replies that Sam Grundy might well give her the five pounds for Larry's cremation, but that he'd '"do it for what he'd like to get out o' me"'. Mrs Bull's response is surely unexpected: '"That's fault with all o' the men. But they don't allus get what they want."' Sexual relations here are not outside the system of exchange – not in an alternative sphere of romance – but are also part of that world of exchange in which negotiation is fundamental. In fact, Mrs Bull has an important role at the end of the novel that had been severely under-rated by critics until a recent article by Jack Windle, for she is the character who continues with Larry's work in offering a critique of the system of Hanky Park.[54] She particularly applies her critique to the position of women. Thus it is no coincidence that, after her unorthodox suggestion to Sally, she immediately refers to the orthodox options available to women in Hanky Park: '"Poor soul wi' a tribe o' kids as lives in next street's bin confined agen … . Couldn't

---

54 Jack Windle, '"What life means for those at the bottom": *Love on the Dole* and its reception since the 1930s', *Literature & History*, 3rd series, 20, 2, 2012, pp. 35–50.

even afford t'pay me for tendin' her i' childbed, an' him working too! Blimey, wot a life Sal, wot a life'" (p. 216). One might also note that, in contrast to Larry for much of the time, Mrs Bull can quite readily make use of the common range of language used in Hanky Park to make her points about the rottenness of the system. As Jack Windle argues: 'Mrs Bull, in the demotic register, takes over Larry's position as a conduit for authorial opinion and in doing so subverts the conventional discursive hierarchy of the novel form.'[55] Not only that, but she can produce living witnesses to the miserable part that women play in the economy of Hanky Park. When Sally returns home, having made her bargain with Sam Grundy, Mrs Bull and Mrs Cranford are there in the kitchen with Mrs Hardcastle, ready to enjoy any resulting spectacle. Sally bitterly reflects that she had thought to be married by now, provoking Mrs Cranford to illustrate her own experience of Mrs Bull's thesis about the typical experience of women:

> 'Married ... You ain't missed nowt wi' missin' that. Oh, God, if Ah'd me time t' go o'er agen Ah'd ne'er get wed. Naow, not t' t' best feller breathin wot hadn't enough to keep me on proper. An' Ah know o' no married woman i' Hanky Park wot wouldn't do same. Marriage, eh? Yaaa. Y' get married for love an' find y've let y'sel' in for a seven day a week job where y' get no pay. Luk at me Sal ... Worritin' me guts out trying t' mek ends meet, an; a tribe o' kids to bring up.' (p. 244)

Mrs Bull suggests that Mrs Cranford is 'naterally dismal' and would benefit from the odd nip of whisky (this is a reworking of Greenwood's earlier short story 'The Cleft Stick', in which Mrs Cranford is so oppressed by her endless toil, her useless husband, her children, and poverty that she tries to gas herself, but cannot for want of a penny for the metre: she takes Mrs Bull's advice and pawns some clothes so she can buy a nip of gin).[56] In fact, as well as this escapist antidote to women's lives, Mrs Bull also consistently offers some other advice about a more lasting improvement in their living conditions – women should limit their families. Windle observes that Mrs Bull 'advises the pregnant

---

55 '"What life means for those at the bottom"', p. 42.
56 See *The Cleft Stick*, p. 70. Remarkably, though in line with the whole collection's strong interest in women's lives, the short story also notes another cause for Mrs Cranford's desperation – the menopause. Mrs Bull advises that the 'change o' life' is 'a bad time for some women – makes 'em feel as though they're going to kick the bucket' (p. 67). However, Mrs Bull also says that this will improve one thing: 'You won't have any more children.'

Helen to "mek this one y'last'" (p. 254) and that she 'here echoes the Women's Co-Operative Guild and the Workers' Birth Control Group who campaigned for smaller working-class families and better conditions for women'.[57] In the same passage Mrs Bull suggests in comic but also forcible vein that men such as Jack Cranford and Ned Narkey should be made to take responsibility:

> 'tain't fair to you an' 'tain't fair t t' child. Luk at Mrs Cranford. One reg'lar every year, an' half of 'em dead. An' Kate Narkey shapin' same way. Yah, them fellers ought to be casterated.' (p. 254)

However, she is also giving serious advice, as the phrase that introduces this speech suggests: 'she stared at Helen steadfastly.' Indeed, like Sally, Mrs Bull is prepared to break taboos about what is 'respectable', knowing full well that the recipients and main beneficiaries of her advice do not want to hear such things discussed: 'Helen shifted uncomfortably, glanced at the clock then said in genuine alarm: "Ooo, luk at the time …"' (p. 254). Helen's discomfort at this topic being referred to seems entirely in line with memories of the period in some striking oral history collected by Nicky Leap and Billie Hunter from a certified midwife, Edith B: 'there wasn't much family planning available then. I think it came on the man's side. They never asked me for advice. No. No. It was a forbidden subject.'[58] Leap and Hunter also interviewed another midwife from the period, Elizabeth C, who said she did give birth control advice: 'Yes, they did ask me how to prevent babies'; but they feel that Edith B's memory probably represents a more common relationship between (even certified) midwives and knowledge about family planning.[59] Indeed, they go on to quote from the May 1934 edition of *Nursing Notes*, which explicitly states that 'advice on the question of contraceptives does not come within the practice or work of a midwife as such; if for health reasons she thinks there is a risk in her patient again becoming pregnant, she should refer her to her doctor.'[60]

How, then, are we, and how was the contemporary reader, to react to the uncertified Mrs Bull's daring but (to many modern ears) sensible

---

57 '"What life means for those at the bottom"', p. 44.
58 *The Midwife's Tale – an Oral History from Handywoman to Professional Midwife* (London: Scarlet Press, 1993), p. 89.
59 *The Midwife's Tale*, p. 89. The authors note that Elizabeth C is the only midwife who recalls giving birth control advice and are wary that she may be recalling a slightly later period, perhaps after the foundation of the National Health Service.
60 *The Midwife's Tale*, p. 90.

advice? Birth control was a political issue in the 1920s and 1930s – or, rather, some mainly women activists tried hard to make it a mainstream political issue:

> Birth control became part of the political agenda in the 1920s when women in the Labour Party fought hard to get their party to support birth control provision. They were to be disappointed though. In 1924, the newly elected first Labour government refused to accept state responsibility for such services.[61]

It seems likely that some contemporary readers would have reacted in a similar way to Helen in regarding this as a taboo topic, or even as a sign of Mrs Bull's dubious respectability. Contraception was often resisted on 'moral grounds [since it] was seen as a temptation to promiscuity'[62] – moreover, there seems to have been some confusion between contraception and abortion, as is evidenced in the discussion in *Nursing Notes* in May 1934 about why birth control was not within the professional domain of midwives, which explicitly states that 'there is a danger of them being falsely accused of being abortionists.'[63] This, of course, is a discussion focused on certified midwives, so there might be an even graver danger that uncertified midwives or 'handywomen' might be associated in the minds of some with illegal practices (especially given that all their paid work relating to birth was in theory outside the law after 1902: see further discussion below of 'handywomen'). However, for other readers, who might well be familiar with the current debates about birth control, Mrs Bull's advice could be seen as progressive. For, despite the Labour Party's refusal to take up the cause at a national level in 1924, there was considerable activism around birth control at a more local level, and notably in Salford itself. In 1926 women activists who were members of the Society for the Provision of Birth Control Clinics established the Manchester and Salford Mother Clinic (the first clinic offering birth control as well as other advice outside London) in the poor Greengate area of Salford. The clinic was also supported by the Women's Co-Operative Guild, which had a more working-class membership.[64] One of the founders was

---

61 *The Midwife's Tale*, p. 84.
62 *The Midwife's Tale*, p. 84.
63 Cited in *The Midwife's Tale*, p. 90.
64 There is a concise account of the clinic's work on the Manchester's Radical History website: <http://radicalmanchester.wordpress.com/2011/04/13/contraceptives-clinics-and-working-class-women-salford-manchester-mothers%E2%80%99-clinic/>, accessed 25 January 2014. This is an article by Sarah Irving (13 April 2011)

Charis Frankenberg (often known as Mrs Sydney Frankenberg), who, as further discussed below, had a public disagreement with Greenwood about his representation of various aspects of Salford life in *Love on the Dole*.[65] Frankenberg in her memoirs certainly recalls public controversy about birth control in Salford in the second half of the 1920s, when an article by the Catholic bishop of Salford that referred to birth control as stemming from the 'powers of evil' and encouraged people to take direct action against the clinic was reproduced in the *Manchester Guardian* (Frankenberg says that the Chief Constable of Salford asked the Bishop's Secretary for moderation, presumably to avoid breaches of public order, but adds that 'there were still strong feelings in 1934').[66] Perhaps as elsewhere in the novel, the humour linked to Mrs Bull herself and to Helen's avoidance of her advice helped to avoid offending some readers while also allowing the novel nevertheless to deal with progressive topics and to introduce them into public conversation. What the comedy does not do, however, is entirely to resolve whether readers should see Mrs Bull more as exploiter or more as the people's friend.

The frankness on Mrs Bull's part may perhaps be contrasted with the novel's other brief reference to contraceptives as something regarded by unemployed young men such as Jack Lindsay as a sign of how low they have sunk: '"Yaa, luk at me, sellin' *these* lousy bloody things," he produced a few packets of cheap contraceptives and a bundle of obscene postcards' (p. 231). Jack is talking to Harry, who shows no interest at all in these goods, but only in what happened to Bill Simmons and Tom Hare. It may be that the novel is again quietly pointing to a lack of insight among the majority of those who live in Hanky Park. However, some more self-interested comments by Mrs Bull in Chapter 6 may cut across this reading of her as a prophetess of progress – here she laments the decline in her income caused by a decline in childbirth and a growth of knowledge among the young:

'Young 'uns ain't having childer as they should … . When Ah was a gel a 'ooman wasn't a 'ooman till she'd bin i' childbed ten times not counting

that draws on Clare Debenham's thesis 'Grassroots Feminism: a Study of the Campaign of the Society for the Provision of Birth Control Clinics 1924–1938' (University of Manchester, 2010). Charis Frankenberg's *Not Old, Madam, Vintage – an Autobiography* (Lavenham: Galaxy Press, 1975), gives her perspective in chapter 15, 'Maternity and Childbirth Campaigning', pp. 128–40.

65 Frankenberg, *Not Old, Madam, Vintage*, p. 124.
66 Frankenberg, *Not Old, Madam, Vintage*, pp. 137–38.

miscarriages. Aach! How d' they expect a body t' mek a livin' when childer goin' t' school know more about things than we did arter we'd bin married years?' (pp. 106–07)[67]

This particular speech, though included in the novel and the play, was specified by the film censor, Miss Shortt, in 1936 as one that would have to be cut were the film to be made since 'it would be impossible according to our standards', presumably precisely because of the subdued reference to contraception.[68]

Mrs Bull is one of the few characters who has a commitment to a political party ('"Ah allus votes Labour and Ah allus will"' [p. 164]) and thus is one of the few who rates Larry for his ideas and activism as well as his usefulness as intermediary. However, even she does not think his speeches will get through to people: '"Taint no use talking socialism to folk. 'Twon't come in our time"' (p. 164). But her progressive sexual politics expressed in the language and context of Hanky Park and in terms of rational self interest may be more effective, and she may be Larry's true successor, as Windle argues:

> In a time of such extreme hardship, Greenwood's message is that to seek an alternative extraneous to the current circumstances is a doomed romance, like Sally and Larry's. By transferring his approach to Mrs Bull, Greenwood suggests utopian politics and traditional conservatism should be sidelined and the working class must focus on survival … Greenwood … agrees and condones Mrs Bull's pragmatic 'use y'head' philosophy'.[69]

This support from Mrs Cranford and Mrs Bull (its radical challenge to assumptions perhaps again slipped under some readers' guards with the use of humour) helps make Sally less the outcast and may prevent

---

67 Historical research on knowledge of birth control among working class-women does, though, sometimes support what appears to be the contradictory picture given by Mrs Bull. *The Midwife's Tale* firmly supports through its oral history interviews the notion that there was very little knowledge about contraception or birth control and also that these were generally taboo subjects, as does an article by Diana G. Gittings, 'Married Life and Birth Control Between the Wars', *Oral History*, 3, 2, Autumn 1975, pp. 53–64. However, Gittings also suggests that new magazines for women began to have some impact on the knowledge of sex and its consequences during the 1930s: 'advice was given on budgeting, housekeeping, childrearing and, later, in the 1930s, on sex and family planning' (p. 57).

68 BBFC Scenario Notes, 1936, p. 42a. Though much of what Miss Shortt wrote has been quoted, not all her comments have been, including this one.

69 '"What life means for those at the bottom"', p. 43.

condemnation, but she is also likely to be found sympathetic because the reader may well share her views about the minimum that anyone in a modern society can expect out of life in the way of material comfort. A review of the play argued that conventional 'virtue' was indeed no longer a stable quality under economic stress:

> In the days before booms and slumps, when virtue was as stabilised as the currency, such a father would have plunged the bread-knife in his daughter's bosom ... [but] are we today to condemn Sally? ... We know that some force in her other than her own luxury and riot is driving her to a career which may not wholly displease her though the man does.[70]

The text of the novel in its closing phases certainly carefully constructs a reading position that sees such material expectations as reasonable rather than deviant or selfish. Indeed, an entirely neglected text by Greenwood that looks back at his own novel suggests that his own view of Sally is that in this sad society it would be unreasonable to expect her to give up an expectation of material comfort in favour of either more authentic romance or conventional moral virtue. The text is illuminating and is worth looking at in some detail. In 1938 Greenwood was invited by the periodical *John Bull* to contribute to a feature called 'Sequels to Great Novels by Famous Authors'. He chose to contribute a short story called 'Prodigal's Return', which a prefatory paragraph says 'shows you his characters as they are today'.[71] The story's focus is very much on Sally and where and who she is now. She is, at a literal level, still with Sam Grundy at his Welsh property, which is envisaged as by the sea and in a place where people come on holiday – indeed, Harry and a friend have visited recently. Sally has not returned home to visit because 'having to expose herself to neighbourly curiosity discouraged her', but she is reflecting on the decision she made:

> Would it have been better for her to have stayed 'respectable' in Hanky Park with her father out of work, her mother a listless drudge, her brother also out of work and father of the child of Helen Hawkins, whom he had had to marry? The thought of such a respectability was revolting. (p. 23)

---

70 Review by James Agate, titled 'A Lancashire Problem', *Sunday Times* 3 February 1935.

71 *John Bull* 29 January 1938, pp. 23–24 in WGC/3/3, pp. 148–49. The story takes up two whole pages and some five columns. It seems remarkable that it has not been commented on before. The *John Bull* page numbers are given in the text after quotations.

Living with Sam Grundy has not been 'without its unpleasantnesses', and he complains about her 'lack of warmth'. But Sally is in no way cowed by him and says she will leave if he wants her to. She still shows independence, a word explicitly used of her by the story: 'She began to feel her power over him; she began to appreciate that her fiery independence was her greatest strength' (p. 23 – the 1970 musical of *Love on the Dole* has a similarly asymmetric future power relationship between Sally and Sam Grundy being predicted by Mrs Bull, Mrs Dorbell, and Mrs Jikes in a number called 'Tiger by the Tail': "'she wouldn't half teach him a lesson ... he'd regret his choice ... the only place he'd be safe from her is jail'"[72]). Sally also places a high price on the patterns of modern consumption that her arrangement brings in compensation and which were so lacking in Hanky Park: 'she revelled in the unusual comforts of the house, the lovely bathroom, the luxurious bed, a well-stocked wardrobe, money in her pockets to take her to the town when she felt like an evening at the movies' (p. 23). However, Harry's friend Chris, a better-off working man, a carpenter from Manchester, is of romantic interest (the story is as interested in that genre as the novel itself) and partly on his account Sally does decide to revisit Hanky Park. Seeing some unemployed mill girls, she at once experiences a clash between what she has now come to feel is normal and what makes up the normality of Hanky Park: 'They all were shabbily dressed – last year's or last year's but one's coats with bits of diseased-looking fur on the collars, cheap print frocks, one-and-eleven-penny silk stockings with runs in them ... a year ago she had been like that ... when she had been "respectable"' (p. 24).[73] Chris asks if she would like to come back to live there, but Sally says that she could not do that and in explaining why makes clear again her view that material well-being should not be merely a dream and that in a properly organised society comfort and authentic relationships should both be possible: "'Oh, no. I couldn't. All this poverty ... Larry was right – he was the boy I should have married. He knew about nice things. He knew it was all wrong for people to live like I was living'" (p. 24). This is, of course, a story written five years later than *Love on the Dole*, and must to an extent be read separately, but it

72 Act II, track 16 on the CD of the 1996 revival of the musical directed by Stewart Nicholls at the Rhoda McGaw Theatre, Woking, Surrey (JTT-1, recorded 4–5 January 1996, and kindly sent to me by the director).

73 One notes that not only her reported thoughts but also Sally's speech have entirely lost any trace of Salford dialect in the 'Prodigal's Return'.

gives a very explicit sense of Greenwood's later thoughts about Sally and suggests a considerable continuity with the way in which her experience is presented to the reader in the novel.

Thus, Sally, explaining why she has taken her decision in the novel's final chapter, 'No Vacancies', picks up on what might seem a minor theme in the novel (but is core to the short story sequel) – the extreme scarcity of the holiday as an experience for those who live in Hanky Park. Directly after Mrs Cranford's speech Sally refuses her way of life: "'That ain't for me … Ah can't; have what Ah wanted so Ah've tuk next best thing. Sick an' tired Ah am o' slugging and seein' nowt for it. Ne'er had holiday i' me life, Ah ain't … Ah'm gonna tek things easy while Ah've got chance'" (p. 245).

Her arrangement with Sam Grundy means that she will, for the first time, apart from rambling with Larry, be able to leave Hanky Park. Indeed, Mrs Jikes specifically envies Sally her 'holiday': "'I wouldn't turn me nowse up at a fortnight's holiday where she's gorn'" (p. 252). In fact, as suggested in the Introduction, there are a surprising number of references in the novel to holidays (or their absence). We first meet the word when Harry imagines that, once he has a job at Marlowe's, life will be 'one long holiday' (p. 29). Then, as well as the mention of Mr and Mrs Hardcastle's once-in-a-lifetime holiday, Harry and Helen's similarly unique liberation from Hanky Park (discussed above), and Larry's equally unique ability actually to take holidays, they are also an important part of the rewards that Sam Grundy can dispense, in return for suitable co-operation. Thus, when Sam buys off Ned Narkey with a job in the police force, holidays are an attractive part of his offer: "'Three ten a week, lodgin' allowance, uniform and boots, an' all y' bloody holidays paid for … on'y for walking about streets eight hours a day'" (p. 189). Ned repeats to himself the phrase 'holidays paid for' and licks his lips. Holidays are understandably associated with mobility – the ability to leave Hanky Park – and thus with Sam, whose money buys him that possibility. For most characters in the novel holidays are an impossibility, but we also observe Larry's thoughts about holidays when he refers to 'little luxuries such as smokes and holidays' (p. 150). Given the increasing expectations among middle-class and working-class people (in work) of an annual holiday, this everyday object of desire is likely to have struck many contemporary readers as an essential one. The lack of holidays and the ways in which the novels' characters crave them is a sign of how far Hanky Park has fallen behind normality, of the extent to which the life it imposes on its people is insupportable. This context in which desire for some material 'luxury' is seen as perfectly 'respectable' is reinforced as even those characters who have criticised Sally's action concede that given the dire circumstances her choice is wholly comprehensible. So, Mr Hardcastle reflects:

> This week-end would see no money whatsoever coming into the house ... What an utter, complete fool he had made of himself in denying the staring, glaring truth of Sally's accusations. *Did* he really wish her to live such a life as her mother had lived; such a life as was in store for young Harry and his wife? No! ... One long succession of dreary, monotonous years, toiling, moiling, with a pauper or near-pauper funeral at the end of it ... . Once begun he found a million excuses for her and a million condemnations of himself. (pp. 249–50)

Sally's ambiguous sacrifice-cum-self-assertion clearly does not fundamentally alter anything in Hanky Park: it gets her out of the trap and removes her and her family from their current poverty (there is a noticeable cluster of legal/financial terms describing her arrangements with Sam: 'sekklement', 'contract', 'independent' [pp. 245, 249, 253]). The few pages of the novel that remain after Sally has handed over to Mr Hardcastle and Harry the letters from Sam Grundy to Mr Moreland at the bus offices reinforce how little the inhabitants of Hanky Park are asking for and that even if their wishes were granted this would not in itself change the system. Thus Harry and his father are overjoyed at the prospect of a job and this bounty enables Helen to look forward to a 'fulfilled' life: "'We've got th' 'ouse at top o' the street. An' we're goin', tonight, t'see about gettin' the furniture on the weekly (the instalment plan). Y'see, Ah'm startin' work agen soon so we'll be able t' pay money off quicker'" (p. 254).

Indeed, one contemporary review of the novel noted that 'Helen's craving for orderliness and a decent home bring her to one room in a slum house.'[74] As the near repetition of the novel's opening sequence at the end suggests, Helen will take up the exact place of Mrs Hardcastle, just as Harry will take that of his father. The reader is likely to end the novel with a strong and sympathetic sense of why the people of Hanky Park are as they are, of their entirely reasonably desires, of why they cannot escape, and of why such a cycle should not be permitted to persist in a decent modern England.

74 *Times Literary Supplement* 29 June 1933, p. 444 (accessed via *TLS Centenary Archive*, 25 July 2012).

V. Mrs Jikes, Mrs Dorbell, Mrs Nattle, Mrs Bull: 'Some folks know how t' make money, by gum they do! Agent for owld Grumpole's clubs, pawnin' for naybores, obligin' ... and selling nips' (p. 105)

There are two final sets of characters to discuss, who were certainly much noticed by reviewers of the novel, as well as of the play and the film, and whose impact is not minor. The first of these is the group of characters who so often appear in the novel together: Mrs Jikes, Mrs Dorbell, Mrs Nattle, and Mrs Bull (who has been to some extent discussed in her own right already). Indeed, advertising for the Jonathan Cape edition of the novel in 1933 identified the group of older women as a selling point for the book, as in this brief advert from *The Sunday Times*, which spent most of its short notice on them: 'A grim picture, lightened by humour, insight and a chorus of bawdy old women' (the film censor, Miss Shortt, did not see the humour and in her plot summary simply said 'there is a trio of very unpleasant old women').[75] The chorus idea quickly caught on – another brief advert by Cape the following week again referred to that idea in its quotation from a review by the novelist Winifred Holtby, and also added what became another common reading of the old women, an association with Shakespeare, in its praise for 'the almost Shakespearian humour of its chorus of old women'.[76] Some reviews (in this case of the play and film respectively) saw the three older women as central to Greenwood's concerns or to the excellence of the piece:

> Now and then three old harpies drift in or out with their gin-bottle, their gossip, their fortune-telling, relieving and delighting the audience by their dark, witch-like drollery, and illustrating, for the dramatist, the innermost difficulties he has set out to discuss.[77]

> [They are] modern equivalents to Macbeth's witches ... their relish in the coarse material of the life around them lift the film to real heights of excellence whenever they appear on screen. Nothing better has come from America or the Continent than the scenes these four play together.[78]

---

75 *Sunday Times* 1933, 18 June 2012, p. 9; BBFC 'Scenario Notes', 1936, p. 42a.

76 25 June 1933, p. 10 (accessed via *Sunday Times Digital Archive*, 25 July 2012).

77 From a review of the play titled 'Garrick Theatre' in *The Times* 31 January 1935, p. 10.

78 From review of the film, *The Times* 30 May 1941, p. 6.

Between them, these adverts and reviews suggest, quite rightly, that these characters play a complex role in the novel: they are a chorus, they bring comic relief, they have alleged literary forbears, they manage at a certain level to thrive in Hanky Park, but they are also deeply part of the system, an 'illustration' of the place's 'innermost difficulties', and they are, as a group, morally ambiguous at the least.

Despite their striking impact as an ensemble, I imagine that many readers then and since share a slight difficulty I have with these characters – I sometimes do not find them easy to hold in my mind individually. There are distinguishing features, which it is useful to summarise:

Mrs Jikes: 'a transplanted sprig of London Pride from Whitechapel' (p. 37); wears a man's cap and a shawl; referred to as 'tiny'; tells fortunes and runs séances; plays the accordion at Mrs Scodger's spiritualist mission. Her husband is alive, but makes little appearance in the novel.

Mrs Dorbell: 'a beshawled, ancient lugubrious woman' (p. 32); pawns items for women too ashamed to visit Price's pawnshop themselves, taking a commission.

Mrs Nattle: 'a tall restless-eyed old woman, who had fetched, in a bassinette [a pram], nine suits, a dozen frocks, any number of boots and shoes, two wedding rings, [and] three watches and chains' (p. 33); she, like Mrs Dorbell, 'oblidges' her neighbours, for a price, assisting with their business at the pawnshop.

Mrs Bull: 'the local uncertified midwife and layer-out of the dead' (p. 57); referred to as 'stout'. Has been married and bereaved, but is now married again, though her husband, 'Jack Bull' is mentioned only once, when Mrs Bull declines to bail him out after the protest march, if he has been arrested. (p. 207)

A sharp-eyed reader may have noticed that the play review and the film review quoted above differ as to the number of this chorus – with the play reviewer opting for three and the film reviewer for four. In fact, the play version cut Mrs Nattle entirely, which reduces the need for an extra actress, but also suggests that Mrs Dorbell alone could represent the function of both in the story. Indeed, the two are not very clearly differentiated in the novel, and more subject to confusion than Mrs Jikes and Mrs Bull. Nevertheless, the film restored Mrs Nattle to her position, distinguishing her more clearly by casting the well-known Irish actress Marie O'Neill as Mrs Dorbell (who is not in the novel represented in any way as being of Irish origin[79]). While the lack of distinctive characterisation between Mrs Nattle and Mrs Dorbell in the novel might be regarded as simply a weakness in the novel, it may also point up something important – that the novel is interested in common and collective experience, and that the chorus-like function of these four women helps to represent this through a certain amount of interchangeability (there may be a related implication of collective representation achieved through different means in the curiously similar names of Harry, Larry, and Sally). The chorus is made up of older women, two of whom must support themselves because they no longer have husbands, but who are able to do so partly through also no longer having children to support, partly because they have widows' or old age pensions, and partly because they have found niches in Hanky Park that they are able to exploit.[80] Mrs Bull is married, but we mainly see her pursuing her own business, and so is Mrs Jikes, but again we see little of her husband, though we learn that he will not go to work until he has been given his 'money for his dinner beer' (p. 37). Mrs Dorbell talks explicitly of her situation:

> 'Thank God as Ah'm a widder an'll me fambly's growd up an' owt o' me sight. Dammum. Not one of 'um ever come t' see me. Yaah! Ah wouldn't have the worrit of 'em agen for a king's ransom. When they've gone, y' can have a nip when y'like wi'out asking anyone's leave.' (p. 208)

Though old age can be a terrible situation for individuals in Hanky Park, it can under some circumstances be a surprising source of relative 'wealth', especially for older women. When searching for Sally and Larry in the hospital, Mrs Hardcastle meets an elderly man who draws attention to what can happen to a poor working man in old age: '"None o'me childer'd ha' me so Ah'd ha' t' come t't' grubber … . They tek y'r pension off y' when y' come in here and the grub's pison"' (p. 211).[81]

---

79 See the extremely informative profiles of the cast included in the 2004 Fabulous Films DVD of the 1941 film of *Love on the Dole* for a brief biography of Marie O'Neill.

80 It is explicit in the novel that Mrs Dorbell and Mrs Nattle have pensions and pension books.

81 Curiously, Greenwood does not gloss 'grubber', which seems as used here to be a genuinely obscure word. From the context, one would expect the word to mean 'hospital', but *OED* does not list any sense that approximates to this meaning. The most relevant sense, especially given the reference soon after to 'grub' (meaning food), is that of 'an eating house'. Perhaps the old man regards the hospital as

But most of the sixteen references to pensions in the novel are linked to women and most show pensions as a source of deep satisfaction in Hanky Park, particularly for Mrs Dorbell and Mrs Nattle. In Chapter 5 Mrs Bull, looking at rows of pawn tickets on Mrs Nattle's kitchen table, observes that unemployment seems to be doing some people some good. Mrs Dorbell, agreeing that things are bad, is inspired to say "'But thank God, unemployment or no, they can't touch me owld age pension. Wot a blessin', wot a blessin''" (p. 162). Mrs Jikes adds that the pension, unlike work "'never gowse on short time'". Indeed, pensions were never threatened even in the 1931 benefit cuts (non-contributory old age pensions of five shillings had been introduced by Lloyd George in a 1908 act for those over 70 and raised to ten shillings a week in 1919, while the Widows', Orphans and Old Age Contributory Pensions scheme, introduced by Neville Chamberlain in 1925, also paid at the same rate: Mrs Dorbell, at least, explicitly refers to her 'owld age' pension [p. 224]).[82]

But for Mrs Dorbell and Mrs Nattle in particular, it is not just the receipt of their own ten shillings a week that makes the pension such a blessing, but also the additional potential it has from a business point of view. Early on in the novel, when we see the women queuing at the pawn shop, the sharp-eyed Mrs Nattle notices Mrs Dorbell surreptitiously pawning her own pension book, though this is explicitly stated to be illegal on the reverse of the document and despite the fact that Mr Price is a magistrate. Further conversation reveals that Mrs Dorbell also pawns the pension books of her clients – a practice that Mrs Nattle is surely also going to adopt since, as Mrs Dorbell explains, nobody "'can't afford to miss ... ten bob pension for sake of half o' crown'" (p. 34), and

mainly a place that feeds him – but, alas, badly – or perhaps the old man shows a sense that an 'infirmary', though by this time a word suggesting principally a hospital, had in the recent past also often indicated a workhouse (see *OED* definition of infirmary).

82 For a brief account of these pension bills, see Mowat, *Britain Between the Wars 1918–1940*, p. 339. There is more detailed discussion of each in Derek Fraser's *The Evolution of the British Welfare State*, 4th edn (Basingstoke: Palgrave Macmillan, 2009), especially on pp. 180–81 and 239–41. The overlap between the two bills was complex, as Fraser makes clear in his discussion on p. 240; we should probably not assume that the pensions referred to in the novel are under the 1908 non-contributory schemes: it may well be that Mrs Nattle's and Mrs Dorbell's 'owld age pensions' are actually derived from their husbands' contributory pensions under the 1925 legislation, which specifically provided benefits for the widow and any children after a husband's death.

it is therefore profitable and, the law apart, low risk. It is to thank Mrs Dorbell for this commercial advice that Mrs Nattle invites her to her home for a drop of something. This is another scheme of Mrs Nattle's – though obviously lacking a licence she retails 'nips' (a word used in this sense on sixteen occasions) at thrippence a time to her acquaintance from a bottle of whisky she always seems to have in her possession (presumably creating a profit sufficient to subsidise her own drinking). But if Mrs Nattle's apparent sociability is really part of her business dealings, it is not without risk, for Mrs Dorbell has an idea about how she might make yet further money by discovering where Mrs Nattle keeps her illegal earnings, so that she can quickly remove them in the unfortunate case of Mrs Nattle's sudden death (see pp. 106 and 224–25). The recurring vision of this event in Mrs Dorbell's mind would, observes the narrator, 'have done justice to a rightful legatee' (p. 225). The curious logic of this perhaps draws attention to the fact that the morality of Mrs Dorbell's ultimate fantasy is no more (but no less) unethical than the origins of Mrs Nattle's 'fortune', for her 'multifarious' businesses are nearly all illegal in themselves, and, anyway, any earnings would, if declared, reduce her widow's or old age pension.

In normal times the ten-shilling pension would hardly constitute a fortune, being less than a third of the average wage in textiles and probably less than a quarter of wages in male-dominated industries at this time – such as the forty-five shillings Larry receives from Marlowe's, which Sally regards as exceptional in Hanky Park.[83] Indeed, the pension was not intended to provide enough to fully cover even subsistence needs, and throughout the 1930s old age pensioners usually had to apply for Public Assistance in addition to make ends meet.[84] But in Hanky Park, with many unemployed or on short time, the regular pension is apparently enough, at least through a comic lens, to make those pensioners *without* dependants into an elite, especially if they are

83 Estimating average wages has various complexities, but my calculation here is based on Mowat's discussion of wages in the inter-war period and his view that in 1935 forty-nine shillings was an average wage for a miner and for those in 'all the main industries', while thirty-six shillings a week was an average weekly wage in the textile industry (*Britain Between the Wars 1918–1940*, p. 491). Reference to Larry's pay is on p. 140 of *Love on the Dole*.

84 In 1939 a quarter of a million people applying for Public Assistance were old-age pensioners – see Fraser, *The Evolution of the British Welfare State*, p. 239 and discussion of the general principle that the pension should not fully cover living costs on pp. 183 and 239.

enterprising enough to develop their businesses from the secure base given them by the pension. It may be ironic in several ways that Mrs Dorbell singles out Lloyd George for criticism in the same speech in which she claims that only the poor help the poor. She is complaining in particular that the pub is not open since it is before noon and in general that everything has got worse since the war:

'Before that started things *was* reason'ble. A body could get a drink wi'hout hinterference wi' this 'ere early closin' and late openin'. But Ah ne'er did hold with Lloyd George nor wi' any o' t' rest of 'em either. Vote for none on'em say I. All same once they get i' Parli'ment. It's poor as 'elps poor *aaaall* world over.' (p. 33)

She is right that laws restricting pub opening hours were introduced in 1914 as part of the Defence of the Realm Act (often known as DORA), and that these provisions were kept in force in the UK after the war (until new legislation in 1988, in fact). Part of the reason for restricting opening hours to was to keep wartime productivity high (and Lloyd George was Minister of Munitions from 1915 to 1916 and prime minister from 1916 until 1922). However, she has no consciousness of another thing Lloyd George was strongly associated with in many working people's minds: the introduction of pensions in 1908 and further welfare and benefit reforms in 1919–21, which have subsequently been seen as the initial basis for the post-1945 welfare state.[85] Her declaration that only the poor help the poor ignores, or is ignorant of, the reforms that resulted in the pension she is so pleased to have. Her lack of understanding may reinforce a central point of the novel – that Hanky Park does need outside help and a larger field of reference – a point that may be further reinforced by the later discussion of politics between Mrs Bull and Mrs Dorbell, which contrasts one's belief in Labour with the other's self-interest and thoughtless nostalgia: '"Me ma and her ma was blue (Conservative) or they wus red (Liberal), just depended on which o't' two gev most coal an' blankets"' (p. 164).

Of course, Mrs Dorbell's views are comic also since she is hardly motivated to do her various deeds by a wish to help the poor. On the contrary, as the chapter heading 'Low Finance' makes very clear, she and Mrs Nattle are seen to be exploiters of the poor and aligned with

---

85 See discussion of how radical the Liberal reform programme overseen by Lloyd George was in the section titled 'Lloyd George and the origins of the Welfare State' in Fraser, *The Evolution of the British Welfare State*, pp. 185–200.

capitalist economics in the emphatic narrative discussion at the beginning of that chapter, her business being 'conducted on very orthodox lines; to be precise, none other than those of the Bank of England's or any other large money-lending concern' (p. 102). Thus she and Mrs Nattle are most akin, except for their apparent sociability and close interaction with their neighbours, to those few other 'elite' and exploitative citizens of Hanky Park, Mr Price, Alderman Grumpole, and Sam Grundy, who similarly make their money precisely from the poverty-stricken economy that the inhabitants of Hanky Park are forced to practise. Mrs Bull is also an ambiguous character, who is often driven by self-interest in her dealings with birth and death, but who can give more disinterested advice on occasion.

These female characters do have, as the reviews with which this section opened pointed out, a range of important functions within the text, which partly result from and partly run alongside their business activities. Thus they do, unlike Price, Grumpole, or Grundy, offer a range of commentaries on Hanky Park, and they are aware of everything that goes on there, making them, indeed, somewhat like the chorus of a Greek play, which remained on stage throughout the events of the classical drama (however, unlike a Greek chorus, they are always on the look-out for themselves too and ready to intervene in events for their own advantage). They are also seen as Shakespearian by some reviewers presumably partly because they make up a comic sub-plot running alongside the often bleak main plot provided by the Hardcastle family, a kind of genre-mixing often associated with Shakespeare's drama, and partly because of a more specific link made between them and the three witches in *Macbeth* (the novel itself, however, never refers to them either as a chorus or as witches, though the novel does quote from Macbeth: 'a tale told by an idiot' on p. 32).[86] Mrs Jikes certainly does her best to be oracular in her fortune-telling activities and in her role as leader of the séance, while Mrs Bull has a unique position in Hanky Park as someone able to deal with entry into the world and exit from it. In fact, just as Larry acts as an intermediary, so too do all four of these women, both in terms of assisting with particular events (pawning, acquiring new clothing, access to charity, prophecy, birth and death) and in terms of helping the reader to

---

86 However, Mrs Dorbell in the story 'The Practised Hand' in *The Cleft Stick* is certainly drawn by Arthur Wragg as looking like one of the weird sisters – see the left-hand figure in the illustration between pp. 200 and 201.

interpret the world of Hanky Park. They are, in several senses of the word, gossips – women who are associated with childbirth and with exchange of news and entertainment (sometimes malicious, sometimes supportive to a degree). They are also, at a low level, an elite group of survivors in Hanky Park in having some spare resources to draw on and in having no dependents (and like Larry in that respect too). However, their moral ambiguity is also notable, and in this respect they are more like Grumpole, Price, and Grundy: they are akin to Collette Colligan's analysis of 'hope' in Hanky Park, in some ways ameliorating life there, in other ways perpetuating its present state.[87]

Mrs Bull's role at the beginning and end of life also contributes to her moral ambiguity, particularly because the novel concisely relates her to a history of midwifery that has been largely forgotten.[88] At her first entry into the novel the narrator identifies her as 'the local uncertified midwife and layer-out of the dead' (p. 57). To the modern ear, these two intermediary functions sit ill together, but there was a long history in which they were carried out by the same person: 'She saw you into the world and she saw you out the other end.'[89] Greenwood's phrase 'uncertified midwife' shows that he has a secure sense of this history, for the phrase refers essentially to the 1902 Midwives Act and subsequent legislation in England and Wales (in 1918 and 1926) that sought to 'establish midwifery as a respectable profession, disassociated from untrained midwives or "handywomen"'.[90] 'Handywomen' went back at least as far as the seventeenth century and did indeed assist with childbirth and preparation for burial, usually for a fee and increasingly for poorer people as birth (at least) became the province

87 '"Hope on, hope ever. One of these fine days my ship will come in"'.

88 See Jean Donnison, *Midwives and Medical Men: a History of the Struggle for the Control of Childbirth* (London: Historical Publications Ltd, 1988; first published by Heinemann Educational Books, 1977); Anne Borsay and Billie Hunter (eds), *Nursing and Midwifery in Britain Since 1700* (Basingstoke: Palgrave-Macmillan, 2012) and Hunter and Leap, *The Midwives Tale*, especially the chapter devoted to handywomen, pp. 19–43.

89 Hunter and Leap, *The Midwives Tale*, p. 19. The quotation is presumably from an oral history interview, but the source is not made clear in this one instance. The footnote at the end of the paragraph refers generally to an unpublished that which may be where the quotation is derived from: Bob Little, 'Go Seek Mrs Dawson. She'll know What to Do – the Demise of the Working-Class Nurse/Midwife in the Early Twentieth Century', Sociology Department, University of Essex, 1983.

90 Billie Hunter, 'Midwifery, 1920–2000: the Reshaping of a Profession', pp. 151–74 in Borsay and Hunter, *Nursing and Midwifery in Britain Since 1700*, p. 152.

of the medically trained.[91] Despite legislation and various kinds of regulation, 'Handywomen were still present at births ... at least in a support role, until the 1940s.'[92] When *Love on the Dole* was published the *Daily Dispatch and Evening News* reported that a well-known Salford campaigner for better health care for women (and a former midwife), Charis Frankenberg, had criticised the novel for misrepresenting Salford in a number of ways, including in its clear assertion that uncertified midwives such as Mrs Bull still worked in the city: 'an uncertificated midwife like Mrs Bull is quite impossible nowadays as her trade is quite illegal.' Greenwood replied sarcastically thus: 'Mrs Frankenberg has established the illegality of uncertificated midwives. And now we know that abortion, ready-money bookmaking, theft, arson and prostitution are "quite impossible nowadays" since they are "illegal".'[93] Greenwood surely has a point, though it may well be that there was increasing access to certified medical assistance for women. It certainly seems very likely that 'handywomen' were still working in some working-class areas in the 1930s, though there may also be other explanations for the characterisation of Mrs Bull as an 'uncertified midwife'. As in other respects, it may be that the novel wants to depict Hanky Park as cut off from modern progress and still following more nineteenth-century styles of deprivation in order to emphasise to readers the stasis of the place. Certainly, visits from a trained and certified midwife would indicate traffic with an outer and more modern world, which would produce a rather different effect from showing Mrs Bull, an insider to Hanky Park, as the only available and affordable medical attendant for women. However, Mrs Bull is noticeably not depicted as an incompetent or dangerous helper in childbirth or in caring for Helen and Harry's baby.[94]

91 Borsay and Hunter, See *Nursing and Midwifery in Britain Since 1700*, p. 26.

92 Borsay and Hunter, *Nursing and Midwifery in Britain Since 1700*, p. 152. It is striking that though there are many references to the term 'handywoman' in the relatively few histories of midwifery, the *OED* currently has no entry for the word, thus missing an opportunity to remember an important aspect of women's and medical history.

93 *Daily Dispatch* 26 September 1937. See WGC/3/3, p. 9.

94 Nor is she like Greenwood's other portrayal of a 'handywoman'. Mrs Haddock, in the story 'The Practised Hand' in *The Cleft Stick*, attends 'in the capacity of usher, to the entrances to this world of all the Salfordians in the immediate vicinity of her home' (p. 201), but she is also willing for a fee to hasten the exit of Mrs Dorbell's sick lodger from the world, so that his landlady can collect his life insurance. In fact, Mrs Haddock may even be a certified midwife, as she displays a certificate and a brass plate, but she nevertheless also (variously) assists

Perhaps she picks up (partly because this also accords with the novel's desire to make these older women ambiguous) on two conflicting views of 'handywomen': the trained and modern midwife's view that she is 'our foe' (a view Charis Frankenberg was, of course, likely to support) and the perception evidenced in oral histories that recalls them as being 'valued and respected within their communities, providing kind, competent care'.[95] Mrs Bull may also share some of the moral ambiguity of Sam Grundy, which will be discussed in the next section: she is an insider who may offer some ways forward, but who is also by no means outside the moral and other economies of Hanky Park. The function of the 'chorus' is clearly complex, but only Mrs Bull emerges from it with some degree of moral authority, and it is notable that she is the last of the four older women to speak in the novel, giving her view of Sally's needs and actions towards the end of the final chapter and telling Mrs Hardcastle that Sally would go 'melancholy mad' (p. 254) and surely commit suicide if she had to stay in Hanky Park.

VI. Sam Grundy and Ned Narkey: 'Honest Sam' (p. 114) and 'Sergeant-Major Narkey' (p. 135)

Though we have already noted the gradations between the 'respectable' (the Hardcastles), the unrespectable (Helen Hawkins' parents), and the exceptional (Larry and Sally), the social hierarchy of Hanky Park is notably flat above that level ('the story is set in a virtual single-class society', observes Constantine[96]). Or, at least, we see very little of it except through glimpses of a few representative figures. In scenes set in Marlowe's there is a single distant reference to 'the manager', who is referred to in a newspaper clipping that Ted Munter has: 'Interview today, the manager of Messrs Marlowe Ltd explained to our representative the possible consequences of the difficulties placed in the way of trade with Russia by the Government' (p. 185). However, this manager is never named (and is hardly therefore really a character) and we do not see him do anything at all, though his decisions must lie behind some of

---

with death and the laying out of the dead. Greenwood adapted this story into a one-act play, a development that a *Manchester Guardian* review of *The Cleft Stick* responded to with horror: 'how a play which any sort of audience could stomach has been made out of it ... passes comprehension' (Thomas Moult, 17 December 1937).

95 Borsay and Hunter, *Nursing and Midwifery in Britain Since 1700*, pp. 152–53.

96 *'Love on the Dole* and its Reception in the 1930s', p. 237.

the events at Marlowe's. There are further references to another manager – the manager at the Employment Exchange – but all in one scene, in which the unemployed cannot believe that all their dole has been cut: 'The manager informed him there was no appeal' (p. 196). Again, this is a nameless individual. Joanna Bourke suggests that there certainly were local communities in the period that were exclusively working class: 'By restricting the individual's activities and social relations to a single locality, low spatial mobility consigns the individual to membership of a local group ... not only were these predominantly working-class localities stable in terms of population, the residents also lived in close proximity.'[97] This seems to apply well to Hanky Park and the novel might be said therefore to represent perspectives from within that community. This necessarily gives it a somewhat restricted viewpoint, and one that is not located within the wider social relations that must still have power over Hanky Park, even if they are exterior to that locality and community. I will return to this point in the conclusion of the book, when I consider Greenwood's ways of thinking about class structure in *Love on the Dole*.

So, despite the opening chapter's somewhat aerial viewpoint of what is allegedly the whole environment, the novel's general viewpoint is much more from the shop-floor in the sphere of work or from the working-class household in the domestic sphere. Thus there is more frequent reference to a number of foremen at Marlowe's. In the main these more numerous figures also remain anonymous (something Harry uses to his advantage by simply fabricating an instruction from 'the foreman' when he initially goes to claim his brass check and thus employment, leaving Ted Munter to guess which of his rivals is plaguing him with new apprentices to process [p. 25]). One foreman is called by a name (Joe Ridge [pp. 69–70]), but, like the two managers, he never becomes a distinct character. In the main the various foremen remain generic figures, even when they are given some rare characterisation, as in the instance when one has (regretfully) to sack Larry after Ted Munter has informed the management about his political activism at work: "'This lousy lot o' devils here, d'y think *they* give a cuss what y'say?'" (p. 186).

The reader does get a more individual sense of Ted Munter, who occupies a position that is perhaps superior in some ways to the foremen, though probably associated with a lack of masculinity, since

97 *Working-Class Cultures in Britain 1890–1960: Gender, Cass and Ethnicity* (London: Routledge, 1994), p. 139.

he is a 'clerk', the Time Clerk to be precise. It is he who listens carefully to the political argument between two young men about capitalism in Chapter 7 ('Dirty Work at the Crossroads'), which leads into Larry's explanation of Labour and Capital. One of the two young men, shortly afterwards identified as Larry's comrade Jim, specifically accuses Ted of being a sycophant: "'Ready to crawl in front of anybody as y'think can do y'a a bit o' good. Ya bloody snake ... go'n report *me* t' t' foreman'" (p. 180). Ted does indeed plan to use such power as he has: if he reports Larry's political activism at work then perhaps Larry will be sacked 'when next the staff was depleted' (p. 184). He also thinks that he can cash in further on this action if he tells Sam Grundy what he has done. Indeed, the portrayal of the inner workings of Ted's mind here gives the reader a sense of how he thinks about Sam Grundy's social position. Ted is pleased to think about possible harm to Sam, but also acutely aware that he is one of the few sources of power and luxury. Thus Ted 'gloated, silently in Sam's discomfiture' (p. 184) when he hears that Sally is to marry Larry. However, he also hopes that passing to Sam the news clipping about the consequences of government intervention in Marlowe's trade to Russia, with its link to the possibility of Larry being discharged, 'would be sufficient to induce Sam Grundy to stand him a couple of double Scotch whiskies' (p. 185). Clearly, Ted is driven by envy: he both dislikes and depends on Sam, but there is little doubt that Sam occupies the highest social position that he can imagine (indeed, his 'lifelong ambition' is that in return for some favour Sam will give him 'a working interest in the bookmaking business' (p. 117).[98]

This standpoint is generally shared by the inhabitants of Hanky Park, but they mainly seem less envious and perhaps attach some more positive hopes to Sam. Sam is called some hard names by both narrator and characters: 'gross', 'notorious', 'the fat pig', 'fat apoplectic', 'the fat bookmaker' (pp. 24, 113, 136, 142, 187). The narrator refers to him as 'the gross street corner bookmaker' (a description that becomes a leitmotif) at his first appearance in the novel, when he is firmly linked to Grumpole

---

98 Ted Munter is a character who seems in some ways close to the heart of Greenwood's writing: he appeared in his first published story 'A Maker of Books', which was republished as the first story of his short-story collection *The Cleft Stick* in 1937 (see Chapter 2). His character is quite consistent in both short story and novel: he epitomises an envious hope, though whereas in the short story he is seen as foolish, by the time of the novel he is seen as malicious.

and Price. However, the narrator also very clearly anticipates aspects of Collette Colligan's idea that the novel is much concerned with the 'politics of hope' when he identifies the social function of these three as that of a 'trinity, the outward visible sign of an inward spiritual discontent; safety valves through which the excess of impending change could escape, vitiate and dissipate itself' (p. 24). This is a primarily negative characterisation of this all too earthly trinity's function: they thrive on an inner discontent in Hanky Park, but do act as a safety valve, so that the inhabitants' desire for positive change from their present state is given somewhere to go, though it is dissipated and corrupted ('vitiated') in the process.[99]

Carl Chinn, in his social history of bookmaking, *Better Betting with a Decent Feller* (2004), certainly sees Greenwood's Sam Grundy as a wholly negative portrayal of a bookie (a general representation of the bookie with which his study often takes issue). Thus in his comments on Sam he says that:

> in his novel, the socialist hero, Larry Meath, is a lonely figure, separated from his fellow workers by his love of books and his determined political beliefs. By contrast, Grundy, the reprehensible backyard bookie, is popular and gregarious and after Meath's death, he gains the socialist's girlfriend ... in portraying this triumph of harsh reality over conviction, Greenwood used all his powerful literary skills to bring to the fore his abomination of bookmakers.[100]

Chinn locates this 'abomination' as part of a widespread hostility to bookmakers largely from outside the working class itself, but which spread across many socialists as well as Christian moralists and middle-class objectors who saw betting as unrespectable, unthrifty, and self-destructive. Indeed, one nationally known Anglican clergyman opposed to betting was based in a Salford parish: Canon Peter Green was vicar of St Philips from 1911 to 1951 and campaigned against gambling from the 1920s onwards, publishing, for example, an article in *The Spectator* in November 1931 entitled 'The Case Against Betting and Gambling'.[101] Indeed, a review of the novel in the Salford newspaper *City News* (17 June 1933) specifically made a link between Canon

99 'Vitiate' is an unusual word for Greenwood to use: *OED* gives several senses mainly to do with corrupting, perverting, impairing, or spoiling.
100 (London: Aurum Press, 2004), p. 155.
101 21 November 1931, pp. 667–68. See also his *Dictionary of National Biography* entry and *Better Betting with a Decent Feller*, pp. xix, 183, 200, 227, 280.

Peter Green and Sam Grundy, though by arguing that Greenwood's novel showed the 'necessity' of bookies in such an environment rather than seeing the portrait as wholly hostile or by accepting the Canon's argument that betting could and should be abolished: 'Canon Peter Green ... the bookmaker's fiercest critic, will be hard put to challenge the psychological necessity of the bookmaker sketched in these pages.'[102] The socialist case against betting is well put by Ramsey MacDonald in a 1904 article that Chinn cites and which seems close in spirit to the novel's comment about how betting 'vitiates' the desire for change:

> To hope ... that a Labour party can be built up in a population quivering from an indulgence in games of hazard is pure folly ... its hazards absorb so much of its leisure; they lead it away from thoughts of social righteousness ... they create in it a state of mind which believes in fate, luck, the irrational, the erratic, they dazzle its eyes with flashy hope.[103]

Chinn sees the authorial dislike as part of Greenwood's (and his mother's) 'upper-working-class status', but also suggests that the novel's placing of the bookmaker may be connected to Greenwood's general strategy of winning over middle-class readers:

> his grim picture was intended to shock his mostly middle-class readers and thus galvanise them into demanding social reform. In order to do this, he had to include points of reference with which his audience was familiar, and that of the gross, flashy and greedy bookmaker was the one which served his purpose best.[104]

Undoubtedly, the novel makes clear that Sam Grundy is part of the system that uses potentially positive human desires to block rather than advance change. However, there is a carnivalesque aspect to him that makes him seem less oppressive than Grumpole and Price to the inhabitants of Hanky Park and possibly to the reader too. Thus, Grumpole and Price seem evidently Dickensian, Scrooge-like characters. Grumpole makes far fewer appearances in the novel than Price and is only briefly characterised physically as a 'fat and greasy citizen' (p. 57). Price, though never explicitly described as thin, is strongly implied to be lacking in the fleshiness that is established for the reader as a

102 From WGC/3/1.
103 'Gambling and Citizenship', in Seebohm Rowntree's *Betting and Gambling: a National Evil* (London: Macmillan, 1905), cited in *Better Betting with a Decent Feller*, p. 154.
104 *Better Betting with a Decent Feller*, p. 157.

characteristic of Sam Grundy. Indeed, 'the cadaverous pawnbroker' is plainly deathly:

> Gaunt, clean-shaven, thin lipped, Mr Price's eyes were like those of a fish, glassy, staring: his high cheek bones, sunken cheeks and sallow complexion ... lent his countenance a deathlike mask ... . Nothing could be more full of life than his skeletonic fingers as they plunged into the heaped money of the cash drawer. (p. 28)

Price's pleasures in life are entirely self-regarding, but also wholly abstract rather than physical: 'he was a magistrate ... and to be giving some cringing wretch a stern talking to was an occupation which inspired in him the greatest pleasure and appreciation of his public spirit' (p. 28). Where Price's surname indicates his relationship with money and Grumpole's suggests grumpiness, Sam Grundy's surname has an ironic reference to the proverbial character Mrs Grundy, who is censorious of anything pleasurable. Sam Grundy, in contrast, is open to anything pleasurable (though a further irony may be that he offers only the hope of pleasure rather than its delivery). Sam Grundy may not be morally good, but in contrast to Price I am not certain that the only perspective on him for the reader is in fact wholly condemnatory (it is noticeable that in the Samuel French acting edition of the play version the 'Description of Characters' says of Grundy: 'A not unpleasant man, though rather stout, and he has the confidence of one who lives on his wits'[105]). There may also be some access to the viewpoint of the people of Hanky Park in which Sam seems a comprehensible-enough figure with the ability to enjoy pleasures that, given the chance, they too would enjoy:

> A buzz of murmured conversation arose from the crowd accompanied by much neck straining as a small fat man, broad set, with beady eyes, an apoplectic complexion, came out of the house, crossed the tiny backyard and stood upon the upturned box, thumbs in waistcoat armholes. Preposterous-sized diamonds ornamented his thick fingers, and a cable-like gold guard, further enhanced by a collection of gold pendants, spade guineas and Masonic emblems, hung heavily across his prominent stomach ... his billycock rested on the back of his head; he wore spats. Self-confidence and gross prosperity oozed from him. (p. 113)

Everything is both overdone and on show – the bookmaker wears on his own well-fed body more portable wealth than any other inhabitant of

---

105 London: French, 1936; 'The Description of Characters' appears on an unnumbered page but it seems to be on p. 5, since the play text proper begins on p. 9.

Hanky Park could ever hope to own in a lifetime. The 'guard' as thick as a cable is a watch-chain, the 'spade guineas' are antique coins last minted in 1813 (worth 21 shillings each when issued), and the Masonic emblems suggest that Sam may have influence among the Brotherhood (including in the police force?), while the billycock hat (a bowler) had become associated with bookies and also distinguishes Sam from the cap-wearing working men.[106] In short, Sam has an exotic super-abundance that is rare indeed in these parts and which may provide spectator and reader alike with vicarious pleasure – not something that could be said of Grumpole or Price, who are merely purveyors of harsh necessities.

Chinn interestingly traces Greenwood's spectacular depiction of Sam back to hostile nineteenth-century portrayals of the 'florid' bookie: 'a thick-set corpulent fellow, the *beau ideal* of a John Bull in appearance', '[exhibiting watch-chains] not to be weighed in the puny scales of a gold smith'.[107] However, it seems possible that Sam, rather than being part of the 'grim picture' that Constantine and Chinn agree is calculated to appeal to middle-class opinion, may also represent a striking contrast to that otherwise all-pervading grimness. Sam is not just a grim necessity, but an entertaining spectacle in himself as well as an apparent source of hope. Thus when he makes his public appearance to present Harry with his winnings, the narrator observes that 'roars of obsequious laughter' greet his question to Harry, '"So, y'thought y'd brek bank, eh, lad?"' and that 'Sam was popular' (p. 113).

One thing that differentiates Sam Grundy from Price and Grumpole, and perhaps also links him to Mrs Bull, is that he is from the people (which does not preclude his exploiting them). For, unlike another character who stands out in Hanky Park, Larry Meath, Sam's life history is made quite clear with some concise allusions to his earlier life by Ted Munter: '"Ah knew him when he'd no breeches arse to his pants. Me an' him ran a crown an' anchor board i' th' army. Pots o' money we made. He saved his, but me, like a bloody fool, as've allus bin, blewed it on women and wine"' (p. 113). Crown and anchor was a gambling game originating in the eighteenth century and played between a banker and

---

106 See *OED* for definitions of 'Spade guinea' and 'billycock'; for references to the bowler hat as frequently (though not invariably) part of the bookie's dress-code; see also Chinn, *Better Betting with a Decent Feller*, pp. 157–60 (also further discussed in my text above).

107 *Better Betting with a Decent Feller*, p. 157. The descriptions are from 1856 and 1874 respectively.

a single or multiple players. It was played with a cloth board divided into six squares containing pictures of a crown, an anchor, and the four card suites – a heart, a club, a spade, and a diamond, and with three dice each similarly marked. The players placed wagers on the symbol or symbols of their choice and then threw the dice: the players won if the dice showed the pictures they had bet on, with the amount won multiplied if the symbol came up more than once (the stake was won back for one symbol, twice the stake for two symbols and three times the stake for three symbols). The game became particularly associated with the Royal Navy and, during the First World War at least, with the British Army.[108] All sources agree that it is a game that always favours the banker, with a consistent advantage of between 7 to 8 per cent, but which also, with the gambler regularly winning back 92 per cent of what he bets, provides enough of an illusion of winning to keep the player addicted and hopeful.[109] Indeed, Chinn gives accounts of several bookies active between the two wars who had started their careers as crown and anchor bankers in the army, including a Mr Nicholls in Birmingham and a Mr McCormick in Salford.[110] Some opponents of gambling after the First World War, such as the Reverend Perkins,[111] saw a direct link between demobilised soldiers and the growth of illegal betting, and Chinn too thinks this is a likely cause for the spread of crown and anchor to civilian society in particular.[112] It was not only that ex-soldiers had acquired a taste for the game, but also that army 'bankers' had often made enough money to set themselves up in this 'business' after the war – a 'bank' being, of course, essential both for that particular game and for other forms of betting, such as those based on horse racing. Chinn specifically refers to Sam Grundy when discussing the role of ex-servicemen in post-war betting, saying that his biography in the novel suggests that such figures must have been 'conspicuous'.[113]

Chinn also notes that many bookies founded their businesses on their army gratuities, and this may suggest a contrast that the novel constructs not only between Sam and Ted Munter but also between Sam and Ned Narkey, who spends rather than invests his army gratuity. Harry observes

---

108 See *OED online* entry for Crown and Anchor. 'House' is another name for Bingo.
109 See *Encyclopedia Britannica* entry: <http://www.britannica.com/EBchecked/topic/1231578/crown-and-anchor>, accessed 24 October 2017.
110 *Better Betting with a Decent Feller*, p. 137.
111 *Better Betting with a Decent Feller*, p. 136.
112 *Better Betting with a Decent Feller*, p. 137.
113 *Better Betting with a Decent Feller*, p. 138.

early in the novel that Ned is popular with the other boys partly because of 'what remained of the gratuity they had given him when he had been demobilized' (p. 22), while later he wonders 'how long Ned's army money would last at this rate' (p. 60). If Sam is not exactly virtuous, the reader is led to see him as having some qualities of foresight and relative civility that Ned lacks. One thing that Chinn certainly misunderstands about the novel is what it is implying about Sam's relationships with women: 'Greenwood's character was also a pimp.'[114] This is based partly on a misunderstanding of the comments made by the crude Bill Simmons about "'one o' Sam Grundy's whores'" in connection with allegedly inside information he has about a horse (p. 56). It is also partly based on Chinn's use of other evidence in which middle-class audiences are invited to see bookies and prostitution as related: 'significantly, in *The Pub and the People*, Grundy's type were discussed under the heading "Singers and Pianists: Bookies and Prostitutes" and it is obvious that the conflation of these two "vice-ridden" occupations had an immediate effect on middle-class readers.'[115] However, on this occasion I am not sure that readers are being recruited to this association. Sam certainly exploits women and treats them as objects – there is no question that he is going to replace his present mistress with Sally without a second thought for her and presumably will replace Sally in turn, as she indeed expects – but he is not a pimp in a more literal sense. In this respect, Sam does conform to Chinn's general view that 'there is no evidence that street bookies were engaged in the organisation of prostitution ... pitch bookies needed the support of their communities if they were to survive in their illegality.'[116] As Chinn makes very clear, most working-class communities saw nothing wrong with street betting and its illegality (a view persisting until 1961 when off-racecourse licensed betting shops were permitted for the first time) was an inconvenience but one with no moral force: 'the outlawing of cash betting away from the race-course was made inoperable by the persistence of working-class punters and bookies in flouting such laws.'[117] Though, as we have seen, there was a strong strand of considered disapproval of betting and bookies among Labour Party leaders, as well as among the 'prudent' middle classes, there was also a view that working people should be able to enjoy the

114 *Better Betting with a Decent Feller*, p. 159.
115 *Better Betting with a Decent Feller*, p. 159.
116 *Better Betting with a Decent Feller*, p. 160.
117 *Better Betting with a Decent Feller*, p. 235.

interest and anticipation provided by betting just as readily as upper-class punters. As Chinn says:

> A vehement disapproval of betting never held sway within the Labour Party as a whole. First, because of the importance of the libertarian socialist tradition, which supported the democratic right of the proletariat to spend their money as they wished; and second, because of a wariness against losing electoral support ... . It is unsurprising that the leadership of the Labour Party felt it prudent to avoid policy statements on betting.[118]

It may be that Greenwood's novel, as so often, is being tactful towards this split in Labour responses to betting and bookies, wishing to keep faith with a broad readership: there are some sharp comments on Grundy in the novel, but he is not always vilified. Certainly, Chinn's sense that Greenwood is wholly hostile to bookmaking does not seem quite right, for Sam Grundy could surely be much more straightforwardly villainous in the novel than he is. Indeed, Greenwood's own later comment about his first published short story, 'The Maker of Books', that writing may be akin to betting, is notable and not unsympathetic to gambling:

> Out of nowhere came the recollection of Sandy Sinclair and his consuming hatred of the Motor Works' factory environment ... in his way was he not like me basically ... searching, like so many, for a way out of intolerable conditions? His desire was to make a book, mine to write one. (p. 205)[119]

This seems comparable to a comment by Jerry White, quoted by Chinn, about betting between the wars: '[it] was scarcely less certain than the daily roulette of economic enterprise'.[120]

Perhaps the novel also refrains from making Sam more villainous because to do so would reduce the reader's enduring sense of Sally's agency and independence, even though this is clearly damaged by Sam's possession of her. It is notable that the novel does not include many scenes showing Sally and Sam together, particularly towards the close, so that we do not have much insight into their relationship or direct experience of how hurtful it is to Sally. If Sam were portrayed as a more

---

118 *Better Betting with a Decent Feller*, p. 166.
119 *There Was a Time* (London: Jonathan Cape, 1967), p. 205. See also my Chapter 2, p. 15.
120 *Better Betting with a Decent Feller*, p. 152; quotation is from Jerry White, *The Worst Street in North London. Campbell Bunk, Islington, Between the Wars* (London; Routledge, 1986), p. 85.

openly 'evil' or melodramatic individual, this might also draw attention away from his function as a role in a self-sustaining system. Perhaps he is more akin to the chorus of older women discussed above, who are exploiters but also ambiguous helpers of their own class. Indeed, we can again draw on Chinn's sense that bookies were often looked up to as benefactors of the community. He quotes a Glaswegian recalling that 'the Bookie and the pawnbroker were respected members of our community – on a par with the local priest as they could bring comfort, hope and help to those in dire need.' However, a Salford reminiscence sees this association as counting against Sam Grundy himself: 'Are all bookies like the one Walter Greenwood wrote about? The answer is a very big "NO". I never met one like that … . Mick McCarthy as Billy [Brady] [was] a good church man and family man who helped many people in hard times.'[121] It is notable that the associations here between bookies and the (Catholic) church are in no way to be found in Greenwood's novel, which in total has only some ten references to the Church in any form, and these mainly associated with selfishness and hypocrisy rather than community ('"an' him bein' a churchgoer an' a magistrate"', of Price [p. 34]). For Chinn's reader of the novel, Sam Grundy is lacking in any sense of community and morality, but it is worth bearing in mind that Mrs Bull, who, as discussed above, has a claim (if an ambiguous one) to moral authority, does speak in Sam's favour: '"He ain't a bad feller at heart"' (p. 216). It may be, among other things, that the novel's reader is imagined as thoroughly secular, and that religion is not one of the markers of 'respectability' to which the novel generally seems so interestingly sensitive (perhaps, like Mrs Dorbell, the imagined reader is assumed '"not t'ave bin' t' church for 'ears an' 'ears"' [p. 34]).[122]

---

121 *Better Betting with a Decent Feller*, pp. 160 and 157. Both quotations come from testimony gathered by Chinn via letter after advertising in newspapers in 'forty-two local newspapers from Aberdeen to Exeter' (p. x). Precise dates are not given for when the testimony refers to, but the correspondents here are Wilson Ditty and John W (see Chinn's endnotes 151 and 166).

122 Harry Hardcastle is the only character – apart from women on the single occasion of their wedding day – who is seen as having any connection with the church. He prays for a new suit (p. 93) and sang in the choir as a boy; but, despite the possibility that the Vicar could help him to a job, he is glad to reject this 'effeminate' sphere together with the pawnshop when he goes to Marlowe's: '"Vicar can get y' job if y'd ask". "Yaah", he replied, impatiently: "I know … Tart's job"' (p. 45). This is a view Sally seems to support too with her contemptuous reference to Harry as a choir boy (p. 18). Only Helen associates the church with respectability in a positive way, thinking that 'all the boys in the choir went into offices' (p. 44).

Certainly, it is also notable that, compared with Sam, his pawn Ned is more explicitly presented as dangerous, antisocial, and (even more) crudely exploitative of women. However, it is Sam's power that advances Ned, even though Sam is alarmed by Ned's physical strength. From early in the novel, when Harry sees Ned and Larry outside Marlowe's, the reader has been led to see Ned as representing a brutish type of working-class masculinity. For readers who might see themselves as 'respectable' working or middle class, he may be an amalgam of their worst expectations of working-class men. It is not coincidental that Ned is usually mediated through the viewpoint of another character. He is first mentioned in the novel by Harry, when he upbraids Sally for having been out with Ned late at night – something he suggests Mr Hardcastle would not consider respectable (p. 18). Harry then sees Ned outside Marlowe's, where, as we have seen, he associates him with unpredictable moods and, through the tattoos of images of naked women on his muscular arms, with what he clearly regards as a far too explicit display of sexuality. Later Harry again makes further links between Ned and excess – in this case with excessive drinking: "'Phoo! The way he could guzzle beer!'" (p. 60). In due course various characters note Ned's swearing (p. 45), "'jazzin''" (p. 72), spitting (p. 113), anger, jealousy, and violence (for example, pp. 133, 135, 145, 188), or accuse him of sexual predation (p. 187). Narkey's rapid loss of control is often emphasised by the narrator and linked to his inarticulacy, especially when he is infuriated by characters who he perceives as trying to assert power over him through speech, as when he seizes Larry to warn him away from Sally ("'you an' y' bloody talk'" [p. 135]), when he quarrels with Sally herself, and when he warns Sam to stay away from Sally. His violence towards Sally after she criticises his treatment of Kate Malloy is especially brutal and shocking: 'He raised his fist and sent Sally reeling against the wall with a blow to her bosom' (p. 167). The novel, as we have seen, sets up literacy, articulacy, and some forms of respectability as highly valued from the reader's perspective and in such a value-system Ned Narkey is the character occupying the lowest possible position.

However, there are aspects of him that do nevertheless have some potential to impress characters and perhaps readers. His stature, clearly regarded as a signifier of traditional manliness, is often remarked: 'his figure rendered him conspicuous' (p. 60). Harry registers ambivalence towards Narkey's bodily presence while also noting its impact on others: 'There was Ned Narkey, a huge fellow with the physique of a Mongolian wrestler … there was something about the beefy hulking brute that repelled one; though Harry admired his strength; according to the boys Ned could lift a girder that four ordinary men couldn't move' (p. 22). Harry also sees Ned's masculinity boosted by being part of the dynamic futurist power that he at first attributes to Marlowe's itself: 'steel platforms from which you saw great muscular men dwarfed to insignificance by the vastness of everything: men the size of Ned Narkey who had charge of the giant crane' (p. 48). This massive display of 'masculinity' is also part of Ned's aura as war hero and he is twice seen falling back on his memory of the war when he feels threatened by the wealthy assurance of Sam Grundy and by the verbal fluency of Larry:

> Blind hate and envy dominated him; his impulse was to snatch at Grundy's throat, fling him to the floor and kick his brains out, as he had done to those German boys, who, scared stiff, he had captured in a pill-box, a feat of heroism which had earned him the medal and the commander's commendatory remarks. (p. 188)

> 'Don't you come the bloody sergeant-major stuff on me, Meath ... Ah fought for such bastards as you. Sergeant-major Narkey that's me. Ay an' Ah wus o'er there while yellow-bellied rats like you wus sleepin' wi' owld sweats wives an' landin' soft jobs for y'selves.' (p. 135)

Just before the second quotation Ned also refers to Larry as a 'white-livered conchie' (that is, a conscientious objector). As with other aspects of Larry's life, there is a gap in the knowledge offered by the text about what he did during the war, so it may be unclear whether the reader is to accept Ned's assertion as true or as part of his general bluster (it seems unlikely that the Larry we have seen in the novel will have taken the opportunity to sleep with absent men's wives – that seems more likely to be Narkey's projection of what he himself would have done). Given the way in which Ned is constructed as savage and inarticulate, it may be that the text is giving the reader the opportunity to regard Larry's possible moral and political stand as admirable, though it does not go as far as to assert this clearly – perhaps again aware that this might split the contemporary readership (one might recall the review of the play which noted approvingly the tiny stage detail of the display of Mr Hardcastle's war medals). Certainly, Ned's account of his act of heroism suggests that the novel may offer the reader some access to the sceptical view of the war and military virtues that the 'War Books Controversy' of the period 1929–30 had bought into the public arena. Greenwood may be fulfilling some readers' expectations about the 'lowest type' of working man, while at the same time challenging ideas about the respectability of patriotism.

Indeed, the way in which Ned becomes a police officer and some continuities in his behaviour suggest that there are in this world some odd connections between violence and law and order. Firstly, it is very clear that Sam Grundy offers Ned the job as a policeman to distract him from the offer of violence towards himself caused by his jealousy of Sam's presumed success with Sally. In fact, it is the hope that there is a policeman nearby to save him from Ned that brings the idea into Sam's mind: he can dispose of Ned as a threat and as a rival by persuading him that respectability ('"but y've got to lay off the skirt"' [p. 189]) can lead him to an immediate job in the police with Sam's help. Ned himself does not initially see it as an idea that makes much sense: '"Me?" ... Ned stared at him dubiously' (p. 189). However, Sam's influence and verbal persuasiveness soon start acting and the pay and conditions as well as the chance to enjoy again his military glory soon seem highly desirable: '"You're an owld sweat and y've Military Medal" ... Ned licked his lips. Seventy shillings a week regular; holidays paid for and clothes free. Better than being in the army for, here, after the eight hours duty, one was a civilian again' (p. 189).[123] It is notable that the pay is more than one and a half times Larry's wages before he was laid off (forty-five shillings a week). Moreover, as Ned soon finds, being in the police may license him to practise the violence he so much enjoys. This is made very apparent to the reader at the march against the Means Test. While Larry and the other speakers address the crowd, Ned ('his magnificent physique set off to perfection in his blue uniform') says to another constable, '"Ah hope t'Christ the bastards start summat"' (p. 198). Soon, his wishes are granted when the police block the agreed route of the march, and he is notably described as repeating an even more vicious version of his earlier assault on Sally: 'a woman whom he struck across the bosom with his truncheon, screamed' (p. 205). It is perhaps surprising that it is not Ned himself who strikes Larry with his truncheon, but another constable – maybe again Ned's apparent 'manliness' and 'bravery' is being undermined here.

123 Barbara Weinberger's *The Best Police in the World – an Oral History of English Policing* (Aldershot: Scholar Press, 1995), p. 13, footnote 19, notes that work by Clive Emsley and Mark Clapson 'shows a variable but high proportion of ex-servicemen in the police throughout the 1920s'. See Clive Emsley and Mark Clapson's article, 'Recruiting the English Policeman c.1840–1940' in *Policing and Society*, 3, 4, March 1994, pp. 269–85, Table 2.

When Harry tells people what has happened he specifically notes that as well as men being knocked unconscious, "'women were coppin' … it too'" (p. 206). Harry relates what has happened at the march after a momentary but significant misunderstanding when he returns home: he sees a policeman in North Street and wonders if he has come to arrest him for having been part of the demonstration. In fact, the policeman is arresting Bill Simmons and Tom Hare for stealing cigarettes – the point perhaps being that this is a more proper role for the police than preventing legitimate protest by workers who despite their privations have kept within the law.[124]

There is a reasonably positive brief portrait of the policeman who strokes the cat and talks to Blind Joe Riley at the beginning of the novel – though even here there are Joe's comments about bobbies being paid to do nothing but walk the streets. Thereafter, the police in Hanky Park are seen mainly to serve the wealthy: they have a special arrangement to keep an eye on Price's pawnbroker's shop (p. 27) and they are rarely to be seen when Sam Grundy is conducting his business in a back entry: 'Two Cities policemen … knew that at any day and the appropriate time, lawbreakers could have been arrested by the score. For some reason or other, their beats took them elsewhere' (p. 111). A policemen is apparently always on duty at the Unemployment Exchange in case of trouble (p. 194), and, indeed, large numbers of police are prominent in the scenes dealing with the demonstration against the Means Test and the cutting of benefits. While the uniformed men line the pavements, the plain-clothes officers mingle with the crowds making notes about the political speeches, but (like Ned) they are conspicuous for their size and are easily identified by the Scottish speaker, who calls them 'traitors to their class', 'enemies of the workers', and 'servants of the boss class'.

For many of the novel's representations of the police there were certainly comparable historical realities of which contemporary readers might have had varying degrees of awareness, as well, of course, as varying views. Thus, the behaviour of the novel's plain-clothes police in making notes about particular speakers and their political views can be compared with the slightly later instruction to his superintendents by the chief constable of Staffordshire that at a march by the unemployed in

124 For a detailed discussion of policing of law and order in the period and a summary of much of the historical literature, see Weinberger, *The Best Police in the World*, Chapter 9, 'Policing Public Order', pp. 171–83.

November 1936 they should 'get the names of any known Communists among the marchers, or other persons likely to cause breaches of the peace'.[125] Clive Emsley argues that in the inter-war period there was an increased tendency for chief constables (and the Home Office) to set the tone for the police forces to believe 'that it was part of their duty to protect "the English way of life" from alien creeds' and that 'for some chief constables ... the most threatening alien creed was that espoused by people on the political left and here they lumped together members of the Labour party and the Independent Labour party as well as communists'.[126] Indeed, the National Council for Civil Liberties was founded in February 1934 precisely to provide observers who would monitor the police's responses to left-wing demonstrations.[127] Interestingly, the way in which Greenwood constructs readers' responses suggests that they may be able to sympathise with a critical view of the police's inability to make distinctions between ordinary working people justifiably protesting and political activists or 'agitators'. However, as we have seen, the novel also suggests through Larry that there is indeed a distinction between the unemployed from Hanky Park and the outside speakers who come to address them. Overall, the effect is to suggest that the police are indiscriminate (a word specifically used of Ned Narkey's use of his truncheon [p. 204]), but that the 'agitators' (whose language clearly marks them as Communists) are also to blame for the conflict. The second point partly concurs with the view that the police leadership itself often took of civil or industrial 'disorder', but the first point about the police being 'indiscriminate' is a more critical view of the police than that generally said to be taken by the Labour Party:

> The leadership of the Labour Party also subscribed to this view of the English Bobby as unique, impartial and non-political ... . Perhaps the Labour leadership sincerely believed that the official view ... was an accurate one; perhaps too, in their determination to present a respectable and responsible

125 Staffs PA Staffordshire Constabulary Memo book 1935–40, Fol. 12. Quoted in Clive Emsley, *The English Police: a Political and Social History* (Harlow: Routledge, 1995), p. 138.

126 *The English Police*, pp. 136–37.

127 WGC/3/3. Mark Lilly's *The National Council for Civil Liberties: the First Fifty Years* (London: Macmillan, 1984), gives an engaged account of the formation of the NCCL by Ronald Kidd and Sylvia Scaffardi, pp. 1–10, while Weinberger, *The Best Police in the World* analyses the policing of both Fascist and leftist marches and demonstrations and the NCCL's charges that the police displayed clear political bias. See pp. 171–83.

image themselves, they were reluctant to criticise those hailed as guardians of the public and of the English way of life.[128]

Greenwood had himself met something like this view of the English policeman as 'one of the finest' in the world in his public correspondence with Mrs Sydney Frankenberg, in which she argued that the scene in the novel where the police hit the marchers with their batons was hardly credible: 'the way the crowd are dealt with is also a gross libel on the police and incredible to anyone with the least knowledge of their training.' Greenwood replied that 'the author was at the head of that demonstration and was subject to blows from a baton'.[129] Indeed, as we have also seen, discussion of this scene in regard to the film also took the view that it was beyond belief and/or could not be seen to happen. Clive Emsley makes clear that this was not an uncommon view and that complaints of police violence were swept aside largely on these grounds, especially if brought by strikers seen as politically motivated:

> Violence by the English police during the interwar period … was an issue on which central government and official journals were both smug and touchy. The implicit argument was that, since the English police were 'the best in the world', they could never, as a body, be unnecessarily violent. … When the ILP's James Maxton raised the question of police brutality against demonstrations by the unemployed in Sheffield and Manchester in 1934, the Home Secretary … replied that he had received reports from the chief constables and saw no reason to take action. Lady Astor enquired: 'Is not the word of a chief constable better than that of a Communist?'[130]

As so often, Greenwood's novel supports some reasonably conservative assumptions that readers might have about public order, while challenging other assumptions about the perfection of the British police quite sharply. In the novel, the relationship between the police and Sam Grundy (perhaps also further enabled by his membership of the Masons) is clearly pointed to as a problem but also as something to be expected. Again, historical sources suggest that this was very much the case, largely

---

128 Emsley, *The English Police*, p. 145.

129 Frankenberg's points are quoted and then responded to by Greenwood in an article in the *Manchester Evening News* 25 September 1937 (the article is headed 'Salford from Two Angles – Unemployed Novelist and Social Worker'. There is further discussion of the material in *The Daily Dispatch* on the following day, 26 September 1937. See WGC/3/3, p. 9.

130 *The English Police*, p. 142. See also Weinberger, *The Best Police in the World*, pp. 171–83, 'Policing Public Order – Marches and Demonstrations'.

because street betting was popular and widely seen as wholly acceptable by working-class people. Most police officers also regarded the legislation against street betting as unenforceable without losing the goodwill of citizens, who, in the main, they policed by consent and through beats carried out by lone officers:

> By the early 1930s, the Police Federation was complaining that it was virtually impossible to maintain a law which was not supported by public opinion ... since eradication was impossible ... the priority became containment, with bookmakers there by permission of the police ... and negotiated deals augmenting police power over the use of public space. As many first-hand accounts testify, the outcome was a formalised relationship and ritual, whereby bookmakers' pitches ... received a certain amount of police protection in return for cash and the charade of a court appearance, the charging of the runner and the fine paid by the bookmaker.[131]

It is of course ironic that Ned, a character who the reader is encouraged to identify as evidently villainous, becomes a police officer: this should show the dangers of Sam's grip on Salford, but nevertheless he seems still somewhat shielded from the direct revulsion inspired by Ned. Perhaps overall, Ned and Sam Grundy sum up the way in which only a few can advance themselves through exploitation within Hanky Park, while the mass of Hanky Park's people are utterly contained by an unjust system. Finally, it is significant that in the last chapter of the novel, which confirms that life in Hanky Park is largely unchanging, Ned Narkey takes the place of the generic bobby in the opening chapter, and his action in kicking the cat may suggest that in this respect Hanky Park is not just unchanging but getting worse.

In the next chapter I will trace the issues raised by the novel about readership and audience through the play and film versions of *Love on the Dole*, which each make significant adaptation decisions related to their perceptions of audience, to their different genres and media, and, indeed, to the dates of their production.

131 Weinberger, *The Best Police in the World*, pp. 165–66.

CHAPTER TWO

Love on the Dole: the Play and the Film –
a Tale of Two Adaptations

I. Walter Greenwood – adaptor: 'It has been said that there
is only one universal language – music. But there is yet
another – poverty and hunger … . It was the universality of
this problem that made Walter Greenwood's novel and play
LOVE ON THE DOLE so popular. Now he has written
another book about some of the same characters'.[1]

We will see in Chapter 3 that the play adaptation of *Love on the Dole*
(1935) was not originally Greenwood's own idea, but one put forward by
a collaborator, Ronald Gow, and that Greenwood's later novel *Standing
Room Only* (1936) may reflect somewhat wryly on having to adopt the
role of 'part-author'. After the play, certainly, Greenwood became an
enthusiastic and sole adaptor of his own work, always eager to consider
conversion from one genre to another.[2] Thus the Walter Greenwood

---

1 Back cover of dust jacket of US edition of *The Cleft Stick* (New York: Frederick
A. Stokes, 1938).

2 He also became a co-author, being invited in 1936 to finish D. H. Lawrence's
three-act play *My Son's My Son*, of which the third act apparently existed only in
a draft form, for a performance at the Playhouse Theatre, London (26 May 1936).
See Keith Sagar's essay, 'D.H. Lawrence: Dramatist', published on the web as a
pdf file and dated 2008 (<http://www.keithsagar.co.uk/moderndrama/lawrence-
dramatist.pdf>, accessed 8 November 2014), particularly Section i, paragraph 1,
the whole of Section vi and endnote 1. Sagar says that the unfinished manuscript
found in 'a box in an attic in Vienna or Berlin' (endnote 1) that Greenwood
was asked to complete as *My Son's My Son* was in fact the same play as the
unpublished Lawrence play now known as *The Daughter-in-Law*, of which a
finished version by Lawrence did exist, as first published in Heinemann's *The*

Collection at the University of Salford contains evidence of numerous of his adaptation projects, some realised, some not. Projects that reached the public realm include his play version of his novel *His Worship The Mayor*, called *Give Us this Day* (1939), his play script of his novel *Only Mugs Work* (1939) and a film script adaptation of his play *The Cure for Love* (play 1945; film 1948).[3] His enthusiasm for widening the market (and/or access) for his creative work is equally abundantly shown by sustained work on projects that were not in the end published or performed or which only finally reached the public after a long genesis. *The Secret Kingdom* is a good example of this: he wrote a play script from the 1938 novel in 1945 and also, sometime during the 1940s, a film script, but had to wait until 1960 before the BBC broadcast an eight-episode television dramatisation from a new script he prepared.[4] Ben Harker's statement that 'Greenwood, like his text, proved adaptable' is not only true, then, of *Love on the Dole* but was a characteristic which persisted through his whole writing career. Harker argues that this adaptability played a key role in the contemporary political impact of the texts of *Love on the Dole* and also in establishing it as a work that has persisted in British culture.[5] Paul W. Salmon makes a related point about Greenwood's enthusiasm for adaptation and the political purposes of his work:

The transformation of *Love on the Dole* from novel to play to film reflects Greenwood's creative versatility and typifies his specific penchant for

---

Complete Plays of D.H. Lawrence in 1965. Greenwood's typescript (WGC/1/4) and his hand-annotated typescript prompt copy for the 1936 production are held by the Walter Greenwood Archive at the University of Salford: WGC/1/4/1. See also the discussion of the text of the play in John Worthen's 'Towards a New Version of D.H. Lawrence's *The Daughter In Law*: Scholarly Edition or Play Text?', *Yearbook of English Studies*, 1999, pp. 231–46. Worthen says that the text was 'revised and at times rewritten by Walter Greenwood'. Presumably Greenwood was thought by the producer, Mr Lion, to be a particularly suitable co-author with Lawrence given their shared working-class background, the working-class setting of the play and its use of working-class/regional dialect.

3 WGC/1/3/4, WGC/1/7/1, WGC/1/8/4, and WGC/1/8/5. For details of the film of *A Cure for Love*, a contemporary review, three clips, and a short discussion by Michael Brooke, see *BFI Screen Online*: <http://www.screenonline.org.uk/film/id/453776/>. As Brooke points out, the *Monthly Film Bulletin* review (17, 193, January–February 1950, p. 8) consisted of just three dismissive words: 'Antediluvian Regional Farce'. However, both play and film were popular successes.

4 See WGC/1/6/2, WGC/1/6/3, and WGC/1/6/4. The TV version was broadcast between May and June 1960.

5 'Adapting to the Conjuncture', p. 56.

adapting his own works from one medium to another. Having emerged from the working class himself, Greenwood remained … dismayed by the disparity between rich and poor: he saw writing as a means of escape from the slum. He did not disdain popular forms and often courted commercial success … nor did he repudiate the power of fiction, film or theater to provide people with an entertaining break from the struggles of their lives.[6]

I think these are all valid points: Greenwood's happiness to contribute to popular entertainment can be seen in what is usually (but incorrectly – see footnote 12) identified as his first filmed story – that for the 1936 Ealing Studios George Formby film about a hapless and poor TT racer who finally makes good, *No Limit*, the plot of which, Ben Harker suggests, might also be seen as echoing Greenwood's own life-story after the success of the novel version of *Love on the Dole*.[7] But it is also the

---

6 In Johnson, *Dictionary of Literary Biography Vol. 191*, p. 133.

7 The film was directed by Monty Banks and produced by Basil Dean's Associated Talking Pictures company, known later (after 1938) as Ealing Studios. See IMDB (<http://www.imdb.com/title/tt0026784/>, accessed 24 November 2014) and 'Adapting to the Conjuncture', p. 65. However, though this has not been noticed by any critical work published on Greenwood, he also seems to have had a hand in the writing of a film partly about rugby league and partly about horse racing, released the year before. *Where's George?* (later retitled *The Hope of His Side*) was directed by Jack Raymond and starred Sydney Howard – see IMDB <http://www.imdb.com/title/tt0136252/fullcredits?ref_=tt_ov_st_sm>, accessed 25 October 2017). The film's protagonist is Alf Scodgers, and also includes Mrs Scodgers, both of whom appear in Greenwood's novel and also in a short story that became part of *The Cleft Stick*, 'Mrs Scodger's Husband'. I am indebted for this information to Tony Collins' online article, 'Where's George? League's Forgotten Feature Film' (<http://tony-collins.squarespace.com/rugbyre-loaded/2013/6/8/wheres-george-rugby-leagues-forgotten-feature-film>, accessed 25 November 2014; originally published in *Forty-20* magazine in 2012). The web version reproduces a film poster that clearly attributes the story to Walter Greenwood. Collins comments that '*Where's George?* has none of the social commentary of Greenwood's other work. In fact it is difficult to find anything of Greenwood in the script' (see also his brief discussion of the film and *Love on the Dole* in Chapter 10, 'The Working-man's Game: Class, Gender and Race' in his book *Rugby League in Twentieth-Century Britain: a Social and Cultural History* (London: Routledge, 2006, Kindle edition location 3802). Like *No Limit*, however, the film does feature a working-class man making it good, if mainly by luck this time, and does feature the Scodgers, who seem to have been comic characters created by Greenwood for whom he felt some affection, as he re-uses them several times. Despite this openness to the opportunities of popular culture, one does, however, wonder what Greenwood made of George Formby's 1935 film *Off the Dole* (Mancunian Film company, directed by Arthur Mertz – see <http://

---

case that the adaptability of texts in the 1930s was very much taken for granted by some, though not all kinds, of authors and audiences. As Lawrence Napper points out in his illuminating study *British Cinema and Middlebrow Culture in the Interwar Years*:

> Adaptability and adaptation … are key features of the middlebrow audience and culture, features which I would speculate the British cinema of the interwar years explored. It should therefore be no surprise to discover that the three films which will form the basis of my argument … are the result not simply of one act of adaptation, but of several. *The Constant Nymph* (1928) and *The Good Companions* (1932) both began life as extraordinarily successful novels, before being transferred first to the stage, and later to the screen. *The Lambeth Walk* (1939) began life as the stage play *Me and My Girl*, which was itself subject to several live broadcasts both on the radio and on the early television service, before being adapted for the screen … . It should be clear, then, that my argument is not concerned with textual purity.[8]

This has many echoes of Greenwood's writing career, with a similar openness to different genres and media. In short, Ben Harker's arguments about Greenwood's and *Love on the Dole*'s particular adaptability can also be put into a wider cultural and historical context where adaptation was both quite usual and took advantage of modern media to expand already large readerships into mass audiences. However, the success of Greenwood as a working-class author in accessing the benefits of this kind of adaptability was probably unique (though working-class performers such as Gracie Fields and George Formby experienced parallel success in moving from music-hall to cinema). Napper places this cultural easiness with adaptability against a kind of authorship and implied readership that is seen as much less relaxed about adaptation:

> Unlike Modernism with its interest in formal purity and experimentation, middlebrow culture was engaged in blurring the boundaries of its media. Traditional modes of representation – realism, pictorialism, theatricality and literary narration – were transferred to new media, and deemed to carry

www.imdb.com/title/tt0151802/>, accessed 25 October 2017), which certainly does not take being on the dole seriously (Formby's benefit is cancelled after he claims that he can only do one job – selling leap year calendars). Curiously the same production company and director then made another film about the dole in 1936 (*Dodging the Dole*) which also seems unsympathetic, this time seeing things from the point of view of a dole office supervisor who is trying to get a work-shy pair to accept some work (see <http://www.imdb.com/title/tt0146634/>, accessed 25 October 2017).

8 (Exeter: University of Exeter Press, 2009), pp. 10–11.

their meanings (and also their cultural status) intact across the adaptation process.[9]

It should be no surprise, then, that, for a range of reasons to do with making a livelihood as a professional writer as well as a political agenda relying on access to a wide audience, Greenwood was keen from almost the beginning to maximise the audience for *Love on the Dole* by translating it into new forms. With the play version, Ronald Gow's perception that the novel could be dramatised pre-empted the author – and Gow's theatrical experience and contacts were no doubt helpful both in the rewriting and the essential process of actually bringing off the play's first production by the Manchester Repertory Theatre. But once the play was a clear success, Greenwood seems actively to have pursued a film version too. Thus during 1935–36 he was in negotiation with the British division of the French film company Gaumont about a film version, but a number of features were famously objected to by the British Board of Film Censors (after they read the play text) to the point where Gaumont felt they could not go ahead with the project. As briefly discussed in Chapter 1, the idea of a film version was resurrected in 1940, leading to the 1941 film of *Love on the Dole*, which will be discussed later in this chapter.

If the reach and reception of the novel was important, so too was that of these adaptations from the original. Richard Overy has produced figures from the Jonathan Cape Archive for sales of the novel, which show that 46,920 copies of the novel were sold in the UK between 1933 and 1949 (there were further good sales in the US too).[10] As we have seen in the Introduction, contemporary sources estimated that more than 1 million people saw the play during 1935 in Britain,[11] while Greenwood himself claimed in 1940 that 3 million people had now seen the play, including the king and queen.[12] As Ben Harker points

9 *British Cinema and Middlebrow Culture in the Interwar Years*, p. 9.

10 Richard Overy, *The Morbid Age: Britain and the Crisis of Civilization 1919–1939* (Harmondsworth: Penguin, 2010; first published by Allen Lane, 2009), p. 71. The sales figures come from the University of Reading Special Collection, Jonathan Cape Archive, Mss 2446 (endnote 80 to Overy's Chapter 2).

11 Stephen Constantine gives an account of contemporary estimates of the possible audience numbers for the play in his '*Love on the Dole* and its Reception in the 1930s'.

12 In a letter to *The Manchester Guardian* of 26 February 1940 (brought to my attention by footnote 1 in Carole Levine's 'Propaganda for Democracy', p. 846. The letter's main purpose was to complain that the censorship and prohibition of

out, some contemporary references to the impact of Greenwood's work in fact referred primarily to the play rather than the novel: 'When, in *The Road to Wigan Pier* (1937), George Orwell cited *Love on the Dole* for yielding real insight into lives of the North's unemployed, he was referring not to the novel but to the stage version, which he assumed his readers had seen.'[13] There are no viewing figures for the film, but, as Overy rightly observes, the sales of the novel alone made it a best-seller by the standards of the day, so that the expansion of this audience to over 3 million through adaptation into play and film certainly made it a work with a wide impact.

Adaptation and theories of adaptation have been the focus of considerable scholarship in the last two decades and some core questions are usefully summarised in the introduction to *Adaptation Studies: New Challenges, New Directions*, by Jørgen Bruhn, Anne Gjeslvik, and Eirik Frisvold Hanssen. They start with the 'unavoidable question of fidelity':

> A central – perhaps even *the* central – question of adaptation studies has been that of fidelity, or the relationship between what has been considered an original and the more-or-less faithful rendering of that form or content into a new product. From the very outset of adaptation criticism ... scholars have criticised the idea that faithfulness is the most interesting or productive instrument with which to confront adaptations ... . Although fidelity discourse has been abandoned, the issue of similarities and differences is still very much present in contemporary research.[14]

My approach to the play and the film will certainly not assume that the novel is the model version of *Love on the Dole* of which they are inherently inferior versions. Nor will the discussion quite assume the complete transferability of the same meaning from one genre or medium to another, so that works could be 'deemed to carry their meanings ... intact across the adaptation process', something Napper suggests contemporary writers perhaps thought possible.[15] I do assume that the three versions of the work have a good deal in common and that many of

the film version of *Love on the Dole* undermined the claim that the war against Germany was being fought to safeguard free speech (indeed, Greenwood likened the British Board of Film Censors to the Nazi propaganda minister Dr Goebbels) – see Levine, 'Propaganda for Democracy', p. 848.

13 'Adapting to the Conjuncture', p. 59. His endnote 22 gives the source of Orwell's observation in *The Road to Wigan Pier* (1937; London: Penguin, 2001), pp. 79–80.

14 (London: Bloomsbury, 2013), p. 5.

15 *British Cinema and Middlebrow Culture*, p. 9.

the issues they raise are shared, but will also assume that adaptation from one genre or medium to another inevitably alters the meaning to a degree, as do changes made in the course of adaptation and because of perceptions of audience. The discussion will therefore indeed focus on similarities and differences between the three versions and will also sustain the focus of Chapter 1 on the reader to explore how the play and film construct the responses of their readers/audiences/viewers, using the particular devices of drama and cinema.

II. The Play – Audience and Ambiguity: 'Presented with the facts, each spectator may for himself select their social or political causes'[16]

As Ben Harker points out in his key essay, there were in fact two versions of the play-text:

> It was published twice in the mid-1930s: the Jonathan Cape edition of 1935 was prepared for publication prior to the London transfer, and reprints the text used for the Manchester performances and subsequent tour; the Samuel French acting edition of 1936 reprints the text as performed in London. What emerges in comparing the two is that the original Manchester adaptation underwent significant further revision *en route* to the West End, and that *Love on the Dole* was adapted for the stage not once but twice.[17]

Some differences from the novel are common to both these versions. Neither includes all the characters from the novel, which is not surprising given the differences in genre: a large cast in a novel adds nothing to printing costs and can be managed through the narrative voice so that both major and minor characters can be introduced and given as much or little space as they need. Thus in the novel Mrs Scodger is a character (deriving from *The Cleft Stick* short story 'Mrs Scodger's Husband') who is hardly vital to the novel's key themes, but who appears more than fleetingly in four chapters, while some characters, such as Joe Ridge, the foreman, appear only once. Clearly, the fact that dramatic texts, when performed rather than read, need to use physical stage space and to represent characters through actors (who also have to be paid) instead of narrative makes a difference to their scale. This general principle relating to the economies of the two forms explains why the casts of the play/s are

16 WGC/3/3, p. 6.
17 'Adapting to the Conjuncture', p. 59. There are some set photographs in the French edition which give some sense of the production, at least.

much smaller than the cast of the novel, and can partly explain why, as discussed in Chapter 1, the four older women (Mrs Bull, Mrs Jikes, Mrs Dorbell, and Mrs Nattle) are reduced to three and why, in the London version, there is one 'agitator' (described thus in the cast list but called Pat O'Leary in the text itself[18]) instead of the two described in the Battle of Bexley Square scene in the novel (in the Manchester version he is simply called 'Young Man'). But some changes to the cast, though no doubt also influenced by these kinds of consideration, seem likely to relate also to aesthetic and/or political decisions about the specific adaptations. One important character in the novel is entirely removed from both play versions: the war hero, crane operator, and then policeman, Ned Narkey (he remained absent in the 1967 Granada TV production too, where Sam Grundy as womaniser becomes the sole villain, unemployment apart). He is replaced in both versions by an unnamed 'policeman' who plays little part in the plot and is perhaps a little more like the generic police constable at the opening of the novel than he is like Ned Narkey. However, the police are represented in the play/s in other ways and I will return to this topic in more detail. There are a few minor characters in the plays who do not appear at all in the novel, particularly the London version's Mr Doyle and Mrs Doyle, while the Manchester version expands somewhat the role of the novel's very minor character Charlie. Charlie works for Sam Grundy and simply gives a sense of Sam's importance, perhaps, while the Doyles seem to have been written to replace a scene from the Manchester version that was dropped from the London version. Harker argues that the introduction of the Doyles is significant partly because they replace a policeman in the Manchester version who is given enough lines to express a political view of the people of Hanky Park: 'The policeman's appearance in Act Two Scene One is cut and replaced by a knock-about comic scene involving a drunken man and his long-suffering wife, a switch which underscores the naturalist motif of Hanky Park's irresistible and brutalising determinism' (Harker notes that 'Gow later recalled that the new scene was written to provide parts for two understudies; 'it covered the commotion', he remembers, 'while the audience returned from the bar', but this perhaps simply helps to reinforce the point that adaptations made for 'practical' reasons still have impacts on the possible range of meanings of an adaptation).[19]

18 See Samuel French's edition, no. 184, *Love on the Dole*, 1936, pp. 54–55.
19 'Adapting to the Conjuncture', p. 63. See also his endnote 45 for details of Gow's recollections, which are referred to in Ray Speakman's notes to Ronald Gow and

Equally important though are changes to the sequence of the story-telling in the plays and to the amount of 'stage time' as opposed to 'page time' occupied by characters. Here there are some major shifts from novel to play. As we have seen, Harry is very much the central focus of the early part of the novel, before being superseded by Larry and Sally as joint protagonists. Neither play-text follows this structure, partly because the sequence in which they tell the story is very different from that of the novel. In the novel the whole of Part One (some sixty-eight pages) is centred on Harry's viewpoint, tracing his growing up through his work at the pawn-shop and then at Marlowe's as an apprentice. Even in Part Two the first two chapters continue to focus on Harry's experiences and his increasing worries about his status. It is not till Chapter 3 ('Raspberry, Gooseberry ...') that we have a chapter focusing on Sally's thoughts and experiences, which also introduces Ned Narkey as a former partner of Sally, and Larry through the political speech which in fact forms the very first lines in both play-texts. As a theatre audience (or even as a reader of the play) we thus jump over a great deal of the plot, character development, and other descriptive detail that we would meet as readers of the novel. This material is skilfully inserted into the plays later: a concise version of Part One of the novel, dealing with Harry's sense of self and the narrative he believes he will surely live out as a working-class adult male is dealt with in some three pages of play-script in Act One. The way in which this rapidly deals with Harry's development and his disillusionment can be illustrated from a brief quotation:

HARRY. Ah've been put on a machine up at the shop – capstan-lathe they call it. That's what Ah've wanted all along, and now Ah've got it. Have y' seen new machines, Larry? By gum, they're wonderful!

LARRY. Aye, they're wonderful. They only need a lad of your years to work 'em ... . But they're not perfect yet, Harry ... . That machine will be perfect when it turns the lever for itself an' Marlowe's can be rid of young Harry Hardcastle.

HARRY (*thoughtfully*). Aye, Ah know that's coming. They turned another hundred fellows off this morning. But Ah'm not worrying. Maybe things'll tek up ... .

Walter Greenwood, *Love on the Dole* (Oxford: Heinemann, 1986), p. 112. Harker notes that Gow agreed to have a lightly edited version of the original scene restored for this 1980s reprint.

LARRY. That's how it is, Harry. The factory wants cheap labour to keep their prices down, and the apprentice racket's a good way of getting it … .[20]

We do not have here the same powerful novelistic effect of getting inside Harry's mind and his world view and sympathising with his very ordinary hopes, while also knowing from quite early on in the narrative that in the society he inhabits these modest desires will be thwarted. Instead we have a well-written piece of dramatic realist dialogue in which ordinary speech appropriate to the context and the characters is also made to carry some of the play's themes: for example, the difficulty that ordinary people in Hanky Park (of whom Harry is representative) have in seeing through the system, and the superior insight of Larry, as well as his ability to explain quite straightforwardly the workings of the system or 'racket'. Indeed, Larry's explanation here is more straightforward for the play audience than it was for the novel reader, who had Larry's sceptical analysis filtered (though not all that ambiguously) through Harry's wish to avoid Larry's complicating advice (see the novel, p. 24).

The main effect of displacing Harry's initial centrality is to refocus the play on Sally and Larry. As Harker argues, this, together with some other adaptation decisions, may have a marked effect on the political possibilities of the play:

> Both stage versions open with Meath withdrawing from the public forum of class politics … a retreat that succinctly pre-figures his trajectory in the play. In both versions he leaves the street to confess his disillusionment, admitting that 'ideals and politics' no longer 'seem to matter like [they] did' and that Sally has 'changed' him … . Both adaptations rework one of the novel's central tropes – that of a potential working-class political awakening – to substantiate this re-casting of Meath from organic intellectual, with optimism of the will, to lapsed idealist now finding an alternative space in the consolations of private life.[21]

Both versions of the play do, indeed, start with scenes set in the domestic environment of the Hardcastle's 'kitchen living-room', from where Sally (at least) can hear through the open door the off-stage Larry delivering a

20 *Love on the Dole – a Play in Three Acts* (London: Jonathan Cape, 1935) (referred to in my text, and following Harker, as the Manchester version), Act I, p. 24. Subsequent references will be to this edition and will be given in brackets in my text (however, references to the French acting edition, or 'London version', will be given in endnotes to reduce confusion).
21 'Adapting to the Conjuncture', p. 61.

political speech in the street. In both cases, Larry's entrance into the house and conversation with Sally may suggest that he is seeking escape from the ungrateful and hard-to-impact public sphere into the more achievable private sphere of romance. Harker links this refocusing especially to the handling of Larry's political speech, which, though it opens both stage versions, is also in other ways reduced in prominence. He rightly notes that both versions, as compared to the novel, reduce Larry's speech in length, and that in the London version a stage direction also states that the exact words are anyway inaudible to the audience: '*We cannot hear his words, but* SALLY *can, and it is interesting to note what he says*'.[22] In fact, in the London version, as Harker also observes, this stage direction states that Larry is '*out of sight and almost out of hearing*'. The speech itself is in both versions identical and much briefer than in the novel – about a hundred words long as compared to nearly three hundred. While some of the speech's words are identical to those of the novel's speech, the final section is clearly newly added and, while it is partly a concise summary, it is also more direct than the novel version in some respects:

> unemployment and pauperdom, that is the legacy of the Industrial Revolution. That is the price we pay for the system. And that is the price you'll go on paying till you waken up to the fact that the remedy's in your own hands. You've got votes – why don't you use them? Why don't you *think*? (p. 14)[23]

Harker argues that we lose the matching of speech to context, whereby the novel gives Larry a chance to teach the reader as much as the people of Hanky Park a lesson about how capitalism works:

> whereas in the novel Greenwood maximises the impact of Meath's teaching by carefully tailoring each lesson to its context – Meath talks about the de-humanising effects of brutal surroundings in his evening meetings held in slum streets and the labour theory of value during breaks from labour in the engineering works – the adaptation compresses Meath's lessons into just one short session, jumbling together a number of his main themes.[24]

This does seem the case, so that to adopt Harker's useful description of the novel version as articulating a 'tempered radicalism',[25] we could agree with him that this radicalism is further tempered by the

---

22 London version, p. 9.
23 London version, pp. 9–10.
24 'Adapting to the Conjuncture', pp. 59–60.
25 'Adapting to the Conjuncture', p. 59.

Manchester version and then again by the London play-text.[26] However, 'tempering' is not the same as removing entirely, especially in the context of what appeared on the mainstream stage in the 1930s (where serious plays about working-class people were few: 'Representation of the working-classes continued to be limited', notes Rebecca D'Monté, identifying *Love on the Dole* as one of a small number of exceptions).[27] I think that *Love on the Dole* in both play-texts still retained some of its capacity to take the audience towards new perspectives, while, like the novel itself, and perhaps more so, avoiding alienating the broad class range it was trying to include in its address. To return to Larry's much abridged political speech, the novel's exhortation that things will go on unchanged 'until you people awaken' is altered in both play speeches to 'till you waken up to the fact that the remedy's in your own hands' and then followed by the direct exhortation that the people of Hanky Park must use their votes: 'You've got votes – why don't you use them?' As in the novel's speech, there is the implication that their situation is partly their own faults for being passive, but there is also a direct instruction to take part in political processes. Admittedly, the stress on voting (and presumably voting Labour) may reassure the audience that Larry is a gradualist seeking change within the current democratic system, but the advice he is giving does not suggest that he has given up on the idea of promoting change.

There are, as Harker notes, some quite large differences in how the speech continues in the opening scenes in the Manchester and London versions. In the Manchester version Larry is visible off-stage and the speech is clearly intended to be entirely audible. Moreover, the dialogue between Larry and his heckler and some more supportive voices in the crowd is clearly also meant to be heard by the audience and gives this version an opportunity to continue to provide, if more briefly, some of the political education that the novel pursues. Thus, when Larry asks his off-stage audience what they do with their dole money, he takes the opportunity to explain (in a compressed way) commodities and labour power, as he also does in the scene in the novel at Marlowe's in Chapter 7 'Dirty Work at the Crossroads':

> LARRY: Yes, you spend it. You spend it on food and clothes. Those are commodities. That's raw material plus labour power. Don't forget that

26 'Adapting to the Conjuncture', p. 60.
27 *British Theatre and Performance 1900–1950* (London: Bloomsbury Methuen, 2015; Kindle Edition), locations 2857 and 2901.

– Labour Power. That's what puts the meaning into capital. So when you talk about doing without it, remember what capital is. (p. 15)

This version of the speech, which imports into the street-setting the discussion of capital and labour from the scene in the novel set at Marlowe's, does still firmly make the radical point that capital is produced from labour power and that it is not therefore a kind of external charitable donation to keep people in work, as Larry's comically undermined critic implies with his repeated but unthinking cry that 'Y'can't do without capickle'. As in the novel, the audience is here made to feel superior to the automatic heckler and thus education and thoughtfulness are aligned by the drama with a socialist analysis.

Similarly, though Harker is right that both versions of the play put more stress on the centrality of Larry and Sally's romantic relationship than does the novel, it is worth looking at the ways in which the dialogue nevertheless resists the idea that this could entirely replace Larry's political vision. Sally plays a clear role in this by showing her explicit understanding of Larry's feelings of defeat and his new-found desire to escape from politics into romance:

SALLY Ah see what y' mean. Ah'm interfering, like. If you feel that way perhaps y'd better not come any more.

LARRY But you don't understand, Sal. I've changed – you've changed me … it makes all I'm fighting for – ideals and politics and all that – it makes it … well, it doesn't seem to matter like it did.

SALLY Then you'd best forget me standing on yon rock and such-like rubbish. (p. 20)

If Larry is tempted to see the personal as a replacement for the political, Sally reminds him sharply in a number of lines that his politics are part of what she finds desirable about him: "'Ah don't know what you're after, proper, only to mek things better. But Ah knows you're a fighter, an' that's good enough for me'" (p. 20). Romance is thus partly recruited to a political purpose (for the characters, text, and audience) rather than replacing politics entirely, though this adaptation does significantly refocus the struggle as less collective and more individual: "'Listen Sal, we're going to fight it, you and me together. We'll be different from the others'" (p. 23). This refocusing, coupled with Larry's death, makes Sally the predominant character throughout the play (as *The Times* review noted of the London production: 'Mr Berkeley's briefer study of Larry – for Larry is killed in a political demonstration – is a clear unsentimentalised accompaniment to Miss Hiller's central portrait'[28]).

With regard to the impact of Larry's speech, it is also worth saying that if professional (and later also amateur) performance was an important way of reaching a large audience, it was not the only way the play could be experienced. The Samuel French acting edition is more specifically designed for acting use, being thinner and lighter than the hardback Cape edition – with 75 pages as compared to 126 pages. Both editions do refer to performance rights (professional and amateur respectively):

> Cape: 'All applications for performance to perform this play should be made to the London Play Company ... the authorised agents of the Dramatist.'

> French: 'The fee for the representation of this play by amateurs is Five Guineas payable in advance to Messrs Samuel French ... who ... will issue a licence for the performance to take place.'

However, unlike the Cape edition, the French edition also includes a five-page 'Property plot' as well as a 'Synopsis of Scenes', photographs of the stage sets and 'The Description of Characters' in the way of practical performance help. [29] It looks likely that the Cape edition does have more than half an eye on a reading audience for the play and in that case many play-readers would in fact have a reading-text with the more radical (or less 'tempered') of the two versions of the speech. But even in the French edition the stage direction suggests that the (truncated) speech should be read to really make sense of the play: 'it is interesting to note what he says'.[30] One might also notice that the Cape front inner dust jacket fold announces that *Love on the Dole* is the first in a 'new play series' and then advertises the next two in the series, both of which have clearly radical concerns with contemporary political issues:

> STEVEDORE ... by Paul Peters and George Sklar. 'A powerful play, dealing with the race problem in the Southern states of America ... '

---

28 31 January 1935.

29 Both editions also include cast lists, but the London version gives a production history and a cast list only for the London Garrick Theatre production (January 1935), while the Manchester version gives the cast lists for the Manchester premiere at the Manchester Repertory Theatre (opened 26 February 1934) and for the touring production that spun out from that (opened at the Theatre Royal, Hanley, 7 May 1934).

30 p. 9.

THE MOON IN THE YELLOW RIVER ... by Denis Johnston. 'A large, strong play ... summarizing ... the struggle of old loyalties, new ideas and mere stupidity in the remaking of Ireland' – Ivor Brown in the *Manchester Guardian*.

This implies an awareness on Cape's part of a potential progressive readership or audience for the play.[31]

A further difference between the two editions suggests another way in which the London edition has been adapted to a fresh 'conjuncture', to use Harker's useful application of a term derived from Gramsci and Stuart Hall. Where the Manchester edition retains the orthographic representation of Salford dialect, the London version replaces this with spelling which suggests Standard English. Thus in the Manchester version Sally early on says to Larry:

'Ah like way y'talk. Y'can talk alright. But ah don't know nowt – Ah mean, Ah don't know nothing about politics.' (p. 15)

In the London version this becomes:

'I like the way you talk. You can talk alright, but I don't know nothing – I mean I don't know *anything* about politics.' (p. 11)

Both versions take parts of a device originally used in the novel's version of this speech to indicate Sally's awareness of the status of 'dialect' and Standard English, revealing this through her swift self-correction ('I was listening. But I don't know nowt – er – anything about politics' [p. 87]). However, the London play version seems problematic because the apparently Standard English that Sally is herself using does not set up the status difference between different kinds of English except through the slip over 'nothing'. In general, reading the London edition is problematic in this respect because a key dynamic in Sally's character and one of the drivers of her interest in Larry is lost with her dialect, as well as many other effects on the reader produced through the representation of dialect. In fact, this adaptation was not, at least, *meant* to be read in quite this way, as is explicitly explained in a note in the London

31 There is some discussion of *Stevedore* (and particularly the part played by Paul Robeson in the British production) in Colin Chambers' article '"Ours will be a dynamic contribution": The Struggle by Diasporic Artists for a Voice in British Theatre in the 1930s and 1940s', *Keywords – a Journal of Cultural Materialism*, 7, 2009, pp. 38–54, pp. 44–46. The Theatre Union premiered the play in the US (see also the unfavourable comparison made by two New York newspapers between *Love on the Dole* and Theatre Union drama referred to below in footnote 58).

edition's material intended to help stage the play. After 'Synopsis of Scenes' there is this:

> Note. – The phonetic spelling of the Lancashire accent, which appeared in the earlier edition of the play, has been more or less eliminated in the present version. This has been done for the convenience of the cast, who may choose to speak in the accent of any other industrial area.[32]

This in some ways again encapsulates the willingness of Greenwood (though here he is, of course, joint author with Gow) to adapt. From its origins as a text specifically about Salford (though with evident resonances for other depressed areas as well as for wider issues about the condition of England), this version is offered as a text for all *industrial* (or *ex-industrial?*) regions. This authorial licence was presumably also potentially liberating and enabling for directors and casts in US, Australian, and New Zealand productions of the play, where a Salford dialect and accent might have been both difficult to achieve and lacking in the specific meanings they originally had in a network of British assumptions about class, education, understanding, and agency.[33] The change also makes French's London version an acting edition in more than just a marketing sense: the note implies that even more than usual this is a script for the play rather than the play itself, since directors and actors are positively invited to change the precise and often Standard English language of the text to something more performable and with meanings appropriate to their particular audience.

However, there are some oddities about how the note's policy is actually applied to the text. The 'more or less eliminated' has some truth in it, for dialect removal is not applied evenly to all the characters. As already suggested, Sally's speech is quite thoroughly standardised (if not always to the same degree), and so is Harry's, while Larry's speech is always, and even more so than in the novel, Standard English. But the chorus of (in this case) three older women are left with lines that, though less specifically 'accented', nevertheless still suggest a less Standard English. Mrs Jikes's lines retain the kind of spelling that in the novel and Manchester version is meant to suggest (as specified in the stage direction) 'a cockney accent': '"We left her having an argument

---

32 Unnumbered page, but presumably p. 4.
33 The British actors who crossed the Atlantic for the first New York production did maintain their dialect performances, but later US-initiated performances such as those in 1936 by the Federal Players at Syracuse New York perhaps did not.

with a lidy'" (p. 24). Mrs Dorbell retains traces of a somewhat generic regional or working-class speech pattern: "'Why if my old ma was alive today she'd turn over in her grave, that she would'" (p. 25), as does Mrs Bull: "'Yah! I don't know what's come over folk these days'" (p. 25). These decisions about the London text imply that there is in effect a class difference between the main protagonists who see that things must change and the rest of the 'passive' population of Hanky Park, and tends to create a hierarchical alliance of Larry–Sally–play-readers (at least, where these identify with Standard English) as superior to the other characters. This alters to a degree the hierarchies in the novel and again pushes Sally into a more dominant position in the read play-text. Indeed, the play makes some further adaptations that reinforce such speech and class hierarchies. Thus, the first scene in the play where the three older women enter and conduct a séance in the Hardcastle house (it is in Mrs Jikes' house in the novel) introduces some further comic 'stage working-class' dialogue, including a link between the gin they are drinking and the responsiveness of 'the spirits', and a malapropism ('Mrs Jikes: "Can't say I care to do it for an antiseptic"' [p. 28]). Sally has in the novel a private reflection on a new distance she feels from this self-made entertainment: 'She shrank from the thought of what Larry would think were he to learn of her having been a party to such a triviality' (p. 101), but in the play this becomes a public speech which marks the end of the scene and act and reinforces a stronger distinction between Larry/Sally and the three older women as a sign of what is wrong with Hanky Park. In response to her mother, Sally says:

> Yes, I *am* getting notions. It's about time some of us at Hanky Park *started* getting notions. You call *them* your friends, that pack of dirty old women. Oh. I'm not blaming them – that's what Hanky Park's done for 'em. It's what it does for all the women ... poverty and pawnshops and dirt and drink! Well, I'm not going that road ... me and Larry's going to fight it – and I'm starting now. (p. 30)

The effect here is readable in different ways. On the one hand, the private embarrassment of the novel's Sally about taking part in this activity, which may be implicitly linked to an emerging consciousness on her part of other perspectives, is replaced by a speech which much more explicitly relates the séance and fortune-telling to the larger political problem of why no-one – and especially women – can escape from their environment: the séance becomes a symbol of both the ideological trickery that keeps people where they are and of their own small-scale attempts at distraction or escape (the film version of the séance loses any such political point, giving Sally a brief comment as she exits that suggests mainly her personal embarrassment at the public speculation about her romance with Larry).[34] In this respect Sally has become, even by the end of Act I, a strong and public critic of the system. But, on the other hand, the speech and the accompanying sense of hierarchy may imply that Sally and Larry will escape as individuals rising above their class rather than as leaders of their class. One character who, however, may perhaps escape this effect (or persists despite it) is Mrs Bull. In the novel she is in many respects both of Hanky Park and yet (sometimes) able to offer independent criticisms of its accepted conventions, and in a reading *or* performed experience of this London version she retains this capacity. Thus she is willing to enjoy the séance, but is indeed sceptical about it and usually sees through habit to the material basis or consequences of everything:

'I knew thou wouldn't need it where thou's gone, and I'm only telling you this so's you'll not think I pinched it …'
'Go on Sally lass, it's only a bit o' fun and it costs nothing …'
'Aye, and I'd be laying you out in a month, drunk to death, fur coat and all.' (p. 28)

In addition to the two performed versions, it is then worth considering the potentially different effects of the London version if used as a reading copy. The Manchester version, which retains the 'representation' of dialect, seems to me to offer a much more satisfactory reading experience because it largely avoids confusing the original set of relationships in the novel between 'dialect' and Standard English with another overlay – but,

34 Sally's view of the séance – which, it seems clear, the audience are assumed to share – as obviously playing on the gullibility of the credulous and also as a sign of embarrassing cultural inferiority, picks up one contemporary negative view of Spiritualism that had been much aired in books and press coverage in the 1920s and early 1930s. Jenny Hazelgrove in *Spiritualism and British Society Between the Wars* (Manchester: Manchester University Press, 2000), makes clear how much public debate there was and gives examples of criticism of Spiritualism as fraudulent by psychiatrists and the clergy as well as by some relative insiders to the world of occultism – see pp. 4, 21, 26–27. However, as Hazelgrove also shows (pp. 15–16), some notable public figures were believers, including the journalist Hannen Swaffer, who nevertheless reviewed the play of *Love on the Dole* so positively (*Daily Herald*, 1 February 1935): he was President of the Spiritualists' National Union from 1930 on, having published an account of his conversion to Spiritualism in 1925.

of course, it still also retains the speech differences in the novel between Larry and the rest of Hanky Park, which impact on how we read him.

However, the edition came after the production and, in fact, as the reviews make clear, the London performance itself did choose to retain speech styles that located the play firmly 'in the north' and which had, in Harker's helpful analysis, some powerful effects on the way the metropolitan audience received the play: 'Headlines such as "London sees Lancashire" [*Daily Mirror* 31 June 1935] encapsulated the novelty of the eventual transfer. This was not a southern re-reading of a northern play, but the real thing which appeared to eschew metropolitan mediation.'[35]

Thus the London *performance* seems to have at least retained some of the effects of the novel and the Manchester version (as both performance and reading-copy) that the London edition may – perhaps in an adaptation to the conjuncture too far? – have risked losing. Some of these effects did indeed reinforce the sense that the play represented 'reality' rather than 'extreme ideology', but that is consistent with the political 'tact' of the novel itself and with the consequent breadth of its impact. In the Manchester version (in both performance and as reading-copy) Sally, at least, is recreated as a paradoxically powerful working-class woman: despite her undeniable material and bodily domination by Sam Grundy, she is seen as having a kind of agency and awareness in a world of highly constrained choices, which is tragic but also a sign that there are perspectives beyond received ideas of 'respectability' and conventional conceptions of 'morality' as stemming from individual and willingly chosen paths.

A further change to the sequence of the novel just before the séance is also worth noting. In the novel Larry and Sally go on their rambling outing to the countryside quite early, and Larry's sacking from Marlowe's comes considerably later. But in the play Larry says during the hike that he has been sacked. This must therefore be the second outing on which Sally accompanies him, because of references to the first ramble in Act I. Thus the only scene suggesting a world outside Hanky Park is heavily overshadowed by Hanky Park's presence and the escape it represents is clearly a very temporary one ('it is as if the cityscape has infiltrated the very landscape of the country … all spaces … seem inextricably bound up with the tensions of society in the 1930s', argues Warden[36]). Slightly

---

35 Square brackets incorporate sources for press responses, but Harker's original endnotes 52–55 give some additional detail and commentary.

36 'Ugliness and Beauty', pp. 4 and 47.

unexpectedly, in that this might reverse one's expectation of what is most likely in the two kinds of representation, the rambling scene is portrayed in the novel only through Sally's account of it to her mother (Part One, Chapter 5, pp. 95–98), while in the play it is presented directly so that the audience witnesses Larry and Sally's conversation on the high moorland thirty miles from Hanky Park (the London version has useful set photographs at relevant points, including one at the beginning of Act I, Scene 3 that shows the stage 'rock' which forms the set for this scene described in the stage direction: 'On the moors. A high cleft between the rocks, commanding a view over many miles of moorland country, stretching towards the sunset' [p. 73]). In the novel the secondhand account perhaps reinforces the general confinement of the characters to Hanky Park itself, while the actual enactment of the scene in the play further reinforces the centrality of Sally and Larry's experience and their developing romantic engagement. But the presence of Hanky Park is reintroduced in several ways, including through some dialogue about whether the beauty of the sunset is paradoxically partly a product of the pollution of the city: 'They say it's the sunshine through the smoke' (p. 75) and comments about a cloud shaped like Sam Grundy. The scene might again refocus the work on Sally and Larry's individual situation, as Harker argues the opening scene does, but there is still some critique of merely individual escape built into the dialogue:

SALLY: Larry, we've got to get out.

LARRY: (*bitterly*) Yes, climb out roughshod over the others, but Hanky Park will still be there. (p. 78 Manchester version)

However, one might also note the disparaging remark that Sally makes about local Labour Party members (taken verbatim from Part 3, Chapter 9 of the novel, p. 193), once Larry has broken the bad news that he has been sacked and rejected the idea of marrying on Sally's wages and his fifteen shillings a week dole money: '"Why don't them Labour councillors as're allus mekkin' a mug out o' y' find a job for y'? They're all right, they are – don't care a damn for us"' (p. 80). This may be modified to an extent by the stage direction '(*hysterically*)', but does seem likely overall to suggest a focus on the personal above the political, and may suggest to some audiences a split between ordinary people and their representatives as well as the inefficacy of political principles.

Another curious note earlier on in this moorland scene has no precedent in the novel version, however. Sally and Larry in effect make a connection between the high place they are in, poetry, and the Romantic sublime: "'Ah'm no poet, Larry, but there's summat in all this loneliness, summat Ah've been wanting'" (p. 76). She then asks Larry a question: "'Do you believe in – God?'" This is notable, as the novel is free of serious engagement with religious belief (despite the early reference to 'churches, chapels and unpretentious mission halls where God is praised', p. 11, there is little further pursuit of religion as the opium of the people, with the exception of the séance, the comically viewed accompaniment provided for hymns at the spiritualist mission by Mrs Scodgers and Mrs Jikes, and the automatic use of the word 'God' in various common idioms).[37] Larry is non-committal and gives no very explicit answer to the question, responding in fact only with his own evasive questions: "'Me? Why? What a funny question.'" It is possible that the literary/ religious motif might allow some audience members to see an openness to spirituality as a sign of insight, sensitivity, and respectability in Larry and Sally, though this would be an optimistic reading of Larry's response (shortly afterwards he may give some assent to Sally's view at the same moment that he denounces any possibility of religion as a force in Hanky Park: "'there's no God there, with all their churches'" [p. 78]). But Sally does on this one occasion express a sense of things beyond the material: "'Here … y' belong to summat big.'" One thing the literary–sublime–religious motif certainly does lead to is an explicit reference to a genre-marker when Sally (unknowingly) links their literal high position with a classical theatrical form: "'It's like as if summat up there was saying – 'Tek care, Sal Hardcastle, as you don't climb too high an' fall'" (p. 77).[38] This foreshadowing of tragedy is picked up again

37 The Spiritualist Mission to which Mrs Scodger and Mrs Jikes contribute the musical accompaniment, together with the séance, could perhaps have been used in *Love on the Dole* as an example of a more profound source of working-class escapism – the Spiritualists' National Union journal, *Psychic News*, claimed in 1932 that there were 500 affiliated societies and 'felt confident that there were approximately 100,000 home séance circles operating in Britain': Hazelgrove, *Spiritualism and British Society Between the Wars*, pp. 14–15. Whatever the reliability of these figures, Hazelgrove makes it clear that there was a great deal of working-class interest in Spiritualism. However, Greenwood's general secularism perhaps inclines him to see Spiritualism as patently fraudulent and comic material, as well as part of a critique of how working-people are deceived.

38 It is these speeches that are presumably being referred to in *The Times* review of the London production, which says 'except for an instance on the moors when rhetoric gets the better of her, every phrase of hers has the spring or, when necessary, the dullness of common speech' (31 January 1935).

at the end of the scene, when it becomes cold and dark and Sally feels a fear of the future. There is no such explicit reference to tragedy in the novel, and this may again point to the more individualist focus of the play versions, although tragic heroes (or heroines – the pre-figuring is immediately of Sally's fall rather than of Larry's) are of course also representative figures.

The events leading to Larry and Sally's fall are also modified in the play versions. In the novel, as we have seen, Ted Munter and Sam Grundy both play a part in Larry's demise, together with managerial decisions at Marlowe's and government decisions about Russian orders, while Ned Narkey is a further source of danger, though in fact it is an unnamed policeman who actually strikes Larry during the demonstration. But in the play two of these parts are deleted from the cast, with a considerable effect on the role of Sam's character (though the newly added character Charlie plays a small part too). While the London edition describes Sam as 'a not unpleasant man' in its 'Description of Characters' and a stage direction, he is in many ways represented as more reprehensible and much less ambiguous in the play versions than in the novel. Here, without the complicating assistance of Ned Narkey and Ted Munter, he becomes a more clearly individual originator of malice as he absorbs some of their functions and, indeed, some of their lines. Sam first enters in Act 2, Scene 1 to pay Harry his winnings and advertise his own reliability as a bookie for whom the sky's the limit – indeed, he takes the opportunity to sell further threepenny trebles: "'tek one for t'wife an' little 'uns too. There's nowt like it. Better'n insurance any day"' (p. 66). Sam is genial while paying out the money and continues in a similar vein when at first he talks to Sally, though the stress remains on the material good he can do for her if she accepts his terms. However, once Sally has named Larry Meath as someone who will defend her Sam immediately becomes more aggressive: "'Turning me down for a white-livered Bolshie! Yah! Y're daft"' (p. 70). These lines, or conspicuous words within them, derive from the novel's Ned Narkey and Ted Munter, who refer respectively to Larry as a "'white-livered conchie"' (p. 135) and to the political activists in Marlowe's in general as "'Bolshies"' (p. 184). Once Sally exits contemptuously, Sam turns immediately to action against Larry through two intermediaries, Charlie and Ted Munter. Charlie is the messenger who is to tell the off-stage Ted Munter that if he uses his influence at the works to get Larry sacked then his betting debts will be cancelled. This simplifies the chain of events that takes place in the novel and makes Sam clearly responsible for Larry's dismissal – in the novel, Ted Munter admits to himself that in fact he doesn't have sufficient influence to get Larry discharged, though he will identify him as a politically active trouble-maker, and then in his envious imagination constructs a scenario where he will collect an unearned reward from Sam for something mainly resulting from more general managerial decisions. Here Sam's power runs more straightforwardly and unimpeded throughout Hanky Park.

In the Manchester version the scene featuring Sam is longer by some thirty-two lines and, after the conversation with Charlie, we see Sam exchanging civil words with a policeman 'who touches his hat to Sam' (p. 71). Sam then offers him a betting tip, but the policeman turns the offer into a joke. The London version omits the conversation in which Sam tells Charlie to talk to Ted Munter as well as the interchange with the policeman. It ends instead at Sally's exit, but where, in the Manchester version, she simply says a contemptuous '"Aach!"' to Sam Grundy, her exit line addressed to the departing bookie in the London version suggests that she is much more aware at this point of her vulnerability and of his power: 'SALLY (*following a step or two; with frightened appeal*). "But, Mr Grundy – Mr Grundy – "' (p. 41). This difference might suggest simply a leaner piece of dramatisation in the London version – the audience can work out that Sam has carried out his threat in the gap between the scenes, and Sally's fear here anticipates her foreboding at the end of the hiking scene. However, this more economical version also loses the detailed basis on which Sam Grundy's power is built, particularly the way in which he is able to profit both when his punters win and when they lose. The final fragment of Act 2 Scene 1 with the policeman might not seem a great loss, but its presence does underline the fact that the police have reached an understanding with Sam and that they are not at all on hostile terms, even if the joking about the betting tip does temper the critical point about the relationship between law-breakers and law-keepers. Even this hint of criticism of the police is removed in the London version of this scene.

Ned Narkey's deletion from the play version constitutes a major difference from the novel – and it is a deletion that in most respects continues on into the film version too (Ned does appear in the film, but, as we shall see, he is hardly the Narkey we have learnt to hate in the novel). His removal reduces the size of the cast, but it seems likely that he might also have been a character who was perceived as highly problematic in a stage or film version. Harker argues that there are some significant adaptations made in the play-versions in their representations of the police and of law, order, and state authority. These topics and possible audience responses to them are the focus of the remaining discussion of the two play-texts. Harker notes that:

> Both adaptations compress and sharpen the tangled novelistic plot by cutting away secondary characters, in particular Ned Narkey … . In the novel Narkey weathers the depression by joining the police force, where he settles old scores, energetically wielding his truncheon during the demonstration against the Means Test on which his old adversary Meath is seriously injured. As a result, Meath's death in the novel is only partly a political matter; in line with the text's ambivalent political readings, the episode hovers ambiguously between an instance of police brutality and more personal plotting … . Paradoxically, the plot-driven adaptation of the novel for the stage generates political overtones that conflict with the countervailing de-radicalising thrust … . In the streamlined play Meath is now unambiguously truncheoned to death by the police and dies promptly on the scene even though 'he was trying to turn men back' from direct confrontation.[39]

If Ned Narkey is a secondary character he is nevertheless an important one, and his deletion, while undoubtedly reducing and concentrating the multiple malicious characters who in various ways threaten Larry, also helps the two adaptations to avoid certain representations likely to offend public opinion, potentially including the range of moderate to progressive opinion they are trying to speak to. Ned in the novel is, of course, presented as undesirably excessive in a number of ways: he is enormously strong, angry, violent, unthrifty, a swearer, a drinker, jealous, sexual predatory, unfaithful, contemptuous of women, and a violent exploiter of them. As suggested in Chapter 1, he may partly represent a nightmarish version of the 'coarse' hyper-masculine working-class man that the novel wants to reassure its readership by rejecting as an abnormality in favour of 'respectable' and more civil working-class characters such as Larry and the Hardcastle family. Paradoxically, though, he is also seen by some (boys, Ned himself, and his former officers) as an admirable working-class type – strong and a war-hero. Though Sam Grundy knows very well that Ned is a source of danger even to him, he exploits this poorly grounded social image to place Ned in the police force and neutralise his danger by making him indebted to his patron. In the novel part of the point of this is clearly about corruption in a literal sense and more widely about a corrupt social order in which the breaker of laws and obligations is most likely to become the guardian of order. Equally, Ned also represents another important

---

39 'Adapting to the Conjuncture', p. 62.

inequality in which the novel shows some interest – the ways in which some working-class men exploit working-class women. His deletion is therefore a loss to the play versions, but this move avoids complicating their representation of working-class men as mainly noble and/or victims ('Greenwood does not cloud their victimhood with negative traits', says Gaughan, even of the novel version[40]), and also perhaps avoids too open a critique of authority and the integrity of its agents.

However, as Harker notes, though avoiding some controversies to be found in the novel, the Manchester version of the play introduces some new material that, while only briefly developed, does generate 'political overtones that conflict with the countervailing de-radicalising thrust':

> Act Two Scene One, which has no equivalent in Greenwood's novel and was cut from the London show, introduces a representative, unnamed policeman who is smugly ignorant and casually authoritarian, if not proto-fascistic … he explains that he sees life as it is, and compares people in Hanky Park to 'maggots squirming in a tin' … . The inclusion of this view foregrounds the authoritarian tendencies of the police behind Meath's death, and lends some credence to the views of the rabble-rousing Communist … who claims that the police are 'Traitors to their class!' … Though the vernacular analysis of Mrs Bull, who describes one policeman as 'a blurry Mussolini', is more typical of the play's idiom, the Manchester production repeatedly aligns the police with the political right.[41]

These political overtones are, however, removed from the London version: 'The policeman's appearance in Act Two Scene One is cut and replaced by a knock-about comic scene involving a drunken man and his long-suffering wife.'[42]

In addition, as compared to the novel, the criticism of the police in both the Manchester and London versions is very much reduced simply in terms of extent, though some traces do remain. In both play versions the march and the subsequent conflict with the police takes place off-stage, which, in some ways, of course, makes the presentation of a crowd scene easier, but also leads to a somewhat clumsy device whereby characters have to enter and exit to provide a running commentary on the events 'outside' (the board of film censors had noted this as an implicitly positive feature of the play that could not reasonably be reproduced in a film: 'The scenes of mobs fighting the

40 'Palatable Socialism or "the Real Thing?"' p. 53.
41 'Adapting to the Conjuncture', pp. 62–63.
42 'Adapting to the Conjuncture', pp. 62–63.

police are not shown in the stage-play, but only described'[43]). Critical comments or behaviour towards the police by Mrs Jikes and Mrs Bull are also reduced in impact by being put in the framework already set up in the play of the three older women as comic stage working-class characters. Thus Mrs Bull's comment linking the police to '"blurry Mussolini"' is followed by lines that pick up material in the novel about the size of the police compared to the unemployed men, but which reduce the seriousness of this contrast: '"Look at him, the big bluebottle! Look at size o' his feet! Ah'd stop indoors wi' feet like that!"' (p. 107). Though it is clear in the novel that Larry wishes to avoid the demonstration turning to conflict with the police, this is presented as stemming from a sense of realism and political strategy on behalf of his fellows as well as a clear sense that the outside 'agitators' do not have their interests at heart – what advantage can come to the marchers from such an outcome? But when the quite long development of this theme in the novel is shrunk down to a few lines and made more explicit as a commentary on what has happened, it certainly reduces its complexity and produces a Larry who is more passively and 'tragically caught', almost as if there by accident: 'HARRY: Copper collared hold o' Larry an' laid him out. Ah saw 'im. An' Larry was doing nowt neither, except he was trying to turn men back' (p. 110). As we have seen, the novel has, directly after the demonstration, a scene in which the police come to arrest Bill Simmons and Tom Hare for stealing cigarettes and which may be read as contrasting this legitimate police action with the illegitimate response to the demonstration (though one could also read it as signalling that unemployed working people are punished whether they work within or without the law). In the play versions there is also a rapid return to the police in a supposedly more normal role – that of helpers in an emergency – when a policeman comes to tell Sally that the injured Larry is asking for her, and later holds back the crowd outside the front door while Mr Hardcastle helps his shocked daughter home (pp. 109, 111). This on-stage police role may have the effect of leaving a final impression of the local police, at least, as more friends than enemies of the working people of Hanky Park and so further neutralising any criticism of the forces of law and order.

The end of the play follows the events and speeches of the novel's conclusion quite closely, with Mr Hardcastle drawing on the language of 'respectability' (though his calling Sally a 'whore' is surprisingly direct

43 Richards, *The Age of the Dream Palace*, p. 119.

and an addition) and Sally questioning whether that sensibility will get them anywhere under current conditions, and whether they or anyone in Hanky Park can afford such a moral code:

> SALLY: Y'd have me wed, would y'? Then tell me where's fellow around here as can afford it. Them as *is* working ain't able to keep themselves, ne'er heed a wife. Luk at y'self ... An luk at our Harry! ... Ah suppose Ah'd be fit to call y'r daughter if Ah was like that an' a tribe o' kids at me skirts. Well, can y' get our Harry a job? No, but Ah can. Yes, me. Ah'm not respectable, but Ah've got influence. (p. 121)

However, Sally, as so often throughout, is more prominent at the end of the play than at the end of the novel. Her final speech here reiterates the idea in the speech quoted above: "'Things are different now t' what y've been used to, an' y've got to face things as they are, not as y'd like 'em to be'" (p. 125). This is much more like a last word than in the novel, where there is still to come a comparison between the joy of Harry at having a job (without reflection on the cost to Sally) and the fate of most in Hanky Park – young men such as Jack Lindsay, who has 'no influential person to pull strings on his behalf' (p. 255) – and the coda which virtually repeats the novel's opening. In the play, Sally's last speech is followed by a supportive speech from her mother ("'they say the country's lovely in t' springtime'") which implies that perhaps Grundy's bargain is too good to turn down, and a final line from Mr Hardcastle that evokes the pathos of his inability to fulfil his conventional masculine role as provider and the need to accept that his daughter's selling of herself as a commodity is the only hope in this abnormal world that is not only tolerated but sustained by those who do have power: "'Ah've done me best, haven't ah?'" (p. 126).

Harker argues that:

> Audience attention is re-directed from dialogic engagement with social, political and structural questions and hidden social forces – capitalism, surplus value, the commodity form – to the realm of the personal and moral within a given environment. Sally's fall, when it eventually comes in Act Three, now plays out as a family tragedy in which a decent working-class character falls into amorality rather than, as in the novel, a blurred but nonetheless grotesquely unsettling narration of alienated labour.[44]

While there is some force in this argument, this ending surely does retain a sense that Sally, Harry, and Mr Hardcastle are individuals

---

44 'Adapting to the Conjuncture', p. 61.

playing roles that they have in no sense willingly chosen in a social system that is indeed grotesque. Sally and her father's conscious alienation from what they would choose to be in an even halfway-decent and equitable society is made clear, as is the way in which the current social system so thoroughly reproduces an impoverished life that has come to be seen as normal and natural rather than ideologically sustained. In this respect I am not sure that the play simply 'reproduced rather than revealed social conditions', but would say that instead it does make a case that present actuality is not real and not only could be, but must be, replaced by a very different possible reality.[45] The plays' radicalism is very much 'tempered' when compared with that of the novel, even though it in its turn has many political ambiguities and displays a strong sense of audiences and a desire for political 'tact'. My reading of the plays' adaptations does in many respects agree with Harker's view: they frequently avoid political risks and controversy and soften the material of the novel further. But there are points, certainly in the Manchester version, and to a lesser extent in the London version, at which adaptation decisions do retain or even introduce some progressive potential, especially given the paucity of political theatre reaching any kind of large audience at this time.[46] Claire Warden argues persuasively that the play, seen in the context of relevant contemporary drama, cannot be seen as either entirely conventional or neutral in its use of setting and landscape:

> [it] cannot be simply consigned to a category of urban melodrama, bourgeois entertainment, or even as part of the early-twentieth century genre of working-class naturalist narratives. In its focus on the landscape and the characters within it, *Love on the Dole* has a significant political agenda, to present the profound and inescapable connections between place and people.[47]

Indeed, Harker's own point about what political bite the plays retained when compared with Greenwood's early writing for popular films (as

---

45 'Adapting to the Conjuncture', p. 65.
46 See Harker's endnote 49, which cites a contemporary Manchester theatre critic making exactly this point: 'Manchester's most radical theatre critic, R.J. Finnemore, cited the play's extended run as evidence of popular demand, poorly served by commercial theatre, for "plays dealing with topics which commercially are regarded as almost taboo" (R. J. Finnemore, 'Is there a crisis in theatre?', *Daily Dispatch*, 17 May 1935).'
47 'Ugliness and Beauty', p. 46.

well as with his mid-1930s experience of trying to adapt his novel/play for cinema) is an important one:

> Even in its West End incarnation ... *Love on the Dole* was another matter [from the story for George Formby's 1935 film *No Limit*]; though shorn of didacticism, its residual naturalist core was true to the novel in stubbornly insisting that material conditions are at some level constitutive, and that the freedom necessary for meaningful personal fulfilment is dependent upon basic conditions being met. The scenario remained structurally incompatible with hegemonic cinematic conventions, and plans for a film adaptation that might have brought *Love on the Dole* back into the type of place it described famously fell foul of the British Board of Film Censors in 1936.[48]

The argument about 'hegemonic cinematic conventions' accords well too with Jeffrey Richards' point about a film with working-class characters considered much more acceptable by the film censors in 1937, and which had two participants with close connections to the play of *Love on the Dole*, but who had to shift conventions to make it into cinema:

> Nothing is more symptomatic of the British film industry in the 1930s than the fact that while film companies were forbidden by the censors to film Walter Greenwood's novel and play ... Ronald Gow who had adapted the book for the stage, and Wendy Hiller, who had made her name in the role of Sally Hardcastle, collaborated on a film comedy, *Lancashire Luck*, about a pools win ... . Instead of the grinding poverty, the clashes between Hunger Marchers and the police and Sally selling herself to a rich man to escape ... we get a pools win, flight from the city to the country and the productive alliance of a working-class family and an impoverished aristocrat ... there is no need to change society – luck and love can make the necessary changes.[49]

It is notable that the working-class fantasy of escape from poverty via gambling is here treated uncritically, while in Greenwood's texts the fantasy's appeal is registered but also critiqued.

What we do not know much about is how Gow and Greenwood worked on the play together – some of the adaptation decisions must

---

48 'Adapting to the Conjuncture', p. 66.

49 *The Age of the Dream Palace*, p. 302. As it happens, *Lancashire Luck* also cast the actor George Carney as the working-class father figure, a role he would reprise as Mr Hardcastle in the film of *Love on the Dole*. Ronald Gow and Wendy Hiller met while working on the play version of *Love on the Dole*; *Lancashire Luck* was released in January 1937 and they married the following month (see also *Oxford DNB* online entry for Wendy Hiller and *IMDB* entry for *Lancashire Luck*).

have been influenced by their joint work on the play-text and to an extent by Gow's as well as Greenwood's political sensibilities. There is some discussion of the issue from Gow's point of view in the Hull *Daily Mail* (9 June 1934, p. 12), where he is recorded as saying:

> Collaboration between two authors is generally supposed to be a temperamental battle, but Greenwood and I were able to work in perfect harmony. I think there are two main reasons for that. The first is that Walter Greenwood is an extraordinarily patient man, and the second is that I spent several weeks reading and re-reading 'Love on the Dole' and studying the conditions of Salford people before I set to work on the play.

This implies that Gow was the main author, taking the lead while Greenwood (class- deferentially) followed, so if this is to be believed than Gow may have been quite influential. Later Gow wrote a substantial piece for the *New York Times* in 1936 which has also not been discussed by critics and which is sub-titled as being precisely about 'how he helped adapt *Love on the Dole* into its dramatic state'. Gow said that he told Greenwood at their first meeting that the play needed to be more entertaining:

> It seemed to me that a play about unemployment would not appeal to the general public. Nor did I feel that the English people cared sufficiently about the tragedy in their midst to see it on the stage. 'But', I said, 'if we can make a British audience laugh … they won't mind how much we make them weep. It's the mixture they love … . Two months later our play was written.'[50]

Perhaps some of the comedy arising from the 'chorus' – for example, the use of malapropism – came from this kind of discussion. However, Greenwood knew from the rejection of some of his early short stories that 'entertainment' was a factor even in political writing, and the novel is not humourless. Gow says that the play was to his mind an 'experiment' to see if the combination of humour and seriousness would work in a play about working-class life and that a 'successful tryout in Manchester gave us the required confidence to … take the play into neighbouring towns'.

Certainly, and like the novel, the play was favourably received by a wide range of reviewers working for newspapers across the political spectrum (a unique exception was a review by Sean O'Casey based on reading the play rather than seeing it, which pronounced that the play 'was either dead before it was taken from the belly of the novel, or the

---

50 23 February 1936, p. XI (main heading is simply *Love on the Dole*).

two drama surgeons killed it as they were taking it out').[51] As for the novel, the play's political ambiguities increased the breadth of its impact as audiences read them according to the politics they were more or less comfortable with: if Greenwood's (and Gow's) aim was to promote gradualist reform through reaching a wide audience this was of course all to the good. Harker summarises a number of such approving reviews from conservative as well more popular centre–left papers, and sees them as tending to use the play to reinforce the *status quo* while allowing a limited expression of liberal guilt:

> Greenwood himself attended the first night where his presence authorised the production. He was praised by London critics for the working-class authenticity which licensed him to speak (he'd been 'kicked around all his life'), for his steadfast commitment to the harsh realities of Salford (he told one reporter that he didn't want to stay in London and 'live soft'), and for his public-spirited political moderation (his constructive political activities as a recently elected Labour Councillor were widely reported).[*Daily Herald* 1 February 1935; *The People*, n.d.] Regional identity and biographical straightforwardness reinforced the sense that his play sidestepped sentimentality, melodrama and extreme ideology in favour of 'plain straightforward statement of fact' [*The Star* 31 January 1935].[52]

A review in *The Times* in many ways exemplifies how reviewers often saw the play as presenting *facts* rather than political argument and somehow found it politically unchallenging, yet also acknowledged it as making a clear, forcible, and reasonable call for change:

> Being conceived in suffering and written in blood, it profoundly moves its audience in January 1935 ... it has the supreme virtue in a piece of this kind of saying what it has to say in plain narrative, stripped of oration ... . The Hardcastles are an honest, hardworking unpolitical family ... Old Hardcastle ... is out of work. His wife ... is baffled by a tragedy for which

---

51 'The Thing That Counts', *New Statesman* 9 February 1935, p. 63. The view was expressed in the 'Current Literature' section, while a much more positive review of the performed play was given by a 'Critic' in the 'Plays and Pictures' section (the context is provided by Brian Cathcart in a 2006 ProQuest online archive of the paper). Some correspondence followed. The review did not prevent Greenwood from defending O'Casey's play *The Star Turns Red* from censorship in a letter to the *Manchester Guardian* on 7 June 1940, p. 10.

52 'Adapting to the Conjuncture', p. 65. I have incorporated the sources and dates of the reviews from Harker's endnotes to make immediately clear the range of approving opinion, but not other material which should be consulted in the original article.

she cannot place the responsibility ... Their son Harry ... finding himself in a world that seemingly has no use for him, does not dispute its theory, but makes love and bets on horses ... . In the foreground are Sally Hardcastle and Larry Meath, pining for escape and seeing none ... . Presented with the facts, each spectator may for himself select their social or political causes. It is the whole strength and merit of the dramatists that they are content to tell their story and to leave gallery and stall to preach to themselves; and the man who can observe the Hardcastles' kitchen without questioning himself a little had better, according to his means, spend the rest of his life in a 'luxury' hotel or at the dog-races.[53]

Here we have almost consciously articulated the way in which the Hardcastle family are regarded as sympathetic 'deserving poor', because they are unthreateningly 'unpolitical' and lacking insight into their own condition, and Sally and Larry are indeed read, as Harker fears, as wanting to escape Hanky Park as individuals only. But at the same time, though the reviewer will not articulate the possible political meanings of the play (it is notable that attention is drawn to the possibility of different social and political interpretations), it is hailed as presenting 'facts' that should have a humanist impact on anyone who sees the play. The audience member who does not question himself is seen as someone who can attempt to escape 'reality' only through luxury or betting (and is thus implicitly compared to Harry, who has tried to escape his reality through betting). However, one review, by Greenwood's 'fairy godmother' Ethel Mannin, did see the play as having more radical potential:

It is a magnificent statement of the case for the overthrow of the capitalist system and I for one would like to compel every supporter of the present regime to sit through its three heart-breaking acts and then ask themselves if they still believed there was no need for a revolution.[54]

Reviews of the Broadway production the following year were also generally approving and saw the play as drawing attention to a problem that must be urgently addressed (of course the New Deal in the US was already addressing unemployment or its symptoms much more

53 31 January 1935, p. 12.
54 WGC/3/3, p. 6. Sadly, the review is one of the few in the Clippings book that is neither attributed nor dated. By 1935 Mannin was a member of the ILP (Independent Labour Party) and her review accordingly reflects a position further to the left than that of the Labour Party (see her entry in the *DNB online*: <http://www.oxforddnb.com/> accessed 2 March 2015).

actively than was the British government). However, two US reviews were much more critical than any British review, mainly because they compared the play with the more explicitly committed work of Theatre Union (founded in 1933) rather than to more commercial drama. The *New York Post* says of *Love on the Dole* that 'neither is it a propaganda play that the Theatre Union might clutch to its bosom wrapped in the red flag ... [the characters] are offered no way out except to get out ... the labour agitator ... is frowned upon by the Hardcastles and their ilk', while the *New York Times* said that the play was 'apologetic and defeatist as well as meek and those are not qualities with which effective protest drama is made'.[55] However, the *New York Times* also acknowledged that its view was a minority one and that other reviews thought the British play more effective than 'bumptious' left-wing drama (a pioneering 1937 work on the Federal Theatre project also took this view, coupling it with the play *Class of 29*: 'the tragic end of the play, like that of *Love on the Dole*, was far more effective than conversion and subsequent salvation, in the manner of crude propaganda, could have been'[56]). The Australian *Workers' Weekly* paper also saw the play's dead end not as defeatist but as contributing to its correct political analysis in a 1935 article about a performance at the Workers' Art Club, Sydney:

> The futility and folly of our present system is further more accentuated by the bitter and ironical climax ... . It is clearly indicated by the author that there is no individual solution to this social disease, and that while a few may salvage themselves, the great majority will remain in Hanky Park.[57]

Of course, readers/audiences can always read a work in different ways – influenced in complex ways by the parameters enabled by the text, the performance, their own ways of reading, and their own political starting points or end points, but it seems likely that the variety of responses to the play is indeed partly produced by its political openness or ambiguity. This ambiguity may well blur the sharpness of the play's political analysis (and so there is a cost), but it also contributed to the breadth of its appeal, especially, though not only, to audiences likely to interpret it through

---

55 *New York Post* 26 February 1936; *New York Times* 15 March 1936; both in WGC/3/1, p. 47.

56 Willson Whitman, *Bread and Circuses: a Study of Federal Theatre* (New York: Oxford University Press, 1937), p. 80.

57 29 October 1935 – the performances were to take place on 24 November, 1 December and 2 December 1935.

centrist, liberal, and moderate-left modes of understanding. As we shall see next in discussion of the film version, these characteristics may also have avoided the censorship issues for the play which blocked the film version for five years.

III. The Film. Censorship and Context:
'A Very Sordid Story';[58] 'Film Was Banned, Now a Triumph'[59]

This section will explore the context of the film version of *Love on the Dole*, while the final section will explore the film text, continuing comparisons with the novel and play versions and sustaining a focus on how viewers were likely to have interpreted this text within the frameworks available to them. The revival of the idea of a film version was not, in 1940, wholly Greenwood's own initiative, but he must have been both pleased and vindicated (he had clearly not forgotten about the project, as the important letter referred to below suggests). The surprising decision to make a film version of *Love on the Dole* in 1940, when the two attempts in 1936 had been subject to extensive and insuperable objections from the British Board of Film Censors, has often been noted. Jeffrey Richards gives the fullest account of the 1936 response to the proposed film. Thus he reports that the British Board of Film Censors' report felt that the film was 'undesirable' in a number of ways. Moral and political issues, which they tended to link rather seamlessly, worried the censors. One, Colonel Hanna, wrote:

> A very sordid story in very sordid surroundings. The language throughout is very coarse and full of swearwords, some of which are quite prohibitive. The scenes of mobs fighting the police are not shown in the stage-play, but only described. They might easily be prohibitive. Even if the book is well reviewed and the stage play had a successful run, I think this subject as it stands would be very undesirable as a film.[60]

His objections are threefold: the representation of a 'sordid' environment on screen, the inclusion of 'coarse' language, and the representation of 'mobs' fighting the police. As we have seen from discussion of both the novel and the plays, and also from newspaper anticipations of possible

58 Richards, *The Age of the Dream Palace*, p. 119, citing British Board of Film Censors' Report 1936/42.

59 *Daily Herald* 28 May 1941.

60 *The Age of the Dream Palace*, p. 119, citing British Board of Film Censors' Report 1936/42.

issues with a film version, Colonel Hanna's problem with the Battle of Bexley Square and the portrayal of the British police was not his alone. Indeed, Richards' discussion of *Love on the Dole* takes place within a section of his book that focuses on the censors' loving protection of 'the entire establishment', and he quotes Colonel Hanna's comment on another 1935 screenplay that included the blackmailing of a senior police officer: 'We never allow the English police to be shown in such a light.' Richards also puts the film into the context of the censors' responses to films dealing with industrial disputes. Thus a 1932 screenplay centring on a strike again leads Hanna to enunciate some general principles:

> Our attitude to the subject has always been very definite. Strikes or labour unrest, where the scene is laid in England, have never been shown in any detail. It is impossible to show such strikes without taking a definite side either with or against the strikers and this would at once range the films as political propaganda of a type that we have always held to be unsuitable for exhibition in this country ... . If therefore the strike is the prominent feature of the story we would consider the subject unsuitable. If the love story is the main feature with a very shadowy reference to the strike in the background, it is possible that the story would be acceptable.[61]

Of course, the workers in *Love on the Dole* are not taking part in a strike, because they are unemployed, but they are expressing a similar dissatisfaction about the *status quo* and to show this social conflict on film would imply that all was not well with the British social system. This quotation and the one above about the police shows clearly the political context of film censorship, which held representations of the *status quo* to be non-political, while determining that anything in any way challenging the *status quo* was to be classed automatically as unacceptably contentious. However, the reference to the love story as a focus that would make a political theme in the background more acceptable is also worth noting in terms of the discussion above of how Sally and Larry's romance is made more prominent in the play versions discussed above, and indeed in the film. Richards also notes that a second censor, Miss Shortt, while equally objecting to the depiction of poverty and the language used, made her key reservation a moral rather than political one: 'I do not consider this play suitable for production as

---

61 *The Age of the Dream Palace*, p. 120, citing British Board of Film Censors' Report 1932/58. The film synopsis was submitted by Gainsborough Pictures and entitled *Tidal Waters*: it centred on conflict between striking watermen and dockworkers who were not on strike.

a film. There is too much of the tragic and sordid side of poverty and a certain amount of dialogue would have to be deleted and the final incident of Sally selling herself is prohibitive.'[62]

It is notable that while Colonel Hanna thinks a film version 'undesirable' Miss Shortt considers the play absolutely unfilmable. After Gaumont British subsequently dropped the proposed film a second company, Atlantic Productions, tried again in June 1936, but with no success. Colonel Hanna found no reason to change his judgement: 'I have read this play a second time, but cannot modify the first report in any way. I still consider it very undesirable.'[63] It is worth noting that Atlantic Productions did not in any way modify the proposal, so that their chances of success seemed slim: both Miss Shortt and Colonel Hanna make it clear in the headings to their typed notes, as well as in Hanna's comment above, that they read not a scenario or synopsis (the commonest form in which film proposals were sent to the censors) but the full text of the stage play.[64] As Richards observes:

> It is clear that the ban on filming resulted from a mixture of moral (bad language, sexual immorality) and political (marchers v. police) considerations. But there is the general impression that it was unwholesome and dangerous to show the masses 'the tragic side of poverty', lest they be stirred up to do something about it, and that is a profoundly political judgement.[65]

Indeed, the historian Ross McKibbin argues that interwar ideologies of class that saw moral and economic behaviours as co-terminous and regarded the middle classes as representing the norm were at the root of an urge to censor any representation of working-class life that might disrupt this normative blending of moral, economic, and political assumption:

> We have seen that from the end of the First World War middle-class Britain

62 *The Age of the Dream Palace*, p. 119, again citing British Board of Film Censors' Report 1936/42. Miss Shortt was the daughter of Edward Shortt, who was president of the BBFC from 1930 to 1935 (see his *DNB* entry <http://www.oxforddnb.com/>, accessed 12 May 2015).

63 *The Age of the Dream Palace*, p. 119, citing British Board of Film Censors' Report 1936/87.

64 All their 'Scenario Notes' for 1936 carefully indicate the type of source they are basing their judgements on: 'Scenario', 'Typed story', 'Script of stage play', or simply, as for *Love on the Dole*, 'Stage Play'. Miss Shortt refers to the need to cut specific speeches indicated by their page numbers in the script, which we can therefore certainly identify as the Cape edition rather than a typed script from the staging process.

65 *The Age of the Dream Palace*, p. 119.

was increasingly motivated by a 'deflationary' ideology fashioned by a particular notion of the working-class and characterised by an acute hostility to working-class politics ... a rather vulgar form of pre-war anti-collectivism was one of its essential features. It thus emphasised the economic centrality of the individual in economic life and the family in social life, while assimilating the financial practices of the family to those of the state. Furthermore, the state, by a developing system of censorship, attempted what it had never specifically done before: to reinforce the economic primacy of the family by moral and social buttresses ... . The refusal of the Board of Film Censors in the 1930s to allow *Love on the Dole* to be filmed is simply the most celebrated example.[66]

Part of the work *Love on the Dole* might be doing in representing so strongly to its audiences the respectability of the Hardcastle family (including Mr Hardcastle's wish to live within their means) is to show them as sharing these 'middle-class' values and being defeated not by 'working-class' failures in family life but by the sheer impossibility of sustaining these values in the current economic and social conditions.

Clearly, these judgements by the film censors of a work that was widely read as a novel and widely seen as a play in Britain must tell us something about mid-1930s assumptions about those media and their reception as compared with their expectations about films and their audiences. Novels in this period were not routinely censored unless a prosecution was brought, but all new plays did have to be sent to the Lord Chamberlain's office before they were licensed for performance (however, one Library Committee, at Crompton near Oldham, certainly *did* discuss withdrawing the novel from circulation, on the grounds that 'many things in the book would not be allowed to be repeated on stage', and when the play was advertised in Britain there was sometimes an advisory notice that it was suitable only for adults[67]). The play of *Love on the Dole* met no major problem with this process, yet was found prohibitive by the British Board of Film Censors. Standards or attitudes must therefore have been

---

66 *The Ideologies of Class: Social Relations in Britain 1880–1950* (Oxford: Clarendon Press, 1994), p. 276.

67 *Manchester Guardian* 15 October 1935, p. 12. Report is headed 'The Crompton Censors'. However, other councillors argued that withdrawal would make the Library Committee 'a laughing stock' and that 'those of them engaged in public assistance work heard actual cases which must be equal to anything in the book'. An advert for the play in the (Tonbridge) *Courier* (22 October 1937, p. 22) stated that 'Not wishing to offend the unsophisticated, I warn my patrons that this is a very outspoken play.'

markedly different between the two bodies – one made up of officials from the Royal household, the other of volunteers appointed by the film industry, though with close ties to the establishment.

Indeed, in as far as there were public statements of general principles by these two different censorship bodies, there were some key differences. A Parliamentary Select Committee review in 1909 of theatre censorship as conducted by the Lord Chamberlain's office recommended some (moderately liberal) principles that continued to be applied for some decades afterwards:

> [There was a] presumption that any play would receive a licence unless it 1) was considered indecent 2) contained the portrayal of offensive personalities 3) depicted living people or people who had died only recently 4) violated religious reverence 5) encouraged crime or vice 6) impaired relations with a foreign power, or 7) was calculated to bring about a breach of the peace.[68]

There is an underlying assumption that a play had to be markedly provocative before censorship could be invoked either in the way of a ban or a request for modification. Greenwood and Gow's play might register marginally against both 1) in that it referred to the arrangement between Sally and Sam Grundy and 7) in that it referred to civil disorder off-stage, but it did pass fairly easily through the Lord Chamberlain's Office. The film censors seem much more protective of their imagined audience, who are thought of as wholly uncritical and perhaps both literally and metaphorically seen as, in effect, 'minors': '[we are guided by] the broad general principle that nothing will be passed which is calculated to demoralize the public ... . Consideration has to be given to the impression made on an average audience which includes a not inconsiderable proportion of people of immature judgement.'[69]

---

68 Anthony Aldgate and James C. Robertson, *Censorship in Theatre and Cinema* (Edinburgh: Edinburgh University Press, 2005), p. 1. See also pp. 1–3 for a helpful and concise account of the operation of the two censorship bodies. Aldgate and Robertson's book may not deal with the play partly because, though it has a chapter on 'Foreign Affairs', there is relatively little material on drama and domestic or class politics.

69 Richards, *The Age of the Dream Palace*, p. 90, quoting what is said to be a BBFC pamphlet *Censorship in Britain*, which was designed to explain its policies to the public. Unfortunately, the date of the pamphlet is given neither in Richards' endnote 4 nor the cited essay by Forsyth Hardy, 'Censorship and Film Societies', in Charles Davy (ed.), *Footnotes to the Film* (London: Lovat Dickson/The Readers' Union, 1938), p. 267. The British Board of Film Censors (particularly the Head of Communications, Catherine Anderson) have been extremely helpful

Nevertheless, in fact the play did provoke in the Lord Chamberlain's Office some similarly negative feelings to those it evoked in the film censors, though at a less alarming intensity. Oddly, the different attitudes to *Love on the Dole* from these two censorship bodies have not been specifically compared before: several standard works on theatre censorship do not discuss the play because it was not a *cause célèbre*, while works on film censorship have not gone back to see if the play met any objection from the Lord Chamberlain's office (and, disappointingly, the case of *Love on the Dole* is not considered in the one work spanning the two media, Anthony Aldgate and James C. Robertson's *Censorship in Theatre and Cinema*, 2005).[70] However, Steve Nicholson in *The Censorship of British Drama 1932–1952* does discuss Greenwood and Gow's play and also quotes from the Lord Chamberlain's report on the play version, which is well worth comparing with the film censors' reports:

There was no significant objection to the stage version of *Love on the Dole* being licensed for the Manchester Repertory Theatre. Indeed, the Office could be said to have anticipated Brecht in indicating that although the depiction of 'reality' within the hidden frame of naturalism might create empathy, it would not encourage an audience to see these conditions as capable of change:

'This play could not fairly be described as propaganda except in so far as any play on this subject must cause a feeling of distress and discontent with present conditions in the beholder. Some things are said in the course of the action which would not appeal to other than Socialist ears, but they come naturally within the framework of the play, and so are justified, aesthetically at any rate'.[71]

in answering my enquiries, but have also not been able to trace a pamphlet of this title, though they were able to locate copies of three pamphlets printed by the BBFC which expressed similar views (Edward Shortt's *Problems of Censorship*, 1935, Lord Tyrrell of Avon's *Film Censorship Today*, 1936 and the same author's *Review of Censorship*, 1937). Clearly, however, the source must date from before or to the year 1938.

70 Thus (perhaps understandably) *Love on the Dole* does not make it into Dominic Shellard, Steve Nicholson and Miriam Handley's *The Lord Chamberlain Regrets: a History of British Theatre Censorship* (London: The British Library, 2004) or David Thomas, David Carlton and Anne Etienne's *Theatre Censorship from Walpole to Wilson* (Oxford: Oxford University Press, 2007).

71 Exeter: University of Exeter Press, 2000, pp. 122–23. The Lord Chamberlain's Office report cited is LCP 1934/12757.

Nicholson goes on to point out that some other plays about unemployment from this period were not licensed for performance, which may again confirm the play's 'tempered radicalism' or suggest how finely its authors had judged its political ambiguity. Nicholson's discussion of the report's logic interestingly intersects with Ben Harker's sense that the play's naturalism constrains its radicalism, and that it loses some features from the novel that might be seen as Brechtian. The report clearly shows its distaste for 'Socialism', but also thinks that 'Socialist' speeches within the play will be picked up only by audience members who are already Socialists and does not therefore see the play as a whole as subversive or propaganda: such political speeches as it contains are accepted as 'natural' for the play's setting. The report thus shows that the theatre and film censors certainly shared some concerns about the work's politics, but that, as seems generally to have been the case, they made different assumptions about the robustness of their audience and indeed about the nature of their own duties. The Lord Chamberlain's play-reader may not personally have liked the play's politics, but was constrained by a sense that he can only censor plays which cross certain lines, and that it is legitimate for a play to cause 'discontent with present conditions in the beholder' (Nicholson observes that, given the establishment's anxieties about the influence of the left, 'it may seem slightly surprising how little the Lord Chamberlain's Office chose to interfere with many plays which overtly addressed contemporary political matter'[72]). The film censors accepted that both novel and play were widely read/seen, but nevertheless felt strongly that the story's generally negative portrayal of British working-class life was too negative for a film audience to be allowed to exercise its own judgement on, even were it not for specific moral objections in addition. The treatment of Greenwood (and Gow's) work thus bears out Richards' general point that the difference in attitudes to plays and films was underpinned by one firm conviction: 'The control exercised over the content of films was far tighter than that exercised over stage productions by the Lord Chamberlain, precisely because the cinema was *the* mass medium, regularly patronised by the working classes and the working classes were deemed to be all too easily influenced'.[73]

However, and under very unusual circumstances, Greenwood's text was eventually filmed. The best account of how, in factual and political

72 *The Censorship of British Drama 1932–1952*, p. 119.
73 *The Age of the Dream Palace*, p. 89.

terms, this impossible film nevertheless became possible is given by Caroline Levine in her article 'Propaganda for Democracy: the Curious Case of *Love on the Dole*'.[74] According to a letter written to *The Guardian* (3 April 1984) by Ronald Gow, co-writer with Greenwood of the play version of *Love in the Dole* (1935):

> in 1940 he and Greenwood were summoned to meet with J. Brooke-Wilkinson, the Secretary of the British Board of Film Censors. 'Brookie' told the two writers that they must turn their dramatic script into a screenplay without delay. 'This film's got to be made', he reportedly told them. 'We've got a tip from someone "higher up". I can say no more.'[75]

Further, Gow recalls that the context was a British sensitivity to criticism in the US, with 'headlines in the American press saying, "Britain Bans Workers' Film"; and in 1940 this was thought to be a bad report from a country fighting for freedom'.[76] Levine's account goes on to identify the 'higher up' as the art historian Kenneth Clark, who had been director of the National Gallery since 1933, but became (for a brief period) director of the Film Division at the Ministry of Information between January and April in 1940. Clark discusses this period in his autobiography, *The Other Half – a Self-Portrait*.[77] Though neither Greenwood nor *Love on the Dole* are mentioned in the autobiography among the wartime films in which Clark had a hand, he admitted to Ronald Gow in 1980 that he had initiated the instruction, following a strongly worded letter to *The Guardian* (26 February 1940) by Greenwood criticising the censorship of his film script in the light of the war against Nazi Germany and arguing that the Board had 'taken upon itself the powers of a Dr Goebbels' and that therefore 'all the talk of the freedom for which we are told we have been fighting [is] so much claptrap'.[78] In fact a little more can be added to Levine's account, for there was continuing press interest (the *Daily Herald* took some pleasure in recording that Britain's wealthiest woman, Lady Yule, the backer of British National Pictures, was funding this 'Slum Film' and quoted Greenwood as saying that 'many of the speeches

---

74 pp. 846–73.

75 Levine, 'Propaganda for Democracy', p. 867.

76 Levine, 'Propaganda for Democracy', p. 867, quoting Gow. However, I have been unable to find any trace of such a US newspaper headline (my thanks to Professor Matthew Steggle for lending his higher-grade digital humanities skills to confirm this lack of result).

77 London: John Murray, 1977, pp. 11–22.

78 See Levine, 'Propaganda for Democracy', p. 848.

have a strong socialist flavour, but Lady Yule wants them all retained').[79] The *Daily Herald* on 27 February 1940 also reported that Greenwood's proposal for the film had again recently run into trouble with the BBFC: 'the author has been informed by the British Board of Film Censors that the film would be "most undesirable" just now, and strongly urged not to proceed with it, at least for the duration of the war. Any completed production "would not be acceptable"'. The article (whose source seems to be Greenwood himself) goes on to say that the film might be seen as undermining the war effort – 'such a film might come within the ambit of security censorship' – but queries why its theme of unemployment is subversive, as 'Mr Churchill tells us that soon there will be none so it will then be a history of the bad old days.'[80] Indeed, the politics of this particular work of adaptation were clearly considered to be of national importance and, as noted in Chapter 1, were in some way brought to the attention of the prime minister himself, since he and Lady Churchill made time to see the film in a special private viewing before its public release on 30 June 1941. The film was, clearly, passed for exhibition this time by the British Board of Film Censors, but sadly the file for 1940 is the one BBFC file that does not seem to survive, so we do not have what would surely have been a fascinating report on why this film was now suitable for universal exhibition.[81]

So far, discussion has covered a good deal of the context of why it was so difficult to get the play made into a film in mid-1930s Britain. The first thing to emphasise is that the film became possible through some very specific as well as some more general political changes that came about because Britain was again at war. In this sense, while the novel and the play were 1930s texts received in 1930s contexts, the film of *Love on the Dole* is markedly a 1940s text whose reception we will need to locate within a new wartime cultural context. Harker articulates this broad change concisely:

> In the mid-1930s *Love on the Dole*'s cinema adaptation was blocked by its resistance to those socially stabilising cinematic conventions that required either consolatory narratives about existing conditions or imaginary resolutions which left structural inequalities untouched. The early war years,

79 13 November 1940, p. 5.
80 The article 'by our film correspondent' is headed '*Love on the Dole* Ban' (27 February 1940, p. 5).
81 My thanks to Jonny Davies at the BFI for confirming this via email on 22 July 2016.

on the other hand, witnessed a shift from defensive to actively 'formative' hegemonic efforts with the widespread cultural circulation of discourses 'disarticulat[ing] old formations' and promising 'a new sort of "settlement"' in the form of the economic, political and social reconstruction considered necessary to secure popular consent to fight and win the war ... . Teamed up with Greenwood ... Baxter created from *Love on the Dole* a semi-official propaganda picture aptly described as 'the opening shot of the People's War'.[82]

This seems entirely convincing: in effect the war (and especially the idea or ideology that it was to be 'a People's War') has made the 1930s part of the past for the film, whereas for the novel and the play the 1930s were still very much the present about which they had much to say. As Peter Miles and Malcolm Smith have observed:

> the film of *Love on the Dole* is infinitely less depressing than the novel precisely because the 1930s figures as 'the past'. The original story is recontextualised by opening and closing rolling captions which seek to remove the intervening narrative from the here and now, re-siting it as a dire object lesson.[83]

A swift series of key material, political, and ideological changes, all closely related to the preparation for and outbreak of war, had rendered the 1930s as suddenly 'past' in ways more fundamental than the mere co-incidence of the change of decade in 1940. Measuring unemployment in the period is complex, but there is general agreement that mass unemployment declined over the period after 1933 and showed further decreases after 1936 before falling further in each of the years 1939, 1940, and 1941. Chris Cook and John Stevenson say that 'From the middle of 1933 the economy began to revive on an upswing which was partially checked in 1937, but continued with rearmament in 1938–9.'[84] The Central Statistical Office provides figures for UK Administrative

---

82 'Adapting to the Conjuncture', p. 67. The 'opening shot of the People's War' reference is to Peter Miles and Malcolm Smith, *Cinema, Literature & Society: Elite and Mass Society in Interwar Britain* (London: Croom Helm, 1987), p. 245. Curiously, Neil Rattigan's *This is England: British Film and the People's War, 1939–1945* (London: Associated University Presses, 2001) does not mention *Love on the Dole* or John Baxter's other wartime films and stated ideals. Neither does James Chapman's *The British at War: Cinema, State and Propaganda 1939–1945* (London: I. B. Tauris, 1998).

83 *Cinema, Literature & Society*, p. 244.

84 Chris Cook and John Stevenson, *The Slump: Britain in the Great Depression* (London: Longman, 2010), p. 16.

Unemployment numbers from 1930 to 1942 that illustrate the trend of the improvement in employment:[85]

Table 1

Year	Numbers unemployed	Year	Numbers unemployed
1930	2,014,017	1936	1,821,700
1931	2,718,325	1937	1,557,000
1932	2,813,325	1938	1,881,367
1933	2,588,367	1939	1,589,800
1934	2,221,067	1940	1,035,325
1935	2,106,125	1941	391,517

In addition to the difficulties of measuring unemployment, public perceptions of the situation also mattered. Though there are, in economic terms, signs of improvement after 1933, unemployment numbers of over 2.5 million are hardly likely to have been seen as resolving the crisis, so that Greenwood's text(s) probably seemed as directly relevant in 1935 and until 1940 as they had in 1933. However, the fall of unemployment numbers by nearly 644,000 to a third of a million by 1941 and the obvious wartime need for maximum mobilisation of the British labour force surely registered firmly that a new (if dangerous) era was at hand.

As well as these economic improvements, there had been significant changes in the government of the country since the outbreak of war in ways that also seemed to signal an end to the 1930s. Paul Addison, in his influential study of British politics during the Second World War, makes clear how strong became the association during the war for a large section of the public between the Conservative Party as led by Chamberlain and the inter-war failure to address either mass unemployment or the international threats posed by Hitler and Mussolini. He summarises the assumptions that underpinned the Conservative and then Conservative-dominated National Governments of the period:

85 James Denman and Paul McDonald, *Labour Market Trends: Unemployment Statistics from 1881 till the Present Day*, Labour Market Statistics Group, January 1996, pp. 10–11, <www.ons.gov.uk/ons/rel/lms/labour-market-trends–discontinued-/january-1996/unemployment-since-1881.pdf>, accessed 2 April 2015.

One of the main factors inhibiting Conservatism between the wars was the taboo of economy in public expenditure, which derived from the opinions of the Treasury and orthodox economists ... . Expenditure on rearmament, which did so much to restore prosperity in the late 1930s, was regarded by Neville Chamberlain, whether as Chancellor of the Exchequer or as Prime Minister, as a terrible burden which threatened inflation, industrial unrest and the collapse of British exports ... . The doctrines of economy and the balanced budget ruled out any major experiment in the cure of mass employment ... . The frankest expression of fatalism came from Chamberlain in his budget speech of 1933, when he announced that Britain must contemplate ten years of large-scale unemployment.[86]

Addison also gives this helpful overview of political change over the period of the 1930s and 1940s:

Between the wars, politics were under the spell of the Conservatives and their ideas: World War II broke into the pattern. In May 1940 Neville Chamberlain's Conservative administration was overthrown in favour of a coalition in which Labour were practically equal partners. In Churchill, the descendant of Marlborough and historian of past glories, the oldest strain of ruling tradition had surfaced. Yet it was from the time that Churchill came to power that the doctrines of innovation, progress and reform began to reassert themselves. 'I am quite certain', Clement Atlee, told the Labour Party conference on 1 May 1940, 'that the world that must emerge from this war must be a world attuned to our ideals'. Churchill's arrival marked the real beginning of popular mobilization for total war ... This experience in turn bred the demand for a better society when the fighting was done, lifted the coalition on to a new place of reforming consensus, swung opinion decisively from Conservative to Labour, dismissed Churchill from office and made Attlee Prime Minister. World War II saw the reformation of British politics for a generation to come.[87]

Churchill's own complicated relationship to the 'People's War' (resulting perhaps partly from very different possible interpretations of what constituted 'the' or 'a' people) is pointed out by Addison, among others:

As leader of the Conservative Party, Churchill failed to lead in any consistent direction. At times, as in his Four-Year Plan broadcast, he stood for a progressive Toryism sharing a great deal of common ground with Labour,

86 *The Road to 1945 – British Politics and the Second World War* (London: Pimlico, 1975, 1994), pp. 31–32.
87 *The Road to 1945*, pp. 13–14.

and possibly allied with Labour in a post-war coalition. At other times, he was amenable to right-wing advocates of a militant party-line, notably Lord Beaverbrook ... . Urging his party occasionally to the right, and occasionally to the left, he refused most of the time to lead them either way.[88]

Some of the prime minister's fractious and negative wartime responses to aspects of the 'People's War' (such as the Beveridge plan and the Army Bureau of Current Affairs' weekly discussion groups with servicemen) suggest his anxieties that such a view of war aims might lead the British people to socialism rather than the 'organic' national unity he probably intended. Thus, he was keen to publicise the democratising progressiveness of the Beveridge plan for an international audience, but apparently acutely worried when it was publicised to the British Army.[89] And when he learnt of the June 1941 proposal for weekly current affairs discussions in the army led by junior officers he sent two memos to the (also disapproving) secretary of state for war: 'Will not such discussions only provide opportunities for the professional grouser and agitator with a glib tongue?'; 'I hope you will wind up this business as quickly and decently as possible and set the persons concerned in it to useful work.'[90] Nevertheless, early in his premiership, the concept of 'the People's War' took a grip on the national imagination and, as part of this, the film of *Love on the Dole* was in effect commissioned with government support. Though Levine interprets the words of the film censor Brooke-Wilkinson – 'this film's got to be made ... . We've got a tip from someone "higher up". I can say no more' – as referring to Kenneth Clark at the Ministry of Information, the cloak and dagger air does make me wonder if there was someone with an investment in the film even higher up – perhaps even Churchill himself? His concern with adverse American public opinion, given his concerted campaign to bring the US into the war against Germany despite the strong isolationist tendencies in some

88 *The Road to 1945*, p. 320.
89 See Angus Calder, *The People's War, Britain 1939–45* (London: Jonathan Cape, 1969; London: Pimlico, 1992), p. 531 and Ian McLaine's *The Ministry of Morale: Home Front Morale and the Ministry of Information in World War II* (London: George Allen & Unwin, 1979), p. 181.
90 Jeremy A. Crang, *The British Army and the People's War 1939–1945* (Manchester: Manchester University Press, 2000), p. 119. See also S. P. Mackenzie's *Politics and Military Morale: Current Affairs and Citizenship Education in the British Army 1914–1950* (Oxford: Clarendon Press, 1992), particularly chapters 4, 5, 6, and 8, and Roger Broad's *The Radical General: Sir Ronald Adam and Britain's New Model Army 1941–46* (Stroud: The History Press, 2003), pp. 135, 147–48, 160, 162–63.

quarters there, and his attendance at a private viewing perhaps does not make the speculation too outlandish.

IV. The Film:
'There are no stars in this film. Nothing is glossed over'[91]

The past that the film revives for its own purposes is very much a recent past and it is clearly assumed that the viewer, of whatever class origin, will recall it readily enough as the film recreates a representative 1930s experience of unemployment and poverty in northern England (Richards points out that several later socially engaged wartime films, including *Hard Steel* (1942) and *The Shipbuilders* (1943), 'were inclined to look backwards in time and were, ostensibly, retrospective in their concerns, while their pertinence to Britain in the 1940s was amply demonstrated'[92]). The black and white film opens with its titles and credits filmed against a painted backcloth of slowly moving clouds and with foreboding music (by Richard Addinsell[93]), which gradually modulates to a more optimistic and romantic theme (used again as a leitmotif linked to Sally (Deborah Kerr) at, for example, her first appearance, when she first meets Larry (Clifford Evans) and during her ramble with him on the moors) before darkening in mood again. A scrolling caption follows, which indeed emphasises the pastness, but only recent pastness, of the 1930s, referring to the 'dark pages' of 'industrial history' and univer-salising while also simultaneously marginalising and deregionalising the experience of industrial poverty as being located not in the centre but on the 'outskirts' of '*every* city' (my emphasis).[94] There is then a significant tense change to the present that takes the viewer back to those times as a period with no clear end in sight: 'where men and women forever strive to live decently in the face of overwhelming odds never doubting that the clouds of depression will one day be lifted'. The caption text here picks

91 WGC/3/2, p. 34. *The Star* 7 May 1941.

92 Jeffrey Richards and Anthony Aldgate, *Best of British – Cinema and Society 1930–1970* (Oxford: Basil Blackwell, 1983), pp. 116–17.

93 As discussed below, the film avoided casting 'stars', but Addinsell had recently become a star among film-music composers with his surprise wartime hit 'The Warsaw Concerto', from the 1941 film *Dangerous Moonlight*. See John Huntley's *British Film Music* (London: Skelton Robinson, 1947), pp. 190–91 ('perhaps the most remarkable piece of film background music ever written', p. 190).

94 See discussion of this effect in Miles and Smith, *Cinema, Literature & Society*, p. 244.

up the visual image of the drifting clouds in the background, as they do indeed darken behind the caption, which specifically dates the beginning of the story to 'March 1930'. The 'decently' and the hopeful optimism emphasise issues of respectability and solidity that we have already met in the novel and the play, but the underlying optimism as opposed to mere dreams of escape seems a fresh note, reinforcing the film's newly retrospective viewpoint. Past and present are, however, finely balanced, partly perhaps because of the peculiar context: the viewer needs to be involved in a live story where the end is both significant and not wholly predictable for the film to work as a text, but equally the wartime present needs to project some sense that it will all end happily (though it is also possible that in some respects this past might now perversely come to feel nostalgic for some viewers – with its 'homely' problems of poverty and domestic politics seeming less catastrophic in retrospect than the anxieties of a world at war).[95] Next there is an establishing shot that shows from an aerial perspective the numerous works' chimneys, one church steeple and the many house rooftops of Hanky Park – providing a cinematic equivalent to some aspects of the novel's Introductory chapter – before zooming in on a particular group of three claustrophobic yards at the rear of three houses. Hanky Park is represented in the aerial view by a set that is clearly drawn rather than real and gives a part-realistic, part-stylised impression of a very darkly lit cityscape (in fact the visual style is, perhaps coincidentally, reminiscent of the monochrome drawings of Arthur Wragg in *The Cleft Stick*, which hover between cartoon and

95 The specific wartime present in which the film was made was mainly between 11 November and 21 December 1940 (Geoff Brown, with Tony Aldgate, *The Common Touch – the Films of John Baxter*, London: BFI, 1991), p. 76 and the present in which the film was viewed was after 30 June 1941, its release date in the UK (Brown, *The Common Touch*, p. 77). The context of this present was also very mixed and the overall picture of the progress of the war very complex: for example, the Battle of Britain had been declared a British victory in October 1940 and the Bismarck had been sunk in May 1941, but equally the Blitz continued until May 1941 (Baxter recalls the film's 'crowd artistes' coming in to film having slept in Underground stations during the Blitz, *The Common Touch*, p. 80) and June 1941 saw the British withdrawal from Crete as well as defeat in Libya with the failure of Operation Battleaxe. In this context, the optimism yet uncertainty of when the hoped-for end might come for the British people that the film evokes could speak in terms of mood to these concerns of the 1940s as much as to the concerns of the 1930s (Wikipedia gives a helpful and concise timeline of the events of the war: <http://en.wikipedia.org/wiki/Timeline_of_World_War_II_(1941)#June_1941>, accessed 15 April 2015).

realism).[96] The yards are a more material set. Though the nearest yard is most clearly visible, the shot registers that each yard (each with identical outside lavatory) is occupied by a woman, each performing exactly the same motion (stooping to collect a shovel of coal), though the viewer can see only the nearest figure clearly because of the claustrophobic dividing walls. The women do not speak to each other and the shot implies that if what we are seeing is a common experience it is also an isolating one. The shot then follows the nearest figure inside the back door of her house, where she throws the coal into a range and then holds a newspaper, the *Manchester Evening News*, in front of the flames till it catches, allowing the viewer to read the headlines and sub-headlines: 'TRADE BOOM IS COMING/Latest Figures Show Big Swing to Better Times/Stock Prices, Sterling and Bank Clearings Advance'.[97] This concisely implies the hope referred to in the opening caption, but also perhaps the disconnection between national economics and local poverty or between what the papers say and the experience of reality for ordinary people in Hanky Park. The rapid combustion of the paper anyway implies that such hope is easily destroyed. The interior set is faithful to the play stage-direction – 'this is not a slum property, but the house of a respectable working man' (p. 13) – and shows dilapidated furniture with some ornaments and crockery that attempt to display respectable domesticity (it is noticeable that in a later scene where Harry (Geoffrey Hibbert) explains to his parents that he must marry Helen the ornaments have disappeared from the fireplace, registering the Hardcastles' further descent from even their initial level of poverty).[98] Mr Hardcastle then returns from his night

---

96 See the dust-jacket image of a factory chimney emitting smoke or the houses in the background of the illustration to 'A Son of Mars' (about Ned Narkey), between pp. 134 and 135, or the buildings in the image for 'The old School', between pp. 214 and 215 (pages with images are not paginated).

97 All references to the film are to the Fabulous Films DVD edition (2004, under licence to the BFI).

98 Nicola Wilson notes that in the novel 'the domestic interior remains static, despite the chronological movement of the text' and argues that 'Greenwood rejects the observer's equation of private domesticity with character and respectability and stresses instead the inevitability of the capitalist cycle' (*Home in British Working-Class Fiction*, p. 97). She also cites Rod Mengham's comparison of the depiction of domestic space in the novel and the film (p. 126, note 37) in his essay 'Anthropology at Home: Domestic Interiors in British Film and Fiction of the 1930s and 1940s', in *Imagined Interiors: Representing the Domestic Interior from the Renaissance*, ed. J. Aynsley and C. Grant (V & A Publishing: London, 2006), pp. 244–55, p. 244. At least one stage production also indicated the growing poverty

shift in the pit, as his coal-dust-covered face makes clear, and, irascible from the start, wakes Sally and Harry for their day shifts by banging on the ceiling with a broom. They share a room and quickly dress before we move to a scene centring on the Hardcastle breakfast table, where several increasingly close-up shots emphasise how Mr Hardcastle carefully divides a hard-boiled egg into three slices, one each for himself, Sally, and Harry (Mrs Hardcastle [Mary Merrall] goes without). The lack of any reaction from anyone (beyond a certain eagerness from Sally in a reaction shot) nicely registers that this is 'normality' for this household. This image of austerity sets the scene for Harry's hesitant request for a suit – he isn't fit to be seen – and for his father's exasperated refusal to enter into weekly payments and his comment that he has "'worked all his blooming life and what have I got?'" This opening sequence sets up, through a range of cinematic devices, the Hardcastles as respectable (there is considerable emphasis on essentially good underlying family relations and, indeed, on washing and cleanliness), hard-working, and habituated to poverty, but under great strain: the family breakfast is disrupted as Mr Hardcastle, clearly in a state of constant anger at his situation, leaves the table, saying he gets no rest at home. The scene ends with a strong affirmation that the family have done their utmost to remain respectable and independent, as Mrs Hardcastle tries to persuade her husband to get Harry a suit and Mr Hardcastle says that they have just kept their heads above water and that he does not want to see her going to the pawnshop every week like some. The following cut to the women of Hanky Park setting off for the pawnshop gives continuity – a device the film uses consistently.

This opening scene's techniques and atmosphere are characteristic of much of the film: it establishes environment, situation, and character very concisely and to an extent in this interior scene looks like a filmed play, with quite frequent use of middle-distance shots that show three or four characters interacting (Geoff Brown refers to the 'theatrical poise' of some of the actors[99]) – though outdoor scenes often use more varied shots and editing techniques, especially when portraying Marlowe's or

---

of the Hardcastle household by removing some of their few treasures as the play progressed, an effect noted by a review in the *Lincolnshire Standard* on 6 October 1945: 'a case of medals, the proud possessions of Henry Hardcastle [is] found empty in the last act when the medals had been pawned' (WGC/3/2, p. 103).

99 *The Common Touch*, p. 80. The reference is to Clifford Evans, Deborah Kerr and Mary Merrall specifically – Brown thinks that George Carney and the chorus of older women give more natural performances.

Harry's search for a new job at a series of works after his apprenticeship finishes. The film is well-regarded by modern film critics: '[the director] John Baxter turned the novel into a serious and moving film.'[100] A book-length study of Baxter's work says that he

> never sought, and never acquired, the 'quality' sheen of respectable British film-making. His style, and his working practices, remained rooted in the factory-belt methods of the 'quota-quickie' studios, where features were shot in ten days ... [however] during the Second World War ... his out-put approached medium-budget respectability: he handled large casts with starry names, and filmed major literary properties like Walter Greenwood's *Love on the Dole*, J.B. Priestley's *Let the People Sing*, and George Blake's *The Shipbuilders*.[101]

Certainly, *Love on the Dole* was completed very swiftly, though partly owing to wartime conditions (the studio had been reprieved from conversion to aircraft production only on condition that it was never left idle).[102] But perhaps the more modestly produced films that Baxter had been making may have contributed something to the film's sense of economy and directness, while the very well-known story, the 'literary' nature of the text, and the wartime shift in the work's possible meanings may have made it easier to resist pressure to make some aspects of the film more conventional. In fact, despite low budgets and his many previous films with musical and or comic elements, Baxter had also shown a consistent interest whenever possible in social conditions, as Geoff Brown and Tony Aldgate's meticulously annotated filmography shows – for example, his now lost 1935 film *A Real Bloke* (George Carney, who plays Mr Hardcastle, starred as the navvy Bill) was praised by *Kinematograph Weekly* precisely for its treatment of this kind of material: 'John Baxter ... has handled this simple study of working-class life with shrewd understanding.'[103] Brown and Aldgate go on to make the point that if *Love on the Dole* mainly used fairly straightforward cinematic devices, it did also draw effectively on other film vocabularies:

> [It] is by far Baxter's grandest production, and the director and his team rise impressively to the challenge of the material. Baxter uses sufficient artistic

100 Anthony Aldgate and Jeffrey Richards, *Britain Can Take It: British Cinema in the Second World War* (London: I. B. Tauris, 1986, 2007), p. 14.

101 Brown, *The Common Touch*, p. 8.

102 Brown, *The Common Touch*, p. 78.

103 Brown, *The Common Touch*, annotated filmography, p. 47, quoting from *Kinematograph Weekly* 28 March 1936, p. 29.

effects to give the film dignity. Michael Chorlton's montage sequences – partly culled from Thorold Dickinson's montage work in *Sing As We Go!* – powerfully convey Blackpool glamour and the drudgery of Harry Hardcastle's search for work; close-ups are used for ironic punctuation (a Tower Ballroom ticket floating in the gutter).[104]

Montage was, of course, a technique much used in documentary film, and one review in *Kinematograph Weekly* did see the film's generally realist aesthetic as giving it membership of the documentary genre: 'Scornful of carping propaganda, it faithfully presents the facts as they are, or rather were, confident of their power to plead their own righteous cause ... it is also a documentary of compelling power and urgent provocation.'[105] This judgement is perhaps influenced by this particular technique, but also presumably by the equation of documentary with socially progressive films based in 'facts' which, in theory, speak for themselves. Miles and Smith also see the film as having points of contact with documentary:

> Even before the ... documentary idea began to have a major impact on the commercial film industry there were to be many points of infiltration in terms of technique and personnel. One has only to compare superficially a film from the early thirties like *Cavalcade* with a film from 1939 or 1940 like *The Stars Look Down* or *Love on the Dole* to notice the change.[106]

Ian Aitken, in his book *Film and Reform*, links Greenwood's novel itself to documentary: 'a number of works ... used a documentary format to represent contemporary social problems. These included ... *Love on the Dole*.'[107] I am not certain that the novel itself does look so strongly like documentary, and it may be more akin to older condition of England novels, which would be consistent with Greenwood's interest in the novels of Mrs Gaskell.[108] However, it is an example that may, as novel,

---

104 *The Common Touch*, p. 80.

105 10 April 1941, p. 20; quoted in *The Common Touch*, p. 81.

106 *Cinema, Literature & Society*, p. 195. However, as my colleague Sheldon Hall has pointed out to me, *Cavalcade* was a Hollywood production, which may equally account for differences in style and approach.

107 *Film and Reform: John Grierson and the Documentary Film Movement* (London: Routledge, 1990), p. 174.

108 See David Cannadine's *Class in Britain* (Harmondsworth: Penguin, 2000) for a number of discussions of nineteenth-century anxieties about the 'two nations' and the condition of England, pp. 82–83, 93, 129, 133. Cannadine's sources include G. D. H. and Margaret Cole's Left Book Club book *The Condition of Britain* (London: Gollancz, 1937), which is a factually based sociological survey, but

play, and, eventually, film, interestingly prove the exception to the rule stated as his following point: 'because these works were sometimes overtly critical of the status quo, they were often treated with hostility by the establishment ... and their use of documentary reportage style was considered as subversive in itself.'[109] Kenneth Clark, as well as deserving credit for intervening to lift the censorship and initiate the filming of *Love on the Dole*, should perhaps also be credited with establishing a Ministry of Information approach to cinema that increased the chances of a film with this kind of realist aesthetic being made in the wartime context:

> In marked contrast to BBFC policy in the 1930s, the MOI required something more than harmless entertainment from the [film] industry. Faced with a plea from the British Film Producers Association for fewer war films ... the MOI expressed its willingness to support all sorts of films, including comedies and dramas, but insisted that they should be of the highest quality and neither maudlin, morbid nor nostalgic for the old ways and old days' and ought to deal realistically with 'everyday life in the factory, mines and on the land'.[110]

If Baxter was beginning to make films with 'starry names' at this time, however, it was an approach he rejected for *Love on the Dole*, a decision linked to an ambition to represent ordinary working people in a realist film. The decision also accorded with the publicly stated wishes of Greenwood himself – the *Star*, among other papers, reported in May 1941 (before the film's general release) that 'The film chiefs wept ... the film people wanted a happy ending and Greenwood would have none of it ... there are no stars in this film. Nothing is glossed over. It is spoken of as the British *Grapes of Wrath* and better.'[111] Baxter had a strong sense, expressed on several occasions, that the film must not be a star vehicle and, though she tried out for the part, he rejected the British film star and dancer Jessie Matthews: '[It] was the sort of subject that would have

whose title suggests some continuity between nineteenth- and twentieth-century concerns across different genres.

109 Aitken, *Film and Reform*, p. 174.

110 Robert Murphy, *British Cinema and the Second World War* (London: Continuum, 2001), p. 63.

111 WGC/3/2, p. 34. The brief article was published on 7 May 1941. Clippings on the same page offer similar versions of the story – perhaps Greenwood was the source, though it also seems conceivable that it was a publicity story put out by the studio to stimulate interest in this film about ordinary people. The comparison with John Ford's award-winning 1940 screen adaptation of John Steinbeck's *The Grapes of Wrath* is apt and clearly intended as high praise.

been artistically unbalanced by big names. A star of her magnitude billed over the title, would have created the wrong sort of interest':[112]

> The question of casting was to my mind all-important. Contrary to the view expressed by distributors and some others, I felt star names should be avoided. The play was famous in itself, and I felt concerned that if I was to secure complete identification on the part of the audience with the character in the film I must remove from their minds the picture of a particular star playing a certain part.[113]

Indeed, as far back as 1935, when the first attempt at filming Greenwood's story was under discussion, 'star identity' was seen as an issue. Gracie Fields, the Lancashire film star, publicly expressed a wish, reported in the *Manchester Guardian*, to play Sally in the film version, but feared, correctly, that she would not be cast because it was a serious role: 'it's too political, they tell me ... they want me to be amusing. And there is nothing to laugh at in the heroine of *Love on the Dole* – it is all too true that story, I can tell you.'[114] In 1938 the name of Gracie Fields was still being linked to the possibility of a film (though perhaps quite unreliably, given the unresolved censorship issue), with the entertainment industry magazine *Variety*'s 'Chatter' column claiming: 'Negotiations still on for "Dole" as Gracie Fields pic, after author turned down $30,000'.[115] Deborah Kerr was finally cast because at audition she was seen as essentially 'ordinary' – a perceived quality that may have partly stemmed from her relative lack of previous public exposure, since she had played only small stage parts and appeared in only one film, the adaptation of Shaw's *Major Barbara*, which, though filmed first, was released in the UK after *Love on the Dole*.[116] She thus

---

112 Michelangelo Capua, *Deborah Kerr – A Biography* (Jefferson, North Carolina: McFarland And Co, 2010; Kindle edition), location 189, citing Matthew Thornton, *Jessie Matthews* (London: Hart-Davis and MacGibbon, 1974), p. 156.

113 Brown, *The Common Touch*, p. 79.

114 2 March 1935, p. 12. See also Rachel Low's *Film Making in 1930s Britain* (London: Allen & Unwin, 1985), pp. 152–53, which discusses perceptions of Gracie Fields' image as a star which linked her firmly to the music hall tradition and limited the film roles she was given to play. The desire to play Sally is not referred to in David Bret's *Gracie Fields – the Authorised Biography* (London: JR Books, 2010).

115 2 February 1938, p. 61 (unsigned round up of theatrical/entertainment industry gossip from London). Accessed via *Entertainment Industry Magazine Archive*.

116 Directed by Gabriel Pascal and made by his production company, *Major Barbara* was released in the US on 4 May 1941, but not till 2 August 1941 in the UK (see IMDB: <http://www.imdb.com/title/tt0033868/releaseinfo?ref_=ttfc_sa_1>,

brought with her no association with previous roles or a 'film actress' identity. Deborah Kerr later recalled that Baxter made some unusual efforts to emphasise to the cast the ordinary 'reality' of the story: 'My first kissing chore [in films] smelled … Clifford Evans … had to kiss me among garbage cans outside my slum home. Our director was a fiend of realism and those cans stank to high heaven.'[117] The film is, indeed, not at all like the kind of fare that Helen in the novel realises are 'cheap opiates': 'the spectacle of films of spacious lives' or 'the shadows [of ideal homes] flickering on a screen' (p. 65).

However, Sally, despite the careful casting rationale, does in fact stand out to a degree from all the other women in Hanky Park – perhaps it would be fair to say that during the film she emerges as a kind of star from the mass experience. In the novel she is not explicitly linked to 'stardom', but in the play Sally specifically says: 'I'm not a film-star, Larry. I can manage as others do', though this may not negate the implication that she is 'special': a 'Readers' Review' submission in *Picturegoer and Film Weekly* said of Deborah Kerr that 'it was not her fault that she looked, shall I say, a little too beautiful for Hankey Park [sic]'.[118] In the film Sally is shown waking slightly tousled, but thereafter her hair is clearly curled and permed, when that of most of the other women is not (Carol Dyhouse records that Mass Observers in 1940 noted that 'straight hair' 'was almost non-existent among

accessed 25 October 2017). Capua, *Deborah Kerr – A Biography* suggests that she was cast in this as the character Jennifer Hill because she looked 'innocent', location 136). John Baxter, in a similar vein, explained that he cast her after his cameraman said that she should get the part because 'She's a girl' – a phrase I have interpreted in the text as referring to youth and ordinariness (see Brown, *The Common Touch*, p. 79). Richards, *The Age of the Dream Palace* has a useful comparison of Jessie Matthews and Gracie Fields as stars, pp. 207–10, and refers to Jessie's try-out for Sally Hardcastle on p. 223.

117 Capua, *Deborah Kerr – A Biography*, location 196, quoting from Jim Meyer, 'Deborah Kerr', *Screen Facts*, 1968, p. 6. Brown, *The Common Touch*, p. 80, quotes a *Kinematograph Weekly* (5 December 1940) studio reporter who praises exactly this aspect of the set (designed by Holmes Paul).

118 As did Kerr herself, gaining enthusiastic reviews for her performance and quickly entering into star territory. Somewhat later (1946) Louis B. Mayer confirmed her status when he invented a jingle to help the studios pronounce her name correctly: 'Her name will rhyme with star and not with cur' (Capua, *Deborah Kerr – A Biography*, location 506). Play quotation is from London version, p. 14, Manchester version, p. 22. The *Picturegoer and Film Weekly* quotation is from a submitted response to the 'Readers' Reviews' column by Miss Dorothy Stuckey, 'Holloway N.7' (11, 532, 2 August 1941, p. 12).

younger women: the fashion was for curls and waves').[119] In addition, she wears a coat (if a slightly shabby one) and a hat, while the other women (including most younger women in crowd scenes, but excluding the older chorus, three of whom do wear individually distinct hats) wear shawls that double as both coat and head-covering. If ordinary, she is much closer to looking like a film star than any other women in Hanky Park, and also therefore more like a 'modern' woman in a consumer society rather than a nineteenth-century mill-girl. It comes as no real surprise when, after accepting Sam Grundy's offer, she returns to North Street wearing expensive clothes, including a fox stole, as if born to it, with hair more elaborately set and, as a close-up of her face shows, made-up more in the manner of a star (an effect particularly

---

119 Mass Observation Archive Topic 18, Box 2, File 1/F, quoted in Carol Dyhouse's *Glamour: Women, History, Feminism* (London: Zed Books, 2010; Kindle edition, 2013), p. 76 (see too p. 81 for an association between the 'perm' and the modern, independent woman). The Wikipedia entry for 'Perms' also gives a useful sense of the link between 'perms', class, and stardom: 'By 1930, the process of permanent-waving was well established and its importance can be gauged if one considers that the majority of middle-class women, at a rough estimate, had their hair set once a week and permed perhaps once every three months as new hair replaced the waved hair. Meanwhile, hairdressers sought to improve the process and reduce the work involved; this meant savings at the lower end of the market and yet more women getting their hair permed. This was also stimulated by pictures of the rich and famous, particularly film stars, who all had their hair permed.' (<http://en.wikipedia.org/wiki/Perm_(hairstyle)>, accessed 22 April 2015). In fact in the film, earlier scenes show women and girls as mainly unwaved and wearing shawls, but towards the end in one scene, where Sally and other women leave the mill, there are some other young women whose dress and hair styles are more like Sally's, though the majority are still wearing the traditional shawl. This scene may be specifically suggested by a discussion of girls' and women's modes of dress on p. 42 of the novel, which describes some wearing shawls and others wearing dresses and 'crimped hair': 'until they married when picture theatres became luxuries and Saturday dances … and cheap finery ceased altogether'. The lack of access in Hanky Park to these increasingly affordable consumer goods for women may visually suggest the way in which its citizens were cut off from a modern British working-class experience by a nineteenth-century style of poverty. However, as elsewhere in Greenwood's work there may be a gap between the representation and the fact: the back cover of Tony Flynn's local history book, *Hanky Park* (Salford: Neil Richardson, 1990) reproduces a series of local advertisements (undated but in what looks like a 1930s newspaper font) one of which is for 'Marie Bayley, 144a Ellor Street, Pendleton', who offers 'Permanent Waving' – however, the price of six shillings might well have limited the range of customers (though a 'trim and wave' is a cheaper alternative at one shilling).

highlighted by the close-up shortly after of her mother's unmade-up, weary, and weeping face).

As with the adaptation from novel to play, so the adaptation to film produces some differences that influence how viewers read this text. Of course, we have already discussed some of the ways in which historical change produced a new perspective within which the film was broadly viewed and understood, but it is important too to look at the detail of adaptation decisions to see how these interact with that context and how these might alter both characterisation and key scenes. The film titles go some way to show the potential complexity of this adaptation, with its several 'originals': 'Walter Greenwood's *Love on the Dole*/From the play by Ronald Gow/Based on Walter Greenwood's novel, *Love on the Dole*/ Screen adaptation by Walter Greenwood in association with Barbara K. Emary and Rollo Gamble'.[120] In some respects the film seems closer to the play versions than to the novel, as implied by these titles, but there are significant differences between all three texts in terms of the sequence of the plot, the portrayal of particular characters, and the handling of specific scenes.

As we have seen, the film, like the novel and the plays, starts with a domestic scene at the Hardcastles, but it does not, like the plays, begin with Larry's off-stage political speech. It is closer here to the routine awakening of the Hardcastle household, as represented in the novel's Chapter 2, but it adds in Mr Hardcastle's return from his night shift, so that the whole nuclear family group are presented to the viewer (suggesting their familiarity and 'normality', while also the abnormal poverty they have become accustomed to). Harry, as in the plays, is already working at Marlowe's, with pawnshop employment in the past. But, where the plays omit the pawnshop scene, the film reintroduces it as it cuts from the Hardcastles to the viewer's first meeting with the 'chorus' of older women. Here a younger boy working for Price reminds those who have read the novel of Harry's recent past, while, for viewers new to the story, he helps introduce the atmosphere of the pawnshop and the complicity between the cadaverous, hypocritical Price and the older women who are obliging their neighbours. As in the novel, the crowd

---

120 This was Rollo Gamble's only credit for a screen-play, but Barbara K. Emary (also known as Emery) frequently worked with Baxter in the 1940s and amassed fourteen writing credits, including for *The Common Touch* (1941) and *Let the People Sing* (1942). See IMDB: <http://www.imdb.com/name/nm0256066/>, accessed 30 April 2015.

of women pushing their way into the shop – composed so as to fill the entire screen – are seen as boisterous and noisy, but hardly the same monstrously female representations of cyclical poverty which in that text we see from Harry's point of view. Instead, their hubbub is used to set up the total and almost sacred silence when the entire crowd is momentarily gripped by the sight and sound of Price tipping his petty change into a dish, and which makes visible how important those few coins are and how humble these women's sense of plenty is. Where in the novel only Mrs Dorbell and Mrs Nattle (Marie O'Neill and Iris Vandeleur) visit Price's, in connection with their business interests, here they are joined by Mrs Bull and Mrs Jikes (Marjorie Rhodes and Marie Ault), who are there on their own business. This allows us the first experience of their banter and the conversation allows some swift introduction of the hand-to-mouth economy in which the pawnshop plays its part (the first two scenes show that the film will include both aspects of what Dave Russell suggests are the two contrary possibilities of 'the North on screen', which 'has tended to be either a comic place where daily hardship was softened by humour, or a site for debating serious moral, economic or social issues'[121]). This scene also offers some strikingly frank comment on one cause of poverty. Mrs Nattle explains that she is pawning Jack Cranford's suit – Mrs Cranford cannot come herself because she is expecting her seventh child, 'and him only working three days a week': Mrs Bull acerbically observes that 'that explains it, Satan finds work you know' (later a frank conversation between Helen and Harry makes it equally clear that pre-marital sex has led to pregnancy – though none of those words is uttered – showing the film's continuing interest in this topic and also the liberating escape from pre-war censorship codes). Clearly, this commentary is the equivalent of Mrs Bull's even franker allusions to family planning and Mrs Cranford's own reflections on her life, though in the novel these come towards the conclusion rather than at the beginning of the narrative. It is a specific example of material that Miss Shortt and Colonel Hanna would surely not have tolerated before the war, and, though it is treated comically, the point does register. From the pawnshop we cut briefly to the street and, via a close-up of her 'naybores oblidged' sign, follow Mrs Nattle to her house, where she sells Mrs Dorbell a nip (it is immediately noticeable that her fireplace is more plushly decorated with ornaments than Mrs Hardcastle's and even

---

121 *Looking North – Northern England and the National Imagination* (Manchester: Manchester University Press, 2004), p. 181.

has a portrait of Queen Victoria above it[122]), and where they are soon joined by Mrs Jikes and Mrs Bull. Again, as in the novel, Mrs Bull's contradictions are brought out; despite her insight into Mrs Cranford's life in the previous scene, she here laments that 'young uns aren't having childer' and that people are laying out their own deceased family, which was not considered respectable when she was young. Her tone implies that the life has gone out of Hanky Park, but it is clear from the scene that these older women are still finding opportunities for both business and pleasure there: their relatively elite status is seen as comic in its pitiful degree, yet also shown as exceptional through their possession of small amounts of disposable income. They are shown possessing what few in Hanky Park have – some autonomy, leisure, and an income. Mrs Hardcastle then arrives to ask about buying Harry's suit with weekly payments and some further conversation about whether Sally should be settling down and marrying leads to another instance of the film's continuity editing, when we next cut to a scene centred on Ned Narkey (Martin Walker), Sally, and Larry.

The scene starts inside a pub, where a man (soon addressed as Ned) asks for another pint, and is told that there'll be no more credit – too many works are on short time and jobs are not safe enough for the landlord to trust in future payment. Ned perforce leaves the pub and finds Larry outside talking on a platform. At first the shot focuses on Ned listening with a surly expression, then moves out to show Larry addressing a small group of men, before moving back to show Ned moving forward from the pub doors to talk to a hitherto unseen female figure who is shown listening more intently to Larry. Ned intrudes rudely, asking why she has kept him waiting and remarking that they were meant to be going 'jazzing' (dancing) tonight. The scene collapses into the present what in the novel is related as having already having happened – Sally did at one time go out with Narkey, but is not doing so when she meets Larry (she and Ned seem here an even more unlikely couple than in the novel, partly because their dress codes mark out what looks like a considerable class or 'respectability' difference). Here it is Larry's speech itself that has delayed her from entering the pub (though she also suggests that it is not a respectable place to meet) and in effect brings her relationship

122 Mrs Bull is allowed some subversion here too – when Mrs Jikes says that nothing has been the same since the old Queen died, Mrs Bull affects not to know which queen and when told says dismissively, 'oh 'er'. The subversion may be aimed both at Mrs Jikes' conservative nostalgia and her devotion to royalty.

with Ned to an end. Strikingly, given the 1935/1936 censorship issues, a frank exchange (if less frank than in the novel) follows in which Narkey says that all his 'trailing her around has been for nothing' and Sally replies that he is a 'dirty dog'. The scene quickly constructs Narkey as a 'rough' and 'ungentlemanly' working man who is dismissive of politics (he refers to the speech as 'muck' and 'blather'), before the shot again returns to Larry delivering his speech, and closes in on his face. Interestingly, he is immediately identified as a Labour Party activist, as the platform includes a sign saying 'East Salford Labour Party' – after Churchill assumed the premiership in 1940, the Labour Party, of course, provided key ministers for the wartime coalition, so this sign in this text of Greenwood's work immediately registers Larry's 'respectability' (as might also his overcoat and trilby, contrasting with the cloth caps and coatlessness of his audience and Ned) and suggests his contribution to national life (in contrast to Ned's selfishness and incivility).[123] The speech differs in some details from that in the novel and those in the plays, though it retains the key tropes from the novel speech. As in the plays, this film speech is much shorter than that of the novel, but here the speaker is both visible and clearly audible: though the scene certainly focuses on Sally's rejection of Ned and her growing interest in Larry, the speech itself does matter. Larry makes the same key points that he does in the novel – that the workers who have toiled for generations should not have to live in the conditions of Hanky Park: 'every individual in the country' deserves 'decent, healthy lives'. However, a new point made in neither plays nor novel is introduced: 'we don't set the blame on any one section of the community, we challenge the system alone which sets man against man and robs all of security.' It is notable (and critics have noted) that the novel does indeed not explicitly blame government nor other class groups for the national disgrace constituted by Hanky Park and other such places; this newly explicit refusal of blame is not, of course, in any way a more radical addition to the speech, but its very explicitness may suggest the change of the context within which the film is being viewed. Now, in wartime, the stress on unity and equality can

123 Steve Fielding's *The Salford Labour Party – a Brief Introduction to the Microfilm Edition of the Salford Labour Party Records* (Wakefield: Microform Academic Publishers, 1997) makes clear that the constituency of East Salford did not come into being until 1950 – before that there were three constituencies, North, South, and West, which is presumably why the film chose the then fictional East Salford Labour Party. See <http://www.microform.co.uk/guides/R97555.pdf>, particularly p. 7 (accessed 25 October 2017).

be framed much more acceptably within the ideal of a united national war effort, rather than as a radical call for the reform of class inequality, though that may also be implied. This social unity is indeed a major theme in this speech, and is underpinned by the democratic processes that Larry draws his listeners' attention to: 'It will go on like this till we people realise that society has the means and the knowledge to allow us to become men and women in the true sense.' There is a small but interesting change here from the novel, as the phrase 'we people' replaces the haughty-seeming 'you people'. Again, this alteration emphasises unity and democracy ('the remedy is in our own hands') as Larry's key values – and these positive ideals are, of course, what Britain is said to be fighting for in its war against Fascism and Nazism. Thus the speech has been transformed in this text from an admittedly guarded socialist critique of the *status quo* to a speech which positively supports the new (theoretical) consensus of wartime. While the film's serious focus on the experience of the 1930s is steadily maintained throughout, there are a number of passing references that may remind viewers of the present viewing context and the frame of the opening and closing captions. Thus, Sam Grundy's side-kick, Charlie (Philip Godfrey), who seems more villainous than his principal in the brief scene at the billiard table where he is the centre of attention, is clearly constructed for the viewer as a (future) draft-dodger, shirker, and black-marketeer; 'because I've been in clink they won't have me in the army when there's another war.' This selfishness puts him outside the film's high regard for unity, community, and equality and links him to other self-centred 'villains' in the film such as Ned Narkey and, presumably, the agitator at the Means Test protest march. Harry, who in the novel and plays seems to aspire only to regular employment and a happy family life, is given slightly more open-ended aspirations in the scene in which he is sitting out with Helen (Joyce Howard) on Dawney's Hill, which aligns his individual ambition for a better life with the film's articulation of a collective hope for a better life: 'I want to do things ... big things. Gosh, I wish I was a boxer or a footballer or something.' Later he says that he will be called a hero if there is another war and he goes into the army.

A number of other additions or rewritings of dialogue in following scenes supports this idea about what the war is being fought for. Thus in its version of the moor scene the play's reference to the sublime and to the possibility of the divine is missing. Instead the contrast between the beauty of the moor and the ugliness of the industrial landscape below leads to a very material focus on what the people of Hanky Park should reasonably expect: Sally says she wishes she 'knew more about people like us' (suggesting a desire to move beyond personal experience to a wider conceptual understanding of working-class lives) and talks of 'nice houses and steady jobs'; and Larry, though worried that the poor have become habituated to deprivation ('we begin to think these things are too good for us'), suggests that equality and unity could bring change – 'if only everybody would lend a hand' (and at this point the shot cuts to Sally and Larry's implied viewpoint – white clouds rolling across the sky – endowing it with optimistic symbolism before fading to the darkly lit chimneys of Hanky Park and North Street). This message is reinforced in a scene entirely omitted from the plays, in which Larry talks about capital and labour at Marlowe's and uses chalk on a wall to illustrate his point (though, disappointingly, in terms of visual teaching aids, he here merely chalks up the signs for pounds, shillings, and pence rather than the novel's 'Raw materials plus labour power = commodities'). Then the explanation of the meanings of capital and labour is followed by Larry's explanation of the underlying problem, which he sees as stemming from a human failing that is magnified by the international extent of economic downturn and unemployment: 'men are afraid of each other', so that next year or the year after or in ten years there will be 'a catastrophe' – clearly the war that is the viewer's present. This seems a humanist (and somewhat sketchy) explanation of the depression and its consequences, rather than an economic or Marxist one. However, Larry briefly implies that the way to transform this dangerous situation is through co-operation and central planning – perhaps on not just a national but even an international scale: 'it takes a disaster to waken people … [but] human conditions are not beyond human control … we can rebuild a new and better world.' As we shall see, this last phrase anticipates the last words spoken in the film.

Ned Narkey, who as we have seen was entirely removed from both play versions, is also reinstated in the film, but his part is heavily amended from that in the novel. We have already discussed his first entry into the film, when he speaks roughly to Sally as she listens to Larry. We next see him at Marlowe's, complaining to Larry (who is welding) that the crane he operates needs repairing and that Larry 'made a right muck of it last time'. Larry tells him to make an official complaint if he wishes, prompting Ned to tell him to stop 'coming the sergeant-major' and to introduce the real topic of his anger – that Sally is going out with Larry. All this is a close parallel to what happens in the novel, but thereafter Ned's role does not develop in the same way. He plays no part in Larry's being laid off and the next time we see him is at the meeting under the arches, after the Means Test and subsequent cuts to the dole have aroused the anger of the men of Hanky Park. Instead of becoming a policeman, he has presumably himself also been laid off and joins in with the agitator in encouraging defiance of the police – he even speaks lines given to one of the 'agitators' in the novel, accusing Larry of 'kowtowing to the boss-class' and saying that 'we're not afraid of the police even if you are' (this is in fact his final appearance in the film, which perhaps does not wish to remind the viewer of his role during the protest in the novel). In effect, Narkey is transformed into a minor character, while his aggressiveness is associated not with the forces of law and order, as in the novel, but with the 'undisciplined' among the workers. Larry and his assistant Jim are set up in contrast as disciplined labour leaders – Larry says 'we don't only not anticipate any trouble, there is not going to be any trouble' and he also asks the protesters to consider the police: 'remember the police have got their job to do just the same as we've got ours.' Indeed, the police are also concisely represented as reasonable in their initial approach to the protest – in place of the novel's representation of constable Ned Narkey's eager anticipation of violence, we instead hear a senior police officer on the phone sending instruction to the commander at the scene – 'Do not contact unless the position looks serious' – an instruction then paraphrased by the officer in charge of the mounted police. Violence breaks out only when the agitator incites the crowd to depart from the designated route and the protestors actively attack the police, dragging some mounted police from their horses. The senior officer on horseback quickly uses his long baton, as do other mounted officers, and the film rapidly cuts between middle-distance shots showing the whole scene and close-ups highlighting particular acts of violence by both police and protesters. It is also clear that Larry and Jim are trying to restrain a portion of the marchers, but they are soon separated and Larry falls to the ground: a closer shot shows a frightened horse rearing over Larry, but the moment of his injury is not seen – instead there is a cut to a lighting streak against a stormy sky, which obviously draws on earlier optimistic and pessimistic uses of the rolling cloud motif. Larry is the victim of an 'accident' rather than a blow from a truncheon as in the novel. There is then a cut to the wrought-iron gates of the Esperance infirmary and thence to Sally at Larry's bedside: the injured Larry reiterates something of his diagnosis of competition rather than co-operation being the chief social problem, as outlined in his teaching session at Marlowe's: 'Everyman for himself. That's what's wrong with the whole world.' What is needed is 'a little effort from everybody ... a new start' (in the novel, he leaves no specific political legacy in his dying words, which are referred to more hopelessly only as 'a low monotonous mumbling' (p. 211).[124]

In some ways, this treatment continues by other means the reduction of any criticism of the police that the play achieves through outright cuts and setting this scene off-stage, but the innovation represented by the scene should not be under-estimated: the historian of policing Clive Emsley says that 'it was the first English-made feature film to show English police wielding batons against a crowd'.[125] However, in other ways the meaning of the scene is transformed by the new reading context. In both novel and play Larry is said to be trying to restrain the protesters, but now representatives of labour, or more particularly Labour Party representatives, are likely to be read as showing unity with an essentially reasonable State of which they are a legitimate part, while the violent protesters are even more than in the novel disruptors of national and social unity. Before the march begins Larry has again reminded the marchers of the democratic nation they are part of, saying that they should have voted against the Means Test: 'You had a chance for that in the last general election' (a direct instruction in fact that they should have voted for Labour rather than for the National Government). However, the scene certainly, and no doubt partly for these reasons, escapes from the pre-war taboo about depicting either demonstrations or violent conflict between police and demonstrators.

Like Ned Narkey, the film's Sam Grundy also has no direct part in either Larry's dismissal from Marlowe's nor his death, and remains, as in the novel (if less so in the plays), an ambiguous figure: played by Frank Cellier, he looks, writes Robert Murphy, 'more like a teddy bear than a repulsive villain'.[126] He seems to me somewhat more predatory than that, however, in the scene towards the end of the film, when he offers Sally the job of housekeeper, as he talks to her from a clear position of power, seated inside his car, smoking his cigar; but, as in the novel, there seems less effort than one might expect to make him into

124 In the play versions there is no hospital or dying scene for Larry, simply a 'cut' from the scene where his off-stage injury is reported to a scene where characters react to his death, something which considerably reduces his presence as compared to either novel or film.

125 *Hard Men: The English and Violence Since 1750* (London: Bloomsbury, 2005), p. 141.

126 *Realism and Tinsel: Cinema and Society in Britain 1939–1949* (London: Routledge, 1989), p. 20.

an outright villain. Sally's refusal of his offer is interrupted in the film scene by Harry arriving to say that Helen is having her baby, and the two Hardcastles accept Sam's offer of a lift in his car. Arriving at Mrs Dorbell's house, Harry is told that he has a daughter, but is immediately also told by his landlady that as they cannot pay the rent they must go at once: Sally overhears not only this through the open door but also Mrs Dorbell's entirely instrumental view that Sally could easily get Harry and his father jobs if she just did what Sam Grundy wanted. Ironically, Mrs Dorbell uses the discourse of respectability/un-respectability to blame Sally for her 'selfishness', saying that she is a 'heartless hussy'. The camera then cuts to Sally, first with a middle-distance shot and then with a close-up of her face and we hear her inner recollections of Larry's dying words ('a new start'), and Sam's promises about replacing 'pinching and scraping' with everything she needs – in each case the sound-track supplying the actual voices of Larry and Sam that she is hearing. She expresses her decision to make a 'new start' – if one with an appallingly ironic relation to the social transformation Larry had in mind – by leaving the house and getting into Sam's waiting car. The decision is clearly based not on 'heartlessness' but on sacrificing herself for her family (Sam's face lit from below seems positively devilish for a moment as she gets into the car, and this is his last appearance in the film – as in the novel and play the emphasis is much more on Sally than on him). We then cut to a version of the conversation in the novel between Mrs Hardcastle and Mrs Bull, where Sally's mother worries about respectability and Mrs Bull reassures her (and no doubt attempts also to reassure the viewer, who may well feel both queasy and dubious) that Sally will take no real harm from Sam Grundy. The following scene sees Sally return to North Street in a taxi with her new clothes and more elaborately waved hair-style. Mrs Hardcastle says that she has changed, grown 'hard,' and Sally replies that you have to be hard to survive. This runs together elements of several chapters in the novel and makes Harry and Helen's plight and her empathy for them the turning point for Sally, rather than her despair that with Larry's death there is little left for her to live for anyway.

The final scenes of the film are closer to those of the play than the novel (indeed, the lines are almost identical), but where the play ends with Mr Hardcastle painfully expressing the fact that his situation makes it impossible for him to uphold his identity as a respectable working man, the film ends with Mrs Hardcastle and some new lines that strongly emphasise the new temporal context of the film: "'Things can't go on for ever like this, Henry. One day we'll all be wanted: the men who've forgotten how to work and the young 'uns who've never had a job. People'll begin to see what's been happening, and once they do they'll be no Hanky Park.'" This, of course, refers to the viewer's present – in the war economy everyone is wanted – and this fact, forming a neat symmetry with the opening of the film, puts the whole story back into the past of the 1930s. However, Mrs Hardcastle's words also look forward to a future not yet achieved and which can only be achieved under two important conditions: that the war is won and that the State will really assume its true and full responsibilities – only then will the inadequate social organisation and environment that constitutes Hanky Park cease to exist in Britain. The last shot moves from Mrs Hardcastle's face to the opening aerial, darkly lit, drawn view of Hanky Park, with its smoking chimneys. Finally, a rolling caption closes the film, this time against a background of dark clouds, which may partly be seen as a product of the smoking chimneys, but with some central brightly lit white clouds, which, of course, represent the hope to which Mrs Hardcastle's words have referred. The caption itself is signed by A. V. Alexander (a Co-operative Society/Labour MP who in 1941 was First Lord of the Admiralty in Churchill's government) and promises the reward of a better society for the sacrifices being made during the war:

> Our working men and women have responded magnificently to any and every call made upon them. Their reward must be a new Britain. Never again must the unemployed become forgotten men of the peace.[127]

Clearly, the adaptation of the film to its new context is carefully and systematically carried through in many details of the film as well as in its overall narrative and architecture.

Discussions of the film that include commentary on the final caption generally assume that it was part of the film released in 1941. However, Simon Baker's concise commentary on the BFI Screen-Online site suggests that the final caption was not added until 1947, presumably for the 1948 re-release of the film.[128] Geoff Brown also feels that 'The sentiment of the postscript makes it clear to me that the postscript was written in retrospect, after the war, and not in 1941 when there wasn't even a glimmer of the war ending, though for absolute proof

---

127 See <http://www.screenonline.org.uk/film/id/485682/>, accessed 25 October 2017.
128 See <http://www.screenonline.org.uk/film/id/485682/>, accessed 25 October 2017.

of that we'd have to look at the original 1941 release print.'[129] If the caption were added later it would still be of great interest, but in a very different post-war historical context, in which it is reinforcing the significance of the 1945 Labour election victory and its keeping of the promises suggested in the film for a better and different post-war Britain. However, some reviews of the film in Australia and New Zealand refer quite clearly to the caption – thus the *Newcastle Sun* review of 1942 (see below) quotes and endorses the caption's promise about the unemployed never again becoming the 'forgotten men and women of peace' (as do some New Zealand newspapers, which reproduce the same review three years later).[130] The archbishop of Sydney, in his letter to a newspaper, states that 'the caption at the end of this picture points us to a moral no less than social duty ... to strive ... to eliminate the possibility of unemployment'.[131] I think we can be sure, therefore, that the caption was present in the 1941 release and that it was, indeed, a bold and futuristic promise.

The film version is usually said to have been a distinct critical success, and some have claimed a degree of commercial success too – Robert Murphy observes that 'Its relevance now rather limited, one might have expected the film to flop. In fact, it generated considerable interest and at least a measure of box-office success.'[132] However, a Mass Observer's very detailed report on 'The Film and Family Life' (dated 13 June 1944) actually ends with the categorical statement '*Love on the Dole* faced the real facts of this situation. It was one of the biggest box-office failures in years.'[133] The context of these final sentences in the report is a sophisticated discussion of the dangers of unrealistic romantic outcomes within predominantly realist films for audiences who may not understand the illusionist devices of realist cinema. The comment is thus making a back-handed compliment to Baxter's film, by arguing that its realist mode includes its treatment of romance too – but we should perhaps therefore be wary of abstracting as a fact the comment about box-office failure. Earlier in the report the

129 Email to the author 8 July 2015 (my thanks to Simon Baker for kindly putting me in touch with Geoff Brown).
130 16 March 1942, p. 4. See also the *Lake Waikatip Mail* 18 October 1945.
131 The *South Coast Times and Wollongong Argus* 6 February 1942, p. 4.
132 *Realism and Tinsel: Cinema and Society in Britain 1939–1949*, p. 18.
133 Jeffrey Richards and Dorothy Sheridan (eds), *Mass Observation at the Movies* (London: Routledge, 1987), p. 298. The mass-observer is Len England and the report is FR2120.

observer, Len England, discusses the 'large number of films dealing with family life on a more serious plane': 'the total number of such pictures is very much smaller than that of the less serious ones, but there is nevertheless a steady flow of them.'[134] The films he lists in this category include *Mrs Miniver* (emphasised as 'the biggest box-office success of 1942'), *Millions Like Us*, *How Green Was My Valley*, *This Happy Breed*, and *Love on the Dole*. This may imply that, at the least, *Love on the Dole* would have been reasonably well-known to cinema audiences as a serious film drama, even if not a favourite. More firmly grounded numerical evidence does not seem to be available, since there do not appear to be any records of audience numbers (Murphy bases his claim to box-office success on a view provided in Michael Balcon's 1943 pamphlet *Realism or Tinsel*).[135] This view is, though, also supported by an important contemporary trade paper, *Kinematograph Weekly*, which in January 1942 listed the four releases from Anglo-American (said to be the year's 'Most Successful British Renter') and ranked *Love on the Dole* as the second most successful of a list in which 'each is a winner'.[136] There is certainly no doubt that the film was as enthusiastically reviewed by as wide a variety of newspapers as the novel and play had been, so that viewers were certainly encouraged to value the film from many quarters.

A number of specialist cinema periodicals rated the film highly, with several notably drawing out political lessons. *Film Notes* (2 June 1941) remarked on the temporal context, but also used this to venture a broad political comment: 'It is a curious time to put it on [but] if this same public has no objection to being reminded of a squalor and misery which we hope we are putting behind us [then the film will be a success].'[137] The *Daily Film Renter* (28 May 1941) is also surprisingly uncommercial in its comment that the film is about 'a phase of British life of which we are not particularly proud ... and which we should stress should never be allowed to continue', leaving *Picture Show* to observe that

---

134 *Mass Observation at the Movies*, pp. 293–94.

135 Sadly, I have not been able to locate this pamphlet – the British Library's copy is now missing. The essay is reprinted but in a 'curtailed' version (p. 66) which does not refer to *Love on the Dole*: see M. Danischevsky (ed.), *Michael Balcon's 25 Years in Films* (London: World Film Publications, 1947), pp. 66–72.

136 R. H. 'Josh' Billings, 'Box Office Stake Results', *Kinematograph Weekly* 8 January 1942, p. 41. I am very grateful to my film colleague Dr Sheldon Hall, who located and brought to my attention this important piece of evidence.

137 WGC/3/2, p. 35.

while it 'makes its message clear and intelligent, [it] has a drab setting and makes no concession to box-office attraction'.[138] *Film Talk* (30 May 1941) focused more straightforwardly on a positive evaluation of the work: 'the most significant and one of the best pictures made since war began'. Among newspapers in general the film was also very well received, with the new meanings suggested by the film-text that we have discussed above being readily taken up in reviewers' interpretations. The Labour-supporting *Daily Herald* (28 May 1941), under the headline 'Film Was Banned, Now a Triumph', saw the movie as signifying the strengths and possibilities of a democratic society capable of progressive development and making clear reference to post-war reconstruction: 'It is good entertainment. But it is also a social document eloquent of democracy's freedom to criticise itself, and makes an urgent demand for a better post-war world.'[139] The Labour Party periodical *The Tribune* (20 June 1941) was equally keen, its reviewer Winifred Horrabin suggesting that 'no one who has ever called themselves a socialist could ever see this film unmoved, and I venture to say not many who have called themselves a human being either.' The *Manchester Guardian* reviewer instead made no political comment, drawing attention to the film as a film: 'its opening is a touch of film-making genius ... the fact that it is throughout photographed in sepia gives it a subtle advantage, the tint being at once warm and prosaic, like the story narrated.'[140] The more conservative *Sunday Times* also printed a favourable brief review by the film critic Dilys Powell, and this too concentrates mainly on cinematic qualities, seeing the film as an improvement on the play version ('the central theme is enlarged and given greater solidity by additional scenes and episodes'), but offering little political analysis. Powell praises the 'skilful visual treatment of the narrative' and notes that the 'background of factory chimneys, machinery, smoke, murk, squalor gives the sad fortunes of mill-hands, mechanics and working women an urgency and truth which I do not remember in the play'.[141] However, the film clearly stayed in her memory, for in her 1947 British Council pamphlet *Films Since 1939* she gave a more politically inflected view of the film, which reinforced Kenneth Clark's judgement that it was important that the film should be made:

138 Both WGC/3/2, p. 36.
139 WGC/3/2, p. 37.
140 28 May 1941 – read via the *Guardian Archive*.
141 1 June 1941; WGC/3/2, p. 37.

Love on the Dole was a brave film to show in the black years of the war: it savagely attacked a social and economic structure which wasted human lives in idleness and poverty, and its picture of the slump in a Lancashire factory town held no flattery for the British. Yet those who most bitterly attacked the conditions it showed could not but praise the public honesty which permitted the showing.[142]

Other conservative papers at the time, including the *Sunday Express* (2 June 1941), the *Daily Mail* (30 May 1941), and *The Times* (30 May 1941), concurred that it was both a good film and one whose values they could broadly agree with.[143] The *Sunday Express* strongly supported the film's view of the social conditions of the 1930s as a terrible mistake, saying that 'it is an attack on the economic bungling of our time' and 'a social thriller of a new kind'. *The Times* agreed that 'the lessons for the future are implicit in every foot of it' (though it had of course been a sustained supporter of the National Government during the 1930s) and also made some acute points about the film as an adaptation:

> Here is an instance of material which has not been spoilt in its transition from one medium to another. Indeed, on the screen *Love on the Dole* has developed a depth and a range which the theatre could not compass: the personal tragedy of Sally and Larry contrives still to be moving and effective, but the emphasis is shifted away from it. Sally and Larry are still there in the foreground, but they are merged in the general pattern of life … in the days of the depression, and their tragedy is part of the general tragedy of the place and the time.[144]

It is notable that, as in Dilys Powell's review, the comparison is with the play rather than the novel, and that this reviewer feels that the individual, romantic focus discussed in the previous chapter has been adapted or re-adapted to give a more collective focus to the film. The review struggles slightly to throw off pre-war views of 'socialists' as disturbers of the peace, but overall reads Larry as part of a new social consensus: 'Clifford Evans as Larry, the agitator who believes in constitutional methods, gives a restrained yet emotional impression of a fighter and an idealist.'

Perhaps even more unexpectedly, the film was praised by papers as wide apart as the society paper *Tatler* and the *Catholic Herald*. *Tatler*'s distinguished drama critic James Agate saw the film as a work of high

142 London: Longmans, Green and co, p. 21.
143 See WGC/3/2, pp. 33 and 35.
144 Read on *Times Digital Archive 1785–2009*.

realism, given the conventions of the movies: 'I pronounce the film to be as near the reality as the business of entertainment permits.'[145] The *Catholic Herald* paid the film the tribute of seeing it as confirming the social analysis of Pope Leo XIII in his encyclical of 1891, *Rerum Novarum* (also the review's headline – though the encyclical is often referred to in English as 'On the Condition of Labour'), which discussed the relationship between the 'social order' and the 'moral order' – a discussion that as the reviewer makes clear was fresh in the mind because it had in turn been recently reinforced in a Whit-Sunday radio address by Pope Pius XII. This endorsement might seem surprising, given Greenwood's general lack of engagement with religion, beyond his comic and critical uses of spiritualism, the film's similar lack of emphasis, and Pope Pius's anxieties about the 'errors and dangers of the materialistic, socialistic conception' of improvements to working-class lives.[146] But the reviewer argued that Pope Pius's address is 'illustrated point by point by every shot of that most poignant and heart-rending British film, *Love on the Dole*' and argued that the film showed how souls are shaped 'from the form given to society'. This review also identified the film's theme of a different future, though it also used the British Board of Film Censors' term 'sordid': 'because it is concerned with reconstruction, its sordidness is painted over bright with hope'.[147]

It is also worth noting that the film was a great success in Australia, building a large audience from an existing sympathetic reception of the novel and the play (which had amateur and sometimes politically committed productions in one state or another more or less continuously between 1935 and 1943): 'it is a great documentary film', said the *Sydney Morning Herald*.[148] The *South Coast Times and Wollongong Argus* reported in February 1942 that three civic leaders had written to praise the newly released film after being invited to a preview at the Wollongong Theatres. These were the archbishop of Sydney, Dr Mowl, Mr J. Moloney, the Chairman of the Australian Boot Trade Employees Federation and Mr S. T. Allen, State President of the Social Credit

---

145 11 June 1941; WGC/3/2, p. 39 (though the cutting is now loose).
146 The text of the radio address by Pope Pius XII was given in *The Tablet* on 7 June 1941 and was formerly accessible on the Tablet's online archive at: <http://archive. thetablet.co.uk/article/7th-june-1941/7/the-whit-sunday-address-of-pope-pius-xii>, accessed 1 June 2015. The quotation is from the fifth paragraph of the text of the address.
147 13 June 1941, WGC/3/2, p. 38.
148 29 December 1941.

Movement. Dr Mowl stressed the essential decency of working-class people but also the damage caused by deprivation: 'I felt greatly moved by this picture, portraying as it does, some of the physical, emotional and sometimes moral consequences of unemployment amongst the working classes of Britain, whose hearts are, in the main, sound and true.' Mr Moloney said that no-one could dispute the film's 'value as propaganda for a more saner state of society' (and promised to reprint the paper's favourable film review in his Federation journal), while Mr Allen was clear that it 'emphasised that it was man's economic system that is at fault more than man himself, and what man has done can be undone'.[149] This encapsulates, though no doubt with a particular Australian cultural flavour, the ways in which the film could speak to a broad audience with differing political and social beliefs. The paper was perhaps keen to gather this kind of support because the film had experienced yet one more censorship problem: the Senior Commonwealth Film Censor, Mr Cresswell O'Reilly, had banned it from public exhibition in Australia on 25 September 1941. All domestic and imported films were censored by O'Reilly, whose 'extreme conservatism manifested itself in decisions which often contributed to an overseas impression of Australian film censorship as among the strictest in the world'.[150] However, the Australian censor's support for the establishment was probably no more pronounced than that of the BBFC, and, indeed, reporting of the ban in Australia, while stressing that the film had been released in the UK, did not show any consciousness that this was after considerable earlier difficulties. The ban led to wide discussion in the Australian press, including speculation about the reasons for it, since the censor, 'following his usual policy', did not state his reasons.[151] The *Newcastle Morning Herald and Miner's Advocate* reported in September 1941 that the film's distributor was to appeal: 'The General Manager of the British Empire Films ... said today that he did not know whether the film was banned on moral grounds or because it dealt too drastically with industrial problems' (both of course part of the BBFC's original objections), but emphasised that in London the press 'had been unanimous about its artistic merit, entertainment value and the timeliness of the theme'.[152] In the UK there was no appeal against the BBFC's decisions, but it was a peculiarity of Australian

149 6 February 1942, p. 4.
150 *Australian Dictionary of Biography online*, 1988– , entry by Joel Greenberg.
151 *Advocate* (Tasmania), 27 September 1941, p. 7.
152 27 September 1941, p. 4.

censorship that while the Commonwealth Censor was powerful because he censored all films entering the country through Sydney (where all films did enter) he was in fact technically subordinate to the Chief Censor in Melbourne, Professor Wallace, to whom appeals could be directed. The film trade are said to have learnt that they could count on Professor Wallace's Appeals Board 'to be far more sympathetic' than the conservative O'Reilly.[153] By 2 October the press were reporting that the appeal had been successful and that the film was now released for 'adult exhibition only'.[154]

Subsequent reviews of the film often referred to the ban ('it is not easy to see why *Love on the Dole* was banned ...') and the publicity undoubtedly did the film more good than harm. It seems possible that it was a more distinct popular success in Australia than in Britain, with widespread screenings and reviews: '*Love on the Dole* made headlines in all states.'[155] Australian readings of the film were also very much in line with British ones, and again covered a political range. The *Worker* (Brisbane) noted the lessons for the future: 'it emphasises ... why a new economic order must arise after this war to do away with such hardships', but so did the *Newcastle Sun* and many other papers:

> No other nation in the world but democratic Britain would have permitted this all revealing story to be brought to the screen – but Britain is determined that never again shall her sons and daughters – now fighting so courageously so that democracy may live – become the forgotten men and women of peace.[156]

However, several reviews do suggest some particular Australian inflections in their responses. For example, the *Empire* implies that some of the living conditions shown in the film are alien to Australians ('in the house there is no bath, and though some laughed when Mrs Hardcastle poured water over her husband ... most appreciated the tragedy of it'), but also notes admiringly as from a distance the wartime conditions of Britain ('the picture too is a tribute to British production, for it was produced

---

153 Ina Bertrand and Diane Collins' *Government and Film in Australia* (Sydney: Currency Press/The Australian Film Institute, 1981), p. 52 (there is discussion of the censorship system at this period, but not the case of *Love on the Dole* specifically).
154 See, for example, *The Telegraph* (Brisbane), 2 October 1941.
155 *The Advocate* (Melbourne), 19 February 1942, p. 20; *The Mirror* (Perth), 29 November 1941, p. 15.
156 25 November 1941, p. 14 and 16 March 1942, p. 4.

in defiance of Hitler's "blitz"').[157] One review, entitled 'Liberty on the Dole', sternly rebukes the authorities in 1941 for patronising Australian audiences and infringing their freedom through their original censorship decision: 'If ... the film was not considered meat too strong for England, it is difficult to understand why Australians should not be allowed to see and judge for themselves'.[158]

In New Zealand, too, the film was a great success, but after even more significant censorship difficulties: the film was rejected both at first submission to the censor and at a resubmission.[159] The exact date of the original censorship is not entirely clear in the sources: presumably the distributors would have tried to release the film in 1941, but the film was not exhibited in New Zealand until 1943. The most substantial account is in Gordon Miram's book, *Speaking Candidly – Films and People in New Zealand*, where he says that the case was one of only three film *cause celebres* in the country up to that date. He suggests that the reason for the issue to resurface in 1943 was due to 'an approaching General Election ... . Political interests were pressing for the film to be released because it was very much a plea for the underdog and an indictment of the political system which produces slumps.'[160] It was finally distributed only after the intervention of the Labour government, when the prime minister, Peter Fraser, exercised his right to replace the entire classification Appeal Board to facilitate a successful appeal against the previous classification.[161] The Labour Party was expecting a very close contest in the 1943 election in New Zealand (and indeed it was a narrow victory for Labour, who won only forty-five parliamentary seats out of eighty): Peter Fraser presumably felt before the election that the film of *Love on the Dole* might help express and sustain Labour values in the contest – giving

---

157 23 March 1942, p. 2.

158 The *Sydney Morning Herald*, 27 September 1941. My thanks to my colleague Professor Matthew Steggle, who located this article for me.

159 See Paul Christoffel's *Censored: a Short History of Censorship in New Zealand* (Department of Internal Affairs, 1989, available online at <http://www.dia.govt. nz/diawebsite.nsf/wpg_URL/Resource-material-Our-Research-and-Reports-Censored-A-Short-History-of-Censorship-in-New-Zealand>, p. 16 (accessed 25 October 2017).

160 Hamilton: Paul's Book Arcade, 1945, p. 84.

161 See the New Zealand Office of Licensing and Classification History of Censorship page: <http://www.censor.org.nz/resources/history/1943.html>, aaccessed 25 October 2017; Barrowman, *A Popular Vision*, p. 24 and Christoffel, *Censored*, p. 16.

Greenwood's text another specific political purpose that has not been well remembered.[162] Part of the censorship appeal process involved 'private screenings for the Prime Minister and Members of Parliament', so we can be sure that Fraser knew exactly what the film was about.[163] However, as Miram points out, by the time the film was passed by the new appeals board the election was over, so that its actual impact as 'propaganda' (his word) was limited.[164] The film was then shown more or less continuously in cinemas all over New Zealand from 1943 until 1946: It did 'good business in our main centres, and better business than was expected in country districts', noted Miram.[165] There were, indeed, adverts in newspapers headed 'The Film Everyone Should See!' (unlike in Australia, the film was 'approved for universal exhibition', but some cinemas added the note that 'the Management considers this Film Unsuitable for children').[166] An article in the *New Zealand Herald* in 1945 was prompted by the previous twelve month's films to look back at film production during the war; it concluded that there had been a decline in quality, particularly in Hollywood films, which focused on 'light entertainment', while there had been some striking British successes, including *Love on the Dole*:

> One of the most controversial films England ever made, and one which was not released here for a long period because of a censorship ban ... it was undoubtedly one of the finest films England ever produced ... [it] dealt with fundamentals and did not hesitate to display political bias – a daring departure from orthodox film practice.[167]

Clearly, the view here is that the film was both an artistic success and a politically radical work, the phrase about 'bias' picking up and reworking the contemporary conservative censor's instinct that only challenges to the *status quo* should be considered as having political content. Other reviews took a similar view to those in British papers two years earlier,

---

162 See Neil Atkinson's *Adventures in Democracy: the History of the Vote in New Zealand* (Dunedin: University of Otago Press/Electoral Commission, 2003), pp. 154–56.
163 Miram, *Speaking Candidly*, p. 84.
164 *Speaking Candidly*, p. 86.
165 *Speaking Candidly*, pp. 16–17.
166 See, for example, the *Evening Post* (Wellington) 4 November 1943, p. 2 and the *Auckland Star* 12 July 1944, p. 8. The advice about suitability for children is from the *Evening Post*.
167 13 January 1945, p. 4.

seeing the film as part of a war for democracy, as a critique of pre-war Britain, and as presaging a new social order in Britain. The immediate political context was, however, somewhat different in the two nations: New Zealand elected a Labour government in 1940 and, after re-election in 1943, it remained in power till 1946. This review from late 1945 presumably endorses not only New Zealand's wartime government but also the 'mother country's' recent political choice. Greenwood's work was clearly influential in Australia and New Zealand, though the censorship issues and public responses to these have remained undiscussed by critics in the UK (I have not found much trace of *Love on the Dole*'s three texts in Canada, though Miram says that film censors there also did not approve the film for exhibition).[168]

It is clear that newspaper responses from a range of political positions in Britain and elsewhere established firmly the idea that the film was a successful one about the lives of many working-class British people in the 1930s, and that it articulated as a chief war aim the imperative to replace that pre-war Britain with something better for the mass of people. Though the narratives of novel, play, and film all leave the story's characters locked into the world of Hanky Park in one way or another, and all construct a reader/audience/viewer who will support the idea that something must be done by those outside Hanky Park, the film is the only text with any certainty that help will come – despite its context in a struggle for national survival the outcome of which is deeply uncertain. Nora Alexander in the *Sunday Pictorial* (1 June 1941) writes eloquently about what we have seen to be the dominant wartime reading of the film, and her fine review nicely sums up the significance of this 1941 version of Greenwood's fertile text:

> Time after time our Censors have waxed apoplectic at the suggestion that Walter Greenwood's *Love on the Dole* was fit subject for a film … . Now with unemployment a minor headache, the moralists have relaxed and the film has been made without a single change. The result is terrific … but it is not depressing. On the contrary, it holds enormous promise for the future. If every man and woman in Britain could see this film, I don't think we would ever go back to the dreadful pre-war years when two million men and women were allowed to rot in idleness. I don't think the censor meant us to feel that way about it. But Walter Greenwood did.[169]

168 *Speaking Candidly*, p. 85.
169 Brown, *The Common Touch*, p. 81. Some of this material about the 1941 film has been discussed in my article about Greenwood's only wartime novel, *Something*

Indeed, though it seems not to have been anywhere cited by critics, the same newspaper two months later carried an article by Greenwood himself titled 'And We Must Win the Peace', in which he both stressed the People's War idea and reconceptualised the whole history of *Love on the Dole* in the terms that the film had so successfully added to or developed out of his earlier work:

> I wrote a book you may remember. It was called "Love on the Dole". Then it became a play. Now it's become a film. In every guise "Love on the Dole" was intended to point to the kind of Britain we don't want after this war. A Britain of unemployment, misery, repression and injustice. This book was intended to be the harbinger of a New Britain.[170]

in My Heart (1944): 'The Army of the Unemployed: Walter Greenwood's Wartime Novel and the Reconstruction of Britain', *Keywords – A Journal of Cultural Materialism*, 10, October 2012.

170 *Sunday Pictorial* 17 August 1941, p. 7.

CHAPTER THREE

Walter Greenwood:
Life and Writings

You may tell me that I am living in a dream world of unreality. In this I could not agree more. Salford and all the filth and threadbare ugliness of north-country industrialism has been, and always will be ... not only a dream, but a hideous nightmare from which the conscience of man will one day awake.[1]

I. Ellor Street to Acceptance Letter: 1903–1933

Walter Greenwood was born on 17 December 1903 at No. 56 Ellor Street, off Hankinson Street, in the 'Parish and Ward of St. Thomas, Pendleton', Salford.[2] Hankinson Street has been not only demolished but thoroughly obliterated: no such street and no such street name exists in modern Salford. The whole of Hankinson Street, with its adjoining streets of decayed nineteenth-century housing, was replaced by the Salford Shopping Precinct in the late 1960s, and the name is now remembered only in the shopping-mall perimeter street, called Hankinson Way (Ellor Street itself is now the site of an adjoining car park). If 'Hanky Park' is one of the most famous locations in Salford it is also a memory that, in some respects, Salford has, quite understandably, wanted to leave behind.[3] However, to understand the world into which Walter

---

1 From the section on Salford in Greenwood's County Books series volume on *Lancashire* (London: Robert Hale, 1951), p. 297.
2 *There Was a Time*, p. 24.
3 As Steven Fielding observes, 'Salford played a distinctive part in Britain's early industrialisation and subsequent deindustrialisation.' See his *The Salford Labour Party*, p. 2.

Greenwood was born we need to go back from the present post-industrial retail park to that industrial urban landscape where generations, as Greenwood said, worked, lived, and died.

Greenwood reflected at the conclusion of his memoirs, written during 1966, on the ongoing demolition of the place where he had spent the majority of the thirty-two years before he became an author:

> Where the wreckers have finished their work only the cobbled roadways and pavements remain to mark the streets which were our childhood playgrounds and where our homes had stood. They were built when the British Empire was at the pinnacle of its wealth and power, and they had sheltered defrauded generations for whom life had been an endless struggle both insulting and deprived.[4]

Hankinson Street was a poor area, in many respects accurately portrayed in the memorable opening of *Love on the Dole*:

> They call this part Hanky Park ... . The district takes it name from a sloping street, Hankinson Street, whose pavements ... have been polished by the traffic of boots and clogs of many generations. On either side of this are other streets, mazes, jungles of tiny houses cramped and huddled together, two rooms alow and aloft. (p. 11)

Like many similar areas in the cities of England, this was a neighbourhood created without the benefit of planning or public health legislation during the extraordinarily rapid urbanisation of the mid and late nineteenth century. In origin, says Asa Briggs, 'Manchester and Salford were twin towns separated by the River Irwell. A tranquil stream in the Middle Ages ... but a "flood of liquid manure" in early Victorian England.'[5] A century later Greenwood calls the city 'a vast sooty spread of incredible streets ... where the proletariat put up a pretence of living'.[6] In that respect, Hankinson Street was no different from parts of Birmingham or Sheffield. However – and this was something Greenwood would have been well aware of as he grew up, given the socialist traditions in parts of his family – Salford might be considered as containing supreme

---

4 *There Was a Time*, p. 250.

5 *Victorian Cities* (Harmondsworth: Penguin, 1963, 1968), 1990, p. 29. There are other references to Salford, but no extended discussion of the city in its own right. The case study on 'Manchester: Symbol of a New Age' in Chapter 3 gives the essential contexts for the growth of the giant Victorian industrial conurbations.

6 Greenwood, *The Secret Kingdom*, p. 10. All subsequent references are to the 1970 edition.

examples of such unrestrained 'free market' development.[7] As Robert Roberts points out in his classic account *The Classic Slum – Salford Life in the First Quarter of the Century*, Engels himself had seen Salford as exemplifying the worst excesses of capitalism and as the nadir of working-class conditions under capitalism:

> All Salford [wrote Engels in 1844] is built in courts or narrow lanes, so narrow that they remind me of the narrowest I have ever seen, in the little lanes of Genoa. The average construction of Salford is, in this respect, much worse than that of Manchester and so too, in respect of cleanliness.[8]

Within Salford there were variations in poverty, and Engels identified particularly atrocious areas, including the Old Town and the district between Oldfield Road and Cross Lane. Robert Roberts' comment on how the classic slum had developed since Engels is very close to the perspective that *Love on the Dole* also gives:

> Through a familiarity so long and close, this district must have become for Engels the very epitome of all industrial ghettos … . He died in 1895 having seen that little world change, develop, 'prosper' even, yet stay in essence the same awful paradigm of what a free capitalist society could produce. By 1900 the area showed some improvement; his 'cow-stable' had doubtless been demolished together with many another noisome den, but much that was vile remained. (p. 14)

Compare Greenwood's overview of Hanky Park:

> The years have brought their changes. Water closets have superseded the earth and tin privies … . Fever is rarer; large families are no longer permitted to live in cellars; instead … they pay much more than their grandparents did for the convenience of living in a single room over a cellar. (p. 12)

Robert Roberts, who was born in Salford in 1905 and grew up there during the same period as Greenwood, stresses social stratification within the working class:

> No view of the English working class in the first quarter of this century would be accurate if that class were shown merely as a great amalgam of artisan and labouring groups united by a common aim and purpose. Life in reality was much more complex. Socially the unskilled workers and their families, who made up about 50 per cent of the population in our industrial

7 See also Claire Warden's discussion of the importance of the play's setting in Salford, 'Ugliness and Beauty', p. 35.
8 Quoted in *The Classic Slum* (Harmondsworth: Penguin, 1978), p. 13.

cities, varied as much from the manual elite as did people in middle station from the aristocracy ... . Born behind a general shop in an area which, sixty years before, Frederick Engels had called 'the classic slum', I grew up in what was perhaps an ideal position for viewing the English proletarian caste system in all its late flower ... . Our own family was in the slum but not, they felt, of it: we had 'connections'. (p. 13)

Roberts outlines the complex caste systems that operated, often with subtle and sometimes mysterious markers, and through which, he argues, a constant, dynamic struggle for social position took place. Though highly relative, a dividing line between respectable and unrespectable played an important symbolic role. Thus Roberts suggests that, among other markers of prestige, casualness of employment was one, giving a descending scale from skilled workers to regularly employed unskilled workers down through dockers, then street hawkers to 'firewood choppers, bundlers and sellers, and the rag and boners' (p. 21). Ewan MacColl's autobiography *Journeyman* gives insight into how in 1930s Salford the status of regularly employed skilled workers like his father (effectively in exile from Scotland because of a long record of political activism) could instantly be eroded by joblessness: 'There's something about an unemployed man, an unemployed craftsman in particular ... he has the demeanour of dog that expects to be beaten.'[9]

That his parents owned a shop gave Robert Roberts, as he says, a vantage point over a certain part of the social system of Salford between 1900 and 1925. The ownership of any (successful) business gave prestige to a family – and, as Roberts makes clear, his mother did indeed exercise considerable social power, with, in her particular case, a strong sense of social and philanthropic obligation wherever it was in her limited means. This context is highly relevant to Greenwood's own early life, as we shall see, since his father's occupation gave a possible entrée to this kind of social and economic status, while descent into lower ranks was also a constant possibility.[10]

Greenwood's parents – and the conflicts between them – might indeed be seen as representing some of the different possibilities of working-class life in the period. Walter's father Tom Greenwood was born in Halifax in 1869, but the 1881 census listed him as living at 35 Barker Street, Salford,

---

9 London: Sidgwick & Jackson, 1990, p. 35.
10 It is perhaps not coincidental that in *The Cleft Stick* there is a strong interest in several stories in those who have risen to become shop or small business owners – see 'A Little Gold Mine' and 'All's Well That Ends Well'.

with the occupation (aged twelve years) of 'hairdresser's assistant' (to his father, also Tom Greenwood, a hairdresser). By the time of his marriage he had opened a hairdresser's shop ('Tom's Hairdressing Saloon'[11]) in his own right at 56 Ellor Street, and married a local woman, Elizabeth Matilda Walter. The character of Robert Treville in Greenwood's 1938 novel *The Secret Kingdom* is clearly a version of his father. Here, having just set up his barber's shop in Salford, Treville considers his prospects:

> Hadn't he established himself as a popular character by virtue of having made himself a favourite at the Palatine Arms? Wasn't he able to bring tears to the eyes of the customers there by way he sang 'the Miner's Dream of Home'? And hadn't they told him he could tell a *risqué* story better than anybody else there? Patrons of the pub became his patrons as a matter of course.[12]

Indeed, as Greenwood explains in his memoir, *There Was a Time*, his father was an 'extrovert' who tried 'without success, to convince my mother that his visits to the pub were "for the sake of business"'.[13] *The Secret Kingdom* details the constant, tragic, and unsuccessful struggle Treville has in choosing between drink and respectability, between a downward and upward social trajectory, and this was certainly a familiar struggle in the early years of the Greenwood household, though it is presented comically in *There Was a Time*: '"nip round to the Temperance Hall and get me a Pledge Form" ... . Father signed this with a great flourish and it was added to the collection' (p. 15). Robert Treville dies young of pneumonia, brought on more or less directly, the novel makes clear, by his chronic struggle with drink; Tom Greenwood also died young, aged forty-five,[14] in 1912, but as a direct result, anyway, of chronic lung disease, probably TB: 'my father was a chronic subject. His condition, like that of all his fellow sufferers, was aggravated, if not

---

11 The name of the shop is clearly painted on the window of the premises in the photograph of Walter Greenwood and his father which forms the frontispiece to *There Was a Time*.

12 *The Secret Kingdom*, p. 25.

13 *There Was a Time*, pp. 13 and 15.

14 Since the 1881 census gives Tom Greenwood's birth date as 1869, he should have been forty-three years old at his death in 1912, but it seems unlikely that Greenwood would have given his father's age at death incorrectly in *There Was a Time*. It seems possible either that Tom Greenwood's father gave an incorrect birth date for his son – not at all uncommon in census records of the period – or that Greenwood's father was himself wrong about his birth year.

caused, by the incessant filth perpetually poured into the atmosphere by industrial and domestic chimneys.'[15]

In his memoir Greenwood represents his parents as consciously seeking to identify themselves with different aspects of working-class culture.[16] His mother came from a family with a strong tradition of socialism, union membership, and self-improvement. Her father, William Walter, was sacked for union membership, probably during the Salford strikes and lockouts of 1911–12, motivated by a quest for a living wage in the face of recent price rises.[17] He is surely recalled in the figure of the staunch old-fashioned socialist and craftsman William Byron in *The Secret Kingdom*, though William Walter died in poverty, while William Byron is portrayed as a highly skilled man who is never close to destitution. Both William Walter and William Byron have book collections, perhaps representing similar values. Here an anonymous neighbour talks of William Byron's reputation in the area:

> Everyone knew him to be a well-read man. He actually had books of his own, *real* books, as became a man interested, as he was, in politics and trade unions. You could see the books in the glass-fronted bookcase in the parlour where he took you when you went to ask his advice.
>
> He knew about music too ... . He and his eldest daughter never went to the variety Music Halls, instead they patronised the Opera Companies, and the Free Trade Hall in Manchester every Thursday when the Halle Orchestra ... played. (p. 14)

As we have seen in Chapter 1, this was the kind of culture of which Elizabeth Greenwood was also part: indeed, she is the literal and spiritual inheritor of her father's books and book case, and they are often consulted in the course of *There Was a Time* (see pp. 117, 139, 245). There was, for Elizabeth Greenwood, nothing contradictory about being desperately poor and working class and having aspirations and an independent sense of self-worth. This sense of dignity is remembered by Greenwood in a dramatic vignette in front of the Poor Law Guardians:

> We went, Mother, Sister and I, to the Board ... the Guardians put their heads together ... then the paymaster ... said: 'very well. Half a crown' ... .

15 *There was a Time*, p. 33.
16 See also some rare discussion of Greenwood's Memoir in Miles and Smith, *Cinema, Literature & Society*, pp. 144–50.
17 See *There was a Time*, p. 57, and for some background Edmund and Ruth Frow's *Radical Salford – Episodes in Labour History* (Manchester: Neil Richardson, 1984), pp. 20–21.

Mother did a startling thing. She left the coin where it lay and electrified the room by announcing in a ringing voice: 'Half a crown? Half a crown for three for a week? ... I would not demean myself. I would sooner sing for our crusts in the gutter. Come along, children.' (p. 69)

Though Elizabeth is shown as having a strong sense of community and is part of the important female self-help network made up of her neighbours Annie Boarder and Polly Myton (who have only a remote resemblance to Mrs Bull and company in *Love on the Dole*), it is notable that Greenwood depicts her as averse to gossip (see the discussion of the importance of 'gossip' in Chapter 1):

> while being anything but unfriendly she, as a general rule, disapproved of standing with groups of neighbours exchanging tittle-tattle in the street. Father on the contrary, loved, when waiting for custom, to stand in his shop doorway ... and greet all who passed with a cheerful wave and jovial comment. (p. 13)

The contrast between the senses of identity (Richards sees these as partly Lancashire identities: 'dominant strong-willed mothers and easy-going good-natured fathers'[18]) inhabited by his parents is consistently presented by Greenwood in *There Was a Time*. As we have seen, Tom Greenwood favoured music hall and variety (he had briefly been a music hall artiste in his youth[19]) and this went with a liking for masculine gossip and social networks in the characteristic settings of the street itself, his own barber's shop, and neighbouring public houses. Unlike his careful wife, Tom Greenwood expresses impatience even with the forms of self-protection that most of the community feels are essential. Some neighbours, the elderly grandparents of Walter's ragged friend 'Mickmac', fall into dire poverty through unemployment and have to go to the dreaded Salford Workhouse, where they do not long survive. When evicted from their house they were disappointed that it is legal for the insurance company to refuse to pay out on their policy because payments have recently lapsed, though they have been paid continuously up until that point for thirty years. At their funeral Tom Greenwood states his preference for pleasure now to deferred 'benefits':

---

18 *Films and British National Identity – from Dickens to Dad's Army* (Manchester: Manchester University Press, 1997), p. 259.

19 According to *There Was a Time*, p. 17, he had appeared occasionally as 'Tom McCann, the singing Irish Comedian'.

'There,' said Dad wryly after the obsequies. 'Slaved all their bloody lives, brought up a family, forked out for death insurance, and they finish up with pauper's funeral. Not that that'd trouble me ... . Come to think of it you can let my burial insurance lapse here and now and let's be having the pennies every week. If I sup it away in beer it'll be one in the eye for those insurance robbers ... *and* the right man will have benefited.' (p. 23)

Elizabeth Greenwood is simply recorded as turning her head aside, closing her eyes, and saying, 'Such vulgarity'.

While such disagreements between his parents are handled with affection and amusement in *There Was a Time*, they are important aspects of different reactions to their circumstances, echoed in some ways in the treatment in *Love on the Dole* of the whole question of whether there is anything beyond the short term, any routes of escape. If the idea of becoming a writer was an important one for Walter Greenwood, and partly derived from his mother's interest in culture and in economies of deferred benefit and investment in the future, his (critical) awareness of the strong pull of the immediate pleasures of working-class life may owe something to his father's attitudes.

However, despite the rich and diverse culture of his home life, Walter's experience of the state's education provision for children of his class in Salford was not positive. *There Was a Time* recalls his being able to leave school early (at thirteen rather than fourteen) by passing the Board of Education's 'Labour Examination', 'open to fatherless boys' so that they could help support their families (p. 107). Greenwood wrote a longer account of his schooldays for a book in which it stood out from accounts written, in the main, by public school boys (and a few public school girls). The invitation to write this essay, 'Langy Road [a Salford Council School]', came from Graham Greene in 1933, directly as a result of the impact of the novel of *Love on the Dole* that year, as Paul W. Salmon notes:

> According to Greene's biographer, Norman Sherry, Greene was deeply moved by *Love on the Dole* and, prior to the publication of his own review of the book in the *Spectator*, wrote a congratulatory letter to the author ... 'Heard from Walter Greenwood ... a pathetic letter referring to the hard life he had' ... Perhaps it was with the prospect of helping him partly in mind that Greene soon solicited an essay from Greenwood.[20]

20 Johnson, *Dictionary of Literary Biography Vol. 191*, p. 134.

Greene was editing a collection of essays for Jonathan Cape to be called *The Old School – Essays by Divers Hands* (published 1934).[21] It was a project that came out of the deep interest of young writers of the time in their own experience of school, and had a broadly leftist agenda. The title referred not only to the notion of the *alma mater* and the old school tie but also to the idea that British schooling in the period discussed (the writers all referring to their schooldays during or just after the First World War) must surely be an anachronism and something that could not go on as it was: 'there can be small doubt that the system which this book mainly represents is doomed', says Greene in the Preface (p. vii). Greenwood's essay is probably there, along with that of H. E. Bates about his grammar school at Kettering, to show that if there was much that was deplorable about the public schools, there was little to be praised in other parts of the highly stratified education system. Greenwood's essay starts by stressing, again, something of his family dynamic and the part played by his parents' perceptions of their class identities: he is very clear that his educational experience has been much affected by what he terms himself 'economic and domestic circumstances' (p. 53). Thus he recounts how his mother made efforts to get him into a better school than the one he would normally have attended: 'maternal ambition was responsible for my enrolment at the Langworthy Road Council School where a "better class" of boy was reputed to attend' (p. 53). Nevertheless, 'In the whole of my school career I never won a prize or an attendance certificate … . To me the Old School was a place to be avoided, a sort of punishment for being young … the teachers' disgust for us was only equalled by our disgust for them' (pp. 56–57). Greenwood felt he did not learn much – though in retrospect he felt the *experience* of attending school in the day and working morning and evenings at the pawnbroker's was a kind of education:

> As I hated school so I hated the shop … . Subconsciously I was being educated, at least, preparing to be educated. It was not until years later that the study of Marxian economics satisfactorily explained the causes of my predicament. Accidentally I discovered a number of pamphlets which had belonged to my grandfather; but much rain was to fall on Manchester and Salford before I made the discovery. (p. 64)

---

21 Graham Greene, *The Old School – Essays by Divers Hands* (Oxford: Oxford University Press reprint, 1984); all subsequent references are to this edition and are given in brackets in the text.

The essay ends with an account of the joyous moment of leaving school: 'I ran out into the schoolyard yelling with triumph' (p. 64). This is closely echoed in the account in *There Was a Time*, though the close of the essay frames the experience slightly differently from the memoir: 'My schooldays were over and I was free to find a full-time job: I was envied' (p. 64).[22] The ironic reference to his school-mates' understanding of his 'freedom' suggests Harry's initially innocent understanding of the blessed state of employment in *Love on the Dole*, while the later account's reference to Marxian economics suggests Larry's more experienced and analytical perspective.

In fact, Walter's own experience of employment was initially similar to Harry's, but subsequently more varied. Unlike Harry, he did indeed progress from part-time hours in the pawnshop into full-time employment there and an exceptionally dreary job it was, involving fifteen-hour days every day except for a half-day on Wednesday and Sunday, and leaving him 'sullenly rebellious against the shop's corroding tedium and its suffocating oppression' (p. 108).[23] He was released after becoming verminous with lice – something that put the pawnshop firmly outside the boundaries of respectability for his mother. A lifelong socialist and 'co-operator', she found him a job as a clerk in the general office of an ideal employer: the local Co-Operative Society (co-operatives had a particularly strong presence in Manchester and Salford from the latter part of the nineteenth century onwards).[24] As the neighbour Polly Myton observes, 'Ten shillings [a week] and a job for life ... what a lucky lad he is!' (p. 109). However, working days included Saturdays and Walter had the same feeling about this job as Harry has about continuing to work at the pawnbrokers – it is not a proper man's job:

22 The essay is reprinted as the last piece in Greenwood's 1937 collection of short stories with illustrations by Arthur Wragg, *The Cleft Stick, or, 'It's the Same the Whole World Over*. However, there are a number of differences in the text, especially at the opening and end, where the boy's date of leaving school is dated precisely to 7 December 1916.

23 It was Ridgeway and Pollit's pawnshop in Pendleton; Greenwood started work there in 1915, aged twelve (see his notes on a later photograph of the shop, WGC/4/4/5).

24 I am not clear exactly which Co-operative organisation Greenwood worked for. Both retail co-operative societies, which ran shops, and the CWS (Co-operative Wholesale Society, founded 1863) had a number of premises in parts of Manchester and Salford. See Victoria Kelley's 'The Equitable Consumer: Shopping at the Co-Op in Manchester', *Journal of Design History*, 11, 4, 1998 for much useful background on the Co-op in the period from the late nineteenth century up until 1914.

Any loving mother, I felt, ought to be only too ready to save her son from this martyrdom ... . I had a catalogue of jobs that would have brought me bliss on top of the necessary wages. Because of man-power shortages apprentices by the score were being taken on at Marlowe's Engineering works; boys were wanted at the London and North Western railway's engine sheds ... . In vain ... I was reminded of the ever-present spectre of short-time, strikes and lock-outs. (p. 110)

Walter never did go to work at 'Marlowe's Engineering works', but, given its importance in *Love on the Dole*, it is worth pausing to discuss Marlowe's before tracing where he did go next.

Though called 'Marlowe's' here and in the novel, the engineering works is based on a major engineering works at the Trafford Park industrial site, where many people from Salford worked.[25] The engineering company's name site changed a number of times owing to several commercial reorganisations in the electrical and heavy engineering industry in Britain between 1918 and 1940. At the period when Walter so envied the engineering apprentices there (circa 1916–18), it was called British Westinghouse and manufactured electrical apparatus such as transformers, arc lamps, meters, switchboards, and control gear.[26] However, in 1919 the company was renamed Metropolitan Vickers (known as MetroVick for short) after its acquisition by the Vickers company and it retained this name into the 1930s and after, so that this was the name behind the Marlowe's of *Love on the Dole*. A number of references in the novel to Marlowe's relate specifically to MetroVick, particularly allusions to their work exporting turbines to the Soviet

---

25 For a history of Trafford Park – the first example anywhere of an industrial park – from its foundation in 1896 until 1996, see Robert Nicholl's *Trafford Park – the First Hundred Years* (Chichester: Phillimore, 1996). Nicholl includes a detailed account of British Westinghouse/Metrovick.

26 There is a full (in-house) business history of the company, *1899–1949 Metropolitan Vickers Electrical Company*, written by the Metrovick engineer John Dummelow to mark the company's 50th anniversary and published by the company in Manchester in 1949. This has now been made available digitally (<https://www. gracesguide.co.uk/Metropolitan-Vickers_Electrical_Co_1899-1949_by_John_ Dummelow:_1899-1909>, accessed 5 January 2018). All references are to the digital (facsimile) version. Discussion of the products manufactured around 1916 is covered on p. 42, while development of products in the 1920s and 1930s is discussed in more detail on pp. 108–15. *Love on the Dole* is clearly factually correct in its statement (see p. 19) about the range of industries 'Marlowe's' is engaged in – though there may be symbolic value too in making it an epitome of heavy industry.

Union, a controversial contract that boosted their trade during the slump, but also involved six of their engineers being tried for sabotage in Moscow when some of the turbines proved defective.[27] Perhaps not surprisingly, the official company history, *1899–1949 Metropolitan Vickers Electrical Company*, gives a rather different impression of being an apprentice at MetroVick from that given in *Love on the Dole* (see, for example, the discussion of the company's apprentice scheme and of its welfare provision).[28] The history does record short-time working and a reduction of the workforce from 11,000 to 7,400 between 1931 and 1933, but also remarks that from 1936, largely as a result of government contracts arising from rearmament, the number of employees rose again (p. 126). The company history does not seem aware that the works were recreated as Marlowe's in Greenwood's novel.

Greenwood himself, since his mother denied him his desired masculine working-class identity, eventually took things into his own hands and escaped from the Co-op by finding a job as a stable lad at the house of a cotton manufacturer who lived at Swinton, three miles from his home (he had been reprimanded at the Co-op for drawing horses on the account books). From there, aged twenty, he went to work at a racing stables out of Salford. The owner, however, lost his money ('the post-war boom was beginning to crack' [p. 157]) and Greenwood returned to Salford. Next came a job with the exploitative 'Boxo Co, Packing Case mftcrs & General carriers' (p. 163), obtained through the offices of Nobby, who had returned from the Army with a distinct entrepreneurial streak ('Just the same in the army. Crown and anchor, the lot he was running. Won a packet' [p. 161]) and who seems to be a partial model for Sam Grundy. Again, this did not last long, and Walter's next job was as a packer at Battersby's and Co, a wholesalers who supplied drapery, bedding, and furniture to retailers across Britain. Here he stayed until at least 1926 and the General Strike, before being laid off as retail orders dried up, especially from Wales, where a great deal of Battersby's orders came from ('the chill winds of economic contraction [blew] through the Welsh mining valleys' [p. 183]). Thus for the first time Greenwood joined

27 *1899–1949 Metropolitan Vickers Electrical Company*, p. 121.
28 *1899–1949 Metropolitan Vickers Electrical Company*, pp. 130–31, 129–30. *Trafford Park* also notes that Metrovick's reputation 'as a trainer of staff ... was unrivalled' and that places at its Trafford Park 'Apprentice Training School [were] heavily sought after' (p. 75). While Greenwood never actually worked for the company or as an engineer, the company history is very much history from above.

'the growing brotherhood of the dole' (p. 184). His wage at Battersby's had been twenty-eight shillings a week; his unemployment benefit was eighteen shillings a week – a drastic reduction in the family's income. His initial reaction was partly that described by a Glasgow doctor and quoted in Chapter 1: 'After falling out of work there is a short period of release (a holiday freedom)'.[29] Walter certainly felt released and released for one main end – to write:

> To me the leisure which unemployment provided was anything but disagreeable. It brought a bubbling sense of freedom at first, a secret elation in being at liberty to indulge in a feast of uninterrupted reading at home, the public library or in those Manchester bookshops where, by tacit consent, the kindly proprietors allowed young men and students to browse among the new books. There was the other motive, the ambition I had been nursing quietly for some time to try my hand at earning a living from writing. (p. 185)

It was around this time that Greenwood met a man he calls James Moleyns, who is probably a part model for Larry in *Love on the Dole* (Larry Finley, another local Labour activist, is suggested as a model by Eddie Frow).[30] Moleyns is introduced as a man with a reputation: 'He soon made himself and his views known to the neighbourhood. It was his views, too freely expressed at his work, that had earned him the sack' (p. 171). Jim, a socialist (and a lover of Wagner and Shaw too), is welcome at the Greenwood house: 'Mother invited him in and, to prove that he was in the presence of the converted, opened our bookcase and showed him her father's treasures' (p. 172). Through Moleyns, Walter's literary and cultural activities while unemployed also assumed a political

---

29 Cited in John Stevenson and Chris Cook, *Britain in the Depression: Society and Politics 1929–39* (London: Longman, 1994), p. 95.

30 See his concise article on Greenwood on the Working Class Movement Library website <https://www.wcml.org.uk/our-collections/creativity-and-culture/drama-and-literature/walter-greenwood-and-love-on-the-dole/>, accessed 25 October 2017. Edmund and Ruth Frow also wrote an entry on Lawrence Finley for the *Dictionary of Labour Biography*, Vol. 4, ed. J. Bellamy and J. Saville (Basingstoke: MacMillan, 1977), pp. 80–81. Finley was unemployed in the early 1930s and 'became active in the National Unemployed Workers' Movement. After the mass demonstrations of October 1931, when the leaders of the Manchester and Salford movement were arrested, Finley took over the leadership and continued the agitation' (p. 80). Unlike Larry, however, Finley remained in good health, joining the Communist Party in 1935 and remaining an active member until his death in 1974. It may be that James Moleyns is a pseudonym for Larry Finley.

aspect, as he typed up the local weekly Labour Party newsletter and was asked by Moleyns to write for it too (Moleyns warned him off being 'all tub-thumping', advising some humour and 'items of local historical interest [such as] Engels' house in Quay Street' [p. 185]). Greenwood's good standard of literacy also brought him several temporary clerk's jobs (including one at Ford's motor works in Trafford Park), where his ability to type was an asset, but the last of these came to an abrupt end in December 1929, since, according to *There Was a Time*, the Wall Street crash directly inspired his then boss to disappear without paying the last three weeks' wages: Greenwood took the firm's typewriter home in lieu of wages.

A longer period of unemployment then followed, during which Greenwood wrote, determinedly aiming both to be published and to earn money for the household (his sister and mother were both in work, but their combined wages were inadequate for the household's needs). The first work his memoir refers to is a novel, rejected by at least one publisher as not suitable for their list (p. 205). Subsequent allusions suggest that he sent out more than one work: 'the discouraging and growing pile of manuscripts had one positive quality – the undeniable proof of practice' (p. 209). Greenwood told an interviewer in the 1970s that the short story 'Jack Cranford's Wife' (later published as 'The Cleft Stick') was his first story but was rejected by an editor for being 'too depressing'.[31] The earliest accepted work was also a short story, which, interestingly, given the importance of Sam Grundy in *Love on the Dole*, is not only about gambling but in Greenwood's mind showed a connection between writing and gambling. Writing, like betting, may be a way out and, at any rate, is a source of hope:

> What about short stories? Out of nowhere came the recollection of Sandy Sinclair and his consuming hatred of the Motor Works' factory environment ... in his way was he not like me basically, in pursuit of the same thing, searching, like so many, for a way out of intolerable conditions? His desire was to make a book, mine to write one. 'A Maker of Books'. There's the title, anyway. (p. 205)

Indeed, this story was his first professionally published, paid for, piece of fiction. It was accepted by *The Storyteller Magazine* in 1931.[32] To its

---

31 'Dole Cue': interview with Catherine Stott, *The Guardian* 2 April 1971, p. 10.
32 *The Story-Teller Magazine* was launched in April 1907 and continued in print until November 1937 (its history is discussed in Mike Ashley in his *The Age of*

author and his family's amazement, the fee was twenty-five guineas
– enough for him to live on for a considerable period – 'a pound a
week for half a year' (p. 215). The story was republished in 1937 as the
title story in his short story collection *The Cleft Stick*, for which it was
probably the starting point (published by Selwyn & Blount with sixteen
fine illustrations by the socialist artist Arthur Wragg).[33] The author's
preface to *The Cleft Stick* adds some details to the later account of
his early authorship. It explains that, with the exception of two recent
stories (and the *Old School* essay 'Langy Road'), the collection is made
up of stories written when he was unemployed between 1928 and 1931
and adds that, though writing was an insecure job, it nevertheless paid
better and was no more 'precarious' (p. 8) than being a working man
at this time. The story itself is about a character, Ted Munter, who
reappears in *Love on the Dole*: 'To Ted the present was always stale,
flat and unprofitable, the past reproachful and vain, but the future –
Ah! The future, that land of rich illusion!' (p. 11). It also refers to Sam
Grundy, for it occurs to Ted that if Sam can make a fortune as a bookie
why, then, so can he. Instead of passing on bets for his workmates
(here in an office rather than at Marlowe's) to Sam, he makes his own
small book – and loses on the venture. He returns to being a client of
Sam's, convinced that if he can just make some capital to start with
he could succeed in becoming a successful bookie like Sam. Having
lost his own money he loses his wife's savings, then the money from
his recently inherited deceased mother's bakery business. During the

the Storytellers – *British Popular Fiction Magazines 1880–1950* (London and New
   Castle, Delaware: British Library/Oak Knoll Press, 2006).
33 Arthur Wragg published a number of illustrated works with Selwyn & Blount,
   often with highly original and strikingly contemporary versions of Christian
   themes. In particular, he had published the controversial *Psalms for Modern Life*
   in 1933, which juxtaposed the texts of the psalms with his stark black and white
   drawings of contemporary life, especially as it related to the increasing risk of
   war. Greenwood might have been attracted to Wragg's *Jesus Wept* of 1934, which
   had many illustrations of the unemployment, poverty, and dereliction of parts
   of contemporary Britain. Two sources discuss Wragg's fascinating and neglected
   work, but without much specific detail on *The Cleft Stick*. See the memoir *Bound
   to Be Read* (London: Jonathan Cape, 1975) by Robert Lusty (managing director of
   Selwyn & Blount, 1933–35) and Judy Brook's *Arthur Wragg: 20th Century Artist,
   Jester and Prophet* (London: Sansom & Co, 2001, 2007), where Greenwood is
   briefly mentioned on p. 89. For selected images from Wragg's books see Chris
   Mullen, 'The Alphabet of Illustrators', *The Visual Telling of Stories*, <http://www.
   fulltable.com/vts/aoi/w/wragg/menuz.htm>, accessed 25 October 2017.

story Ted oscillates between despair and hope and, at the end, he is slave to a kind of hope, as he still thinks that: 'the logical move was for him to become a maker of books himself' (p. 27).

This success encouraged Walter's writing ambitions, which were a way out for him and his family, but also in his mind absolutely linked to telling of the plight of the people in his community and others like it:

> This beguiled me down flowery paths into the siren land of 'If' where riches I had never known before would be mine if I found a home for one or two stories a month. Around me, in the poverty-stricken helplessness of those both in work and out of it, was material in abundance. Burning as I was with political bias for the establishment of social reform, I assured myself, ignorantly, that this fervid desire would be shared by editors in London ... . Now and then a kindly disposed editor would add a note to his rejection slip saying that, while he thought the story good of itself, its subject matter was not the sort of thing to interest readers who paid their money for romance, entertainment and excitement. If I cared to send something of a lighter nature, he would be happy to read it. Efforts I made in this direction foundered; my heart was not in them. (pp. 215–16)

In the preface to *The Cleft Stick* Greenwood says that at least one editor suggested that he write 'football stories', but that he had no 'feeling for such subjects'.[34] In his memoir this period of literary and pecuniary disappointment coincides with the 1931 national financial crisis, the fall of Labour and the election of the National Government. The next chapter recounts the reaction of men on the dole to the subsequent cuts in benefit and tells of the events in Salford of 1 October 1931, also dramatised in *Love on the Dole*, known as the Battle of Bexley Square.[35] Later chapters discuss further how the various texts of *Love on the Dole* deal with this major manifestation of discontent by the unemployed of Salford. In his memoir Greenwood recounts how the demonstration, led by the Salford branch of the NUWM (National Unemployed Workers' Movement), was prevented from marching to

34 Author's Preface, p. 9. In his interview with Catherine Stott (*The Guardian* 2 April 1971) Greenwood specifically linked the football request to his story 'Jack Cranford's Wife'.

35 Eddie Frow, who was arrested during the march, gives a brief account in *Radical Salford*, pp. 29–31, and, with Ruth Frow, a fuller account in *The Battle of Bexley Square: Salford Unemployed Workers' Demonstration, 1st October 1931* (Manchester: Working Class Movement Library, Manchester, 1994). I have not found any discussion of Bexley Square in national histories of unemployment in the period, but see the following note for a wider context.

the town hall as planned, and was broken up first by mounted police and then by the fire brigade:

> people cowering, tottering, stumbling, the drenched mass breaking into retreat … . The 'mob' dispersed, became individuals with names, Mrs Boarder, Michael McBride, James Moleyns … . With the exception of those who were taken to the cells or by ambulance to hospital they retreated in groups … making their sullen way home. (p. 222)

This was part of a national wave of protests led by the NUWM between September and December 1931, with many involving marches to town halls, and generally meeting the same kind of police response.[36]

Greenwood, on reduced benefit and then without any income at all after a Means Test (because his mother and sister were in work), continued to hope for at least a subsistence level of literary success: he now held out the 'threadbare hope' (p. 223) of having two stories a year accepted. On his daily walk he passed what he hoped was a precedent for Salford literary success: the shop in the Crescent on which the successful local author Harold Brighouse was said to have based his well-known play *Hobson's Choice* (first performed in 1915).[37] Greenwood's situation had not much changed by December 1932, though he now earned £1 per week as a collector for a clothing business very like the Good Samaritan clothing company. He was by this time working on a novel, which made him feel at least different from the 'scarecrow spectres' (p. 240) on street corners who had no occupation. He recalls being utterly gripped by this particular tale – 'theme, characters and development flowed' (p. 246) – and, a period of writer's block overcome at the close, the typescript was sent off to two publishers simultaneously (a practice generally thought unprofessional by publishers).

36 See Wal Hannington's *Unemployed Struggles 1919–1936* (London: Lawrence and Wishart, 1936; reprinted 1977), p. 228 and pp. 223–29 for an account from 1936 of the national situation, which refers to protests against the economy measures between September and December 1931 in cities including Blackburn, Bolton, Coventry, Glasgow, Manchester, and London and in the counties of 'Fife, North Staffs, West Riding, Wigan, Tyneside and Yorkshire'. Stephen Constantine's *Unemployment in Britain Between the Wars* discusses the impact of the NUWM, pp. 42–44.

37 Brighouse was born in Eccles; *Hobson's Choice*, along with others of his plays, established a school of Manchester realism. He wrote regularly for the *Manchester Guardian* from 1913 onwards and published a number of works in the 1920s, including a novel about a mill-owning family, *Heppelstalls* (1922) and *Three Lancashire Plays* (1920). See Brian Hollingsworth's entry on Brighouse in *DNB* (online edition, 2008).

One of the two publishers returned the typescript in December 1932 with the bittersweet news that 'We have read your novel with great interest. Unfortunately our Spring List is to include a book on a similar theme translated from the German, Mr Hans Fallada's *Little Man, What Now?*' (p. 249). The publisher in question was George Putnam, and the novel had originally been published in Berlin in 1932 as *Kleiner Mann, Was Nunn?* The novel, portraying the increasingly difficult lives of an unemployed couple in Weimar Germany, was a success in its original language and equally successful in British and US translations. The US edition was selected as a Book of the Month Club book and a film version was quickly made, being released by Universal Pictures in 1934. Interestingly, Graham Greene praised Fallada's novel, as he was to praise *Love on the Dole*, reviewing both for the *Spectator*: 'Finished *Little Man What Now?* with intense respect', 'Everything that gives pleasure costs money … there are chapters which pluck the nerves with the agony of those who are insecure.'[38] Some of the success of Hans Fallada's novel took place after *Love on the Dole* was itself published, but even in 1932 this news and rejection combined might have suggested to Greenwood that his belief that there would be readers interested in his book about the unemployed was in principle correct. But 'in principle' was little good, when so much of immediate practical as well as longer-term consequence hung on an actual acceptance.

However, January 1933 brought a letter from the second publisher, Jonathan Cape, which Greenwood quotes as starting simply, 'Dear Sir, We will publish your novel.' The memoir comments, 'I was on the threshold of a wonderful year, though this I did not know' (p. 249). In fact this is the memoir's last comment on the 1930s, for the remaining brief chapter of the memoir looks back at Hanky Park from the time and place of the 1960s demolition site that is preparing the ground for The Salford Shopping Precinct. This ending, with its comparison of the period 1900–1933 with the period of the post-war welfare state

---

38 The first quotation is from Greene's diary, 10 April 1933; the second is from his *Spectator* review, 21 April 1933, p. 579. See Sherry's *The Life of Graham Greene 1904–1939*, Vol. 1 (London: Jonathan Cape, 1989), p. 468. For discussion of *Kleiner Man Wass Nunn?* see Jenny Williams' *More Lives Than One: a Biography of Hans Fallada* (London: Libris, 1998), especially chapter five: 'Success 1931–33', pp. 114–51. There is an essay comparing the two author's novels of unemployment: A. V. Subiotto's '*Kleiner Mann-was nun?* and *Love on the Dole*: Two Novels of the Depression' in Alan F. Bance (ed.), *Weimar Germany: Writers and Politics* (Edinburgh: Scottish Academic Press, 1982), pp. 77–90.

and 1960s prosperity in particular, is clearly making a point about the ending of that impoverished world (as it seemed), and also a point about Greenwood's own life: with the publication of *Love on the Dole* he left that life behind and took up the desired life of a writer – and that is a story he does not wish to pursue in his memoirs beyond this founding point.

II. Professional Writer: 1933–1944

In fact, very few others have wished to pursue Greenwood's life as a professional writer much beyond the publication of *Love on the Dole* either. The focus of this case study is itself that important text in its three main manifestations, and my next task is to give an account of how its publication impacted on Greenwood's life – a story that his memoir leaves us to fill in very broadly for ourselves by leaping over the space between 1933 and 1966. However, I will also give a reasonable outline of his writing career up until the end of the war and a more concise account of the remainder of his career, which continued in various respects into the 1960s. If *Love on the Dole* remains his most significant work, ignoring his other work of the 1930s as well as his later work has sometimes left him as a rather contextless author – accepting in effect his own memoir's rhetorical closure of his life in 1933, and also perhaps a stereotyped view of working-class writers as able to write only a single successful work directly from experience (a view that played a considerable part in some reviewers' responses to his novels after *Love on the Dole*). It is also important to note that Greenwood's later work often referred to or reworked *Love on the Dole*, so that this work – and its 1930s origins – were often kept in readers' minds in the 1930s, 1940s, and 1950s.

The public impact of this unemployed man's novel of unemployment was striking, as we have already seen. 'Judged by the highest standards, this is an impressive, a deeply moving book', said Graham Greene in *The Spectator*.[39] Or there is the *Manchester Guardian* review, written by Harold Brighouse himself:

> We passionately desire this novel to be read; it is the real thing. Mr Greenwood is a Salford man ... he has been on the dole. He knows and he can tell ... . In a first novel he communicates with an ease which makes him, in sheer readability, the superior of most experienced novelists.[40]

39 Quoted by Croft in *Red Letter Days*, p. 108.
40 30 June 1933.

Perhaps this sympathetic response from the *Manchester Guardian* is no surprise, but papers such as the *Daily Mail* and the *Telegraph* were also positive about Greenwood's work. The *Telegraph* said that 'It brings home to us the tragedy of unemployment' and, while the *Mail* did not review the novel in 1933, looking back on it in 1944 in his *Daily Mail* literature column, Peter Quennell wrote: '*Love on the Dole* was a genuinely impassioned book – a cry of pity and indignation, a protest against the barbaric behaviours of so-called civilised society.'[41] That this positive view of the novel was widely shared is suggested by its publication history, as Andy Croft points out: 'The enthusiasm was not limited to the review pages. *Love on the Dole* went into a second imprint a month after it was published, a third in the next month, and two more in the following year.'[42]

Greenwood's life was certainly not instantly transformed, as his letter to Graham Greene suggests: soon after the novel had been published Greenwood reports that he is living on a wage of 30 shillings a week. This was presumably the now slightly increased income from his work for the clothing club. The *Daily Dispatch* reported on 15 June 1933 that Greenwood had received letters praising his novel from two well-known novelists – Graham Greene and Naomi Mitchison.[43] Subsequently, Greenwood met Naomi Mitchison (a Labour Party activist as well as author), who, according to one of her biographers, helped him negotiate an advance with Cape for *Love on the Dole* – something that made a considerable financial difference to him. However, Mitchison's other biographer says that Greenwood first met Naomi in 1934 when she was planning to write a book on slum housing and he escorted her around Salford; perhaps she was able to help him retrospectively reach a more helpful financial understanding with Cape rather than negotiate an advance?[44] As Christopher Hilliard has pointed out, even politically sympathetic publishers did not always show a good understanding of the conditions under which working-class writers produced their writing, or their need for immediate payment, so it is quite possible that Greenwood could have benefited from such an intervention.[45]

41 20 June 1933; 7 October 1944, p. 2.

42 *Red Letter Days*, p. 109. This Book Guild edition is in the author's collection.

43 See WGC/3 – vol. 1 of Greenwood's clippings book.

44 See respectively Jill Benton's *Naomi Mitchison – a Biography* (London: Pandora Press, 1990, 1992), p. 89, and Jenni Calder's *The Nine Lives of Naomi Mitchison* (London: Virago Press, 1997), p. 125.

45 See his 'Producers by Hand and by Brain: Working-Class Writers and Left-Wing

The reliability of *There Was a Time* itself has sometimes been doubted: [the memoir] 'seldom mentions specific dates and because of its strong novelistic quality, several critics have questioned its value as autobiography'.[46] Certainly there are omissions: though the support of his mother and sister is clear from the memoir, it is also said that he was encouraged by others not credited in the memoir, including the Salford Labour councillor James Openshaw and the Reverend Samuel Proudfoot, vicar of the St Thomas Church, Pendleton, in whose parish Greenwood was born. He is also said to have written much of *Love on the Dole* in the presumably conducive environment of the Ashfield Labour Club.[47] Similarly, though not referred to at all to in his memoir, an established writer, Ethel Mannin, says firmly in her own memoir of 1971 that she helped Greenwood achieve the status of author in a significant way:

> Walter Greenwood used to declare that I was his 'fairy godmother' because it was I who encouraged him to write the novel which made his name. He had sent me, out of the blue, some short stories – it is something which is liable to happen to authors ... but this was material from someone who could obviously write. I replied suggesting it be used as a novel, for I couldn't see it finding a market as short stories.[48]

Greenwood did refer clearly to her help in the 1937 'Author's Preface' to *The Cleft Stick*: 'Miss Ethel Mannin, a complete stranger to me at that

Publishers in 1930s Britain', *The Journal of Modern History*, 78, March 2006, pp. 37–64.

46 Paul W. Salmon, *Dictionary of Literary Biography Vol. 191*, p. 133, probably referring to Geoffrey Moorhouse's entry in the *DNB*.

47 According to the Working Class Movement Library website entry on Greenwood: <https://www.wcml.org.uk/our-collections/creativity-and-culture/drama-and-literature/walter-greenwood-and-love-on-the-dole/>. James Openshaw, who was Mayor of Salford in 1955–56, is also mentioned as defending Poplarism (a generous attitude to spending on unemployment benefit adopted by the council of Poplar in London) in the *Salford Reporter*, in John Henry's article on 'The Politics of Pauperism in Salford in the 1920s', *North-West Labour History Journal*, 33, pp. 27–36. *Love on the Dole* is mentioned, but only to observe correctly that it belongs to the period after the Poor Law was replaced by the later arrangements of the Public Assistance Committee. Derek Tatton, in his essay 'Literature, Culture and the Workers' Education Association', says that *Love on the Dole* began life in a WEA writing class, but does not cite any source, and I have not so far found any evidence for this (see Stephen K. Roberts (ed.), *A Ministry of Enthusiasm: Centenary Essays on the Workers' Educational Association* (London: Pluto Press, 2003), p. 250.

48 *Young in the Twenties – a Chapter of Autobiography* (London: Hutchison, 1971), p. 143.

time, was good enough to read the collection and to advise me to write a novel using some of the characters. I followed her advice and *Love on the Dole* was the consequence.'[49] The short stories were clearly those written between 1928 and 1931 that became *The Cleft Stick* and which included characters who also appear in *Love on the Dole*. Greenwood will surely have known of Mannin's leftist but in many ways romantic and popular novels and shorter fiction of the 1930s (including perhaps *Ragged Banners* and *Bruised Wings and Other Stories*, both from 1931) and presumably identified her as someone likely to be sympathetic to his stories of working-class life. The need for such help from a more established writer was, as Andy Croft has pointed out, a common pattern for working-class writers in the period.[50]

By 1934, and with whatever help from those close to home and those in the business of writing, his situation must have been changing considerably as he began to achieve his dream of making a living from his writing. *Love on the Dole* enjoyed continued success, his second novel, *His Worship the Mayor*, was accepted for publication by Cape (coming out in September of that year), and he had a number of commissions and journalistic work (including his *Old School* essay and a November 1934 story for *The London Mercury*).[51] With further professional assistance from Graham Greene and Naomi Mitchison, who sought help from the Society of Authors on his behalf, he must have gradually begun to live more comfortably and to feel that he had future prospects as a writer.[52] During 1935 he began a correspondence with Edith Sitwell, after she wrote to him praising both *Love on the Dole* and *His Worship the Mayor*, an action reinforced in public by her positive review of his writing in a *Sunday Referee* article called 'Here is a Dickens of Our Time'.[53] Sitwell wrote him a further six letters between 1935 and 1937,

49 *The Cleft Stick*, p. 9.
50 See *Red Letter Days*, pp. 178–79. After his own reputation was established, Greenwood in turn was reported by the *Salford Reporter* as acting as patron to another local working-class writer, E. A. Hibberd, whose first novel, *The Brittlesnaps*, was published by Duckworth in 1937.
51 'The Practised Hand', later included in *The Cleft Stick*. See WGC/7/2/8.
52 The article is held in the Greenwood archives at Salford University, 'The Practised Hand', WGC/7/2/8; Paul W. Salmon notes Norman Sherry's account of how Greene wrote to Naomi Mitchison about the Authors' Society and Greenwood. See respectively Johnson, *Dictionary of Literary Biography Vol. 191*, p. 134 and Norman, *The Life of Graham Greene*, Vol. 1, p. 478.
53 Eight letters from Edith Sitwell to Greenwood are held in the Greenwood Archive holdings of Correspondence (WGC/1/1/1–8). The first is dated 25 February 1935

all expressing support for his writing, often in considerable detail, and often more generally reaffirming the value of his writing, as when she says she will invite Siegfried Sassoon (from whom *Love on the Dole* takes one of its epigraphs) to see the play version, together with her brother Osbert, or when she defends him from a critical review by a 'Mr Brophy' of *The Cleft Stick*.[54] Such support must have been valuable in these early stages of his career as a writer. As we shall see, by the end of the year he had been associated with many of the most prominent liberal, left, and working-class writers of the time through being selected as a delegate to the 1935 International Writers' Congress. In May 1935 *Left Review* named Greenwood as one of the thirty-eight authors who are signatories to a 'Protest against the Jubilee' – which argued that celebration of the king's reign from 1910 to 1935 was both a poor use of public money and inappropriate given the losses of the First World War and current mass unemployment. However, apart from a mention in August 1935, Greenwood is not thereafter referred to at all in *Left Review* and it reviewed no more of his novels after A. L. Lloyd's mainly negative review of *His Worship the Mayor* in November 1934 – though Edgell Rickword, co-editor of *Left Review*, much later recalled Greenwood's work as ground-breaking: 'Until *Love on the Dole* there wasn't much expression of the situation.'[55] Further journalistic commissions followed elsewhere in 1935, including two pieces for *The Spectator* in 1935 and 1936 (one on 'Poverty and Freedom', the other called simply 'On the Dole') and in March 1935 a (critically unnoticed) short story for the TUC periodical, *Labour – a Magazine for All Workers*, called 'Return of a Revolutionary'.[56]

In February 1935 the *Salford Reporter* in its regular 'Salford Men and Matters' column noted that Greenwood had been a guest on the

---

and the last 26 December 1941. The *Sunday Referee* article was published on 24 February 1935 (WGC/3/34/2).

54 See WGC/2/1/1, 2/1/7. There is a further letter from Renishaw Hall, the Sitwell's house in Derbyshire, dated 26 December 1944. 'Mr Brophy' had said of *The Cleft Stick* that Greenwood was 'not an artist but a competent popular journalist'. Sitwell included in her letter to Greenwood the letter she had written to the *Daily Telegraph* dissenting from this view and stating that instead Greenwood was 'not only an artist, but an exceedingly fine artist' (WGC/2/1/7).

55 See *Left Review*, I, 8, May 1935, p. 191; I, 11, August 1935, p. 463; and I, 2, November 1934; see Alan Young and Michael Schmidt, 'A Conversation with Edgell Rickword', *Poetry Nation*, I, 1973, pp. 1–9, p. 8: <http://www.pnreview. co.uk/cgi-bin/scribe?item_id=3979>, accessed 26 October 2017.

56 (London: TUC, March 1935), pp. 150–51.

BBC radio programme 'In Town Tonight', where 'he spoke briefly but interestingly of his early days of struggle ... [and] then the writing of *Love on the Dole* in all sorts of odd corners, upon scraps of paper, including wall paper'.[57] This clearly suggests Greenwood's status as a topical and nationally known figure – indeed, his name and works recur a number of times in the BBC periodical *The Listener* between 1933 and 1941 – in 1935 he features with other authors in a substantial discussion by W. E. Williams of two different kinds of contemporary fiction: that with more inward-looking aesthetic concerns, and that which, like *Love on the Dole*, focuses on 'concern for the world's griefs and inequalities'.[58] In fact, Greenwood's BBC radio profile has been under-estimated in discussions of the reach of his public reputation in the 1930s and afterwards: the Northern Region broadcast an eight-minute extract consisting of the whole of Act Two, Scene Two from *Love on the Dole* as early as March 1936, and also broadcast a fifteen-minute extract from *Give Us This Day* (the stage adaptation of *His Worship the Mayor*) the same year.[59]

Other things also became possible for him: in 1933 he stood in the local council elections in the Seedley Ward (adjoining Pendleton to the West), but lost to the Liberals (by 1,400 votes to 1,000), who were the current holders of the ward. Greenwood's election leaflet contains an address that bears considerable resemblance to that of Larry in *Love on the Dole* in squarely blaming the voters:

> The people responsible for the present chaos in affairs local and national are yourselves. It was your votes which placed the National Government in office; it was your votes which gave the Tory-Liberal-Independent Coalition their present majority in the Council Chamber. Consequently you are all directly responsible for the present cuts in the social services.[60]

57 See WGC/3/3, p. 34.
58 Reported in an article 'Salford Men and Matters' in the *Salford City Reporter*, 15 February 1935 (a copy is in WGC3/34/1). *The Listener* carried a number of adverts for Cape, including for the cheaper Florin editions, in which both *Love on the Dole* and *His Worship the Mayor* were reprinted (see, for example, 10 April 1935, p. vii and 14 April 1937, p. 721). W. E. Williams' article is 'Style and Purpose in Literature', 24 July 1935, pp. 169–70.
59 BBC Written Archive, Walter Greenwood Scriptwriter, File 1, 1934–62, letter from Greenwood agreeing terms for himself and on behalf of Gow (20 February 1936); Walter Greenwood File 1, RCONT1, 1936–1962, letter from Copyright Section to Greenwood, 31 February 1936. It was a Northern region broadcast scheduled for 2 April 1936.
60 Leaflet in author's collection (the Greenwood archive also has a copy) dated 12 October 1933.

As Matthew Worley, the historian of the Labour Party, observes, 'In Salford ... there existed a number of obstacles to the extension of Labour support amongst its poorest inhabitants [for example] ... the threat of increased rates and rents appear to have limited the party's appeal in the town's "slum" districts.'[61] Nevertheless, Greenwood stood again the following year in the desperately poor St Matthias ward, winning it for Labour by 750 votes.[62] Greenwood remained a city councillor for a year and drew heavily on that experience for his second novel, *His Worship the Mayor* (the *Salford Reporter* records that a fellow Labour councillor, W. W. Crabtree, played a part in the eventual Manchester Repertory Theatre play version of this second novel and suggested some improvements to its Means Test scene).[63] The novel tells a story of local politics through a narrative focused on the rise to influence of Edgar Hargreaves, a tailor whom it suits the local elite of the Two Cities to support, initially for their own ends. Edgar's experience is up to a point based on Greenwood's, though Edgar is without any political belief beyond one that he should have his share of the advantages accruing to the ruling clique of the city. Unlike *Love on the Dole* (which does little to justify its 'Tale of Two Cities' sub-title), the novel does show a wider social panorama than just the microcosm of Hanky Park, and particularly shows the world of commercial success and local politics in parallel to the lives of the poverty-stricken and the unemployed:

> Acres of plate glass glare forth with electrical extravagance when darkness descends ... as though the street is making a concentrated endeavour to divert one from making the accidental discovery of crouching slumdom behind.
>
> For it *is* there, this slumdom ... a shabby, ugly, obscene consort to the Two Cities' worldwide reputation of boundless wealth ... and like ragged skirts the dreary acres of dilapidated slumdom spread out in all directions, a mocking, derisive and damning indictment of the practical application of that economic theory to which Manchester gave its name.[64]

61 *Labour Inside the Gate – a History of the British Labour Party Between the Wars* (London: I. B. Tauris, 2000), p. 43.
62 Information drawn from Working Class Movement Library website entry on Greenwood: <https://www.wcml.org.uk/our-collections/creativity-and-culture/drama-and-literature/walter-greenwood-and-love-on-the-dole/>, accesssed 9 January 2017.
63 'Councillor's New Role', short article published 6 December 1935 (WGC3/34/5).
64 (London: Jonathan Cape, 1934), p. 12; all subsequent references are to this edition and will be given in brackets in the text.

The novel shows that there is much that needs attending to, but has little faith in the will of local politicians and their hangers-on (what are here called 'Progressives' are presumably meant to represent Liberals) to address anything but their own ambitions:

> Frequently horse-drawn lorries passed whose sides were decorated with huge calico banners saying: 'HARGREAVES. The People's Friend,' and such like; lorries full of dirty, ragged, ill-fed slum-children waving penny Union jacks and singing … . Mr Crawley … said, with a gesture towards the songsters: 'You see, Edgar, the distribution of cast-off clothing to the unemployed is paying a good dividend.' (p. 156)

In some respects Winifred Holtby's novel *South Riding*, published in 1936, which also took local government as its theme, similarly sees local politicians as often motivated by self-interest, but it also suggested that civic and social progress can be made through even these imperfect instruments.[65] Such unintended consequences have little place in the more cynical story of *His Worship The Mayor*, which sees Sam Grundy as, if anything, one of the more honest of the elected officials of Salford:

> Sam Grundy, the bookie … was standing as Progressive candidate … . Everybody knew Sam … 'I ain't no eddicated feller … I'm just plain Honest Sam Grundy … with a motto, "Sky's the limit" and all paid fair and square and no argyment'. Holding aloft his election address written by Mr Crawley: 'An I'll do all it says on t'paper.' (p. 157)

One wonders if this treatment of local democracy, even if aimed primarily at Conservative and Liberals, did much to please Greenwood's friends in the local Labour Party (not to mention the vicar of St Thomas, Pendleton, given the collusive role in the novel of the Vicar of the 'Ward of St Margaret' [p. 148]). The novel's sympathies are mainly focused on the unemployed miner, Jo Shuttleworth, who cannot believe that the local pit is shutting forever: 'Jo Shuttleworth was looking at the men demolishing the head-stocks. It frightened him … he could hardly grasp the significance of what he saw' (p. 162). This novel, too, was generally well reviewed by newspapers and periodicals with widely differing viewpoints.

---

65 For some discussion of Winfred Holtby's representation of local government see Chapter 1 of my *English Fiction in the 1930s* and my chapter '"Frustrated Spinsters" and "Morbid Degenerates"? Women and Men in Winifred Holtby's *Truth is Not Sober* (1934)', in *A Woman in Her Time: Winifred Holtby in Context*, ed. Lisa Regan (Cambridge: Scholar's Press, 2010).

As Andy Croft notes, the independent Marxist adult education journal *Plebs* praised the novel for its 'implicit condemnation of social injustice' and argued that it was likely to be 'worth 1,000 Socialist propaganda speeches'.[66] It was also liked by the *Daily Telegraph* reviewer, who thought it 'magnificent' and 'not an inch behind that grand book' [*Love on the Dole*], and who seems to read Hargreaves' story as well as that of the Shuttleworth family with sympathy: 'Mr Greenwood gives us a double story of a struggling little draper who, through a legacy and graft, becomes Lord Mayor of the Two Cities, and of the heart-rending struggles of an unemployed miner and his family for mere existence.'[67]

Despite the general critique of local politics, however, Hargreaves' thoughts about his entry into a new world may also reflect something of the changes which Greenwood too was experiencing at this period: 'He revolved hitherto unsuspected pleasant aspects of his present environment. New significances, potentialities began slowly to unfold; a strange sense of unhampered freedom, of there being no obligation to stay in the Two Cities against his will' (p. 196). Greenwood's status as a politically committed working-class writer certainly led to what may have been his first trip abroad in 1935, when, as Andy Croft notes, he travelled to the International Writers' Congress in Paris, which was particularly dedicated to opposing the growing menace of fascism: 'The British delegation of E. M. Forster, Aldous Huxley, John Strachey, Christina Stead, Ralph Fox, Walter Greenwood, Winifred Holtby, Storm Jameson, Naomi Mitchison and James Hanley met with writers from 38 other countries.'[68]

His entry into celebrity enabled him to come to the attention of a wide range of variously influential people over the next few years, many but not all on the left. Thus a full-page article by Hannen Swaffer about the play version of *Love on the Dole* in the *Daily Herald* on 1 February 1935 lists a number of people who have explicitly praised the play to him, including 'Herbert Morrison, Gordon Selfridge, Lord Ronsonby, Susan Lawrence, Dick Mitchison, Lady Cripps, Jim Middleton and Dick Sheppard' (who asked to be introduced to the author).[69]

---

66 The first quotation is Croft's interpretation of the views of the periodical, the second is a verbatim quotation from *Plebs* itself. See *Red Letter Days*, p. 248.
67 Quoted on the dust jacket of the novel.
68 *Red Letter Days*, p. 51.
69 See WGC/3/1. It is likely that Greenwood subsequently met Arthur Wragg through Dick Sheppard.

Morrison, Lawrence, Middleton, Lady Cripps, and Dick Mitchison (Naomi's husband) were all strongly linked to the Labour Party, Sheppard was a pacifist (and at this point in the process of founding the Peace Pledge Union), and Gordon Selfridge was, of course, a successful (for the moment) capitalist who had founded the famous department store. *Tribune* reported on 28 May 1937 that Greenwood was the guest at a reception where he met Professor Harold Laski, the left-wing writer and public intellectual, the more conservative travel writer, Stephen Graham, and Kingsley Martin, founding editor of the labour/dissenting left periodical *New Statesman and Nation*. It is worth noting that the success of his more political novels did not make Greenwood feel that he must separate himself from other forms of popular culture: in 1937 he contributed 'additional dialogue' to a revue, *It's in the Bag* (by Cecil Landeau and George Frank Rubens), which tried out at the Manchester Palace. The *Daily Mail* claimed this was a 'rebellion' against being labelled a 'writer of sordid, low-life dramas'.[70] The *Manchester Guardian* reviewer liked a number of the performers (who included Margaret Rutherford and Doris Hare) and several of the songs, but felt that the story, which was meant to link (fairly loosely) the sketches and musical numbers, was in need of urgent pruning.[71] However, the revue did move to the Saville Theatre in London and was regarded by an American reviewer as an 'instantaneous success'.[72] Presumably Greenwood's contribution bought in some further income.

Some acquaintances were apparently worried about his sudden fame, his displacement from his own class, and, indeed, his interest in the world of entertainment. His collaborator-to-be Arthur Wragg records in a letter to Canon Dick Sheppard his own and the prominent Labour politician Stafford Cripps' concerns about Greenwood:

> [Cripps] says that W.G. [sic] is in danger of having his head turned by success & that I must keep in touch with him 'and keep him up to the mark' … he asks me to remember what obscurity in the past must mean to anyone like W.G. once success comes … he said that the old friends, who still suffered, had estranged themselves subtly from W.G. and his success … and therefore that he needed friends who could appreciate all this & exchange ideas with

70 'Mr Greenwood Rebels', Harold Conroy, *Daily Mail* 11 September 1937, p. 6.
71 *Manchester Guardian* 13 October 1937. *The Stage* explains that Greenwood was responsible for 'additional dialogue' and that the revue was novel precisely because there was a story to link the sketches and songs together (14 October 1937, p. 13).
72 Bert Ross in *The Billboard*, 4 December 1937.

him … . Cripps is afraid that a fine mentality which W.G. has is meeting too many people in film & theatre who worship his success.

The letter is, like all of Wragg's letters, undated, but clearly comes after Wragg and Greenwood had been introduced and before they had actually started work on *The Cleft Stick*, and so was probably written in 1935 or possibly 1936. Wragg is conscious that the patrician and wealthy Cripps is their patron and indeed that there may be an element of the patronising: [Cripps] 'may be too fond of "looking after one" & "instructing".'[73] It seems unlikely that Greenwood would have found this anxiety about contact with the world of popular entertainment sympathetic and another 1936 letter from Greenwood suggests, on the contrary, his relish for the successful entertainer. The letter is written from Gracie Fields' villa, Canzone del Mare in Capri, telling a friend about 'this magic villa' and explaining that 'the nuisance is I've got to come home. Gracie told me to stay on for 6 months!'[74]

One further consequence of his fame and relative fortune was a change in his personal plans, which in due course took him away from Salford for good. In 1934 he was sued for breach of promise by Alice Myles, his fiancée at the time of publication of *Love on the Dole*, and, according to Greenwood's *Dictionary of National Biography* entry, a model for Sally Hardcastle. He had broken off the engagement before meeting an American Broadway dancer, singer, and actress who took film roles in two movies released during 1933 and who had also appeared in the musicals *The One Girl* at the London Hippodrome and *That's a Pretty Thing* at Daly's Theatre in New York, both during 1933; she is said by one US newspaper to have insured her legs for '$100,000 and saw that the newspapers heard about it' while appearing at Daly's.[75] This was Pearl Alice Osgood – Greenwood met her at a

---

73 Photocopy of letter identified by a later marking as letter 'R45', part of the V&A Archive's holdings of Wragg's uncatalogued papers: AAD/2004/8 (folder labelled 'Good copies of some of Raggie's Letters to Dick'). The letter is from The Warren Polperro and includes a long discussion of Cripps' views of Greenwood on pp. 2–3.

74 Letter in author's possession, undated, but referring to the upcoming rehearsal of Greenwood's one act play *The Practised Hand* in July 1936, which was the reason why Greenwood had shortly to return home from Capri. The letter is addressed to 'Hannah' and was kept in association with a first edition of *Love on the Dole*, inscribed by Greenwood to a Henrietta Russell, August 1933.

75 Her Broadway credits include *Ziegfield Follies* of 1931, while her film credits are *For Love of You* and *Yours Sincerely*. In the latter movie she sang two songs that were commercial hits in 1933. The second film was made by Warner Brothers

theatrical party while visiting New York in April 1936 to assist at the new Broadway production of the play of *Love on the Dole*.[76] When asked by newspaper reporters in 1937, Greenwood simply said: 'I met Miss Osgood when I was in New York for the production there of *Love on the Dole*.'[77] Breach of promise (that is, the breaking of a promise to marry) carried legal consequences for men partly because an engagement was considered to be a legal contract and partly because such a breach was generally very damaging to a woman's reputation and hence financial and matrimonial prospects. Alice Myles' legal case against Greenwood was reported in *The Salford Reporter* ('Action Against City Councillor', 22 November 1934) and followed up the next week with a report that he had settled out of court: 'Breach of Promise Action settled' (29 November 1934). A striking detail of the settlement featured in the sub-headline may suggest that Greenwood was really quite well off by this time: 'City Councillor to pay £700 damages and costs' (remember that his first professional writing fee of twenty-five guineas was, he reckoned, enough for him to survive on for six months).[78] Some press reports were less accurate – the *Washington Post* reported that 'Arthur Greenwood' was 'almost back on the dole' after Alice Myles was awarded '£3,500 damages'.[79] Greenwood seems to have given Alice a copy of the first edition of *Love on the Dole* with the inscription 'To my dear Alice in remembrance of "all our yesterdays". Walter. August 19th 1933', so presumably the breach between

in the US, while the first was a British film made by Windsor. See IMDB <http://uk.imdb.com/name/nm0651880/> and IBDB <http://www.ibdb.com/person.php?id=55236>, accessed 26 October 2017. *The One Girl* was reviewed in *The Times* on 22 February 1933 and was said to benefit from a strong cast, including 'the amusing vitality of Pearl Osgood, who immensely enjoys herself as a would-be siren' (accessed via *The Times Archive*, 12 July 2010). The US *Star* newspaper (22 September 1937) tells the story of her insuring her legs as part of its coverage of her wedding to Greenwood (see WGC/3/1). Pearl later acted in some of Greenwood's stage plays.

76 His visit to New York is reported by the *New York Post* (25 April 1936), who arranged for him to visit an unemployed New York family to see their standard of living while on relief: Greenwood is reported as concluding that 'the standard of destitution is higher' in the US. See WGC/3/1.

77 *Manchester Evening News* 23 September 1937. See WGC/3/1.

78 See Greenwood archive WGC/3/34/3 and WGC/34/4 <http://www.salford.ac.uk/__data/assets/xml_file/0007/530476/Greenwood.xml>, accessed 9 January 2017.

79 29 December 1935. Arthur Greenwood was, of course, a Labour MP and at this time Deputy Leader of the Labour Party.

them went back to the year of publication of his novel.[80] He and Pearl married in London on 22 September 1937 – the wedding was keenly reported in both British and US papers, suggesting that he and Pearl had a considerable joint-celebrity status (Arthur Wragg, the illustrator of *The Cleft Stick* and a celebrity in his own right, was best man).[81] Some reporting was fairly frivolous: the *Daily Mail* could not resist 'Love (not) on the Dole', while the *Daily Dispatch* reported that after the wedding Pearl said '"Eee, I am glad", uttered in a mock Lancashire accent'. Another (unidentified) paper reported that afterwards Pearl had visited Walter's birthplace (Ellor Street) and quoted what is in effect her more serious, but rather optimistic, reading of his novel: 'Perhaps Walter was right after all in *Love on the Dole*. I think Salford people are wonderful to be so plucky and spick-and-span. They've got back-street courage. But something should be done to find better homes for them.'[82] Pearl subsequently appeared in some of Greenwood's plays, including the stage version of *Only Mugs Work* in 1939.[83]

These personal developments were also partly the basis for his third novel, which also dealt, if in a distinctly comic mode, with Greenwood's transformation into a professional writer. *Standing Room Only or 'a Laugh in Every Line'* was published by Jonathan Cape in 1936. The *Times Literary Supplement* reviewer thought it:

A pity that he has been lured from Manchester and Salford; his previous books have made him a name as a chronicler of contemporary life ... but in his new book he deserts reality and gives pictures of a world in which he is as little at home as his hero Henry Ormerod ... the chicanery which goes on behind the scenes should be interesting to youthful playwrights if not to the general public.[84]

80 Information found in description of this 'association copy' of *Love on the Dole* on the website of the Antiquarian Booksellers Association, seller Nigel Williams Rare Books (see <http://www.aba.org.uk/dole.html>, accessed 24 June 2010).

81 Greenwood's clippings book has several pages of articles from both UK and US newspapers reporting the wedding. The *Manchester City News* (24 September 1937) reports that Arthur Wragg was best man.

82 *Daily Dispatch* in WGC/3/2, p. 42; second quotation is from an unattributed clipping, p. 42, perhaps dating from 24 November 1934.

83 See Greenwood archive items under WGC/3/13/1–37 (reviews of the stage version of *Only Mugs Work* from March 1939).

84 *Times Literary Supplement* 18 July 1936, p. 598. The reviewer is Leonora Eyles, who specialised in reviewing 'New novels, cookery, slums and social problems; sex & marriage'. Article and reviewer information accessed via the *TLS Centenary Archive*.

There are several things to say about this response to the novel, which in several ways might be said to deny Greenwood the possession of his own experience. It clearly identifies Greenwood as a 'chronicler' – a recorder – of working-class life in Salford and Manchester, but seems unwilling to give him much credit as a creative writer who has to sustain a career as a professional author. Could he simply write (and could he get a publisher to publish?) another novel 'chronicling' life in Salford without some development, some shift in angle or viewpoint? As a matter of fact, the novel does not simply abandon Salford, for much of it is set there, including much of its exploration of the world of the theatre and, indeed the *business* of theatre, which was by no means alien to the life of the two Cities. What the reviewer seems to mean is that this novel does move on from the Salford that she would want to see again – a Salford that symbolises only urban working-class poverty. The idea that Greenwood 'deserts reality' presupposes that Hanky Park is the only reality to which such a writer can have access. While lamenting what the book is not about, the comment that the novel 'gives pictures of a world in which [Greenwood] is as little at home as his hero Henry Ormerod' does almost catch what it is actually doing. For if it is not another *Love on the Dole*, *Standing Room Only* does engage in its own way with the question of the status of a working-class writer and with the problem of deracination that Greenwood had already begun to hint at in *His Worship the Mayor*. Ben Harker's argument about Greenwood as a professional author is borne out (if not for its fictional playwright Henry Ormerod) by the kinds of issue broached in *Standing Room Only*: 'Greenwood, like his text, proved adaptable; he was not a proletarian dupe fleeced of his work by an unscrupulous culture industry, but an emerging professional writer actively participating in the re-articulation of his text.'[85] Henry Ormerod is clearly based to an extent on Greenwood himself and on his own recent transformation from unemployed working man to author, and contemporary readers would surely have recognised this. However, the novel's would-be author does not have the support of his family. Henry lives with his mother, works at a drapers called Duckworth's (presumably based to an extent on Greenwood's experience at Battersby's), and is, without evident enthusiasm on his part, identified as a likely husband by Edna Armstrong, also a Duckworth's employee. Henry's ambition to be a playwright is especially scorned by his mother and Edna, who jointly regard it as both unachievable and a delusion

---

85 'Adapting to the Conjuncture', p. 56.

that distracts him from fulfilling the roles of satisfactory son, fiancé, and breadwinner. Their sustained campaign against Henry's alleged lack of realism about his talents brings out sharply their view that the very act of harbouring such a desire is transgressive – a dereliction of his proper class identity and a pointless aping of his betters:

> You spend too much time talking to that Mrs Duckworth. She's no right to encourage you as she does. And I don't think Mr Duckworth likes it, either. What does she want, putting ideas into your head and lending you play books. It's only wasting your time. You've got to be *educated* to write plays ... .[86]

However, Henry can counter-attack by implicitly pointing out that actually people they know *do* go in for drama, as keen members of an amateur drama society, and that they have already performed his play along with those of serious (and popular) playwrights: 'Dilys Richmond says its the best part she's *ever* had. And she's played lead in nearly *all* the plays the Society's put on. *And* we've done Shaw and Galsworthy' (p. 27).[87]

This kind of conflict between Henry and his kith and kin may draw on some of the differences between his father and mother that Greenwood later explored in his memoir. For, if Elizabeth Greenwood fully supported her son's writing of serious fiction, the scenario is somewhat altered in this novel merely by making Henry a writer of a play. Mrs Ormerod suspects his play of being part of what she regards as a more frivolous tradition of theatrical entertainment. It is the influence of Mr Ormerod she fears most: 'Your father had ambitions. And what became of him? ... Gave up a safe job in the warehouse to dress himself up like an idiot and act like a fool on the stage ... . Home life? Ha! Once in a blue moon he comes home' (pp. 29–30). Ormerod Senior is, in fact, a musical hall or variety artiste, whose 'turn' as 'a juggling act' means he is very little at home (p. 81). Henry's play, on the other hand, is clearly 'legitimate theatre' in the sense that it is a complete play rather than an 'act' or 'turn', but it is also very plainly an 'entertainment', a comedy, so that its place in a cultural hierarchy of seriousness is ambiguous. This is an issue at the centre of the novel and, it seems reasonable to guess, very

---

86 *Standing Room Only, or 'A Laugh in Every Line'* (originally published London: Jonathan Cape, 1936; reprinted London: Howard Baker, 1970), pp. 26–27. All subsequent references are to this 1970 edition and will be given in the text.

87 See also below, note 91, for further discussion of the Dylis Richmond character.

much part of Greenwood's negotiation of his own experience as a newly published author who needed to continue to find his way in the business of making a living through his writing. Indeed, when Greenwood's fiction works were listed on the dust jackets of later editions, such as that of his 1944 novel, *Something in My Heart*, they were divided into 'novels' and 'entertainments', a distinction perhaps derived from Graham Greene's similar categorisation of his output (*Standing Room Only* is listed as an 'entertainment', as is *Only Mugs Work*).

However, if his commitment to writing as 'social reform' was important, each of his works up to this point had also incorporated much that was likely to be entertaining as well as instructive, including a strong comic strand. And, despite the *TLS*, *Standing Room Only* was generally well received – the Chief Librarian of the Wellington Public Libraries in New Zealand, for example, thought it had 'all the qualities which made *Love on the Dole* such a success' and chose it as his Book of the Week in a newspaper review in 1936. It is significant that he ended his review by emphasising that Greenwood's writing provided 'entertainment of the best kind', a view also articulated somewhat more cautiously by Sheffield's influential City Librarian, J. P. Lamb, in a report on the value of both 'classical' and 'semi-standard' fiction stock held in the city in 1936–37:

> the semi-standard group includes … scores of modern writers of considerable gifts – Vera Brittain, Ethel Mannin, Russell Green, P. Bottome, E. Boileau and W. Greenwood – for example … they give mental refreshment to highly-intelligent and well-read library-borrrowers, they are 'introductory readers' to those newly finding an interest in reading … they widen vocabulary, extend horizons, stimulate ideas, and often add factual knowledge.[88]

Of the three further novels Greenwood published before the outbreak of war, two at least might be said to have a predominance of entertainment over instruction, and draw strongly on popular genres. Thus *Standing Room Only* is a comedy set in theatre-land, with a strong romance interest, while *Only Mugs Work* (1938) is a gangster novel, which adapts an American hard-boiled mode to the streets of London, though its ending is strongly romantic. His third pre-war novel, *The Secret Kingdom*,

---

88 *Evening Post* (Wellington), 24 October 1936, p. 28; the 80th Annual Sheffield City Libraries Report (1936–37), 'The Reading of Fiction', was located and drawn to my attention by Val Hewson – the full report can be read on the *Reading Sheffield* website: <http://www.readingsheffield.co.uk/the-reading-of-fiction-sheffield-city-libraries-80th-annual-report-1936–37/>, accessed 4 January 2018.

also of 1938, does return to Salford as its pre-dominant setting and is the most evidently committed of these works, with its focus on the life of the socialist Byron family (nevertheless, it too has a firmly romance-based plot and emotional atmosphere). Greenwood, needing to maintain both his income and standing as a professional author, may have been exploring, with sometimes mixed success, how he might sustain his writing career using popular or middlebrow genres during these years.

Standing Room Only may then be in itself a less 'serious' work than *Love on the Dole*, but it also begins to explore through comedy some of the challenges that a newly arrived working-class writer might meet. First of all, there is the question of who controls the financial aspects of the writer's own labour. Henry Ormerod (somewhat like Greenwood with the typescript of the novel of *Love on the Dole*) has sent his play to two different theatrical agents, who are long-time rivals. However, one, McPherson, accepts the play not so much because he is impressed with the play's original genius as because it suits his plans to manipulate a wealthy patron into backing a play as a vehicle for a starlet in whom he is interested. The other impresario, Henry Ellis, is motivated by rivalry and through taking at face value his sneaked glance at the flattering acceptance letter that McPherson has sent to Henry Ormerod.

In fact, McPherson has a reader's report on the play that suggests that the play has some potential, but will also need rewriting: 'This could be made into a highly diverting play' (p. 35). His rival Henry Ellis takes the same view, feeling it needs the attention of a 'play doctor',[89] whose job it is to work up submitted play scripts into a satisfactory form for commercial production. Such a procedure immediately undermines the notion of the author as originating genius and sole source of artistic origin, and, indeed, suggests that the author of the play script is not its absolute owner.

The play doctor theme recalls, and is presumably based to an extent upon, Greenwood's own experience with the adaptation of the novel of *Love on the Dole* into a play – since he was, indeed, not sole author of

---

89 *OED* defines the term as meaning 'a professional improver of other people's plays', and gives the first recorded usage as having a US source: 'If Shakespeare lived today he would have waited four years to have his first comedy read and accepted, after which it would have been re-written by the stage-carpenter and the leading lady and put on … with a play doctor in the rear of the theater keeping track of the laughs with a hand comptometer' (*Evening Telegram*, Elyria, Ohio, 2/3 July 1912).

the play version of what was indisputably his novel. All editions of the play bear the following attribution of authorship:

Love on the Dole

A Play in Three Acts

By RONALD GOW & WALTER GREENWOOD

(Adapted from WALTER GREENWOOD's novel of the same name).

Ronald Gow was a teacher at Altrincham Grammar School during the 1920s and 1930s (Altrincham being part of the Manchester Metropolitan Borough of Trafford). He had become interested in using film for educational purposes and wrote and made several such films during the 1920s. In the 1930s he had a number of short plays performed on BBC radio and subsequently published, and then had a success with his play, *Glorious Gallows*, about the slavery abolitionist John Brown (produced in London in 1933 and New York in 1934, published by the leftist publisher Gollancz in 1933, and followed by a US film version in 1938[90]). A photograph exists of Gow acting in a 1930 production by the Altrincham Garrick Society amateur drama group, and, indeed, the Society had performed a number of Gow's own plays over the previous decade.[91] As a local amateur actor and a successful playwright Gow

---

90 *The Playwrights' Database* lists useful information about Gow's long career, plays and publications – see <http://www.doollee.com/PlaywrightsG/gow-ronald. html#14170>, accessed 16 February 2010. Some brief information about Ronald Gow is given in Alex Jennings' *DNB* entry for Dame Wendy Hiller, who married Gow after starring as Sally in the play of *Love on the Dole*; there is some further information about Gow's film career on the IMDB database: <http://www.imdb. com/name/nm0332921/>, accessed 2 February 2010.

91 The photograph of Gow shows him in *Song of* Drums by Ashley Dukes (first published by Ernest Benn in 1926), and a list of productions shows that the Society performed ten plays by Gow between 1921 and 1934 – when his success with *Love on the Dole* presumably took his attention elsewhere. The productions included one of *Gallows Glorious* in the 1932–33 season. It is interesting to note that Galsworthy and Shaw were popular playwrights for the Altrincham Garrick Society, which accords with Henry Ormerod's implication that these are favourite 'serious' authors for an amateur drama society of the period. Harold Brighouse was another favourite at the Altrincham Garrick. See Pamela Knox's *The Flame Still Burns – the Story of Altrincham Garrick Theatre* (Altrincham: Altrincham Garrick Theatre,1993), p. 15 and pp. 101–02.

presumably had contacts with the Manchester Repertory Theatre, then based at the Rusholme Theatre:[92] certainly, it was his idea to adapt the Salford novel as a play for the Manchester theatre company. Thus Gow invited Greenwood to a meeting: '"Watch out for a hungry-looking chap with a red tie", he wrote': 'Over coffee we agreed about the play ... but with one condition. We were to make money out of it, so it mustn't be a high-brow piece. I think he had an idea I was some sort of egg-head!'[93] In fact, Gow's agent, Lawrence Fitch, told Greenwood that, though it was brilliant, he would eat his hat if such a play made any money during the Depression (Fitch later said he was grateful not to be held to this).[94] Perhaps, there was a sense on Greenwood's part that there were class and educational differences between Gow and himself and that he was having to share his own work, which was already selling well (Gow remained keen to make clear the co-authorship, asserting it in a letter to the BBC in 1960).[95] At any rate, in the *Standing Room Only* reworking of the motif Henry Ormerod's play is taken over by the producer Mr Ellis (who persuades Henry to sign his contract before meeting with his rival McPherson) and his play doctor: 'Here's my offer. Fifty pounds down for six months' option on the play ... providing you'll agree to collaborate with one of my play doctors' (p. 59). Ellis has already, as part of his pitch, apparently sympathised with Ormerod's position as a working-class writer: 'It's a marvel to me ... that you've done as well as you have

92 For an account of the Rusholme Theatre see the Arthur Lloyd History of Music Hall and Theatre website: <http://www.arthurlloyd.co.uk/ManchesterTheatres/RusholmeTheatreManchester.htm>; and the Rusholme and Victoria Park Archive website <http://rusholmearchive.org/a-tour-of-wilmslow-road>, both accessed 20 February 2011.

93 According to the quotation of this account by Gow in a *TV Times* article by Laurence Marcus about the 19 January 1967 Granada TV adaptation of the story, starring Anne Stallybrass as Sally. See <http://www.televisionheaven.co.uk/love_on_the_dole.htm>, accessed 2 February 2010. There is an account of the meeting differing in some details in a solo interview given by Gow to the *New York Times* 23 February 1935, from which the quotation about the red tie comes. Greenwood's red tie (or one of them) has recently turned up for sale together with a signed first edition of *Love on the Dole* (now in author's collection, purchased from J and M Books, Towcester).

94 Obituary of Ronald Gow by Lawrence Fitch, *The Guardian* 10 May 1993.

95 BBC Written Archive, Caversham Park, Ronald Gow Copyright File 1, 1927–1962. In a memo (25 February 1960) from Gow to the Head of Copyright and Editor of Radio Times, he asks that the forthcoming (24 April 1969) TV adaptation of *Love on the Dole* be jointly credited in all publicity, and not credited to 'Walter Greenwood alone'.

done ... . I'd like to see the kind of stuff those play doctors of mine'd turn out if *they* had to work like you' (p. 58).

In this instance the play doctor is a Miss Helen Carlisle, who in fact has somewhat higher standards of behaviour than Mr Ellis, asking him: '"Have you got the author's consent to the revisions?"' (p. 19). Ellis replies, '"Don't worry about the author."' Nevertheless, like everyone else, Helen Carlisle needs to take her cut: '"I'll do it as soon as he gives consent ... and I'll want the usual agreement: an eighty-twenty division of royalty with the customary advance"'. As it turns out, Helen Carlisle has socialist sympathies and has even read the pamphlet on 'Artists and the Collective System' (p. 133) written by the novel's leftist theatre director, Roger Morden. Nevertheless, phrases such as 'on condition that', 'providing that' and so on are frequent in Henry's negotiations with those who will transform his play-text into public performance, with Henry nearly always in an inferior position. It is Ellis who makes the '"library deal for five thousand quid"', who decides on '"a touring show ... *two* companies ... twice nightly we'll run it"', and who commissions the play-doctor to cut the touring version to 'two hours including interval' (pp. 228–29). Thus Henry loses control of the text of his play and also of its finances, with everyone taking far more money out of it than he does (even his father, returning from touring his music hall act, insists on being Henry's agent, on taking his 5 per cent commission and, in short, on offering his 'lifelong experience in matters theatrical' [p. 81]).

Henry is, in return, though, transported to London's theatre-land and a world of apparently Hollywoodesque glamour and intrigue. Meeting his Salford acquaintance, the former amateur actress Dilys Richmond, who is to be cast as the leading lady in his play, 'He breathed the faint perfume which hung about her: it was delicious; he eyed appreciatively, the set of her shoulders and the blonde knot of hair done stylishly at the nape of her neck' (p. 124).[96] However, he soon finds that class issues

96 Dilys Richmond's story perhaps draws on the career of Ruth Dunning, a member of the Altrincham Garrick Playhouse's amateur company, who in 1934 was cast as Sally Hardcastle at the Garrick Theatre, London, in her first professional role, taking over from Wendy Hiller when she went to New York for the first US production of *Love on the Dole*. Ruth Dunning went on to a long and successful TV and film career, being especially remembered as Mrs Grove in *The Grove Family* (BBC TV 1954–57), a TV serial which has been described as the first British 'soap'. See Knox, *The Flame Still Burns*, pp. 25 and 100 and filmography on the IMDB: <http://www.imdb.com/name/nm0242959/>, accessed 16 February 2010).

are not left behind just because he is now an 'author': 'Dilys, he saw, was fraternising with Rupert Fotheringay, her leading man ... wryly he supposed she was taken in by his being a West End star. Eighty quid a week for a profile, a university accent, and enough sex appeal to thrill the women' (p. 132). Moreover, Rupert is not the only rival – there is also Sir Walter Brierley,[97] who has financed the show precisely with the aim of making Dilys 'grateful' to him, and finally Lord Donithorne. Despite Henry's romantic interest in Dilys, it all becomes too much for him – the constant intrigues, the financial advantage everyone seems to expect to extract from the play – and soon the most comforting word he can imagine is 'home': 'The moment Henry sat down in the train he felt happier: it was as though he had left London far behind.'

In the end Henry agrees, in a moment of inattention, so glad is he to be home, to marry Edna. However, he lacks any real commitment and, indeed, their new suburban home, funded by the weekly royalty cheques from his play, which is at last bringing him some money too, is not what he meant by the word 'home'. The truth is that he now feels he fits in nowhere, something summed up by the car which Edna insists on:

> That 'thing' stood as a barrier between him and his old friends. Before its arrival they had been uncomprehending of the significance of his new profession: it did not mean anything. He had used the tramcars and buses as themselves and had stood with them in the queues for these vehicles. He now had a vehicle to himself ... . Sometimes he passed a group of his friends as they stood chatting at the street corner. Once he saw them nudge each other as his car approached ... he secretly yearned to join them again in those carefree evenings at the theatre or cinema. (p. 285)

There is misogyny here in blaming Edna for Henry's own ill-considered decision to run away from London, but clearly the end of the novel laments Henry's sense of exclusion from his origins. It is a conclusion that, as we have seen from his breach of promise case and his marriage to Pearl Osgood, notably represents a course which is the opposite to that which Greenwood in fact chose. Perhaps the marriage of a suddenly successful provincial playwright to a successful London actress would

---

97 The naming of this country squire as Walter Brierley is presumably a joking reference on Greenwood's part to his fellow working-class writer and ex-miner from Derbyshire, Walter Brierley, whose novel *Means Test Man* had a considerable impact in 1935, the year before the publication of *Standing Room Only*.

have seemed too like a fantasy-romance ending? Or perhaps he felt such an ending would too evidently remove him from the more ordinary lives of his imagined readers or damage his reputation as a northern working-class novelist (though Henry's job as a draper as well as his translation to a more modern suburbia does, anyway, suggest a rather different social milieu from that of Hanky Park).

There is very little written about *Standing Room Only*, but clearly it is not a text without interest from the point of view of understanding Greenwood's own self-representation and his career as a writer of working-class origins. As usual, Paul W. Salmon is the exception and he suggests some interesting links between this novel and one of the two works Greenwood published two years later in 1938:

> There are several connections between *Standing Room Only* and *Only Mugs Work* that actually point up the weaknesses of both. The two works share the laudable ambition of revealing to the reader the dark side of certain social strata (the world of the theater in the former and the London underworld in the latter). But in both books this documentary impulse clashes with stereotypical conventions and especially with the kind of simplistic genre tropes one would expect a social commentator studiously to avoid. The authenticity of the portrait of gangsters in *Only Mugs Work* is undermined by the pervasiveness of gangster film iconography and of Greenwood's incongruous weaving of a romantic plotline into the work. Similarly, *Standing Room Only* abounds with stock characters such as Henry's self-willed and shrewish mother and Edna ... . Exemplifying the awkward tensions ... is the character of Roger Morden, the director of the stage production of Henry's play. Morden espouses socialist views that echo Greenwood's own and that point up the grasping selfishness rampant in the world of the theatre. Yet, although Morden almost emerges as worthy of the reader's attention, this more complex character finds himself in a world of stock characters, rather like a good actor trapped in a bad play.[98]

Certainly, Morden emerges as a critic of the commercial system that overrides artistic considerations ('you know how popular I am with managements because of my opinions' [p. 223]), but, despite his ability to analyse the force of money, he is still very much part of that commercial world and dependent on it. He does contribute to the novel's reflections on authorship, art, and commerce, but I am

---

98 Johnson, *Dictionary of Literary Biography Vol. 191*, p. 136. See also, however, discussion of this novel's representation of north and south in Dave Russell's *Looking North*, pp. 96–97.

not certain that he rather than Henry is at the centre of the novel. Greenwood does often draw on comic characters who have elements of the stock character about them (this is surely the case too with the chorus of older women in *Love on the Dole*), and, just as his mother is part-shrew, so too Henry is part-ingénu, and Morden the artist-forced-to-compromise-with- society. Overall, it seems a successful comic novel about what happens to a provincial working-class author who is taken up by the numerous agents who are part of the processes of publication and performance.

I do, however, agree with Salmon's view of *Only Mugs Work*, which seems to me the least successful of all Greenwood's writings of the 1930s. The blending of hard-boiled, American-influenced gangster novel and sentimental romance is not well-handled and incongruous is, indeed, the word. Oddly enough the book was received more kindly than *Standing Room Only* in the *Times Literary Supplement*, though this may be largely because it was reviewed *as* a thriller rather than as a novel, together with three detective novels. The distinction between detective novels and thrillers/crime stories was an important one in the 1930s, which has been variously discussed,[99] but this reviewer, at any rate, was completely certain that the Greenwood's book exemplified the distinction, so that, having discussed the three detective novels, which she liked in varying degrees, she ended with *Only Mugs Work*:

> This is a very satisfactory batch of stories: the plots are ingenious enough to hold attention to the last page, and the characters are sufficiently real to arouse sympathy.
>
> Mr Greenwood's story belongs to an entirely different category. Since it deals with criminals it can be called a crime story, yet here is no pleasant escape from reality but an incursion into a reality that would be scarcely credible in this country if it were not for newspaper reports of recent happenings that occur to the reader. While this is not in any sense one of the repellent stories to which attention is drawn in another place ... it is horrifying in its own way as it takes us behind the scenes of the Soho gangster world and reveals the activities of men who prey on prostitutes, beggars [and] pedlars ... who do not draw the line at mild torture and

---

99 See my discussion of Eric Ambler's exploration of what he sees as the differences between the escapism of the detective novel and the insights into the frightening actuality of contemporary life in his novel *The Mask of Demetrios* (1939) in 'Leftists and Thrillers: the Politics of a Thirties Sub-genre', in *And in Our Time: Literature of the Nineteen Thirties*, ed. Anthony Shuttleworth (Lewisburg PA: Bucknell University Press, 2003), pp. 147–62.

murder ... Mr Greenwood's talent for portraying horrifying people and making them seem credible is as strong as in his *Love on the Dole* and it either adds to the thrill of the story or makes it distasteful according to the temperament of the reader.[100]

From the point of view of Greenwood's writing career, this would-be thriller (unfortunately it does not seem to me very thrilling) again suggests that he is exploring the possibilities of popular forms as ways of both making a living as a professional writer and of finding new topics to write about. However, as the review suggests, there is an uncertainty about the use of the genre that may have left the novel satisfying no-one, neither devotees of romance nor detective novel fans nor hard-boiled thriller addicts nor readers expecting from the author of *Love on the Dole* something more socially concerned in nature.[101] Nevertheless, when Hutchinson published Greenwood's only wartime novel, *Something in My Heart*, they linked it to both *Love on the Dole* (discussed on the back page of the dust -jacket) and *Only Mugs Work*, laconically referenced on both the dust-jacket spine and rear with the words under Walter Greenwood's name: 'Author of "Only Mugs Work" (5th Thousand)'. It may have had its fans: it was reprinted in a cheap edition in 1947 and I have a copy of this once in the stock of 'the Silver Library' with date stamps showing that it was borrowed by forty-one readers (at four pence per week) between 9 March 1948 and 24 June 1949.[102]

It is notable that 1938 was the first year in which Greenwood published two novels, and the first time he had published with a company other than Cape. Thus while *The Secret Kingdom* came out under the Cape imprint *Only Mugs Work* was published by Hutchinson, who were perhaps more downmarket than Cape, though often adept at finding highly popular authors.[103] As the 1930s publisher Sir Robert Lusty recalled:

100 *Times Literary Supplement*, Saturday, 22 October 1938, p. 681. The reviewer is again Leonora Eyles, who knew Greenwood's work well, since she had written the *TLS*'s review of *Love on the Dole* in 1933 and that of *Standing Room Only* in 1936.

101 See the response of a member of the Reading 1900–1950 Reading Group at <https://reading19001950.wordpress.com/2016/07/18/only-mugs-work-1938-by-walter-greenwood/>, accessed 26 October 2017.

102 This is based on the first edition dust jacket of *Something in My Heart*, which also records that the novel cost 9/6 'including extra war costs'.

103 Characterising the market niches and literary values of publishers is, of course, a difficult venture. Cape was by no means only a high-brow publisher, nor was it uninterested in popular writers; nevertheless, it seems broadly reasonable to

the imprint of Hutchinson may not have been exactly revered in the book world of the time. 'Too highbrow' was a favoured justification for rejection by Mr Walter [Hutchinson] ... but the list was never negligible ... . Philip Gibbs, Gilbert Frankau, Rafael Sabatini, Eden Philpotts, Geoffrey Moss, Cosmo Hamilton were all continuing stars in a crowded constellation.[104]

In fact, *The Secret Kingdom* was to be Greenwood's last Cape book (with the exception of his 1967 memoir *There Was a Time*), and he remained a Hutchinson author for the rest of his career, as far as fiction publication was concerned.

The Secret Kingdom returned to Salford for its setting and to a focus again on a socially engaged kind of fiction that might find sympathy among a broad range of readers. However, despite apparently heeding advice from earlier reviews about returning to the streets of Hanky Park, responses were not all positive. The review in the *TLS* of *The Secret Kingdom* praised his continued engagement with working-class life, but is unimpressed by the literary technique and quality of the novel:

> It is pleasant to find that Mr Greenwood has not abandoned in imagination the working-class scene. Once more he writes of poverty and insecurity in the mean streets of Salford, of the response of different types of character to hard and ugly conditions of life. It is less pleasant to record that this latest book of his is a disappointment ... . The chief trouble ... is an all too evident willingness to use the conventional and the ready-made. Paula Byron's struggles to maintain the ordinary decencies of life, her courage and tenacity in the face of the handicaps that often daunt the slum-dweller, her yearnings towards the secret kingdom of Shakespeare, the Iliad and the Emperor Concerto – all this was potentially the stuff of a novel as true and revealing as *Love on the Dole*. Paula, as she is drawn here, is a ghost of a woman, not a person at all, but a personification of conventional working-class virtues ... . Mr Greenwood has demonstrated plainly enough his talent for much better things.[105]

suggest that there was a difference of status as compared with Hutchinson. Michael S. Howard comments that 'from the first they [Cape's books] bore that stamp of quality and style which expressed the personality of G. Wren Howard. It is harder to perceive that mark of Jonathan [Cape's] own character in the catholicity and range of the books themselves' (Michael S. Howard's *Jonathan S. Cape, Publisher* (Harmondsworth: Penguin, 1977), p. ix). See Parts One and Two of that book for further guidance on Cape's list and style during the 1920s and 1930s.

104 *Bound to Be Read*, pp. 36–37.
105 *Times Literary Supplement*, Saturday 21 May 1938 (accessed via *TLS Centenary*

One might, of course, say that all literary works do draw on conventions, have some degree of ready-madeness, but equally 'literary' readers do generally accept a principle of value that rates highly originality in writing, either through going beyond existing conventions to some extent or at least redeploying them. This is, indeed, a distinction often used to define (though this is highly problematic) the difference between popular culture and 'art', and between 'middlebrow culture' and 'real culture', as the *OED* definition of the adjectival form of the important term 'middlebrow' suggests: 'demanding or involving only a moderate degree of intellectual application, typically as a result of not deviating from convention'.[106] Of course, to say that something does not work is not quite the same thing as saying it is 'middlebrow', but the review does seem to say that between *Love on the Dole* and *The Secret Kingdom* Greenwood has fallen from the position of original writer to that of merely conventional writer. However, it may well be that in fact much of Greenwood's influence comes, from the very beginning – from *Love on the Dole* onwards – from a certain middlebrow position in the literary marketplace: he created novels that a very wide readership recognised as readable yet serious literary works (it is important to recognise that 'middlebrow' novels may also be read by working-class readers).

However, the titles of his later 1930s and 1940s novels are notably different from those of his earlier works and may indicate a shift further into middlebrow territory. *Love on the Dole* may derive its title from a phrase, 'marriage on the dole', referred to in contemporary discussions of the conditions of life under unemployment (used, for example, in the Carnegie Trust research report *Disinherited Youth* [1939]). Replacing the word 'marriage' with 'love' gives a concise preview of the novel's attractions to romance, but also its highly anti-romantic working out of its two romance and marriage plots (though Greenwood seems to have hesitated over the title – a surviving printer's final copy has a title page bearing the words *The Lovers* and an alternative page with the title, *They Call it Love* crossed out and replaced with the pencilled final title

Archive, 7 June 2010). The reviewer was R. D. Charques, author among other works of a leftist critical book *Contemporary Literature and Social Revolution* (London: Martin Secker, 1933).

106 *OED online edition.* My thanks also to Mary Grover, Erica Brown, Faye Hammill, and other members of the AHRC funded Middlebrow Network for numerous discussions about this term.

in Greenwood's hand).[107] *His Worship the Mayor* also suggests an ironic rewriting of the original meaning of its title phrase, since it is very much about *quid pro quos* in local politics. *Standing Room Only* is a colloquial phrase, while *Only Mugs Work* is, like the thriller which it titles, meant to suggest hard-boiled American with a London accent. Both *The Secret Kingdom* and *Something in My Heart* (published 1943) seem more openly to promise romance, mystery revealed, and perhaps escape in their titles, and may imply pathos rather than irony.

The reader will not be disappointed in this respect. After an introduction to the setting of *The Secret Kingdom* and the family of the principal female protagonist, Chapter iii is called 'Mystery at Number One'. Alternating chapters introduce two characters who stand out from their environment: Bert Treville, who has come to Palatine Street, Salford, from as far away as Manchester and is thus a romantically interesting stranger; and Paula, eldest daughter of the Byron family, who has mysteriously disappeared from Palatine Street for six months, as well as being a member of a family known for their strangeness in the whole district, for William Byron the father 'had books of his own, *real* books … . You could see the books in the glass-fronted bookcase in the parlour where he took you when you went to ask his advice' (p. 14).[108] Paula has, in fact, and despite what the neighbours all think, absented herself to work as a parlour-maid and to recover from her refusal of a proposal of marriage:

> She could think of John Blake now without a pang. As for the other men … there didn't seem to be any chivalry in them. Good manners were something to be shy, if not ashamed of. What then remained for her to satisfy her desire for colour and romance but Italian opera, Shakespeare, the poets and the classical novelists? There were, of course, that most secret and cherished release from reality, dreams.
>
> Dreams! Impalpable things that could be, and often were, more real than reality. In these she could believe, whereas all that which she saw about her … was altogether incredible and alien to her nature. Who could countenance the mean lives of Lancashire workers, the endless dreariness of the streets, the dirt, poverty, weeping skies, the feeling of imprisonment, of no escape and the never-ending uncertainty of everything? (pp. 35–36)

107 Details from sales description of the copy (and image) by J and M Books, Towcester <http://www.pbfa.org/books/d/love-on-the-dole/121611>, accessed 12 June 2015.

108 Morley-Baker reprint, Leeds, 1970. All subsequent references are to this edition and page numbers are given in brackets in the text.

Bert Treville, who has come to Salford to open his own barber's shop, is equally romantically inclined, but in his case towards Paula: "'Paula, oh Paula! So removed from collective woman; a creation apart, a thing unique, a shining light far away'" (p. 27).

So far, I have not suggested any reason for disagreeing with the *TLS* reviewer's sense that this novel draws on the 'conventional and the ready-made'. The novel does indeed quickly establish modes of interpretation for itself that are likely to be readily identified by its reader: it could not be called highbrow or difficult. Nor is it obviously lowbrow, with a dwelling on sensation or emotion in its own right. Though it is wholly about working-class families in Salford, one can also see that it might not necessarily have struck contemporary readers as having the kinds of feature they might expect of working-class fiction. It does, instead, seem best described as 'betwixt and between', and with a notable reference to markers of 'culture' that its readers are expected to show knowledge of, a kind of bookishness that Mary Grover has suggested is an identifying feature of the middlebrow, a keenness to display a certain ownership of cultural capital.[109] It is a text well-caught in some respects by Q. D. Leavis's description of the 'middling novel' as: 'All on the traditional model, and therefore easy to respond to, yet with an appearance of originality; they deal in soothing and not disturbing sentiments, yet with sufficient surface stimulus to be pleasing ... their readers are left with the agreeable sensation of having improved themselves without incurring fatigue.'[110] However, I have slightly misrepresented the novel thus far in that it does have features which, if not requiring high modernist decoding at the level of style, are nevertheless not quite as conventionally 'middling' and easy as Leavis's description suggests, at the level of content. For example, the opening scene-setting chapter (highly reminiscent of the opening of *Love on the Dole*) talks of the way in which the Two Cities can be differently understood from ideological and actual class viewpoints:

Let it pass that children are taught that Manchester is a place at which

---

109 See her monograph, *The Ordeal of Warwick Deeping: Middlebrow Authorship and Cultural Embarrassment* (Madison: Fairleigh Dickinson Press, 2009), especially the section entitled 'Deeping's Changing Use of Cultural Touchstones' in the final chapter (pp. 169–75). Grover argues that his strategies suggest a readership who were curious about high culture and anxious about how they stood in relation to it.

110 *Fiction and the Reading Public* (London: Chatto & Windus, 1932), pp. 36–37.

anybody can point with pride as an illustrious example of national wealth, municipal enterprise and public-spiritedness … . All this is, alas, only one side of the picture …

A stranger's reactions to the districts surrounding the city's centre will depend on two things, his or her social position and social conscience … . Streets of houses where the proletariat put up a pretence of living: … cotton mills, engineering works, cheek by jowl; main streets lined with pettifogging shops that change hands ceaselessly, bankrupting each successive optimist; railway bridges, dripping arches, canals; dog-racing tracks, football fields, cheap dance halls and super cinemas. Of this there is no end. (p. 10)

This may not be revolutionary rhetoric, but neither is it obviously encouraging an easy acceptance of the status quo or avoiding entirely any disturbance to readers who may not share this kind of social analysis. This was, after all, a world in which, to quote Edward Upward, 'even saying the word "capitalism" was to damn you, so not much was said',[111] and presumably the word 'proletariat' here would have a related effect for uncommitted readers. Similarly, if in some ways Paula Byron is unimpeachably 'respectable' in her aspirations to high culture and her distaste for industrial Salford, she is also unimpeachably socialist in her beliefs. Thinking about her daily walk to work at her mill at 6 a.m., and the daily sight of the night-soil men emptying the 'pestiferous ordure tins' from Baxter Street, 'aroused that other side of her nature, the fiery, indignant side which leapt in ardent response to the political debates and speeches in the Labour Club and the Manchester Free Trade Hall. This other side, as practical as the looms in the mill, dismissed her romantic dreams as silly' (p. 37). Paula is, in many respects, the novel's central character, but her plot-line is also balanced throughout the novel by a plot-line centred on a male character, first that of her suitor Bert Treville and then, after Bert's premature death through drink and pneumonia, that of her son Lance, a talented pianist. Though the novel is strongly interested in romance, it does also seem keen to provide points of entry for male readers (allowing them opportunity to enjoy the romance too, perhaps). Thus though Bert's struggles with the demon drink are, in the end, fatal, they begin with fully realised accounts of the part that the pub plays in his community

---

111 From an interview with Edward Upward by Nicholas Wroe, *The Guardian* 23 August 2003; available at <http://www.guardian.co.uk/books/2003/aug/23/featuresreviews.guardianreview10>, accessed 26 October 2017. Upward refers to his experience as a Communist Party member who also taught at a public school, Alleyn's school, Dulwich.

for men as their main social focus, and his pleasure in this is explored sympathetically, although he eventually fails to hold the line between 'respectable' social drinking and ruinous neglect of his family and his own health. Equally, after Bert's death, Lance's engagement with the literary and musical education his mother scrimps to provide him with is balanced by insights into his struggles with other attractive forms of working-class masculine identity:

> Lance was fed up with this school business. Gosh! Look at Billy Waring and the gang; all wearing overalls, talking professionally about capstan lathes, foundries, machine shops, castings, shell-cases, big guns, oh, and all the romantic things associated with the war!
>
> … and mother always harping on studying and winning a scholarship. As though it wasn't bad enough having to study the piano … . If he were wearing overalls would Aunt Anne have the nerve to ask him to be bringing her new baby to the mill every day at noon? (p. 338)

At the end of *The Secret Kingdom*, after a long period of unemployment, Lance makes it as concert pianist when he is broadcast live by BBC radio (the Byrons have to borrow a wireless). *The Secret Kingdom* of the title is, it seems, a sustaining inner resource of higher things – a combination of socialist principles with high cultural participation.

In many ways this is a classic Greenwood ending or event (reminiscent of his own *deus ex machina* acceptance letters for his early short story and his first novel). The dire way out of Hanky Park through Sally's becoming Sam Grundy's mistress at the end of *Love on the Dole* is here replaced by a positive rescue for the impoverished Byron family coming out of the wider world from a (still newish) national cultural institution. There is a strong sense, despite Greenwood's own experience, of which the reader is likely to be reminded, that there is an element of the wish-fulfilment, easy-way-out ending to this. However, there is also for Paula a sense of the rest of her class abandoned, left behind by her individual advance: Paula 'saw herself … being rescued from the inhospitable desert island of poverty on whose shores … all the imaginable downtrodden were silently congregated, their unenvious eyes following her dumbly as she receded' (p. 412). This does feel as if we are, at the closure of the novel, back, though not straightfor-wardly, with Leavis's 'soothing and not disturbing sentiments'. It is also a significant ending in terms of some issues about Greenwood's class and gender identifications. If Lance feared earlier that there was a feminising element in his mother's cultural aspirations for him, and even if these were dealt with partly by his own participation in the masculine world of the dole-office queue, there is nevertheless a sense here that he does, and his family with him, leave behind a world of manual labour characterised as masculine for a more feminised, bourgeois way of living.

It is a running theme in criticism of *Love on the Dole* (from Stephen Constantine's seminal article and my own past work to a recent piece by Matthew Gaughan[112]) that Greenwood has a tendency to soften things that might frighten off the middle-class audience who are implied or, at least, catered for as readers. Thus Larry in *Love on the Dole* is a lone working-class intellectual, rather than one among organised union or party members, and is feminised and somewhat middle-class-seeming in his speech and in other features compared with, for example, the brutal portrayal of the villainous Ned Narkey. A desire not to disturb is undoubtedly, and even more so, also an aspect of *The Secret Kingdom*, which gives in some respects a softer-edged view of working-class life than does its predecessor. However, if it is, in the respects I've suggested, a text that fits in many ways into the cultural ambit of the 'middlebrow', look what it does manage to get into that world and into the mental universe of its readers. It depicts a whole family who live by socialist principles, transmitted from their father William Byron, a lifelong union member and activist, through his three daughters, and it suggests very fully that the deprived life of Hanky Park is not at all the only kind of working-class life possible. If Paula's cultural tastes and aspiration might look partly calculated to make her an appealing heroine for middle-class or uncommitted readers, and to make her socialism more palatable, they may also genuinely suggest to such readers that working-class life and aspirations were not a world apart, that this could be a culturally rich and in that sense independent life in its own right. Harold Brighouse was again a champion of the novel in the *Manchester Guardian* and his review brought out nicely what was new about it:

> It lacks the raw force and passionate drive of that specifically 'depression' book and goes calmly about its gentler business of telling the life-story of a

112 Both as it happens in the same journal. See Constantine's '*Love on the Dole* and its Reception in the 1930s' and Gaughan's 'Palatable Socialism or "the Real Thing"?', pp. 47–61. See also Chapter 3 in my *English Fiction in the 1930s: Language, Genre, History*, pp. 43–50, 'Dialect and Dialectic: Region and Nation in Walter Greenwood's *Love on the Dole*'.

Salford working woman. Comment is subdued, facts as a rule are allowed to speak for themselves ... [it is] the deeply moving story of Byron, Socialist, and craftsman, and especially it is the story of Paula.[113]

One might also speculate that Greenwood is himself by this stage somewhat further from his roots in Salford, and that he is now recreating from a temporal, social, and geographical distance what was once his own immediate experience. The rescue of Lance by both his own artistic talents and a national cultural institution is, as in *Standing Room Only*, a version of Greenwood's own escape from Hanky Park. By 1938 he had been a professional writer for five years, and had been living in Cornwall and London for two years. Indeed, by 1938 he had become not just an author but himself an agent for a variety of kinds of creative artist, for in that year he co-founded with his accountant, a Mr Park, his own stage and film agency and production company, called Greenpark, after its two originators.[114] Its 'memorandum and articles of association' stated that the company was founded to 'Carry on the Business of Producers and Promoters of Electric Cinematograph Pictures, Picture Theatres, Music halls, Stage Plays, Operas, Operettas, Burlesque, Vaudevilles, Ballets, Pantomimes, Revues, Concerts, Spectacular Piece and Bioscopic Pictures'.[115] This range of cultural production seems highly appropriate to an author who expressed interest in a wide variety of cultural products. It also seem significant to note before going on to discuss the single novel which Greenwood wrote during the 1940s that the company went on to make government information films during the war.[116] It seems possible that this activity, and perhaps even more direct contacts with the wartime Ministry of Information (see discussion of the film in Chapter 2) may have influenced the shape and message of *Something in My Heart*, which so interestingly and insistently revisits *Love on the Dole*

113 'New Novels', 24 May 1938.

114 I assume this is the James Park from Salford to whom Greenwood's 1950 book on *Lancashire* is dedicated, and who by 1950 was, as the dedication makes clear, an Alderman of Salford.

115 Greenpark still exists and since 1997 has been mainly a company marketing its film and picture archive under the title Greenpark images. This history and quotation are taken from the company website <http://www.greenparkimages. co.uk/Company-History/I9.htm>, accessed 9 June 2017.

116 Two Greenpark films, *Summer on the Farm* (1943) and *Five Towns* (1947), can be seen in the BFI DVD set *Land of Promise: the British Documentary Movement 1930–1950* (BFIVD756, London, BFI: 2013), and are introduced in the useful accompanying booklet.

from the perspective of the war (Kunitz and Haycraft indeed wondered in a 1942 literary–biographical entry 'what difference the war and the social changes actuated by it will make in his writing').[117]

The story opens in 1937 and initially concerns three main characters from Salford: Helen Oakroyd, who works in a textile mill, and Harry Watson and Taffy Lloyd, both of whom are on the dole. Harry, Helen, and Taffy reproduce aspects of the roles of Sally, Harry, and Larry in *Love on the Dole*, as well as reusing two names from that novel (Harry and Helen). Confusingly, however, the Harry here broadly corresponds to Larry, Helen to Sally, and Taffy to Harry Hardcastle. Harry Watson is clearly a self-educated and politically active working man, Taffy is consciously less articulate than Harry Watson ('I can't put it into words like Harry' [p. 8]), while Helen is a 'beauty' on 'twenty-five bob a week',[118] who craves romance and feels a thus far unrequited love for Harry. The names themselves are, of course, pointing the reader back to *Love on the Dole*, but so too do many other allusions in the opening chapter. Thus Taffy, thinking about his situation, not only echoes Mr Hardcastle's 'oh God, gimme a job!' but also summarises the sense that *Love on the Dole* gives so strongly of the impossibility of an ordinary life for the unemployed and the sense of hopelessness:

> Blimey! A job! A quid in your pocket and a decent suit of clothes to your back. Aye and married to a girl like Helen. Aw, but chuck it man. How many more mugs are there like you in Britain thinking the same thing? Millions of 'em and all signing on the dole like you and Harry. Most of 'em like you, too, young, strong and with the best part of their lives supposed to be in front of them. All being robbed of it, robbed of something that could never be replaced. (p. 7)

The themes of love and marriage on the dole raised by Taffy are also strongly picked up by the other two characters in the first few pages. Helen thinks about how much she likes Harry Watson, but also shows her independence by asserting that she does not necessarily need a conventional marriage relationship. She also observes that Harry does not seem to notice her and reprises some of the romance/class dynamic between Sally and Larry in the earlier novel:

---

117 Stanley J. Kunitz and Howard Haycraft (eds), *Twentieth Century Authors: a Biographical Dictionary of Modern Literature* (New York: H. W. Wilson, 1942), p. 574.

118 Morley-Baker reprint, Leeds, 1969, p. 8. All subsequent references are to this edition and will be given in brackets in the text.

When, every Thursday, he was taking his class in economics at the Labour Club, she was among those present. Maybe he *did* guess how she felt and maybe this avoidance was his unspoken answer. No, no it wasn't that ... . He was too interested in his political activities; *that* was the reason. She found herself hating them and his other studious interests. Yet, it was partly because of these he was so different from the other fellows; this was the quality in him that was the mainspring of her love. (p. 6)

In fact, Harry shortly afterwards articulates his own refusal to respond to her as stemming partly from political commitment and partly from an assumption that romance and domestication will inevitably erode the single man's 'freedom' to engage with politics:

You'll find yourself enmeshed ... Instead of waiting for you at the street corner you'll find her at your house and, maybe, when you feel like studying ... . Romance? Love? Who's taking about these things? As well ask a soldier about those things when he's in the middle of a battle. You're in the same fix as a soldier – except that no battle can last long ... . Some of your fellow dole-birds have been out of work for ten years. A dreary, weary, spirit-breaking battle in the concentration camp of empty pockets. (p. 10)

The comparison of unemployment with military service and, indeed, combat has a particular resonance of course, given that this is a wartime novel. Indeed, the first edition rear dust jacket makes this very clear, referring to Harry and Taffy as 'two of that vast army of the unemployed' who have now joined the RAF. The meaning of unemployment is thus shifted towards something more heroic than the hopelessness represented in *Love on the Dole*.

Indeed, though the evocation of Greenwood's first novel is strong, there are also some differences between it and *Something in My Heart*. Where the 1933 novel often implies that the people of Hanky Park are in many respects stuck in poverty very like that of the nineteenth century, this novel suggests both a more modern England and also characters who are not quite so wholly stuck in the endlessly reproducing and reproduced system into which they are born. Thus aspects of consumer England and modern leisure seem to be more often referred to, even if they are no longer possible for most of the characters, and there is a greater knowledge of the wider world:

Just look at 'em, patent leather and pointed toe: the only ones I've got left and what I used to go jazzing in. Aw! I'm no blooming Red. I'm an ordinary guy, a skilled mechanic out of a job ... . But I can fix any blasted, broken-down car or machine with the next man. (p. 8)

There is also, notably, less use of dialect and a greater use of contemporary idioms – often cinema- or popular-fiction-derived Americanisms such as 'dough'. These are unemployed citizens, but citizens nevertheless of England rather than of just Hanky Park (indeed, the fact that Taffy is Welsh widens the picture of unemployment in itself, though this may also be a reference to the 1941 film, in which Larry is played by the Welsh actor Cliff Ellis with a clearly Welsh accent). Though Taffy and Harry are trapped for the moment, there are even some possible ways out. Thus, Harry is, among other things, good at boxing: 'Lightweight champion of the Salford Lads' Club three times running ... . You could have been British professional champion if you'd wanted and be walking about with a pocketful of dough just for poking somebody in the kisser. Turning the promoter's dough down like you did' (p. 9). However, Harry has 'other fish to fry', for he is studying through his union 'for the Ruskin College scholarship' (p. 9). Both these escape routes, in their different ways, suggest a representation of unemployment in 1930s Salford as less isolating than the version depicted in *Love on the Dole*. Where in the earlier novel Larry seems to be the only union activist in Hanky Park, an odd exception whose origins and history are not revealed in the novel, and the unemployed youngster Harry Hardcastle has in the end only the street corners to go to, here Harry Watson is part of a society that does have some collective working-class institutions which can help the unemployed: boys' clubs, a Labour Club (p. 6), a union which can fund study, and a national college for working people, to which some can aspire.[119] The contained stasis of Greenwood's earlier novel is to a degree opened up to a more national and even international culture here. The 'ignorant' and passive inhabitants of Hanky Park have been succeeded by much more politically conscious beings; during a political discussion about how Hitler came to power in Germany on the back of unemployment and loss of hope, Harry reminds Taffy of their joint attempts to do something: 'We've collected for the people of China and Spain and the Vienna workers. You were at the meeting for Sacco and Vanzetti' (p. 21). The escape route through professional boxing is, of course, a more traditional one and perhaps more like the 'escape' that Ned Narkey makes into the local police force through his physical strength and aggression, or, as a working-class sport, like the dream-version of escape Sam Grundy offers through gambling.

---

119 Ruskin College, Oxford was founded in 1899 as a college where working-class men (originally) might have access to higher education.

Overall, this seems a slightly more hopeful Salford, even though the mass experience, as we are frequently reminded, is one of deprivation through joblessness. Another means of escape offered as a last resort in *Love on the Dole* is now seen as a focus of both mobility and, indeed, modernity. In a moment of desperation, Harry Hardcastle thinks his only course may be to join the army, but both Harry Watson and Taffy Lloyd share an obsession that is, if marginally, at least contactable for unemployed men from Salford. At the very opening of the novel Helen sees two ragged men and knows how they have spent their day: 'they had signed on at the dole late this afternoon and thence had walked to Barton aerodrome to watch those who could afford it take lessons in flying' (p. 5). Flying was deployed as a potent symbol of a number of things during the 1920s and 1930s – including escape, modern mobility, technological mastery of nature, the possibility of individual liberation from mass experience, and, particularly towards the end of the period, a symbol of Fascist domination.[120] Here it certainly symbolises escape for Harry and Taffy, but is also associated with the modern, with resistance to fascism, and with individual and national recovery. Thus the once desperate Taffy comes back to Salford to see Harry, who is still studying to get to Ruskin, having completed his (pre-war) RAF training as an Observer: 'Taffy Lloyd stood on the doorstep, sunburnt and grinning. A winged "O" was on the breast of his uniform … . The same Taffy and yet – what a difference! Bright eyes, straight shoulders, a living air about him' (p. 28). Where the civilian social order has failed him, the RAF has transformed him: 'I'm telling you … the way they never taught us *anything* at school … the education in the RAF … those instructors, they really *want* you to learn' (p. 29).

These transformations and modernisations of *Love on the Dole* are key to this wartime novel's message. What was a call for help from the forgotten region of Hanky Park is here put into a larger perspective: the road to war and thence to a hoped-for better post-war Britain. This perspective makes *Something in My Heart* precisely a progressive narrative in several senses, where *Love on the Dole* is often a circular one, except

120 The meanings associated with flying in the period are discussed in a number of sources. See, for example, Valentine Cunningham's *British Writers of the Thirties* (Oxford: Oxford University Press, 1988), e.g. pp. 186–87, 203; Susan Ware's *Still Missing: Amelia Earhart and the Search for Modern Feminism* (New York: W. W. Norton and Co, 1993), and my *English Fiction in the 1930s* (Chapter 10, 'Flight, Gender Dystopia: Katherine Burdekin's *Swastika Night*, Storm Jameson's *In the Second Year*, Rex Warner's *The Aerodrome*').

for the bitter progress for the Hardcastle family achieved through Sally's submission to Sam Grundy's 'patronage'. Just as the war led to a transformation of the meanings of *Love on the Dole*, and hence the possibility of a film version, so here the war, partly through rearmament, can put an end to unemployment, poverty and loss of purpose. What was the identity-sapping nothingness of unemployment is here being written into a history – and a highly critical one – of pre-war government failure to manage this social and economic disaster and, prospectively, of what must replace such failures. In fact, it seems likely that there is a feedback loop here through which Greenwood is influenced to an extent by the belated film version of his own first novel. Greenwood proposed a radio adaptation of the novel to the BBC in 1944 (though it was not in the end pursued) and Val Gielgud in an internal memo reads the novel's concerns very much in this way:

> I am sure there is the basis of an interesting contemporary serial dealing with one of the most curious of modern sociological problems: when a country can educate, feed and clothe its young men to die in war and is apparently unable to do the same thing to enable them to live in peace. This, of course, is likely to be a burning question of widespread popular interest within the next twelve months.[121]

There is, though, some curious political ground to traverse in the novel. Here is a novel expressing sympathy for the unemployed workers of the 1930s and which in many respects also makes clear its socialist and particularly Labour Party sympathies. The rather fluid and sometimes opposed meanings attributed to 'flying' thus need to be made to serve the cause of democracy and to disseminate the idea that post-war Britain must be a very differently organised place from 1930s Britain. Though there has been no previous critical discussion of the novel, *Something in My Heart* was not alone either in needing to transform the imagery of flying or in its focus on the RAF as a symbol of the national and social unity created by the war effort. A recent pioneering study by Martin Francis, *The Flyer – British Culture and the Royal Airforce 1939–1945*, has detailed just how important (and how variously representable) the RAF was to wartime British culture:

> Traditionally, debates about how far British society became more egalitarian (in both subjective and objective terms) between 1939 and 1945 focused on

121 BBC internal memo from Gielgud to Stephen Potter 8 November 1944 in BBC Written Archives' Walter Greenwood Scriptwriter File I, 1934–62.

the home front, following the lead of Angus Calder's classic *The People's War* ... . However, recently there has been more attention paid to the relationship between service life and social change in wartime ... . With Colonel Blimp dead and buried, the military was no longer a safe haven for those who wished to escape the democratic and populist impulses of the modern world.[122]

Greenwood's wartime sequel to *Love on the Dole* should certainly be approached very much in these kinds of terms. Its address to national unity and reform is made clear even by the first edition's rear dust-jacket 'blurb', which records how Harry and Taffy serve together with their 'RAF friend, Rupert Hardcastle, wealthy son of a great industrialist'.[123] In fact, this cross-class friendship is achieved only after considerable initial class-hostility displayed by Rupert – resolved after Harry not only shows his superior judgement and flying skills but also knocks Rupert down in an impromptu bout of boxing (p. 57).

Social unity under the stress of war and in its comradeship is a strong theme throughout the rest of the novel, but this consensus is presented as a new, even revolutionary development: there is much criticism of the pre-war social order and much looking forward to a very different post-war society. This cluster of topics is a frequent topic of thought and conversation across the class range of characters in the novel. Thus the indubitably upper-middle-class Group Captain Donaldson reflects, 'Well, if Watson was an example of working class "ignorance" then the possessing classes had better do something about their own ignorance, for in the future they certainly wouldn't be able to patronise men like that' (p. 109). In short, the novel is dedicated (perhaps none too subtly, though the 'middlebrow' periodical *John O'London's* referred to it as 'an important novel of ideas'[124]) to supporting the war as a People's War, based on a promise that Britain would never go back to the 1930s (there was a translation into French in 1946, called *Mais des Hommes Aussi*, which presumably also offered hope for a better life in liberated Europe).[125] The role of the film in

---

122 Oxford: Oxford University Press, 2008, p. 5.

123 Again, Greenwood re-uses a name from *Love on the Dole*, though somewhat oddly given that it is transferred from the unemployed family to the rich industrialist.

124 Quoted on the inside dust jacket of the Morley-Baker 1969 reprint.

125 The title, which might literally be translated 'But There are Also Men', presumably suggests that humans should come before economic (or ideological?) systems – it seems no worse a title than Greenwood's own rather uninformative one. The

marking a wartime political shift – or the promise of a shift – towards greater class consensus and the founding of the welfare state has been much discussed, as we shall see – but clearly this novel was another important, and more explicit, contribution by Greenwood towards this agreement on the need for major post-war social and political change. It is also a novel that shows how important *Love on the Dole* continued to be in the 1940s as a national reference point for an unacceptable past and a hoped-for, planned, future.[126]

III. New Writing, Adaptations, and Revivals 1945–1974

The lack of interest shown by critics in Greenwood's work between 1933 and 1945 is equally the case for the rest of his career (apart, again, from Paul W. Salmon's concise account). Given the 1930s and 1940s focus of this study, this is not the place to discuss in full his post-war career, but since this is at present the only book-length study of Greenwood, this section should give some account of what was still a very active writing career, should note his continuing strong interest in diverse forms of creativity – fiction, plays, film, and television – and should outline some continuities and developments. It is important to note, too, how firmly *Love on the Dole* remained in the national repertory during the war and the post-war period. The main focus of critics on Greenwood as a 1930s author has sometimes made it appear that he simply stopped writing in the 1940s – as the neglect of *Something in the Heart* (1944) suggests. Indeed – and unlike the case for most 1930s writers – existing accounts do not even give much account of how he spent the war years, let alone of his writing from that period. There are gaps in the public record of his life at this period, no doubt partly due to wartime conditions, but some at least of these gaps can be usefully filled. We know from a letter from Edith Sitwell (26 December 1941) that his London house was damaged by bombing and that Pearl was in some way injured in the blitz (the couple also divorced in 1944: Greenwood, nearly thirty years later, said that they were both like 'erupting volcanoes').[127] The damage

---

translation was by H. Delgove and Cl. Vaudecrane and was published in a paper cover by the Paris publisher Correa in 1946. Quite a few copies seem to be on the market, suggesting a reasonably large imprint.

126 For a more detailed discussion of the novel see my article, 'The Army of the Unemployed'.

127 'Dole Cue', 2 April 1971, p. 10.

to the house must have been considerable, as the draft manuscripts of two volumes of his unpublished historical novel trilogy, *The Prosperous Years*, were 'destroyed in the blitz'.[128] Biographical material included on the website for the Walter Greenwood Collection states that he served in the Royal Army Service Corps during the war.[129] The RASC was responsible during the war for supply and transport for British army units, and was also responsible for 'providing clerks for headquarters units'.[130] Since Greenwood was thirty-five in September 1939 he would have been subject to call-up under the National Service Act passed that month. However, a letter Greenwood wrote to Val Gielgud, head of Radio Drama at the BBC, records that he was not called up until 1943: 'just as I was about to begin the final draft of the novel I spoke to you about [presumably *Something in My Heart*] I was called into the army.' The letter is headed with his army service number and address: '14653657, P[riva]te Walter Greenwood, Basic Course 400, X Coy, 12 TB (clerks) RASC, Buller Barracks, Aldershot'.[131] Employment as a clerk (again) may well not have filled Greenwood with immediate enthusiasm – and perhaps the events described below might be linked to his being made to return to an occupation he strongly disliked. He is recorded as passing his Army 'Class III Trade Test for Learner Clerks', but it seems legitimate to wonder if this was the best use the country could make of the man who had co-written the script for the film of *Love on the Dole* two years previously and who was engaged in other useful creative activity.[132] The only public reference to his war service is in a post-war (Glasgow) *Evening News* report about the genesis of his 1945 play and 1952 novel *So Brief the Spring*, which refers to his initial training in Glasgow:

> The new play is a result of a six-year-old promise made to [the actor] Robert Newton on a pre-war holiday in Cornwall. Robert went into the Navy and

128 Note by Greenwood on the surviving second volume, WGC/1/1/1.
129 See <http://www.salford.ac.uk/__data/assets/xml_file/0007/530476/Greenwood.xml>.
130 According to a website that reproduces an undated but probably World War II training manual for the RASC: <https://www.forces-war-records.co.uk/units/4495/royal-army-service-corps/>.
131 BBC Written Archives, Caversham Park, Walter Greenwood Scriptwriter File 1, 1934–62, Letter, 3 September 1943 (there is a stamped date on the letter, presumably of receipt at the BBC rather than date of composition, and while the month and year are clear, the day is not).
132 On his 'Record of all Casualties' and also on his B200B form.

Walter to the Army and part of the writing was done in an exercise book ... while Walter was training at Maryhill Barracks.[133]

Greenwood's Army Service record shows that during his service he was admitted to the Sutton Emergency Hospital in Surrey on 24 September 1943. He remained in hospital for more than twenty-one days, triggering under regulations his transfer on 16 October 1943 to the 'Y-List' (meaning that if he regained fitness he could be posted to a new rather than his existing unit).[134] The Sutton Emergency Hospital (ironically a former workhouse and then a 'Training Centre for the Unemployed') had at the beginning of the war been designated a 'Neurosis Centre', designed to treat psychiatric injuries as a consequence of bombing, but it had returned to a general medical role by this time, though it became a specialised psychiatric hospital again in 1946, so perhaps it retained some specialists during the war. Greenwood's illness certainly seem to have been diagnosed as a serious psychological one – he is recorded as suffering from a 'Disability – Psychopathic Personality' and hence discharged 'as permanently unfit for any form of Military Service' on 15 November 1943, after serving since mid-August 1943. I am uncertain what to make of this diagnosis. The standard history of British Army psychiatry during the war (written by the wartime Deputy Assistant Director of Army Psychiatry) notably discusses the 'psychopathic personality' in a chapter on 'Disciplinary problems' and regards the 'psychopath' as someone who is antisocial and unable to fit into army life (the phrase 'psychopathic delinquent' is used, though even the author does query whether behaviours resulting from a 'disability' can be treated as disciplinary offences). It seems clear that the 'psychopathic' diagnosis was used to discharge men who were considered to be misfits or not useful to the army, especially as the war went on.[135] However, Greenwood's military

133 10 October 1945, 'Cinema Topics' by Maurice Crichton, clippings book, WGC/3/2, p. 120.

134 From his 'Record of All Casualties' form. For a brief explanation of the 'Y-list' system see <http://www.bbc.co.uk/history/ww2peopleswar/stories/32/a8594832. shtml>, accessed 26 October 2017.

135 See Robert H. Ahrenfeldt's *Psychiatry in the British Army in the Second World War* (London: Routledge & Kegan Paul, 1958), particularly Chapter V and pp. 104–05. Ben Shephard's more recent *A War of Nerves: Soldiers and Psychiatrists 1914–1994* (London: Cape, 2000) is more interested in psychiatric combat injury than in the wider experience of mental illness in the army and does not discuss the term 'psychopath', though there is a reference to a soldier who has been given that label on p. 257. The discussion of the novelist Rayner Heppenstall's horrified response

conduct is recorded as 'Good', which does not suggest an obvious disciplinary problem in his case.[136]

So, for most of the war, Greenwood's contribution was made mainly through his writing. In addition to *Something in the Heart*, he was also involved in other kinds of project, including theatre and documentary film production. Greenwood's Army Service Record lists his 'Trade on Enlistment' as 'Film Producer and Author', which suggests his continuing direct involvement in the work of Greenpark Ltd.[137] The company produced a considerable number of 'information' films (probably about thirty) between 1942 and 1950, some short, some more substantial.[138] There is not space here to discuss all the films, but *Summer on the Farm* and *London 1942* in 1943, *Make Fruitful the Land* in 1945, *Proud City – a Plan for London* in 1946, and *Five Towns* in 1947 give a reasonably representative sample. *Summer on the Farm* was one of a set of 'four seasons' short films by Greenpark about farming and was scripted and directed by Ralph Keene, who worked on a large number of Greenpark films (Greenwood may well have known Keene already, since newspapers in 1939 announced that this documentary filmmaker had been asked by Michael Balcon to produce *His Worship the Mayor* for Ealing Studios, but sadly the film was never made).[139] Jez Stewart suggests that *Summer on the Farm* was a 'public relations exercise for rural workers, aimed at

to army life and his deliberate campaign to be discharged on psychiatric grounds on p. 260 may perhaps have some relevance.

136 My thanks to the Army Personnel Centre, Support Division Historical Disclosures for providing a copy of Greenwood's Army Service Record made up of: Army Form B.102, Army Form B200B, Army Form B 200 d, Army Form B 200 D and a 'record of all casualties'. Information about the Sutton Emergency Hospital is from the Lost Hospitals of London website: <http://ezitis.myzen.co.uk/belmont.html>, accessed 26 October 2017.

137 Army Form B200B.

138 The invaluable TIDA (Travel and Industrial Development Association)/British Council catalogues, now available as facsimiles online (see <http://timeimage.wikispaces.com/Book+-+Films+of+Britain+%28series%29>, accessed 26 October 2017), list Greenpark (and other company) productions from 1939 to 1950. However, the catalogue does not seem to list all Greenpark productions, and lists some Greenpark–Verity Films co-productions under Verity's name only. See listing of Greenpark films in the Bibliography for twenty-nine titles – though there may be others too. Many of the Greenpark productions can be watched online at the British Council Film website: <http://film.britishcouncil.org/british-council-film-collection>, accessed 26 October 2017.

139 *Daily Mail* 21 February 1939, p. 8; *New Zealand Herald* 27 May 1939, p. 14. His Army Form B200b records the 'Trade on Enlistment'.

the millions of industrial workers in towns', and was probably intended to show the equal importance of urban and agricultural work to the war effort.[140] *London 1942* was directed by Ken Annakin, with Ralph Keene as producer: it reflects visually and verbally on the state of London after three years of war and constructs the city as a centre for the people's war and a model for communal values: 'Every man, woman and child has a job to do', 'everyone gets a fair share', 'Here is the ordinary citizen, one of the worldwide brotherhood of men and women ... who will fight till the lights go up again on a world freed from want and fear.'[141] *Make Fruitful the Land* was an informative and in fact entertaining film about the history and practice of crop rotation, made in technicolour and making imaginative and innovative use of illustrations, paintings, and animated diagrams as well as dramatic reconstruction and live footage.[142] *Five Towns* was directed by Terry Bishop (with a script by the communist poet Randall Swingler) and shows the London fiancée of a man from the potteries being introduced both to his family and the region. Themes include post-war reconstruction and the living craft of pottery-making ('using excellent actuality footage of pottery production'), a focus which, together with the Arnold Bennett milieu of the film, Greenwood would surely have found sympathetic.[143] Ralph Keene directed and scripted another Greenpark production in 1946, *Proud City – a Plan for London*, the topic of which inevitably gives it an even stronger focus on post-war reconstruction: the rebuilding of the capital.[144] Though Greenwood's interest in film has been noticed, his commitment to film production may have been underestimated during and after the war. Most of the Greenpark films had sponsors who were interested in either agricultural production or in post-war reconstruction, but at the very least he is likely to have found these sympathetic topics to be involved with.

140 *Land of Promise: the British Documentary Movement 1930–1950*, accompanying booklet, entry for *Summer at the Farm*, p. 41.

141 The film can be seen at the British Council Film website: <http://film.british-council.org/london-1942>, accessed 26 October 2017.

142 The film can be viewed at the British Council Film website: <http://film.british-council.org/make-fruitful-the-land>, accessed 26 October 2017.

143 *Land of Promise: the British Documentary Movement 1930–1950*, accompanying booklet, entry for *Five Towns* by Patrick Russell, p. 64.

144 For basic details see BFI <http://www.bfi.org.uk/films-tv-people/4ce2b6a3bd643>, accessed 26 October 2017; the film is available on the *London Pride* DVD (40s Britain, Panamint Cinema, PDC2029, nd) and on *The Guardian* news website: <https://www.theguardian.com/uk-news/davehillblog/2014/mar/22/london-county-plan-abercrombie-forshaw>, accessed 26 October 2017.

Some obituaries and also his *Dictionary of National Biography* entry record without any further detail that Greenwood wrote a script in 1944 or 1945 for a film called *Six Men of Dorset*. This seems in fact not to have been made, but we can reconstruct its subject matter quite precisely and also why Greenwood might have found it an attractive project. The *Evening News* reported on 3 October 1945 that the actor and director Bernard Miles had told their film critic that he had recently been working 'with Roy Boulting and Walter Greenwood on a script for *The Six Men of Dorset*'.[145] This was to be part of an ambitious programme of post-war British film production by the Two Cities company. The *Evening News* saw no need to say anything further about 'The Six Men of Dorset' because it could presume that many readers would have heard of the play on which it was based – Miles Malleson and H. Brooks' play *Six Men of Dorset*, published in 1934 to celebrate the centenary of the Tolpuddle Martyrs being sentenced to transportation for forming an agricultural union in 1834 and their subsequent pardon after mass demonstrations. The play was performed during commemorations at Tolpuddle in August–September 1934 and published by Victor Gollancz, who also published a second edition in 1937 for the Left Book Club (the only other play published by the LBC, also in 1937, was Clifford Odet's *Waiting for Lefty*).[146] A number of features of the play would no doubt have appealed to Greenwood, including its theme of indisputable social injustice enforced by the haves on the have-nots and the contrast between the standard English of the landowners, vicars, lawyers, and judges and the Dorset dialect of the six martyrs. Unlike *Love on the Dole*, the play explicitly represents a step forward for social justice in England, as radical MPs successfully press for pardons and legal reform in parliament, supported by national mass protests, including one in London. Famously, the actual London protest was conducted without any disorder and this is emphasised in the play too: 'There's going to be trouble in the minds and consciences of the Cabinet, and nowhere else', says the radical leader Wade.[147] This might well have appealed to Greenwood as an opportunity to

145 WGC/3/2, p. 103.

146 See Glasgow University Library's complete listing of the Left Book Club titles in their Special Collection: <http://www.gla.ac.uk/services/specialcollections/collectionsa-z/leftbookclub/>, accessed 26 October 2017.

147 Left Book Club edition, p. 92. The Tolpuddle Martyrs' website gives a clear account of the historical events: <http://www.tolpuddlemartyrs.org.uk/story>, accessed 26 October 2017.

revisit an act of social democratic resistance somewhat like the Battle of Bexley Square, but one with a different and more effective outcome. The fact that he was working on this project during 1944–45, and his collaboration with the filmmaker Roy Boulting (who, in partnership with his brother John, was 'socialistically inclined' and 'wanted film to have serious connections to social reality') again confirms his continued political activity during the war (as does his 1945 reference to a play he is planning about the International Brigade in Spain called *Scipio*).[148] The managing director of the Two Cities film company, Filippo del Giudice, a distinguished producer of British wartime films, including *In Which We Serve* (1942), told *Kinematograph Weekly* that the completed script for *Six Men of Dorset* was 'a most satisfying film treatment'.[149] Del Giudice is said to have given his writers, directors, and actors 'an exceptional degree of creative autonomy', but he sold a controlling interest in his company to Rank in order to fund his production of Laurence Olivier's classic 1944 film of *Henry V*. Thereafter Rank took over increasingly tight control of the Two Cities company – two senior Rank employees seem to have taken upon themselves the task of making Del Giudice work in a more straightforwardly 'commercial' manner, and it may well be that *Six Men of Dorset* was a victim of this take-over and change in ethos.[150] It is a pity that Greenwood, Boulting and Miles's script was not filmed – the story of the Tolpuddle Martyrs had to wait until 1986 for Bill Douglas's film *Comrades*.[151]

After 1945 Greenwood published a further four novels, all with Hutchinson. Between 1952 and 1956 he completed his Trelooe Trilogy, made up of *So Brief the Spring* (1952), *What Everybody Wants* (1954), and *Down by the Sea* (1956). The trilogy was set in Cornwall, where

---

148 The *Stage*, 4 October 1945 in WGC/3/2, p. 103. See BFI Screen-Online for a concise account of the work of the Boulting Brothers, from which these quotations about them come: <http://www.screenonline.org.uk/film/id/446435/>, accessed 26 October 2017.

149 27 September 1945, pp. 5 and 17 (in WGC/3/2, p. 103).

150 See the BFI Screen-Online concise biography of Del Giudice: <http://www.screenonline.org.uk/people/id/476932/>, accessed 26 October 2017; and Geoffrey McNab's *J. Arthur Rank and the British Film Industry* (London: Routledge, 1993), pp. 87–90. Neither refer specifically to *Six Men of Dorset*, but give accounts of the growing differences between Del Giudice's creative approach to film-making and that of Rank's senior managers in the mid to late 1940s.

151 *Comrades*, produced by Skreba Films, has a BFI entry at <http://www.screenonline.org.uk/film/id/450592/> (accessed 26 October 2017) and was re-released by the BFI in a new restored dual-format edition in 2012.

Greenwood had holidayed since meeting Arthur Wragg in the 1930s and where he was then living. For much of his career Greenwood had been keen wherever possible to turn novels into stage versions (he had adapted *Only Mugs Work* in 1938 and *His Worship the Mayor* in 1940, the stage version being called *Give Us This Day*). In the 1950s this process was reversed: *So Brief the Spring* originated as a play as early as 1945, as did Greenwood's final novel *Saturday Night at the Crown* (1959), which was an adaptation of a play first performed in 1956 (a *Guardian* review of the play thought it a 'mild concoction ... [but] a show-case for Thora Hird' and the novel is dedicated to her as 'the inimitable Ada Thorpe' in the play).[152]

The Trelooe Trilogy clearly sold steadily and is still highly readable. However, there were no longer reviews in major national newspapers such as *The Times* and the *Manchester Guardian*, though Hutchinson placed display adverts for the novels in these papers.[153] Instead, the novels' covers quote from regional newspapers and magazines; an extract from a review in *The Lady* of *What Everybody Wants* is reasonably representative, though it under-represents a strand of serious social comment that is still present in the novels: 'All takes place in a Cornish village. The shrewd humour is unfailing. Recommended for holiday reading.'[154] All three novels actually show a strong sense of the changes brought about after the war: there are frequent references to increased taxation, the National Health Service, nationalisation, and the welfare state by richer and poorer characters alike. The attitudes of the novels to these developments sometimes seem neutral: they work through characters' thoughts without the kinds of explicit authorial narrative intervention in *Love on the Dole*. However, there are clear distinctions suggested between the post-welfare state respectable and unrespectable poor and, indeed, the post-welfare

---

152 The script of the 1945 *So Brief the Spring* is held in the Greenwood Collection as WGC/1/10/1. The *Manchester Guardian* reviewed the play's premiere at Morecambe on 8 June 1954 and again on its post-novel revival at the Garrick, London, on 10 September 1957 (the quotation is from the later review). The title *Saturday Night at the Crown* and the setting of the story in a pub echo a well-known 1930s novel called *Saturday Night at the Greyhound* (London: Hogarth Press, 1931), by John Hampson, though the details of the two novels are rather different. See my article on Hampson in Johnson, *Dictionary of Literary Biography Vol. 191*, pp. 163–70. *Saturday Night at the Greyhound* is also discussed in Steven Earnshaw's *The Pub in Literature: England's Altered State* (Manchester: Manchester University Press, 2000), pp. 246–47.

153 For example, see *The Times* 2 April 1954, p. 18 or 5 July 1956, p. 13.

154 From the dust jacket of the Hutchinson edition, March 1955.

state honest and dishonest wealthy. The three novels share a number of characters, but each also introduces new characters who interact with the population of the fictional Cornish village of Trelooe; each novel spends considerable effort on portraying everyday life (perhaps something in the manner of a 'soap opera'), but also contains one much less ordinary adventure or event. A character who helps knit all three novels together is Randy Jollifer. Greenwood borrowed the name from a small boat that he bought to go sailing with the actor Robert Newton in Cornwall (Newton played Jollifer in the 1945 stage version of this story and the novel is dedicated to him – and indeed the character is based on some aspects of Newton's life).[155]

Randy is the central character in *So Brief the Spring*, though this is not at first obvious. He has wealthy relatives: his father, the miserly Arky Jollifer, acquires the local manor house and its farm through marriage, but disinherits Randy after his wartime marriage ends in divorce. Having served in the Royal Navy during the war (as did Newton), Randy now earns a modest living as a fisherman and by taking holiday-makers on fishing trips. He lives contentedly in a cottage and some features of his life suggest that he is rural-maritime-post-war kin to Larry Meath: his cottage boasts filled bookshelves, a typewriter, a radiogram, and a gramophone, as well as records of 'Bach, Handel, Mozart, Beethoven and Chopin'.[156] The bookshelf is regarded as 'astonishing' in such a man's house by the female character who appears at first to be the novel's central figure – Ann Halstead (p. 74). This recalls Sally's observation of Larry's bookshelf and, indeed, Ann initially looks as if she is a new version of Sally. She is in Trelooe on holiday alone to think about her future – she is doubtful about marrying her fiancé and dreads living in a small flat in London, but is enraptured by Trelooe and especially the half-ruined manor house. Her discontent resembles Sally's to an extent, but her dreams from the beginning have a more material aspect. She is attracted to Randy, but wants to acquire 'his' manor-house as well. In the course of winning the favour of Arky as part of a longer-term stratagem, she receives an offer of marriage from the miserly father and accepts it (something which seems surprising and unconvincing in the novel, but which revisits Sally's 'arrangement' with Sam Grundy). So besotted is Arky that he alters

155 See *Daily Dispatch* article about the play version of *So Brief the Spring*, 2 October 1945 (WGC/3/2, p. 117).
156 (London: Hutchinson, 1952), p. 38. All subsequent page references are to this edition and will be given in brackets in the text.

his will in her favour (now disinheriting his two exploited farm-hand nephews Sam and Eb) and tells her that the cellar of his semi-ruinous house is full of biscuit-tins packed full of treasury notes and three cider-barrels of gold sovereigns – all the fruit of tax evasion via cash dealings during the First and Second World Wars and since. However, Arky dies of a heart attack as Ann accepts his proposal, and Sam and Eb, long on the look-out for their uncle's hidden treasure, manage to knock over a lantern and set the house ablaze as they struggle to enter the cellar first. Amended will and treasury notes are destroyed – but Randy eventually inherits the melted mass of gold sovereigns. The moral seems to be that what was a desperate choice in the 1930s for Sally is an avoidable choice in the 1950s – material need is different from material greed, and the context is now a different one. Though Ann happily marries a doctor friend of Randy's, he marries a concert pianist who frequently plays on BBC radio. Culture is still part of *The Secret Kingdom* referred to in his 1938 novel, which features the BBC and musical ability as ways out of poverty rather than alternatives to avarice.

Randy Jollifer presumably represents a middle way – he is content to labour and deserves his fortune (which does not seem to alter him). But if the novel is critical of the money-obsessed rich, it also has some comment on the 'idle poor', and revisits 1930s themes of 'respectability'. A 'disreputable family from the town slums', the Connors, who have spent the war living in a house requisitioned in a 1939 from an absentee owner, get very short shrift:

> The mother was a slut and the father a servile loafer, content to draw the dole ... . As his shiftless wife could depend on her swarm of undisciplined children being fed at school, he could always find a customer for his meat ration coupons, which paid for some of his drink and cigarettes ... he thought it just and proper that all who worked hard and were thrifty should be taxed severely to pride him and his with 'my rights'. (pp. 39–40)

The language directly picks up the discourse of respectability *versus* unrespectability of which *Love on the Dole* is so often critical (it is sadly notable too that this model 'bad family' are given an Irish surname). These may be the thoughts of Randy, who is the next-door neighbour, rather than directly those of an authorial narrator, but he is normally the trilogy's centre of sound judgement. This early example of what could be called a 'Benefits Street'-style discourse of hostility towards 'undeserving' benefit claimants might seem very surprising in a novel by the author of *Love on the Dole*. But the point is presumably that things are now changed: this family are not like the Hardcastles, but more like Helen Hawkins' parents, and they are not beset by the same pressing needs as the inhabitants of Hanky Park. The implication is that they could choose differently in a post-war welfare state with full employment. However, later in the book Randy talks of being made up of several different personalities – one of whom is an idealist: 'Wants the stars as playthings – up in arms against a lot that passes for respectability in this world' (p. 88). Two sets of characters who are dismissive of the post-war working classes certainly are implicitly criticised in the novel. The miser Uncle Arky comments on some hired workers: 'Skulking, idle, good-for-nothings. Welfare State! I'd Welfare State 'em if I had my way' (p. 17). Randy's other neighbours are exposed to his criticism to an extent when they complain of the Connors: 'they're giving them a council house and providing them with furniture out of the rates. Everybody's up in arms. *We're* all paying for this – out of the rates' (p. 41). Randy accuses the speaker of malicious gossip. The speaker is Miss Perrow, who, with Mrs Duckett, does indeed recall the 'gossips' in *Love on the Dole*, though their number is now reduced to two. They also appear in each novel in the trilogy, but Greenwood's view of gossips seems to have darkened: the pair seem less ambiguous, are never helpful, and are more malicious and less comic than their 1930s forebears (they are naturally in competition, but also positively hate each other, despite their apparent friendship). They are as materialistic as Arky and as dishonest, and their views of the welfare state and taxation are entirely opportunistic. They operate at a lower level in society than Arky does, but are equally greedy. In the second novel Mrs Duckett offers help to an old man in a similar way to a predecessor in Greenwood's 1930s story (and one-act play) *The Practised Hand*: having realised that old Garnet has a £1500 hidden in his mattress (he does not trust banks) she takes him in and hastens his end with frequent applications of whisky.

Happily married by the end of the first novel, Randy is the stable core of the second two, but displaced in both from the star role of working man made good by the character of Darky Durrant. He is a tough character on the margin of Trelooe society (perhaps damaged and isolated by his combat experience in the war). He is a 'gypsy' and a poacher with a distinguished war record (naturally of a slightly irregular kind: he was a Commando who was awarded a number of medals). He lives hand to mouth in a semi-ruinous cottage, and a number of the characters, and clearly the novel itself, admire his close relationship to the natural world, despite his disregard for many property laws. When it comes to real moral questions, however, Durrant always makes the right choices (he rescues the boy Mungo from crooks who steal horses to butcher and sell as beef). In *What Everybody Wants* he marries a capable orphaned servant girl who, during the course of the final novel, *Down by the Sea*, brings him to an extent back into contact with society, opening his cottage as a tea-room for tourists. As the language used in reviews of the trilogy suggests, it has many features (including happy endings for the good, and pastoral tendencies) that we might call middlebrow. Where, earlier in his career, Greenwood is happy to use popular conventions allied with an urge for social reform, there is in these 1950s novels less pressure from social issues, though there is always a running commentary on obsession with money as a perversion of a satisfying life. In some ways, the trilogy picks up but allows fulfilment of Harry and Helen's hopeless fantasy on their trip to Blackpool in *Love on the Dole* – that they could live there simply in a cottage and support themselves by growing vegetables and by Harry working on a fishing boat. However, Trelooe is not idyllic – the fishermen have to sign on the dole to make ends meet and the mean and self-interested are always with us, unfixed by post-war British social reform.

Greenwood's final novel *Saturday Night at the Crown* is set entirely in a Manchester pub over the course of a single day, and its urban, wholly working-class setting makes it more easily comparable to his pre-war fiction. It follows the fortunes of the landlord Harry Boothroyd, the barmaid Sally Earnshaw, the cook Maudie, and a number of customers, including the dominant Ada Thorpe and her husband (who does not get the chance to speak for the entire course of the novel), her son Bert Thorpe and his new girlfriend Jean McLean, the extended Hardy family, who have hired a room after the funeral of the clan's mother, old Mrs Hardy, and a group of US troops from a nearby base. This is a story notably set in a new world of 1950s working-class prosperity. Some of the younger characters (added since the original play version), such as Bert Thorpe, work in the thriving successor to *Love on the Dole*'s Marlowe's works ('Metropolitan-Electric's products … found their way all over the world'), making use of its sports facilities and even owning their own expensive racing cycles.[157] Not everyone has enough money for everything they would like, but all the characters have enough

---

157 (London: Hutchinson, 1959), p. 10. All subsequent page references are to this edition and are given in brackets in the text.

surplus to make quite a night of it at the Crown. Indeed, this is a world with resemblances to that of Alan Sillitoe's *Saturday Night and Sunday Morning* (with which its representations of 1950s working-class life might fruitfully be compared). However, there is considerable reference to the pre-war world, and sometimes in quite specific ways to the world of *Love on the Dole*. A narrative voice notes that near the Crown is 'what had once been the pawnshop':

> But the larger part of the shop's trade in these days of full employment, better pay and other financial advantages of the Welfare state, consisted in the sale of cheap clothing, appallingly ugly and badly-made furniture, radio sets and television receivers all bought and sometimes paid for ... 'on the never never'. (p. 14)

There may still be things to criticise, but things are relatively better. Older characters are shown as more aware of the changes in their lifetime, though so too is the one younger character who is interested in politics, the significantly named Sally (Greenwood again recycles a few of his favourite names). She refutes the landlord's casually expressed view that politics never make any difference, saying:

> 'You of all people ... . How many kids do you see running abut now, down-at-heel, shabby and half-starved like many of them were when I left school? ... and nearly four million men on the dole ... . Look at the children running about now, fine and healthy from vitamins and orange juice when they were babies ... these things ... had to be fought for. They weren't just dished out like prizes in a silly TV quiz. (p. 46)

It is noticeably now a world where everyone has access to a national culture of radio and TV – Bert dreams that he and Jean's singing at the pub might be noticed by a talent scout: 'Somebody from the BBC or commercial TV ... their own weekly programme on TV ... [Eventually] a film "The Bert and Jean story" ... Look at Tommy Steele and the rest' (p. 2).

There are thus some new kinds of working-class dreams (though there is still betting going on in the pub) and, if not all are achievable, many seem much more possible than was the case in Hanky Park. If *Love on the Dole* was an anti-romance or a novel about the impossibility of romance for working people under current economic conditions ('the tragedy of a lost generation who are denied consummation, in decency, of the natural desires and hopes of youth', Greenwood had said of *Love on the Dole*), then *Saturday Night at the Crown* is a novel dependent on the practical possibilities of romance.[158] It is interested in marriages disrupted by greed (those of the Hardy siblings arguing about their inheritance) or by unequal power (that of Ada and Herbert Thorpe), but also the potential of future relationships based in equality and good economic planning. In the end Bert will have his Jean, Maudie will have her Scottish lorry driver Jock McCall and a jointly owned transport café, and Sally will have her Harry Boothroyd and the country pub she has bought for him with her savings in place of the urban Crown. There are still things characters have to worry about (including the atom bomb, under-age sex, old age, greedy relatives, snobbery, vanity, dominant wives, and skiffle bands), but this seems a world of working-class possibility where decent people can apparently make it. It is surely intended to be read (as various echoes suggest) with a memory of *Love on the Dole* in mind. Simon Baker has suggested that the chorus of older women in the film of *Love on the Dole* 'presage the gossiping Ena Sharples, Minnie Caldwell and Martha Longhirst in the early *Coronation Street* (ITV 1961–), especially in the scene where they sit in their local's private bar criticising their neighbours'.[159] Indeed, Baker is not the only one to see affinities between Greenwood's work and *Coronation Street* – the reviewer Keith Dewhurst saw a certain kinship in a 1971 *Guardian* article, but said that, compared with *Love on the Dole*, '*Coronation Street* is not really serious'; while another 1970s reviewer remarked that a revival of *The Cure for Love* 'looks and sounds like wartime *Coronation Street*'.[160] More recently, a sense of similarity is quite frequently expressed in viewers' internet reviews of the film of *Love on the Dole*: 'Fantastic drama. I think the early *Coronation Street* actors must have studied the same technique'; 'a lovely old film predating early *Coronation Street*, but more earthy'.[161] Of course, the stories share a background in working-class Salford, if at very different periods. Indeed, the two versions of Salford shared quite a number of actors too at various points – Betty Driver, who played

---

158 Cited in '*Love on the Dole* and its Reception in the 1930s', p. 235; originally from *Manchester Evening News* article in WGC/3/1.

159 In his commentary on the film on BFI Screen-Online: <http://www.screenonline. org.uk/film/id/485682/>, accessed 26 October 2017.

160 *The Guardian* 2 April 1971 and Nicholas de Jongh in *The Guardian* 21 September 1978, p. 10.

161 Reviews of the *Love on the Dole* DVD (Fabulous Films, 2004) posted on Amazon in 2009 and 2014 by James W. Turner and John Sutcliffe respectively (<https://www. amazon.co.uk/Love-Dole-DVD-Deborah-Kerr/dp/B00019HOM2>, accessed 26 October 2017, italics added.

Mrs Bull in the 1967 Granada TV adaptation of *Love on the Dole*, was a long-term Coronation Street actress, playing Betty Williams/Turpin from 1969 until 2011, while four others of the Granada cast appeared in Coronation Street either occasionally or regularly in the 1960s (George A. Cooper [Sam Grundy], Ronald Cunliffe [Harry], Eve Pearce [Mrs Hardcastle], Martin Shaw [O'Leary]) and even Geoffrey Hibbert, Harry in the 1941 film, made several guest appearances in the Street in the 1960s.[162] This may partly have been because the adaptor of the Granada production, John Finch, was also an early writer for Coronation Street (from 1961 onwards), and perhaps formed a hub for a network of actors mainly of authentic working-class origin. However, beyond the general atmosphere (in which the Crown surely does presage the Rover's Return) three early Coronation Street gossips may have more specific partial models in the 'chorus' of older women in *Love on the Dole*: Ena Sharples, Martha Longhurst, and Minnie Caldwell (Ena Sharples, with her job as caretaker of the Mission Hall, may draw to an extent on Greenwood's Mrs Scodger and Mrs Jikes, who are habitués of the Spiritualist Mission in Hanky Park).

Theatre also took up considerable energy in the post-war period, with the production of several original plays including *The Cure for Love: A Lancashire Comedy in Three Acts* in 1945 and *Too Clever for Love* in 1952 (both of these had a number of BBC radio productions in the 1940s and 1950s). Two post-war theatrical friendships were important to Greenwood – with the actor Robert Donat and the actress Thora Hird. Donat directed and acted in *The Cure for Love* in its 1945 premiere before putting much energy into getting the 1949 film version made, while Thora Hird, who played Mrs Dorbell in that film, went on to act in other plays Greenwood wrote – including *Happy Days* (1959), which was written with her in mind (the first draft was preserved in a folder marked 'Thora's New Play').[163] Later there were further adaptations, including

---

162 See Dennis Barker's obituary of Betty Diver (*The Guardian* 15 October 2011) and for Geoffrey Hibbert see IMDB: <http://www.imdb.com/name/nm0382504/bio?ref_=nm_ov_bio_sm>, accessed 26 October 2017. For *Coronation Street* parts played by Cooper, Cunliffe, Pearce, Shaw see their various entries in Wikipedia, Coropedia and IMDB.

163 For further information on the film of *The Cure for Love* and three clips see the BFI Screen-Online entry: <http://www.screenonline.org.uk/film/id/453776/>, accessed 26 October 2017. For the *Happy Days* folder, dating to 1958, see WGC/1/10/1; Thora Hird appeared in a production at the Grand Theatre Blackpool in 1959, together with the future *Coronation Street* actress Pat Phoenix (see WGC/5/4/1).

his last work for theatre – a stage version of his memoir *There Was a Time* (later produced under the title *Hanky Park*), performed in 1967 and revived in 1971.[164] Equally, the theatrical career of *Love on the Dole* continued, with innumerable productions at larger and smaller theatres in Britain since 1945 (as well as in the US): the National Theatre listed the play in its One Hundred Plays of the Century in 1999.[165] There was also a musical version produced at the Nottingham Playhouse in 1970 (with a book by Terry Hughes based on Gow and Greenwood's play, lyrics by Robert A. Gray, and music by Alan Fluck).[166]

Greenwood was the co-writer (with Ara Calder Marshall and Paul Rotha) of a 1947 documentary about post-war Manchester directed by Rotha and called *A City Speaks* ('a film about local Government') – a fact noted by historians but not by Greenwood's literary critics.[167] Like

---

164 *Too Clever for Love* was originally called *Never a Dull Moment* and produced under that title at the Oldham Repertory theatre; the second production under the new title was at the Morecombe Repertory Theatre. Details of BBC radio productions of *The Cure for Love* and *Too Clever for Love* can be found by searching for their titles in the BBC Genome Project. The production history of stage versions of *There Was a Time/Hanky Park* is complex (see the Walter Greenwood Collection under 'Manuscripts and Typescripts' for numerous revised scripts) – but the first production under the first title was at Dundee Repertory Theatre on 23 October 1967 and the first production under the second title was at the Mermaid Theatre, London 1 April 1971.

165 The Walter Greenwood Collection's holding of posters and programmes gives a sense of the frequency of productions of *Love on the Dole*, though this is representative rather than comprehensive. See WGC/5 (<http://www.ils.salford.ac.uk/library/resources/special/Greenwood.xml#Theatre Programmes, Playbills, etc; accessed 17 July 2010). For National Theatre Hundred Best Plays see <http://www.nationaltheatre.org.uk/11741/platforms/nt2000-one-hundred-plays-of-the-century.html>, accessed 16 July 2010.

166 There was also an amateur revival with a revised script and music by the Just-the-Ticket Theatre Company, Roda McGraw Theatre, Woking, 1995, directed by Stewart Nicholls (who very kindly provided me with a recording of the show). For details of both Nottingham and Woking productions see the Musical Theatre website: <http://www.musical-theatre.net/html/justtheticket/loveonthedole.html>, accessed 17 July 2010.

167 The film is listed by IMDB under Greenwood's writing credits, but they have little information on the film: <http://www.imdb.com/name/nm0339405/>, accessed 26 October 2017. There is a substantial discussion of the film in Charlotte Wildman's 'A City Speaks: The Projection of Civic Identity in Manchester', *Twentieth Century British History*, 23, 1, 2012, pp. 80–89. The BFI has recently made the film available on BFI player (see <http://player.bfi.org.uk/film/watch-city-speaks-1947/>, accessed 26 October 2017.

Paul Rotha's 1946 documentary *Land of Promise*, the film centres on the topic of post-war improvements, though in this case with a focus on Manchester rather than the nation as a whole. Charlotte Wildman suggests that there is a 'relative lack of a narrative of "reconstruction"' in the film, but it seems to me its strong interest in the replacement of nineteenth-century slums with modern planned housing, and in the provision by local government of employment, social services, and healthcare (indeed, post-war Manchester is represented as a welfare state in its own right) is very much a focus on post-war reconstruction.[168] These topics Greenwood would surely have found, like his collaborators, sympathetic, but his association with the film (he is one of the narrators too) perhaps also helped to underline the distance travelled since *Love on the Dole* and the fulfilment of the 1941 film's promise – though the documentary is clear that there is still work to do: 'let the lessons of yesterday not be forgotten in the plans of tomorrow'. Greenwood also wrote two post-war feature-film scripts. The highly watchable *The Eureka Stockade* (1949) had what might seem an uncharacteristic setting for Greenwood in 1850s Australia (though his script for *Six Men of Dorset* might form a possible bridge, given its Australian scenes, and he would presumably have been aware of the positive reception of the film of *Love on the Dole* there), and focused on a key event in the development of Australia as a democracy, when gold miners suffering taxation without representation rebelled against the governor of Ballarat, Victoria.[169] They took an armed stand in a hastily built stockade and were quickly defeated in a bloody battle with the police and a British military detachment. Afterwards, much public opinion across Australia turned against the governor and democratic rights were granted to the miners and all other white adult males to elect representatives to the Victoria parliament. Though this has not

---

168 'A City Speaks', p. 98.
169 It was an Ealing Studios film and clearly an ambitious production with a large budget, as there is a large cast, including the Australian film star Chipps Rafferty, who plays Lalor, and complex sets and outdoor locations in Australia. The director was the documentary maker Harry Watts, who would also have found the story's democratic and activist focus of great interest. See IMDB for factual details of the film: <http://www.imdb.com/title/tt0041340/?ref_=ttco_co_tt>, accessed 26 February 2015. Sadly, Harry Watts' memoir, *Don't Look at the Camera* (London: Elek, 1974) makes no reference to the film. For an account of the events behind the film, see, for example, Manning Clark's *History of Australia* (1962; London: Pimlico, abridged, 1993), pp. 254–65.

been previously noticed, the story gave Greenwood a curious chance to revisit an aspect of *Love on the Dole*: the historical miner's leader, Peter Lalor, is depicted as a moderate who tries to negotiate with the governor and who repeatedly tries to dissuade the miners from more radical politics and from armed revolt. He becomes their leader only when the governor refuses to negotiate, and is in the end elected as their MP: the scenes in the film strongly suggest that Peter Lalor and the Eureka Stockade are seen as reprising Larry and the Battle of Bexley Square, except that in this case the authorities push him into more radical activism and he survives to become a democratic political leader. Perhaps this is partly a response on Greenwood's part to some criticism that Larry had been too passive a political figure? More obviously characteristic in that it returned (if in a somewhat different post-war context) to the themes of co-operation between labour and capital discussed in *Something in My Heart*, was the 1950 film *Chance of a Lifetime*. This was directed by Bernard Miles and caused considerable controversy because of its story-line about the absolute need for co-operation between workers and management. While the film's urge for consensus now seems moderate – in line with Greenwood's lifelong Labour Party membership – rather than revolutionary, film distributors were unable to see this, as Fintan MacDonagh explains:

> Reacting against its perceived socialist agenda, the major film circuits refused to show it, and it was even castigated as 'propaganda for communism and workers' control' by the Ministry of Labour. The President of the Board of Trade, Harold Wilson ... personally intervened to impose its release on the Odeon circuit. Regrettably it was not a financial success, though Miles later spoke of his pride in making a film to 'speak for England'.[170]

The *Film Bulletin* Review took the opposite view, praising the authentic portrayal of the working-class engineering workers as unusual in English cinema, but suggesting that the consensus it portrayed would 'displease the more extremely left'.[171] For Greenwood it was perhaps something of a return to the imagined life of Marlowe's engineering works – a number

---

170 See the brief article on the film by Fintan MacDonagh at the BFI Screen-Online website: <http://www.screenonline.org.uk/film/id/476987/index.html>, accessed 14 July 2010). Clips from the film are also accessible. See also Robert Murphy's similar discussion in his *Realism and Tinsel*, p. 80.

171 The anonymous *Film Bulletin* review is from Vol. 17, issue 195, 1950, p. 43. Available at the BFI website: <http://www.screenonline.org.uk/media/mfb/1378357/index.html>, accessed 14 July 2010.

of discussions about managers and money by the workers in the works' yard recall somewhat Larry's impromptu lessons there – as well as to the continuing need for cross-class co-operation.

Greenwood also continued to be engaged in both radio productions and in the new possibilities provided by television, often working with adaptors. *Love on the Dole* remained a firm favourite for adaptations during his lifetime (as well as after), holding the record for the most-produced play in the BBC's 'Saturday Night Theatre' programme, which ran from 1943 until 1996 (BBC productions of the play included six separate versions in 1942, 1945, 1949, 1955, 1965, and 1972, with further productions after Greenwood's death, in 1980 and 1987).[172] There was also a BBC TV production of *The Secret Kingdom* in eight parts in 1960, while versions of *Love on the Dole* were produced by BBC TV Sunday Night Theatre in 1960, by Granada TV in 1967, and again by the BBC in 1969.[173]

Though *Saturday Night at the Crown* (1959) was Greenwood's final novel, he wrote one further successful (and indeed impressive) prose work: his memoir *There Was a Time*, published by Jonathan Cape in 1967 (its popularity was confirmed by a Penguin paperback edition later that year). It was praised as a twentieth-century working-class autobiography evoking a now unimaginable world, though also some feelings of nostalgia for an imagined lost community: 'Will we get, sixty years on, a fond memoir of the gamey, rich broth of a life people are living in our new vertical villages? ... His Hanky Park is not yet drowned deep as Atlantis, but it seems a remote, almost enchanted land.'[174] As in *Saturday Night at the Crown*, Greenwood felt confident here that much better times for working-class people were now irrevocably established:

Meritorious children of my contemporaries ... are graduates of Oxbridge, Red-brick and the local school of Advanced Technology. Yesterday the

172 Information of radio productions derived from the invaluable Saturday Night Theatre website <http://www.saturday-night-theatre.co.uk/>, accessed 14 July 2010), which gives a list of all the plays produced in the series from 1943 onwards. *Love on the Dole* seems to have been the most often produced for Saturday Night Theatre.

173 Information for TV adaptations derived from the IMDB: <http://www.imdb.com/title/tt1387593/>, accessed 26 October 2017, from the Greenwood collection (WGC/1/2/4) and from the Television Heaven website: <http://www.television-heaven.co.uk/plays_2.htm>, accessed 14 July 2010. ITV has the complete tape of the 1967 Granada TV production and very kindly provided me with a copy.

174 Peter Eckersley, *The Guardian* 12 May 1967, p. 9.

Depression and lo! By a hop skip and a jump the Space Age and a Welfare State. A five-day, forty-hour week, holidays with pay, superannuation pension schemes, lunch vouchers and works' canteens; an inrush of immigrants to fill the rising tide of jobs ... and organised Labour in conference with employers on equal terms. (p. 251)

He seemed less confident by the 1970s. In an interview for the *Guardian* with Catherine Stott on the occasion of the opening of *Hanky Park* (his play version of his memoir) at the Mermaid Theatre, London, in 1971, Greenwood is reported as 'gloomily' foreseeing 'another slump just round the corner' and as being at work 'on a novel about contemporary Manchester': 'from the dark hints he dropped, he still finds plenty of social atrocities to write about'.[175]

In an amateur interview with Greenwood filmed in Salford in 1973 (his appearance seemed to have changed surprisingly little since his first publicity photos in the 1930s) he expressed the view that overall there had been 'a marvellous change for the better', and referred several times to the benefits of the post-war welfare state, especially improved child nutrition and health, and access to education. However, he regretted the loss of 'neighbourliness' and had sharp reservations about high-rise flats.[176] Some of the footage is taken outside 'Walter Greenwood Court', the fifteen-storey-block built to replace the demolished Hanky Park area in 1964 and named in his honour. The building, which was by then a hostel housing otherwise homeless young people, was the setting of a 1994 documentary that, taking *Love on the Dole* as a benchmark, compared the lives then lived in Walter Greenwood Court with those lived in Hanky Park in the 1930s.[177] In refraining from overall 'authorial' commentary, the programme is truer to purer forms of documentary than the novel of *Love on the Dole* – we hear from the residents and from the hostel manager via a mainly neutral interviewer, but must come to our own conclusions. These might well be bleak: while the material conditions of the people living in Walter Greenwood Court seem indisputably superior to those who lived

175 'Dole Cue', 2 April 1971, p. 10.
176 The sixteen minute interview is posted on YouTube as part of the Kersal Flats local history channel: <https://www.youtube.com/watch?v=J1xr1UwLbQo>, accessed 26 October 2017.
177 *Close Up North: Love on the Dole*, directed by Lyn Webster Wilde (Halcyon Productions, BBC North, 28 minutes, 1 December 2004, WGC/7/18/3; can be watched on YouTube: <https://www.youtube.com/watch?v=E25CcYw4s8M&noht ml5=False>.

in Ellor Street sixty years earlier, their aspirations, possibilities, and future expectations seem painfully low. Walter Greenwood Court was demolished in its turn in 2001.

The 1971 production of *Hanky Park* also gave Keith Dewhurst an opportunity in *The Guardian* to look back over Greenwood's career. He argued that he was 'a writer of interest' for several of his works, 'but that with *Love on the Dole* he is far more':

> he is part of English literature and of the history of English society and taste ... [he] is not a great highbrow master like D.H. Lawrence, but he is and always has been a truly popular writer – a man of the people who entertains all sorts and conditions and appeals instantly and directly to their hearts ... . The paradox and fascination of the book is that although the anger of the situation gave Walter Greenwood a pen of fire it is his approach to fiction that makes his work a classic.[178]

This is acute and accords with Greenwood's own rare reflections on what made his first novel both successful and effective:

> I was burning up inside with fury at the poverty around me ... it was a burning hatred but I realised this was no way to go about writing it down. This would be carrying a torch. I knew the most convincing way to present it was to get the characters right and a good story to tell it through.[179]

His obituaries were to take a similar view, though they sometimes under-rated his artistry and the ways in which he belonged to, and carefully adapted, literary and popular culture traditions (Dewhurst, on the contrary, had noted Greenwood's 'flair' and 'cunning' as a 'shrewd judge of the world, who went very assuredly from Hanky Park to Broadway').[180] *The Times* said that:

> His plays and novels owed nothing to modern, nor any other, theories of literature and drama. The stories he told, he convinced both readers and theatre audiences, were the inevitable result of the situations which faced the people he created. He was ... a primitive, a literary equivalent to L.S. Lowry.[181]

In 1971 Greenwood was awarded the honorary degree of Doctor of Letters by the University of Salford, to which he had donated all the

178 'Greenwood's Grass Roots', 2 April 1971.
179 'Dole Cue', *The Guardian*, 2 April 1971, p. 10.
180 2 April 1971.
181 16 September 1974, p. 16. Unsigned.

papers now forming the invaluable Walter Greenwood Collection. He died peacefully in bed at his home on the Isle of Man on 11 September 1974, having spent over forty years of his life as a successful, popular, significant, and influential author.

Conclusion

Walter Greenwood's *Love on the Dole* was clearly very influential in all three of its forms in the period from novel publication in 1933 to film release in 1941 and on into the later 1940s. It was frequently described or called upon as a work based in fact and one that truly documented real conditions, a point Matthew Gaughan illustrates from a number of newspaper reviews of the novel: 'a faithful representation of the unemployed', 'a "social document"', 'facts, facts, facts, all the way'.[1] At least one US economics journal referred to the novel, in December 1934, as a source of valid testimony: 'the reaction on family life is strikingly portrayed in a recent novel by Walter Greenwood, *Love on the Dole*'.[2] Ten years later a well-known social worker still saw the text as giving a total recall of the Depression: 'readers who wish to recapture the atmosphere of these years can achieve this unpleasant experience by re-reading Walter Greenwood's *Love on the Dole*'.[3] It was claimed when the play was performed at the Salford Empire that local audiences recognised 'not only local scenes, but the vivid realism of life as portrayed here'.[4] The texts do, indeed, all draw on an environment and a reality which Greenwood knew well (in as far as anyone can fully 'know' any reality), and putting each of these versions of *Love on the Dole* back into their historical and aesthetic contexts is productive. But contexts are never single nor simple, and historicising the

---

1 'Palatable Socialism or "the Real Thing"?', pp. 47 and 48. The quotations are from *The Sunday Chronicle* 3 August 1933), *The Times Literary Supplement* 29 June 1933, and the *New Clarion* 8 July 1933).

2 Footnote 55 in Helen Fisher Hohman, 'The Status of Unemployment Insurance in Great Britain', *Journal of Political Economy*, 42, 6, December 1934, pp. 721–52, p. 749.

3 Mary Danvers Stocks (later Baroness Stocks), *Fifty Years in Every Street* (Manchester: Manchester University Press, 1944), p. 81.

4 *The Stage* 29 June 1939, p. 2. Unsigned brief review referring to the June 1939 production at Salford.

text does not tell us what it meant, but rather opens up a range of possible things it might have meant at the times of publication and reception. Indeed, 'realism', whether descending from nineteenth-century forms of the novel or drama, or the newer forms of written and film documentary, is always a matter of illusion, of creating a rhetoric or representation of 'reality', inevitably through the manipulation of devices and discourses, inevitably with conscious or unconscious purposes on the part of the author, partly determined by the possibilities of genre or sub-genre, and open to the varying interpretation(s) of the reader(s)/the audience(s)/ the viewer(s) within their reading frameworks and contexts. So while Greenwood's texts have often been seen as message-bearing ('fiction with a definite social aim', said the novelist and critic Phyllis Bentley[5]), they have also been seen by many critics as highly interpretable in various ways, particularly because the critics have often had reservations about their coherence. As early as 1934, a US newspaper reviewer of the novel, Peter Monro Jack, raised this issue:

> Mr Greenwood is not yet clear about his attitude. He inclines to off-set his pathos with a touch of facetiousness in his chapter titles, an unnecessary and silly device. He may as well accept his experiences and form his convictions from them. He can stand on his own two legs, heeding neither the clamour of party, nor the lure of popularity. It is something to have written the most moving tale of mean streets since the war.[6]

One might suspect that, in fact, the texts often do steer a subtle path between popular appeal and serious political intention, and one that is not inevitably a result of confusion or uncertainty. However, a number of critics working on the novel and play versions of *Love on the Dole* since have also seen them as containing contradictions arising from divided purposes. Roger Webster argues that these 'contradictions' are part of a deliberate and anti-bourgeois aesthetic: 'some critics have attacked Greenwood for propagating middle-class values and retaining unquestioningly the bourgeois form of fiction, that of the traditional realist novel', [however his] 'divided language is not a form of collusion but rather a reflection and revelation of the divisions in literary and social processes'.[7] Matthew Gaughan suggests that contradictions are

5 'Contemporary British Fiction', *The English Journal*, 28, 4, April 1939, pp. 251–61, p. 257.
6 *New York Times* 26 August 1934, p. 8; read via *Pro-Quest Historical Newspapers* database.
7 '*Love on the Dole* and the Aesthetic of Contradiction', in *The British Working-Class*

produced by the novel's attempt to do too many things at once, arising from uncertainties about its purpose and hence its effect on an imagined readership:

> The novel attempts to present *and* represent Hanky Park's ... poverty, culture and politics to an audience unfamiliar with those qualities, leading it into a series of contradictions: between a positive representation of the author's community and a damning of its political indifference; between an authentic account 'faithful' to the life of his community and an account which will appear both authentic and appealing to a middle-class and southern readership; and between a novel which is a socialist polemic and a novel which describes ... part of its community's conservatism.[8]

Carole Snee too sees the novel as so heavily inflected by middle-class sensibilities that it cannot give a convincing or coherent representation of a working-class community. John Kirk also argues that the novel's very popularity then and since is closely related to its lack of radicalism:

> it is not surprising that one of the least radical novels of the 1930s ... should outlive the decade ... . *Love on the Dole* is more acceptable to the dominant culture and its literary institutions, recuperable to a liberal reading which robs the narrative of any oppositional class discourse.[9]

However, Kirk does admit that, nevertheless, the novel's avoidance of direct confrontation still leaves 'a barely submersible message of the need for radical change, even revolution, to alter what are depicted as almost insupportable conditions of existence'.[10] Ben Harker too suggests the potential – if not fully realised – radicalism of the novel, and then the ways in which this is, in the main, 'tempered' or diminished in the play versions and reworked by the film in a fresh context. Overall, the arguments proposed by the pioneer of research on Greenwood, Stephen Constantine, still seem key to understanding the work: 'Greenwood was writing directly for a middle-class audience and ... this targeted audience made Greenwood limit the socialist politics of the novel' (however, as we have seen, his assumption that all theatre audiences were middle-class may not be right).[11]

Novel in the Twentieth Century, ed. Jeremy Hawthorn (London: Edward Arnold, 1984), pp. 49–61, p. 54.

8 'Palatable Socialism or "the Real Thing"?', p. 50.

9 *Twentieth Century Writing and the British Working Class*, p. 51.

10 *Twentieth Century Writing and the British Working Class*, p. 39.

11 Cited in 'Palatable Socialism or "the Real Thing"?', p. 49; see also '*Love on the Dole* and its Reception in the 1930s', p. 235.

Indeed, while Constantine's argument is still persuasive, I think that there may be some further nuances to add to it. I am not sure that the imagined or actual readership or audience was that narrow, but would see it rather as spanning working-class readers (especially those with rising expectations in the new consumer-based 1930s economy), middle-class, and indeed upper-class readers as a central part of the work's project, an idea which, as so often, Miles and Smith suggest: 'in certain respects Greenwood did surrender the purest status as proletarian novel for his book ... but he surrenders it not for a mess of pottage, nor in deference – but in a project of communication, and for the act of intervention that his text historically achieved.'[12] This is in line with their persuasive argument about Greenwood's alleged 'bourgeois tendencies', and for proper understanding of his roots in a working-class tradition of literacy:

> The Shakespeare, Wordsworth and Dickens floating below or on the surface of Greenwood's texts are distinctively-read writers, read for their relevance to working-class conditions and represented to the reader with their elements of radical vision accentuated ... In short, the fact of Greenwood's using literary allusion to texts domesticated within a middle-class canon need not be regarded as cultural appeasement when those texts also have a separate mode of existence within literate working-class consciousness.[13]

This does not contradict Webster's argument that Greenwood uses but also exposes limitations in the bourgeois novel form – particularly through *Love on the Dole*'s insistence that its characters are in a contradictory world where there are discourses of moral choice but no true individual choices. Indeed, though I agree that Greenwood's socialist politics as represented through the (complex) text are certainly carefully handled, this is not quite the same thing as saying that he is limiting what he would like to say. Behind the novel is a strong discontent with the situation of the people of Hanky Park and those living in similar conditions elsewhere in Britain (his 'actuating motive is indignation' said a standard literary reference work in 1942) and an urge to alter contemporary stereotypes about the unemployed.[14] It is useful at this point to think about how discontent is bound up with new social visions and perceptions of class. David Cannadine in his book *Class in Britain* argues

---

12 *Cinema, Literature & Society*, p. 152.
13 *Cinema, Literature & Society*, pp. 149–50.
14 Kunitz and Haycraft, *Twentieth Century Authors: a Biographical Dictionary of Modern Literature*, p. 574.

that 'discontent causes some people to see their society in an alternative way ... and establish (for a time) new identities':

> For most politicians from Wilkes to Cobbett, from Cobden to Gladstone, Lloyd-George to Baldwin, Thatcher to Major, one of the most important tasks was to persuade people to see their society differently and to persuade people to see themselves differently: in short to change their sense of identity, which in practice meant moving them from accepting one vision of British Society to embracing another.[15]

Cannadine argues that the best way to approach the history of class in Britain is by studying the ways in which different models of class description have declined or become dominant, been disputed, espoused, or revivified. He argues that actually a limited number of models have been deployed:

> When Britons have tried to make sense of the unequal social worlds they have inhabited ... they have usually come up with versions or variants of ... three basic and enduring models: the hierarchical view of society as a seamless web; the triadic version with upper, middle and lower collective groups; and the dichotomous, adversarial picture, where society is sundered between 'us' and 'them'.[16]

Love on the Dole in all three of its versions is a political text precisely because it represents a source of discontent in a way that is intended to strengthen or bring into being in its readers/audiences a desire for a different and more inclusive vision of British society. However, as noted in earlier discussions in Chapter 1, there are, for a political text, unusual features in the novel's portrayal of class, though these may partially arise from the actual situations of some working-class communities. It presents a very shallow class hierarchy and, though there are some clearly blameworthy characters (Grumpole, Price, Ned Narkey) and some ambiguously blameworthy/helpful characters (Sam Grundy, Mrs Dorbell, Mrs Nattle, Mrs Bull), the novel does not very clearly identify or personify a dominant class or classes who bear the responsibility for Hanky Park. Thus, the novel (and equally the play and film) do not, as Constantine pointed out, obviously hold the upper and/or middle classes responsible (unless these are solely and actually quite weakly represented by Grumpole, Price and Grundy), but seems rather to see Hanky Park as a result of an impersonal system (a view the film explicitly articulates

15 *Class in Britain*, Kindle edition, location 3671.
16 *Class in Britain*, p. 19.

through Larry's political speech in the street).[17] In terms of Cannadine's 'vernacular' models of class description, the text does not seem to see its society as a 'hierarchical seamless web', nor really as 'the triadic version with upper, middle and lower collective groups' – for it to use either of those models it would need a wider cast of characters across the whole hierarchy or class system – as do, for example, socially panoramic novels such as Elizabeth Gaskell's *Mary Barton* (1848) or Henry Green's pseudo-proletarian novel *Living* (1929), which is set in a large works like Marlowe's and represents all classes from directors through managers, clerks, foremen, foundry-workers and their families. Rather, Hanky Park contains overwhelmingly one kind of people: working people, and then what seem a few odd exceptions, rather than classes of people. These include Price and Grumpole, who we might assume to have partly inherited status, though we are given very little background for them, and who maintain their position through exploitation of the working people. There is also Sam Grundy, who has 'risen above' his class through entrepreneurship and exploitation (Sally might be considered to have also risen above her class at the close of the novel, also through a kind of 'entrepreneurship', but by self-exploitation rather than the exploitation of others). Larry is a potential leader of his class, as perhaps is Mrs Bull, though she may also be an exploiter. Hanky Park itself may be a single-class community because anyone who is of a class 'above' this level of the working class moves out (as Sam Grundy does). But, nevertheless, even such a community must interact with or be affected by other social groups, and one could imagine a novel like *Love on the Dole* that did show the whole range of classes and their place in the system, perhaps with a focus on Marlowe's and the differing places in Salford and Manchester (the two cities of the novel's sub-title) where its workers lived. In this sense, the text is deliberately giving its readers a constrained perspective, and in giving us so little access to the whole system seems to be much less interested in the only remaining class model: 'the dichotomous, adversarial picture, where society is sundered between "us" and "them"'. However, I think that actually this probably is the underlying, if suppressed, class model that *Love on the Dole* draws on. The model remains implicit because the text wishes to emphasise the unity of 'us' and not the dichotomous and adversarial split from 'them': here 'us', as suggested by the texts' careful approaches to their readerships, is constructed as a wide range of 'ordinary' people (working, middle, upper) which they hope to bring into

17 See *'Love on the Dole* and its Reception in the 1930s', p. 237.

a consensus about what is a reasonable and achievable standard of living that should be available to all. This may accord with a 1936 article about 'Unemployment in the USA' written by Greenwood on his return from Broadway: 'there were signs of a growing conscience, signs that people of moderate means were taking unemployment to heart.'[18] The 'them' may be represented in an abstract way through Larry's perspective, at least, as the National Government, which so remotely and impersonally allows Hanky Park to continue as it is and even worsens its plight through measures such as the Means Test. But this agency has little real presence in the text – partly because the people of Hanky Park mainly do not see how it might be responsible, partly because the text itself is concerned to build identification and therefore suppress blame. The central dynamic of the text stems from its strategy of trying to overcome and replace a different and obstructive conception of 'them' and 'us', one which at the period, as Ros McKibbin has argued, aligned the upper and middle classes and if possible the 'respectable' working classes against the deviant and failing 'unrespectable' working classes, who were seen as victims of their own bad choices. Greenwood's texts need to detach readers from that perspective and provide a scenario that both vividly voices discontent and gives the opportunity for attachment to a larger sense of 'us'. His text must redraw ideas of respectability and conceptions of free choice without splitting its audience through provoking reattachment to an obstructive conception of 'them' and 'us'. This intervention took place in a particular historical context in which, while mass unemployment might seem clearly to signify a gross increase in class division, there was, paradoxically, as David Cannadine points out, a competing belief that hierarchy as the natural order was declining in favour of a more equal society in Britain. Thus he quotes J. B. Priestley's argument in *English Journey* in 1934 that, despite the obvious inequalities, modern British society was 'without privilege' and 'as near to a classless society as we have yet got', as well as the sociologists A. M. Carr-Saunders and D. Caradog-Jones, who questioned in 1937 if 'it [is] not a misreading of the social structure of this country to dwell on class divisions when, in respect of dress, speech and use of leisure, all members of the community are obviously coming to resemble one another?'[19] Such a view was, of course, highly disputable,

18 *Manchester Guardian* 13 April 1936, p. 11.
19 *Class in Britain*, pp. 129 and 130–31, citing *English Journey* (London: Victor Gollancz, 1934), pp. 401–03 and *A Survey of the Social Structure of England and Wales*, 2nd edition (Oxford: Oxford University Press, 1937), p. 67.

but I think something like it may underpin *Love on the Dole*'s strategies in trying to construct its readerships' perspectives on Hanky Park, and all other communities like it, as a gross anomaly that should be removed from a British society that could readily be reconstructed as a democracy in which all could have access to at least minimum material and thence cultural standards.

Indeed, perhaps the novel, plays, and film are best seen as aiming at influencing and/or helping to construct a more broadly based version of what Arthur Marwick identified as political 'middle opinion' in an important historical article of 1969:

> It is the aim of this paper, first of all, to stress in a way previous commentators have not done, that there was in fact a very large groundwork of social and political 'agreement' in the thirties; and then to show that it was from this groundwork that there arose the ideological structure which took Britain safely through the forties and brought her to rest in the fifties. That is to say the mixed economy … all-party acceptance for a welfare state, all-party rejection of the nineteenth-century vision of state planning as a horrible evil, were concepts which received their vital nurture in the 1930s.[20]

This unity of the 'middle' seems consistent with one strand at least of the interwar and wartime Labour Party's self-conception:

> Those on the left believed that the Labour Party existed to promote class war in the interests of the workers; but those on the right rejected the idea that Labour represented only one class, and discounted the Marxist theory of class war and class struggle. As Arthur Henderson put it in 1919, 'Labour is in politics not in the interests of a class, but to further the interests of the community as a whole'. During the 1922 election Philip Snowden rebutted the widespread accusation that 'the Labour Party exists for the benefit of one class'. It was the 'very opposite of a class party' … for its objective was 'justice for all men and women of every class who live by honest and useful work' … . Hence Labour's alternative vision of British society, built round co-operation and harmony.[21]

Of course, the 'honest and useful work' criterion does suggest that there are some, presumably in the upper classes as well as among the 'criminal classes', who are neither honest nor productive, and thus this

20 'Middle Opinion in the Thirties: Planning, Progress and Political Agreement', *The English Historical Review*, 79, 311, April, 1964, pp. 285–98, p. 286. Constantine also cites this article (*'Love on the Dole* and its Reception in the 1930s', p. 244), but I think we could slightly expand his sense of the classes making up the 'middle'.

21 *Class in Britain*, pp. 139–40.

vision of cross-class solidarity still draws on a model of 'us' and 'them'. An entirely neglected interview in a TUC magazine with the actor Julien Mitchell, who played Mr Hardcastle in the 1934 touring production of the play, certainly suggests that he saw the play as appealing to a broad middle ground:

> As far as I understand the purpose of this play, it is to intended to bring home to the man-on-the-street the tragedy of worklessness ... . I cannot doubt that this great play will serve its purpose with the enormous majority of people ... . All of us who have the privilege of taking part in it feel that in interpreting our parts we are conveying a message which, in the present state of affairs, is bound to reach the heart of every right-minded thinking man and woman.[22]

There is one more year beyond 1933, 1935, and 1941 closely connected to the mobilisation of such a body of middle opinion that we should look at as a concluding act in this exploration of *Love on the Dole*: 1945. The novel and the play certainly had considerable impact in the US in 1934 and 1935–6 and neither were forgotten (a 1938 newspaper report on a sociological study of newly-weds drawing relief could be titled without explanation, 'Love on the Dole is Un-American, Chicago Relief Survey Shows').[23] The *Economist*'s US correspondent claimed in a 1942 article about American perceptions of wartime Britain that, with one exception, these were dominated by rural images from popular fiction:

> What is the picture painted for Americans by British films, novels, belles-lettres, lectures? Amazingly it is of a predominantly rural country with a large rentier population living on the profits of empire ... . There die the baronets ... who are found slain in libraries and country house bedrooms ... . The only important shadow cast on this idyllic picture is that thrown by grim and 'powerful' novels and plays of the depressed areas. 'Murder in the Country House' and 'Love on the Dole' – that is all that many Americans know of the eastern bastion of their own security.[24]

Ironically, however, given that the film's production was enabled by a wartime anxiety about public opinion in the US, the film was not in fact released in the States until October 1945, giving US viewers a

---

22 *Labour – a Magazine for all Workers*, TUC, March 1935, p. 151.
23 *Washington Post* 26 December 1938, p. 3.
24 'American Survey' 4 July 1942, pp. 11–12 ('by a Correspondent lately returned from the Unite States').

different viewing context.[25] The reasons for this later release in the US are not completely clear, though reviewers did speculate about it: 'Release of the picture, made in 1941, was deferred on the other side at the understandable request of the Churchill government. For different reasons, its release in this country was something that entailed a bit of negotiating with filmdom's regulatory powers.'[26] The first claim we know not to be true, but it reflects interestingly a reading of the film as in opposition to the wartime coalition (which is, at least on the surface, incorrect, but may show application of a sense of Churchill's reservations about post-war reconstruction, probably to be located in the June 1945 election campaign rather than in the 1941 People's War period). The second claim suggests that, yet again, the film had met censorship issues. Another reviewer noted the speculation ('assorted rumours'), but assigned a primarily commercial motive: 'the most reasonable [motive] seems to be that few people would be interested in a picture about unemployment and poverty at a time when jobs were plentiful.'[27] These assorted observations, though, help to highlight the different reading context of 1945. One reviewer, perhaps less well-informed about Britain, concludes that 'as such things normally go', the film is 'a serving of strong dramatic meat that offers no solid solution of the problem it attacks',[28] while another links it firmly to the 1945 Labour election victory and the current British government:

> Coming at a time when England's new Labour Government is beginning to experience some of the labor-management unrest prevalent in this country, 'Love on the Dole' has a peculiar timeliness and significance, notwithstanding that it was filmed four years ago … . Being a discourse on the depression years … [it] is critical of an economic system that does not produce jobs for people who want to work and fails to provide a decent wage for those who do have employment. The implication is that a strong Labour party could work out a system whereby the monied and the working interests could both benefit. Current events have provided 'Love on the Dole' with

25 The US entertainment industry magazine *Variety* did publish a brief review of the film by its London correspondent in April 1941 and clearly expected that the film would shortly be released in the US too, as it predicted 'a good deal of attention from patrons both here (England) and in the US'. *Variety* reprinted an extract from this review on the actual US release in October 1945 (see issue of 10 October 1945, p. 22).

26 Nelson B. Bell in the *Washington Post* 24 October 1934, p. 9.

27 'T.M.P.' in the *New York Times*, 13 October 1934, p. 21.

28 *Washington Post* 24 October 1934, p. 9.

curious sociological and political overtones. As a result it might be taken as a hindsight observation of conditions that brought the Labor party to power in England, or it might be taken as a warning of unhappy days to come in America unless labor and management finds a way to pull together.[29]

Here the film is not being seen in the temporal context originally intended (and discussed in Chapter 2 above), but the reviewer does nevertheless pick up all the cues and reads the film as a successful prediction in 1941 of the post-war settlement of 1945. It is notable too, how, without much textual warrant, he reads the film as a lesson for labour/management co-operation of the kind in which Greenwood was to show such interest in his 1949 film with Bernard Miles, *A Chance of a Lifetime*.[30] On this occasion, the promises of what was, in some senses, a 'propaganda' film are seen as actually fulfilled.

I have suggested previously in this book that Greenwood's most famous text has often been read with insufficient regard to a number of productive contexts. One such set of contexts is his own literary career and his public presence not only in the 1930s but afterwards, and beyond the film's release: the British public remained interested in his celebrity and his work after 1941 (when in a discussion between John Gielgud and Frank O'Connor in the *Listener* about whether English drama could include both 'poetry' and 'real life' they could take it for granted that readers would have the play of *Love on the Dole* still firmly in mind).[31] Early in 1942, and probably designed to pick up new readers from the 1941 film release, there was a new Book Guild edition of the novel, which lists as 'In preparation' a 'novel and play' by Greenwood called *England Arise!* (though Hannen Swaffer in the *Daily Herald* in June 1941 said it was to be a film script). While clearly based on Edward Carpenter's socialist hymn of 1896, this work by Greenwood never appeared in any genre, but shows his continuing political commitment during the war.[32] By 1944 Greenwood was able to reconfirm and encourage what he saw as a democratic turn in British society by confidently publishing a novel, *Something in My Heart*, that was a sequel to *Love on the Dole*. It articulated a widely shared vision and cheerfully advocated not only the prospect but

29 'T.M.P' in the *New York Times* 13 October 1934, p. 21.
30 Discussed in Chapter 2.
31 'The Actor Answers Back', 6 February 1941, pp. 192–93, p. 193.
32 Croft, *Red Letter Days*, p. 109. The Book Guild edition is in the author's collection; Hannen Swaffer refers to Greenwood's projected *England Arise!* in the *Daily Herald* 25 June 1941, p. 2.

the actuality of sweeping changes to the nature of British government, and further encouragement of an already emerging egalitarian class structure. The contemporary reviews in 1944 of *Something in My Heart* make it clear that the majority of reviewers certainly identified the novel as linking a critique of the 1930s to a discussion of wartime and post-war reconstruction. They generally saw at once the link to *Love on the Dole*: 'Here is a warm-hearted story which may be ranked almost as a sequel to *Love on the Dole*' (the *Daily Telegraph*),[33] and, across a wide range of newspapers, there was sympathy with the view taken by the novel that state planning was the way to ensure that the social crisis of the 1930s could never return:

> Mr Greenwood has nothing good to say of the England in which such material [i.e. the unemployed workers of Salford] was allowed to go to waste, but much hope of a post-war England which will make better use of its heritage of brains and character. (*Daily Telegraph*)[34]

> The situation obviously allows Mr Greenwood opportunity for sharp comment on the economic follies of the past and our hope for a more humane and rational system in the future. (*Western Mail*)[35]

Some reviews of the novel also suggest a public awareness that there are some official barriers to discussion of the future and anxieties that hoped-for promises might not be fulfilled. Thus the *Irish Times* detects a difference between the hope and confidence of Greenwood's main characters and authorial uncertainty: 'This confidence seems not altogether shared by the author, who continually reminds one of their past, and occasionally hints that another slump might occur after the war. He quashes his bouts of pessimism, however, by a few references to the Beveridge Plan.'[36]

In what seems to have been the longest review of *Something in My Heart*, in *John O'London's Weekly*, the novelist Pamela Hansford Johnson suggests that the issues it raises need to be more widely discussed, and also regards it as articulating views typical of those in the services:

> Let me say ... that this is an important novel of ideas, and that it ventilates a good many worries that are apt to fester in confinement. If future generations want to know what the fighting men were thinking during the Nazi war,

---

33 20 October 1944, unsigned; p. 64 of WGC/3/2.
34 Also 20 October 1944.
35 31 October 1944. Review by H. M. Dowling, p. 64 of WGC/3/2.
36 28 October 1944. P. 65, WGC/3/2.

they will get a good deal of enlightenment from any copy of *Something in My Heart* ... that may remain extant.[37]

The novel seems to be a specific intervention in the debate about post-war reconstruction, which voices a not uncommon suspicion that the government, or sections of it, might not follow through the radical reforms that it had somewhat inadvertently sponsored, and supplies its readers with a clear historical and personal narrative of why such reforms are necessary, possible, reasonable, and deserved by the British people.

This novel, therefore, as well as the preceding three versions of *Love on the Dole*, plays a part in what Ian McLaine diagnoses as the 'most important single reason for the failure of [wartime] class resentment to assume threatening proportions ... its absorption into the public's post-war aspirations'.[38] It is odd that Greenwood's wartime novel has received no recent attention at all: certainly, it is a novel that in itself may suggest how important *Love on the Dole* continued to be in the 1940s as a national reference point for an unacceptable past and a hoped-for, planned, future. Indeed, one striking newspaper review in July 1945, while not directly about Greenwood at all, showed how strongly his writing was associated with a kind of realism that could tell the truth and with actively putting that past behind us:

> I wish more people could have had the chance to see the excellent show which the ABCA (Army Bureau of Current Affairs) play unit put on at the Arts Theatre last week ... . 'Where Do We Go From Here?' is Walter Greenwood's *Love on the Dole* all over again, plus another wartime lesson – the value of planning our economy to prevent a repetition of the years which followed 1918. I can understand why these plays have been so popular with Army audiences. The dialogue and the situations would ring true to anyone who had been brought up in a working-class home.[39]

Ignoring Greenwood's own literary career also means that the popular success of another wartime work, the play *The Cure for Love* (first produced in Oldham in 29 January 1945 and then in London on 12 July 1945, actually *during* the election), and its role in keeping *Love on the*

---

37 20 October 1944. Page 63 of WGC/3/2 (p. 32 of *John O'London's Weekly*).
38 *The Ministry of Morale*, p. 178.
39 *New Statesman and Nation* in WGC/3/2, p. 82. The review makes it clear that 'Where Do we Go From Here?' was a 'Living Newspaper' type drama. Penelope Summerfield refers to it as a play about post-war reconstruction in her article, 'Education and Politics in the British Armed Services in the Second World War', *International Review of Social History*, 26, 2, August 1981, pp. 133–58, p. 143.

Dole alive in people's memories, has been forgotten.[40] The play again revisits some Hanky Park favourites (though some seem to be hardly the same characters) and also has some commentary on the possible shape of post-war Britain. Thus, a somewhat more agreeable Ted Munter reckons that 'this country's going to be worth livin' in after the war … what with the dole, Beveridge Report, Public Assistance and Old Age Pensions at two quid a week. I wouldn't mind being a workin' man myself again.'[41]

There is further direct evidence of the continuing interest in *Love on the Dole* itself in wartime. There is testimony from Mass Observation reports during the war that the novel continued to be widely read. Thus a Mass Observation Literature Questionnaire from 1940 (or the commentary deriving from it) notes that:

> [it] must be clearly realized that within fiction, too, there are a good many books which are in fact social and sociological documents, or serious works stimulating thought about present, past or future times. Books like 'How Green was my Valley', 'And Quiet Flows the Don', 'Love on the Dole' and 'The Grapes of Wrath', which are among the most popular fiction books for borrowing and buying[,] are works of fictions which really belong to the serious class.

'Books and the Public – a Study of Buying, Borrowing, Keeping, Selecting, Remembering, Giving and Reading Books' from July 1942 (File Report 13332, section XXXI) also mentions *Love on the Dole* as one of twenty-five fiction books borrowed from libraries that were 'most popular at the time of this investigation'. In Section XVII of the same report (about book-buying habits), an observer notes that 'One of the waitresses at the snack counter is very keen to get a copy of *Love on the Dole*, but it seems difficult to get.' Though this is not noted in *Mass-Observation at the Movies*, the Commentary on the Literature Questionnaire also observes that a film version of a novel may boost sales or library loan popularity and specifically mentions *Love on the Dole* among others, seeing it as having a particular appeal then to 'C and D class people': that is, to what this class-categorisation system defines as lower–middle-, skilled-working- and working-class readers and viewers:

---

40 See, for example, the unsigned review of the play at the Westminster Theatre, London, in *The Stage* 19 July 1945, which says precisely that the play will be popular, despite what it thinks are some thin elements, and refers to *Love on the Dole* as a more serious 'sociological' work by Greenwood.

41 London: Samuel French, 1947, acting edition no. 2102, Act III, p. 71.

It will be seen that a very wide range is covered, naturally. If there is one notable characteristic, it is for people who buy fiction to buy books which have already been filmed. The most frequently bought fiction books, especially by C and D class people, are definitely those which have been filmed, like 'Hatter's Castle', 'The Grapes of Wrath', 'Love on the Dole', 'Rebecca', 'North West Passage', 'Gone with the Wind', etc. Here again we come to the souvenir and permanent value of the book … . Having seen a film, people like to keep [it] in some permanent form by buying the book.[42]

It is notable that the class-range of the audience identified here does co-incide with some of the range which I have suggested above as a possible readership, and certainly suggests an interest in both the novel and the film of *Love on the Dole* beyond simply the 'middle classes'. Jonathan Cape too clearly thought there was continuing interest in the novel of *Love on the Dole*, for they published a new edition in 1945 (a copy signed by Greenwood survives in which the author has annotated the epigraph 'The Time is Ripe, and rotten ripe for change;/Then let it come … ' with the words: 'And this is what I think too!').[43]

The novelist Marghanita Laski certainly took it for granted that any general reader would have known and remembered Greenwood's work when in 1944 she published her successful satire *Love on the Supertax*, which, through a sometimes very exact parody, purports to show a Britain where, owing to wartime social change, the once-rich are now in the position formerly occupied by the people of Hanky Park:

> This is a story of the spring of 1944. But it does not tell of that jocund season as you know it in Finsbury and Hoxton, where after their day's work is done, clear-eyed, confident men and women meet to discuss the Trades Dispute Act or to visit the latest exhibition of paintings by left-wing artists at the Klassical Kinema … . This is not a story of that spring of 1944 as it came to strong vigorous citizens with an ample presence and an assurance of the future, but of spring as it came to the needy and the dispirited, to the fallen and the dispossessed, spring as it came to Mayfair.[44]

Laski's satire is quite complex partly because it is a satiric dystopia and partly because the reversal of the class hierarchy makes it open to question as to which of her characters matches which of Greenwood's, though many equivalences are certainly on offer. Her heroine, Clarissa,

---

42 From *Mass Observation Archive online*, Matthew Adams, accessed 15 February 2012.
43 Copy offered for sale on Abe Books UK by booksellers Peter Grogan, London, 17 July 2016, now in author's collection.
44 Marghanita Laski, *Lover on the Supertax* (London: Cresset Press, 1944), p. 5.

daughter of an impoverished ducal household, is undoubtedly the Mayfair equivalent of Sally. But of her two suitors, either the well-off worker and Communist activist Sid Barker (though most obviously read as Larry) or the businessman Sir Herbert Porkington might, in this world turned upside-down, be the equivalent of Sam Grundy, who can take her away from all this. One thing is clear, however – though the plot and characters of this satire are creatively and often precisely derived from the novel and play of *Love on the Dole*, it is reacting in its satiric portrayal of social change specifically to the film version and to its promises about the consequences of a People's War. Clarissa, once she has realised that a life-long relationship with Sid is impossible because of their different class backgrounds, accepts an offer from Sir Herbert Porkington to join him both in marriage and in fighting to preserve the interests of their own class against democracy – the old ways of capitalism and hereditary privilege.[45]

The play too had life in it: though the original touring production(s) ended in 1937, there were a number of different productions between May and September 1939, including at the Attercliffe Palace, Sheffield, the Salford Hippodrome, the Norwich Hippodrome, the Wood Green Empire, the Prince's Theatre, Manchester, and the Royal, Ashton-Under-Lyme, with the latter said to be sold out with its first live production after reverting from cinema to theatre.[46] My own copy of the

---

45 It is difficult concisely to represent the nature of Laski's novel, which for a sympathetic reader of Greenwood may be quite a disturbing experience at first, despite its comedy: it looks on the surface like a Waughesque satire against an 'unnatural' inversion of class-hierarchy and snobbery, before coming round at the end to an ominous warning that the ruling classes will never let go of their power without a struggle. Already, Sir Herbert says that his secret organisation has achieved several important victories against social progress, including 'the withdrawal of the A.B.C.A. pamphlet on the Beveridge plan', 'the shelving of the Barlow, Scott and Uthwatt Reports', and 'the emasculation of the Socialists through continued coalition Government' (p. 120). See above and Chapter 2 for discussion of Greenwood's wartime novel *Something in My Heart* (1944), which indeed does fear that the wartime government may not deliver on its post-war promises. Laski was, of course, the daughter of the prominent leftist intellectual Harold Laski, who was an admirer of *Love on the Dole*. I am grateful to Dr Erica Brown and the *Reading 1900–1950* reading group at Sheffield Hallam University for drawing my attention to Laski's novel – see the review by a reading group member on their blog at <https://reading19001950.wordpress.com/2014/02/17/love-on-the-supertax-by-marghanita-laski-1944/>, accessed 27 October 2017.
46 Salford production discussed in *The Stage* 29 June 1030, p. 2; Wood Green Empire Programme for week commencing 21 July 1939 (production reviewed in *The Stage*

1938 edition of the Samuel French acting edition of the play of *Love on the Dole* is, as it happens, inscribed to a previous owner, 'With love and best wishes from Frances, Xmas 1941', and there was a wartime production in Britain in September 1944, while Australian prisoners of war captured by the Japanese and held in the Changi prison in Singapore put on a production of Greenwood and Gow's play in March of the same year.[47]

I suggested in the Introduction and Chapter 3 that Greenwood's radio profile needed to be taken much more notice of – *Love on the Dole* featured a good deal on 1940s radio (and, indeed, if the radio scripts had survived there would be a fourth version of the text to consider). Correspondence at the BBC Written Archive records that a ten-minute extract from *Love on the Dole* was broadcast as part of the magazine programme *Everybody's Scrapbook* on 15 June 1941 (with a recorded repeat on 20 June 1941).[48] There was also the first full radio version of the play broadcast in the series 'Radio Theatre' (No. 14) for the BBC Eastern Service (the service for listeners in India, the Middle and Far East) on 22 June 1942, followed the same year by selected scenes (with Wendy Hiller as Sally and Robert Donat as Larry) in a 'Saturday Matinee' for the Forces Programme on 19 September 1942. A second full production was broadcast in BBC Radio's Saturday Night Theatre slot on 20 January 1945 (which may be a reasonably significant year for the play to have a new airing, with the end of the war in Europe in sight and political decisions about post-war reconstruction now needing to be made).[49] The

3 August 1939, p. 3); Ashton-Under-Lyme production discussed in *The Stage* 21 September 1939; Manchester production reviewed in *The Stage* 10 August 1939, p. 11, Norwich production discussed in *The Stage* 15 June 1939, p. 13.

47 The British production was at the Queens Park Hippodrome – see *The Stage*, 28 September 1944, p. 2. For the Changi Prison production, there is a surviving typed script and an attractively designed programme featuring smoking industrial chimneys, perhaps influenced by the dust jacket of the Cape edition of the novel, though also creative in adding a wall displaying a peeling poster for the play in Hanky Park itself – see <http://changipowart.com/archives/703>, accessed 27 October 2017. The programme was drawn by Dan Bettany, the production was by the 'Red Rose players' and the producers were Ken Dowbiggin and Martin English.

48 See the memo from Frances Worsley to Copyright Section, 9 July 1941 and the agreement between the Corporation and Gow and Greenwood for use of the play. Some rewriting must have been involved, as Gow is to be paid for 'his work on the script'.

49 My thanks to Trisha Hayes at the BBC Written Archives in Reading for finding the 1942 production and for confirming that the scripts for the two

Radio Times felt able to alert its audience to the discontent in the play, warning listeners in 1945: 'Don't expect light entertainment from this play ... It will make you feel uncomfortable; and it will probably light in you some of the holy anger in the author's heart that life for some people can be such a warped and inexplicably cruel business'.[50] The New Zealand newspaper the *Alexandra Herald and Otago Gazette* noted a year later in an article about the Lancashire actress Belle Chrystall (who played Sally) that this broadcast 'scored a record for drama listening figures'.[51] The *Sunday Times* reviewer Desmond Shawe-Taylor must have

1940s adaptations do not survive (email 17 March 2016). The record of the Saturday Matinee performance can be found on the BBC Genome project at <http://genome.ch.bbc.co.uk/c4bd61ec0b804991b222ae9a27d71fb7>, accessed 27 October 2017. See also the *Saturday Night Theatre – a Tribute to BBC Radio Drama* website, which usefully lists all plays broadcast and their dates from the very beginning of the series on 3 April 1943 onwards: <http://www.saturday-night-theatre.co.uk/broadcasts.php>, accessed 22 February 2012. My thanks to Ben Harker for suggesting the potential importance of the date of the broadcast. The 1942 and 1945 radio versions are credited to Greenwood, Gow, and Cynthia Pughe: presumably both broadcasts used the same adaptation by Pughe, though they had different producers (Pughe worked on many BBC radio adaptations over a long period: she is first credited as a writer for fifty-three Saturday Night Theatre adaptations in the years from 1943 until 1961 (see Saturday Night Theatre broadcast dates website: <http://www.saturday-night-theatre.co.uk/broadcasts. php>, accessed 27 October 2017). Saturday Night Theatre broadcast further productions of *Love on the Dole* on 21 May 1949, 9 January 1965, 20 May 1972, 19 July 1980 and 7 November 1987 – the last being in honour of Ronald Gow's 90th birthday (information derived from Saturday Night Theatre website and email from Trish Hayes at the BBC Written Archives). The 1941 broadcast on the Eastern Service seems to have been adapted by the BBC producer John Burrell, who had some Indian connections (see BBC card index of productions of *Love on the Dole*, BBC Written Archives, and Burrell's *DNB* entry). Scholarly work on Orwell's BBC years may suggest that the Eastern Service broadcast of the play might not have had a large audience, since wireless ownership was limited in India and reception difficult in the Far East: see, for example, Peter Davison's *George Orwell – a Literary Life* (Basingstoke: Macmillan, 1996), p. 117.

50 Commentary in *Radio Times* by Stephen Williams located via a search in the BBC Genome project: <http://genome.ch.bbc.co.uk/search/0/20?adv=0&q=love +on+the+dole&media=all&yf=1923&yt=2009&mf=1&mt=12&tf=00%3A00&tt =00%3A00>, accessed 27 October 2017.

51 18 September 1946, p. 3. The article tells us that Chrystall had joined the BBC Repertory Company in 1941: she had appeared in film versions of *Hobson's Choice* and *Hindle Wakes* in 1931, so was perhaps a clear choice for Sally (see IMDB: <http://www.imdb.com/name/nm0160779/>, accessed 27 October 2017).

been recalling the recent broadcast when he commented in his Radio column on 11 February 1945 that:

> listening to *The Corn is Green* or *Love on the Dole* I feel sure that the radio-diffusion of standard drama is a good thing. Thousands have discovered a brand-new interest in the drama and many will visit a theatre for the first time if a play which they have enjoyed on the air should come their way in the flesh.[52]

There was in fact something of a revival of productions of the play during 1945–46, both before and after the July 1945 elections: Greenwood's clippings book has notices of four amateur productions, including one by the Bradford Co-Operative Society's Education Committee (*Co-Operative News*, Manchester, 13 April 1946). There is a significant reference in the Glasgow *Evening Times* of 17 August 1945 to a political rally at the 'Cosmo Cinema' by the successful North Lanark Labour candidate (Margaret McCrorie Herbison), which included a screening of *Love on the Dole*, presumably as a way of marking that its aspirations had, indeed, been met with the electorate's firm approval of the Labour Party's post-war plans.[53] Greenwood was himself interviewed by R. B. Marriott for *The Stage* in October 1945 for his views on what 'the theatre of peace' would be most interested in: he thought that there would be a focus on 'ordinary people', particularly in 'the provinces', since, 'with the growing consciousness of social and political things, there is emerging a large audience with a taste for plays dealing with current topics'.[54] The movie version was one of a number of British wartime films featured in the *Daily Mail*'s 'What Do You Know about Films?' quiz in 1946, which was linked to a popular poll (the National Film Award) to judge the best British film made between September 1939 and September 1945 – readers were told that they were bound 'to remember the heart-rending story of poverty, relieved with humour'.[55] In 1948 theatre productions of *Love on the Dole* were again touring quite steadily, and Pathé's re-release of the

---

52 Desmond Shawe-Taylor, *Sunday Times*, 11 February 1945, p. 3.

53 See WGC/3/2 for the article. See the *DNB* online for information about the MP Margaret Herbison. Her father was a miner and she had been a National Council of Labour College lecturer in economics and an English and History teacher during the 1930s, so it is perhaps not surprising that she took an interest in *Love on the Dole*.

54 4 October 1945, p. 1. The article is entitled 'Theatre of Peace – Walter Greenwood Looks Ahead'.

55 13 March 1946, p. 3 (accessed via the *Daily Mail* archive). Readers were asked to name the film company, director, producer, and main actors.

film in April 1948 must also attest to a feeling that the film's view of the future – and now the present – was a still significant one.[56]

An unattributed cutting in Greenwood's clippings book from 1933, headed: 'Young Novelist's Plans', says of the novel that 'He began it as propaganda for the Salford Labour Party and it developed from there.'[57] Certainly, *Love on the Dole*'s complex uses and varying mediations of local actualities and images, of political aspirations, persuasive argument, and national imaginings are key factors in what made it work on the imaginations of its readerships and audiences, and what continues to make it a significant and enduringly remembered work of the 1930s and 1940s. The ambiguities and complex representations and the political tact of the first two versions, the novel and the play, were and are contributing factors to what makes it a rich and re-readable work, while the greater certainty of the message in the film suggests the degree to which the novel and play's appeal to 'middle opinion' had become a dominant national theme during the course of the war and after. The claim made in 1935 by a *Daily Telegraph* reviewer of Greenwood's second novel, *His Worship the Mayor*, suggests the novel's ability to reach readers who might otherwise be resistant to progressive ideas, and also makes a claim which for both author and novel still seems valid: 'I know of no new author more "important" than Walter Greenwood, or one who has written a better first novel than *Love on the Dole*.'[58]

One final thing to say: though this book constitutes the fullest discussion of Greenwood's writing and career so far, there is still a lot more to say about him and his contexts, and an enormous amount of material still to explore, including lost short stories and even an unpublished novel. To explore some further aspects of Greenwood's literary life, the reader may wish to visit my WordPress site, *Walter Greenwood: Not Just Love on the Dole*, at https://waltergreenwoodnotjustloveonthedole.com/home/. The site is designed to provide further resources for understanding and studying the whole story of Walter Greenwood and his times, and is intended to be useful and attractive for students, teachers, and lecturers – but above all for readers of all kinds who want to know (even) more about Walter.

---

56 For theatre productions see issues of *The Stage*, such as those from January to April 1948; see the IMDB *Love on the Dole* entry for the film release dates: <http://www.imdb.com/title/tt0033853/releaseinfo?ref_=ttfc_ql_2>, accessed 27 October 2017.

57 WGC/3/1, p. 1.

58 Quoted in a Jonathan Cape advert for *His Worship the Mayor* in *The Listener*, 1935.

Bibliography and Filmography

Primary Sources

Archives
BBC Written Archive, Caversham
British Film Institute Ben Reuben Library (British Board of Film Censors'
    Scenario Notes 1936)
British Library Music Collections
Daily Mail Historical Archive
Entertainment Industry Magazine Archive
Gale News Vault
The Guardian and *The Observer* online archives
Mass Observation Archive online, Matthew Adams, 2012
National Library of Australia online newspaper archive (http://trove.nla.gov.au/)
National Library of New Zealand online newspaper archive (https://
    paperspast.natlib.govt.nz/)
The *Sunday Times* Digital Archive 1822–2006
The Times Digital Archive 1785–2016
The Times Literary Supplement Historical Archive
Walter Greenwood Special Collection, University of Salford (see description
    of contents: http://archiveshub.ac.uk/data/gb427-wgc)

Fiction, Plays, and Art
Brierley, Walter, *Means Test Man* (London: Methuen: 1935).
Brighouse, Harold, *Hobson's Choice* (London: Samuel French, 1916).
Fallada, Hans, *Little Man, What Now?*, translated by Eric Sutton (London:
    George Putnam, 1933; originally published as *Kleiner Mann, Was Nunn?*,
    Berlin: Rowohlt, 1932).
Gow, Ronald, and Walter Greenwood, *Love on the Dole* (London: Jonathan
    Cape, 1933; Harmondsworth: Penguin, 1969, 1992).

Gow, Ronald, and Walter Greenwood, *Love on the Dole – a Play in Three Acts* (London: Jonathan Cape, 1935).

Gow, Ronald, and Walter Greenwood, *Love on the Dole – a Play in Three Acts* (London: Samuel French, 1936).

Greenwood, Walter, *His Worship The Mayor* (London: Jonathan Cape, 1935).

Greenwood, Walter, *Standing Room Only, or 'A Laugh in Every Line'* (Jonathan Cape, London, 1936; Howard Baker, London, 1970).

Greenwood, Walter, *Rêves Sans Provisions* (translated by Charlotte Neveu, published in a special issue of the periodical *La Petite Illustration* (no. 418, 1937).

Greenwood, Walter, *The Cleft Stick, or, 'It's the Same the Whole World Over*, with illustrations by Arthur Wragg (London: Selwyn & Blount, 1937).

Greenwood, Walter, *The Cleft Stick* (New York: Frederick A. Stokes, 1938).

Greenwood, Walter, 'Prodigal's Return' *John Bull* (29 January 1938), pp. 23–4.

Greenwood, Walter, *The Secret Kingdom* (London: Jonathan Cape, 1938; Leeds: Morley-Baker, 1969).

Greenwood, Walter, *Only Mugs Work* (London: Hutchinson, 1939).

Greenwood, Walter, *Something in My Heart* (London: Hutchinson, 1944; Leeds: Morley-Baker, 1969).

Greenwood, Walter, *The Cure for Love* (play) (London: Samuel French, 1947).

Greenwood, Walter, *So Brief the Spring* (London: Hutchinson, 1952).

Greenwood, Walter, *What Everybody Wants* (London: Hutchinson, 1954).

Greenwood, Walter, *Down by the Sea* (London: Hutchinson, 1956).

Greenwood, Walter, *Saturday Night at the Crown* (London: Hutchinson, 1959).

Greenwood, Walter and Ronald Gow, *Love on the Dole* (Hereford Plays) (Oxford: Heinemann, 1986).

Hampson, John, *Saturday Night at the Greyhound* (Richmond: Hogarth Press, 1931).

Holtby, Winifred, *South Riding* (London: Collins, 1936; London: Virago, 1988).

Laski, Marghanita, *Love on the Supertax* (London: Cresset Press, 1944).

Malleson, Miles and H. Brooks, *Six Men of Dorset* (London: Gollancz, 1934).

Orwell, George, *The Road to Wigan Pier* (London: Gollancz, 1937).

Orwell, George, *The Lion and the Unicorn* (London: Secker & Warburg, 1941).

Priestley, J. B., *English Journey* (London: Heinemann, 1934).

Wragg, Arthur, *Psalms for Modern Life* (London: Selwyn & Blount, 1933).

Wragg, Arthur, *Jesus Wept* (London: Selwyn & Blount, 1934).

Films, DVDs, and TV Programmes

Andrew Marr's *The Making of Modern Britain* (Episode 5, 'Little Britain', Director: Francis Whately; first broadcast 25/11/2009).

Chance of a Lifetime (Director: Bernard Miles; Pilgrim Pictures, 1959).

A City Speaks (Director: Paul Rotha; Films of Fact/Paul Rotha Productions, 1947).

The Common Touch (Director: John Baxter; British National Films, 1941).

The Eureka Stockade (Director: Harry Watt; Ealing Studios, 1949).

Five Towns (Director: Terry Bishop; Greenpark/Board of Trade, 1947).

Land of Promise the British Documentary Movement 1930–1950 (BFIVD756, London, BFI: 2013).

London Pride DVD (40s Britain, Panamint Cinema, PDC2029, nd).

Love on the Dole (Director: John Baxter; British National Films, 1941; Fabulous Films DVD, 2004).

Love on the Dole (Director: John Baxter; British National Films, 1941; Fabulous Films, with cast and crew biographies, VFB 14867 DVD, 2004).

Love on the Dole (Director: John Baxter; British National Films, 1941; BFI remastered re-release on DVD/Blu-Ray, 2016).

No Limit (Director: Monty Banks; Associated Talking Pictures, 1935).

Off the Dole (Director: Arthur Mertz; Mancunian Film, 1935).

Proud City – a Plan for London (Director: Ralph Keene; Greenpark, 1945).

The Proud Valley (Director: Pen Tennyson; Ealing Studies, 1940).

Summer on the Farm (Director: Ralph Keene; Greenpark/ Ministry of Agriculture/Ministry of Information 1943).

Greenpark Films (in order of production to 1950)

Those marked * can be viewed online at the British Council Films website; the BFI website has some information for most of the titles. *The Documentary Newsletter* No. 3, 1944, is also informative and is available online at: https://archive.org/stream/docum56film/docum56film_djvu.txt. The fullest, though incomplete, listing is on the *IMDB*: http://www.imdb.com/company/coo103177/?ref_=ttco_co_1.

*London, 1942** (Director: Ken Annakin; 1943).

Spring on the Farm (Director: Ralph Keene; Greenpark/Ministry of Agriculture/Ministry of Information, 1943).

Summer on the Farm (Director: Ralph Keene; Greenpark/Ministry of Agriculture/Ministry of Information, 1943; viewable on BFI Screenplayer; http://www.screenonline.org.uk/film/id/1316156/).

Winter on the Farm (Director: Ralph Keene; 1943).

The Crown of the Year (Director: Ralph Keene; 1943).

The Grassy Shires (Director: Ralph Keene; 1944).

Cornish Valley (Director: Ralph Keene; 1944).

Crofters (Director: Ralph Keene; 1944; viewable on BFI Screenplayer http://www.screenonline.org.uk/film/id/841963/).

North-East Corner (Director: John Eldridge; 1944).

*Make Fruitful the Land** (Director: Ken Annakin; 1945).

*A Farmer's Boy** (Director: Peter Price; 1945).

Proud City – a Plan for London (Director: Ralph Keene; 1945).

*We of the West Riding** (Director: Ken Annakin; 1945).

It Began on the Clyde (Director: Ken Annakin; 1946).

Cyprus is an Island (Director: Ralph Keene; 1946; sponsored by the Ministry of Information; viewable online at: http://www.colonialfilm.org.uk/node/4511).

*English Criminal Justice** (Director: Ken Annakin; 1946).

Fenlands (Director: Ken Annakin; 1946).

United Harvest (Director: Ralph Keene; 1946).

Five Towns (Director: Terry Bishop; sponsored by Board of Trade, 1947).

Park Here (Director: John Eldridge; 1947).

Waverley Steps: a Visit to Edinburgh (Director: John Eldridge; 1948).

Three Dawns to Sydney (Director: John Eldridge; 1949).

The Frasers of Cabot Cove (Director: Humphrey Swingler; 1949).

This Farming Business (Director unknown; 1949).

Pearl of the Gulf (with Film Producer's Guild; sponsored by Bahrain Petroleum Co, 1950?).

A Bridge in Persia (Director: James Mckechnie; 1950).

No Man's Friend (Director: Joe Mendoza; 1950).

Fifty Acres (Director: Peter Plaskett; 1950).

Nines Was Standing (Director: Humphrey Swingler; 1950).

Newspapers and Periodicals

Advocate (Melbourne)
Advocate (Tasmania)
Alexandra Herald and Otago Gazette (New Zealand)
Auckland Star (New Zealand)
Catholic Herald
Co-operative News (Manchester)
Daily Dispatch
Daily Express
Daily Film Renter
Daily Herald
Daily Independent (Sheffield)
Daily Mail
Daily Mail (Hull)
Daily Mirror
Daily Telegraph
Empire (Australia)
Evening Times (Glasgow)
Evening Post (Wellington, New Zealand)
Film Bulletin
Film Notes
Film Talk

Guardian
John Bull
John O'London's Weekly
Kinematograph Weekly
La Petite Illustration (France)
Manchester City News
Manchester Evening News
Manchester Guardian
New Clarion
New York Times (USA)
New York Post
New Zealand Herald
Newcastle Morning Herald and Mining Advocate (Australia)
Newcastle Sun (Australia)
Nursing Notes
Observer
Picturegoer and Film Weekly
Picture Show
Radio Times
Salford Reporter
South Coast Times and Wollongong Argus (Australia)
Spectator
Star
Sunday Express
Sunday Pictorial
Sunday Referee
Sunday Times
Sydney Morning Herald (Australia)
Tatler
The Listener
The Mirror (Perth)
The Stage
The Storyteller Magazine
The Tablet
The Telegraph (Brisbane)
The Times
Times Literary Supplement
Tribune
Tribune (Australia)
Washington Post (USA)
Worker (Brisbane, Australia)
Workers' Weekly (Australia)

Record and CDs

The Film Music of Richard Addinsell (London: Chandos LC 7038, 2003).

Love on the Dole (song by Parsons and Fase from Unity Theatre Production, *Babes in the Wood*), Decca F.6933, 1939.

Love on the Dole – a Musical Play: recording of the musical directed by Stewart Nicholls at the Rhoda McGraw Theatre, Woking, Surrey (JTT-1, recorded 4–5/1/1996).

The Rise of Communism (London: Opal CD 9856, nd).

Secondary Sources

Articles and Essays

Bentley, Phyllis, 'Contemporary British Fiction', *The English Journal*, Vol. 28, no. 4. April 1939, pp. 251–61.

Chambers, Colin, '"Ours will be a dynamic contribution": The Struggle by Diasporic Artists for a Voice in British Theatre in the 1930s and 1940s', *Keywords – a Journal of Cultural Materialism*, Vol. 7. 2009, pp. 38–54.

Colligan, Collette, '"Hope on, hope ever. One of these fine days my ship will come in:" The Politics of Hope in Walter Greenwood's *Love on the Dole* (1933)', *Postgraduate English: A Journal and Forum for Postgraduates in English in the UK and Europe*, Vol. 3. March 2001: <http://community.dur.ac.uk/postgraduate.english/ojs/index.php/pgenglish/article/view/11/10>, accessed 10 September 2011.

Constantine, Stephen, '*Love on the Dole* and its Reception in the 1930s', *Literature and History*, Vol. 8. Autumn 1982, pp. 232–47.

Davies, Andrew, 'The Police and the People: Gambling in Salford, 1900–1939', *Historical Journal*, Vol. XXXIV, no. 1. 1991, pp. 87–115.

Davies, Andrew, 'Leisure in the "classic slum" 1900–1939', in *Workers' Worlds: Cultures and Communities in Manchester and Salford, 1880–1939*, ed. Andrew Davies and Steven Fielding (Manchester: Manchester University Press, 1992), pp. 102–32.

Emsley, Clive and Mark Clapson, 'Recruiting the English Policeman c.1840–1940', *Policing and Society*, Vol. 3, issue 4. March 1994, pp. 269–85.

Fowler, David, 'Teenage Consumers? Young Wage-earners and Leisure in Manchester, 1919–1939', in *Workers' Worlds: Cultures and Communities in Manchester and Salford, 1880–1939*, ed. Andrew Davies and Steven Fielding (Manchester: Manchester University Press, 1992).

Gaughan, Matthew, 'Palatable Socialism or "the Real Thing"?: Walter Greenwood's *Love on the Dole*', *Literature and History*, Vol. 17, no. 2. 2008, pp. 47–61.

Gittings, Diana G., 'Married Life and Birth Control Between the Wars', *Oral History*, Vol. 3, no. 2. Autumn 1975, pp. 53–64.

Harker, Ben, 'Adapting to the Conjuncture – Walter Greenwood, History and *Love on the Dole*', *Keywords – a Journal of Cultural Materialism*, Vol. 7. 2009, pp. 55–72.

Henry, John, 'The Politics of Pauperism in Salford in the 1920s', *North-West Labour History Journal*, Vol. 33, 2008, pp. 27–36.

Hilliard, Christopher, 'Producers by Hand and by Brain: Working-Class Writers and Left-Wing Publishers in 1930s Britain', *The Journal of Modern History*, Vol. 78. March 2006, pp. 37–64.

Hohman, Helen Fisher, 'The Status of Unemployment Insurance in Great Britain', *Journal of Political Economy*, Vol. 42, no. 6. December 1934, pp. 721–52.

Hopkins, Chris, 'Dialect and Dialect: Region and Nation in Walter Greenwood's Love on the Dole', *Literature of Region and Nation*, Vol. 3, no. 4. 1993, pp. 1–8.

Hopkins, Chris, 'Leftists and Thrillers: the Politics of a Thirties Sub-genre', in *And in Our Time: Literature of the Nineteen Thirties*, ed. Anthony Shuttleworth (Lewisburg PA: Bucknell University Press, 2003), pp. 147–62.

Hopkins, Chris, '"Frustrated Spinsters" and "Morbid Degenerates"?: Women and Men in Winifred Holtby's *Truth is Not Sober* (1934)', in *A Woman in Her Time: Winifred Holtby in Context*, ed. Lisa Regan (Cambridge: Scholar's Press, 2010), pp. 149–71.

Hopkins, Chris, 'The Army of the Unemployed: Walter Greenwood's Wartime Novel and the Reconstruction of Britain', *Keywords – A Journal of Cultural Materialism*, Vol. 10. October 2012, pp. 103–24.

Hunter, Billie, 'Midwifery, 1920–2000: the Reshaping of a Profession', in *Nursing and Midwifery in Britain Since 1700*, ed. Anne Borsay and Billie Hunter (Basingstoke: Palgrave-Macmillan, 2012), pp. 151–74.

Kelley, Victoria, 'The Equitable Consumer: Shopping at the Co-Op in Manchester', *Journal of Design History*, Vol. 11, no. 4. 1998, pp. 295–310.

Levine, Carole, 'Propaganda for Democracy: the Curious Case of *Love on the Dole*', *Journal of British Studies*, Vol. 45. October 2006, pp. 851–65.

Lopez Ortega, Ramon, 'The Language of the Working-Class Novel', in *The Socialist Novel in Britain*, ed. Gustav Klaus (Brighton: Harvester, 1982), pp. 122–44.

Marwick, Arthur, 'Middle Opinion in the Thirties: Planning, Progress and Political Agreement', *The English Historical Review*, Vol. 79, no. 311. April 1964, pp. 285–98.

Napper, Lawrence, 'No Limit: British Class and Comedy of the 1930s', in *British Comedy Cinema*, ed. I.Q. Hunter and Larraine Porter (Abingdon: Routledge, 2012), pp. 39–40.

Salmon, Paul W., Entry on Walter Greenwood in *Dictionary of Literary Biography* Vol. 191 (Detroit, Michigan: Gale Research, 1998).

Snee, Carole, 'Working-Class Literature or Proletarian Writing?' in *Culture and Crisis in Britain in the Thirties*, ed. Jon Clark, Margot Heinemann, David Margolies and Carole Snee (London: Lawrence and Wishart, 1979), pp. 165–91.

Stott, Catherine, 'Dole Cue', *The Guardian*, 2 April 1971, p. 10.

Summerfield, Penelope, 'Education and Politics in the British Armed Services in the Second World War', *International Review of Social History*, Vol. 26, no. 2, August 1981, pp. 133–58.

Tatton, Derek, 'Literature, Culture and the Workers' Education Association', Stephen K. Roberts (ed.), *A Ministry of Enthusiasm: Centenary Essays on the Workers' Educational Association* (London: Pluto Press, 2003).

Tichelar, Michael, 'The Labour Party, Agricultural Policy and the Retreat from Rural Land Nationalisation during the Second World War', *Agricultural History Review*, Vol. 51, no. II. 2003, pp. 209–25.

Warden, Claire, 'Ugliness and Beauty: the Politics of Landscape in Walter Greenwood's *Love on the Dole*', *New Theatre Quarterly*, Vol. 29, no. 1. February 2013, p. 40.

Whitworth, Michael H., 'Enemies of Cant – *The Athenaeum* (1919–21) and *The Adelphi* (1923–48)', in *The Oxford Critical and Cultural History of Modernist Magazines, Vol. I Britain and Ireland 1880–1955*, ed. Peter Brooker and Andrew Thacker (Oxford: Oxford University Press, 2009), pp. 364–88.

Wildman, Charlotte, '*A City Speaks*: The Projection of Civic Identity in Manchester', *Twentieth Century British History*, Vol. 23, no. 1. 2012, pp. 80–89.

Windle, Jack, '"What life means for those at the bottom": *Love on the Dole* and its reception since the 1930s', *Literature & History*, 3rd series, Vol. 20, no. 2, 2011, pp. 35–50.

Worthen, John, 'Towards a New Version of D.H. Lawrence's *The Daughter In Law*: Scholarly Edition or Play Text?', *Yearbook of English Studies*, 1999, pp. 231–46.

Books

Addison, Paul, *The Road to 1945 – British Politics and the Second World War* (London: Pimlico, 1975, 1994).

Ahrenfeldt, Robert H., *Psychiatry in the British Army in the Second World War* (London: Routledge & Kegan Paul, 1958).

Aitken, John, *Film and Reform: John Grierson and the Documentary Film Movement* (London: Routledge, 1990).

Aldgate, Anthony and Jeffrey Richards, *Britain Can Take It: British Cinema in the Second World War* (London: I. B. Tauris, 1986, 2007).

Aldgate, Anthony and James C. Robertson, *Censorship in Theatre and Cinema* (Edinburgh: Edinburgh University Press, 2005).

Ashley, Mike, *The Age of the Storytellers – British Popular Fiction Magazines 1880–1950* (London and New Castle, Delaware: British Library/Oak Knoll Press, 2006).

Atkinson, Neil, *Adventures in Democracy: the History of the Vote in New Zealand* (Dunedin: University of Otago Press/Electoral Commission, 2003).

Bance, Alan F. (ed.), *Weimar Germany: Writers and Politics* (Edinburgh: Scottish Academic Press, 1982).

Barrowman, Rachel, *A Popular Vision: the Arts and the Left in New Zealand, 1930–1950* (Wellington: University of Victoria Press, 1991).

Baxendale, John and Chris Pawling, *Narrating the Thirties: a Decade in the Making 1930 to the Present* (Basingstoke: Palgrave-Macmillan, 1995).

Beale, H. (ed.), *Memoirs of the Unemployed* (London: Victor Gollancz, 1934).

Bellamy, J. and J. Saville MacMillan (eds), *Dictionary of Labour Biography*, Vol. 4 (London: MacMillan, 1977).

Benton, Jill, *Naomi Mitchison – a Biography* (London: Pandora Press, 1990, 1992).

Berlin, Isaiah, *Personal Impressions*, ed. Henry Hardy (London: Hogarth Press, 1980; Kindle edition, 2008).

Berry, David, *Wales & Cinema: the First Hundred Years* (Cardiff: University of Wales Press, 1994).

Bertrand, Ina and Diane Collins, *Government and Film in Australia* (Sydney: Currency Press/The Australian Film Institute, 1981).

Briggs, Asa, *Victorian Cities* (Harmondsworth: Penguin, 1963, 1968, 1990).

Borsay, Anne and Billie Hunter (eds), *Nursing and Midwifery in Britain Since 1700* (Basingstoke: Palgrave-Macmillan, 2012).

Bourke, Joanna, *Working-Class Cultures in Britain 1890–1960: Gender, Cass and Ethnicity* (London: Routledge, 1994).

Bret, David, *Gracie Fields – the Authorised Biography* (London: JR Books, 2010).

Broad, Roger, *The Radical General: Sir Ronald Adam and Britain's New Model Army 1941–46* (Stroud: The History Press, 2003).

Brooks, Judy, *Arthur Wragg: 20th Century Artist, Jester and Prophet* (London: Sansom & Co, 2001, 2007).

Brown, Geoff (with Tony Aldgate), *The Common Touch – the Films of John Baxter* (London: NFT Dossier No. 5. BFI, 1989).

Bruhn, Jørgen, Anne Gjeslvik and Eirik Frisvold Hanssen, *Adaptation Studies: New Challenges, New Directions* (London: Bloomsbury Academic, 2013).

Calder, Angus, *The People's War, Britain 1939–45* (London: Jonathan Cape, 1969; London: Pimlico, 1992).

Calder, Jenni, *The Nine Lives of Naomi Mitchison* (London: Virago Press, 1997).

Cannadine, David, *Class in Britain* (Harmondsworth: Penguin, 2000).

Capua, Michelangelo, *Deborah Kerr – A Biography* (Jefferson, North Carolina: McFarland and Co., 2010).

Carr-Saunders. A. M. and D. Caradog-Jones, *A Survey of the Social Structure of England and Wales*, 2nd edition (Oxford: Oxford University Press, 1937).

Chapman, James, *The British at War: Cinema, State and Propaganda 1939–1945* (London: I. B. Tauris, 1998).

Chinn, Carl, *Better Betting with a Decent Feller: A Social History of Bookmaking* (London: Aurum Press, 2004).

Christoffel, Paul, *Censored: a Short History of Censorship in New Zealand* (Department of Internal Affairs, 1989), available online at <http://www.dia.govt.nz/diawebsite.nsf/wpg_URL/Resource-material-Our-Research-and-Reports-Censored-A-Short-History-of-Censorship-in-New-Zealand>, accessed 24 October 2017.

Clapson, Mark, *A Bit of a Flutter: Popular Gambling and English Society 1823–1961* (Manchester: Manchester University Press, 1992).

Clark, Jon, Margot Heinemann, David Margolies and Carole Snee, *Culture and Crisis in Britain in the Thirties* (London: Lawrence and Wishart, 1979).

Clark, Kenneth, *The Other Half – a Self-Portrait* (London: John Murray, 1977).

Clark, Manning, *History of Australia* (1962; abridged, London: Pimlico, 1993).

Cohen, M., *I was One of the Unemployed* (London: Gollancz, 1945).

Collins, Tony, *Rugby League in Twentieth-Century Britain: a Social and Cultural History* (London: Routledge, 2006; Kindle edition 2006).

Constantine, Stephen, *Unemployment in Britain Between the Wars*, Seminar Studies in History (Harlow: Longman, 1980).

Cook, Chris and John Stevenson, *The Slump: Britain in the Great Depression* (London: Longman, 2010).

Crang, Jeremy A., *The British Army and the People's War 1939–1945* (Manchester: Manchester University Press, 2000).

Croft, Andy, *Red Letter Days: British Fiction in the 1930s* (London: Lawrence and Wishart, 1990).

Crusher, Richard, *We Refuse to Starve in Silence – a History of the National Unemployed Workers' Movement, 1920–1946* (London: Lawrence and Wishart, 1987).

Cunningham, Valentine, *British Writers of the Thirties* (Oxford: Oxford University Press, 1988).

Danischevsky, M. (ed.), *Michael Balcon's 25 Years in Films* (London: World Film Publications, 1947).

Davies, Andrew, *Leisure, Gender and Poverty: Working-class Culture in Salford and Manchester 1900–1939* (Buckingham: Open University Press, 1992).

Davies, Andrew and Steven Fielding, *Workers' Worlds: Cultures and Communities in Manchester and Salford, 1880–1939* (Manchester: Manchester University Press, 1992).

Davison, Peter, *George Orwell – a Literary Life* (Basingstoke: Macmillan, 1996).

Davy, Charles (ed.), *Footnotes to the Film* (London: Lovat Dickson/The Readers' Union, 1938).

Day, Gary, *Class*, New Critical Idiom Series (London: Routledge, 1991).

Debenham, Clare, *Grassroots Feminism: a Study of the Campaign of the Society for the Provision of Birth Control Clinics 1924–1938* (PhD Thesis, Manchester: University of Manchester, 2010).

Dictionary of National Biography (online).

Disinherited Youth, Carnegie UK Trust (London: Constable, 1943).

D'Monté Rebecca, *British Theatre and Performance 1900–1950* (London: Bloomsbury Methuen, 2015, Kindle edition, 2015).

Donnison, Jean, *Midwives and Medical Men: a History of the Struggle for the Control of Childbirth* (London: Heinemann Educational Books, 1977; London: Historical Publications Ltd, 1988).

Dummelow, John, *1899–1949 Metropolitan Vickers Electrical Company* (Manchester: Metropolitan Vickers, 1949; published online by Jim Lawton, nd, and available via Grace's Guides to British Industrial History: <http://www.gracesguide.co.uk/Metropolitan-Vickers_Electrical_Co_1899–1949_by_John_Dummelow:_1929–1939>, accessed 24 October 2017).

Duncan, Robert, *Pubs and Patriots: the Drink Crisis in Britain During World War One* (Liverpool: Liverpool University Press, 2013).

Dyhouse, Carol, *Glamour: Women, History, Feminism* (London: Zed Books, 2010; Kindle edition, 2013).

Earnshaw, Steven, *The Pub in Literature: England's Altered State* (Manchester: Manchester University Press, 2000).

Emsley, Clive, *The English Police: a Political and Social History* (Harlow: Routledge, 1991, 1995).

Emsley, Clive, *Hard Men: The English and Violence Since 1750* (London: Bloomsbury, 2005).

Encyclopedia Britannica

Fielding, Steve, *The Salford Labour Party – a Brief Introduction to the Microfilm Edition of the Salford Labour Party Records* (Wakefield: Microform Academic Publishers, 1997) online at <http://www.microform.co.uk/guides/R97555.pdf>, accessed 24 October 2017.

Flynn, Tony, *Hanky Park* (Salford: Neil Richardson, 1990).

Flynn, Tony, *The History of Salford Cinemas* (Salford: Neil Richardson, 1987).

Fox, Pamela, *Class Fictions – Shame and Resistance in the British Working-Class Novel, 1890–1945* (London: Duke University Press, 1994).

Frances, Martin, *The Flyer – British Culture and the RAF 1939–1945* (Oxford: Oxford University Press, 2008).

Frankenburg, Charis, *Not Old, Madam, Vintage – an Autobiography* (Lavenham: Galaxy Press, 1975).

Fraser, Derek, *The Evolution of the British Welfare State*, 4th edn (Basingstoke: Palgrave Macmillan, 2009).

Frow, Edmund and Ruth, *Radical Salford – Episodes in Labour History* (Manchester: Neil Richardson, 1984).

Frow, Edmund and Ruth, *The Battle of Bexley Square: Salford Unemployed Workers' Demonstration, 1st October 1931* (Manchester: Working Class Movement Library, 1994).

Greene, Graham, *The Old School – Essays by Divers Hands* (London: Jonathan Cape, 1934; Oxford: Oxford University Press reprint, 1984).

Greenwood, Walter, *How the Other Man Lives* (London: Labour Book Service, 1940).

Greenwood, Walter, *Lancashire*, County Book Series (London: Hale, 1951).

Greenwood, Walter, *There Was a Time* (London: Jonathan Cape, 1967).

Grover, Mary, *The Ordeal of Warwick Deeping: Middlebrow Authorship and Cultural Embarrassment* (Madison: Fairleigh Dickinson Press, 2009).

Hannington, Wal, *The Problem of the Distressed Areas* (London: Gollancz, 1937).

Hannington, Wal, *Unemployed Struggles 1919–1936* (London: Lawrence and Wishart, 1936, 1977).

Hawthorn, Jeremy (ed.), *The British Working-Class Novel in the Twentieth Century* (London: Edward Arnold, 1984).

Hayward, Ian, *Working-Class Fiction from Chartism to Trainspotting* (London: Edward Arnold, 1997).

Hazelgrove, Jenny, *Spiritualism and British Society Between the Wars* (Manchester: Manchester University Press, 2000).

Hibberd, E. A., *The Brittlesnaps* (London: Duckworth, 1937).

Hilliard, Christopher, *To Exercise Our Talents: the Democratization of Writing in Britain* (Cambridge, Massachusetts/London: Harvard University Press, 2006).

Hopkins, Chris, *English Fiction in the 1930s: Language, Genre, History* (London: Continuum, 2006).

Howard, Michael S., *Jonathan S. Cape, Publisher* (Harmondsworth: Penguin, 1977).

Hunter, Billie and Nicola Leap, *The Midwife's Tale – an Oral History from Handywoman to Professional Midwife* (London: Scarlet Press, 1993).

Hunter, I. Q. and Larraine Porter (eds), *British Comedy Cinema* (Abingdon: Routledge, 2012).

Huntley, John, *British Film Music* (London: Skelton Robinson, 1947).

Johnson, George M. (ed.), *Dictionary of Literary Biography Vol. 191: British Novelists Between the Wars* (Detroit, Michigan: Gale Research, 1998).

Kirk, John, *Twentieth Century Writing and the British Working Class* (Cardiff: University of Wales Press, 2003).

Klaus, Gustav, ed. *The Socialist Novel in Britain* (Brighton: Harvester, 1982).

Knox, Pamela, *The Flame Still Burns – the Story of Altrincham Garrick Theatre* (Altrincham: Altrincham Garrick Theatre, 1993).

Kunitz, Stanley J. and Howard Haycraft (eds), *Twentieth Century Authors: a Biographical Dictionary of Modern Literature* (New York: H. W. Wilson, 1942).

Leavis, Q. D., *Fiction and the Reading Public* (London: Chatto & Windus, 1932).

Lilly, Mark, *The National Council for Civil Liberties: the First Fifty Years* (London: Macmillan, 1984).

Low, Rachel, *Film Making in 1930s Britain* (London: Allen & Unwin, 1985).

Lowell, James Russell, *The Writings: Miscellaneous Poems* (London: Macmillan).

Lusty, Robert, *Bound to Be Read* (London: Jonathan Cape, 1975).

MacColl, Ewan, *Journeyman* (London: Sidgewick & Jackson, 1990).

Mackenzie, S. P., *Politics and Military Morale: Current Affairs and Citizenship Education in the British Army 1914–1950* (Oxford: Clarendon Press, 1992).

McKibbin, Ross, *The Ideologies of Class: Social Relations in Britain 1880–1950* (Oxford: Clarendon Press, 1994).

McLaine, Ian, *The Ministry of Morale: Home Front Morale and the Ministry of Information in World War II* (London: George Allen & Unwin, 1979).

McNab, Geoffrey, *J. Arthur Rank and the British Film Industry* (London: Routledge, 1993).

Madge, Charles and Tom Harrison, *Britain by Mass-Observation* (Harmondsworth: Penguin, 1939).

Mannin, Ethel, *Young in the Twenties – a Chapter of Autobiography* (London: Hutchison, 1971).

Miles, Peter and Malcolm Smith, *Cinema, Literature & Society: Elite and Mass Society in Interwar Britain* (London: Croom Helm, 1987).

Miram, Gordon, *Speaking Candidly – Films and People in New Zealand* (Hamilton: Paul's Book Arcade, 1945).

Mowat, Charles Loch, *Britain Between the Wars 1918–1940* (London: Methuen, 1955, 1968).

Muggeridge, Malcolm, *The Thirties: 1930–1940 in Great Britain* (London: Weidenfeld and Nicolson, 1989).

Murphy, Robert, *British Cinema and the Second World War* (London: Continuum, 2001).

Murphy, Robert, *Realism and Tinsel: Cinema and Society in Britain 1939–1949* (London: Routledge, 1989, 1992).

Napper, Lawrence, *British Cinema and Middlebrow Culture in the Interwar Years* (Exeter: University of Exeter Press, 2009).

Nicholl, Robert, *Trafford Park – the First Hundred Years* (Chichester: Phillimore, 1996).

Nicholson, Steve, *The Censorship of British Drama 1932–1952* (Exeter: University of Exeter Press, 2000).

Overy, Richard, *The Morbid Age: Britain and the Crisis of Civilization 1919–1939* (London: Allen Lane, 2009; Harmondsworth: Penguin, 2010).

Oxford English Dictionary (online).

Phelan, James, *Living to Tell About It – a Rhetoric and Ethic of Character Narration* (London and Ithaca, New York: Cornell University Press, 2005).

Pollard, Sydney, *The Development of the British Economy 1914–1980* (London: Arnold, 1983).

Powell, Dilys, *Films Since 1939* (London: Longmans, Green and Co for the British Council, 1947).

Pythian, Graham, *Blitz Britain: Manchester and Salford* (Stroud: The History Press, 2015; Kindle edition, 2015).

Rattigan, Neil, *This is England: British Film and the People's War, 1939–1945* (London: Associated University Presses, 2001).

Reeve, N. H., *The Novels of Rex Warner* (London: Palgrave Macmillan, 1989).

Richards, Jeffrey, *The Age of the Dream Palace: Cinema and Society in Britain, 1930–1939* (London: Routledge, 1984; New York: I. B. Tauris, 2010).

Richards, Jeffrey, *Films and British National Identity – from Dickens to Dad's Army* (Manchester: Manchester University Press, 1997).

Richards, Jeffrey and Anthony Aldgate, *Best of British – Cinema and Society 1930–1970* (Oxford: Basil Blackwell, 1983).

Richards, Jeffrey and Dorothy Sheridan (eds), *Mass Observation at the Movies* (London: Routledge, 1987).

Robb, George, *British Culture and the Great War* (Basingstoke, Palgrave, 2002).

Roberts, Robert, *The Classic Slum – Salford Life in the First Quarter of the Century* (Harmondsworth: Penguin, 1978).

Roberts, Stephen K. (ed.), *A Ministry of Enthusiasm: Centenary Essays on the Workers' Educational Association* (London: Pluto Press, 2003).

Ross, Stephen A., 'Authenticity Betrayed: the "Idiot Folk" of Love on the Dole', *Cultural Critique*, Vol. 56. December 2004, pp. 189–209.

Russell, Dave, *Looking North – Northern England and the National Imagination* (Manchester: Manchester University Press, 2004).

Shellard, Dominic, Steve Nicholson and Miriam Handley, *The Lord Chamberlain Regrets: a History of British Theatre Censorship* (London: The British Library, 2004).

Shephard, Ben, *A War of Nerves: Soldiers and Psychiatrists 1914–1994* (London: Cape, 2000).

Sherry, Norman, *The Life of Graham Greene 1904–1939*, Vol. 1 (London: Jonathan Cape, 1989).

Shuttleworth, Anthony, *And in Our Time: Literature of the Nineteen Thirties* (Bucknell: Bucknell University Press, 2003).

Stevenson, John, *British Society 1914–1945*, Penguin Social History of Britain (Harmondsworth: Penguin, 1984).

Stevenson, John and Chris Cook, *Britain in the Depression: Society and Politics 1929–39* (London: Longman, 1994).

Stocks, Mary Danvers (Baroness Stocks), *Fifty Years in Every Street* (Manchester: Manchester University Press, 1944).

Taylor, A. J. P., *English History 1914–1945* (Oxford: Oxford University Press, 1965; Harmondsworth, Penguin, 1970).

Thomas, David, David Carlton and Anne Etienne, *Theatre Censorship from Walpole to Wilson* (Oxford: Oxford University Press, 2007).

Thorpe, Andrew, *Britain in the 1930s: the Deceptive Decade* (Oxford, Blackwell, 1992).

Thorpe, Andrew, *The British General Election of 1931* (Oxford: Clarendon Press, 1991).

Tilley, John, *Churchill's Favourite Socialist – a Life of A.V. Alexander* (Manchester: Holyoake Press, 1995).

Topman, J. and J. A. Hough, *The Co-operative movement in Britain*, with foreword by A. V. Alexander (London: Longmans, 1944, 1948).

Tressell, Robert, *The Ragged Trousered Philanthropists* (London: The Richards Press, 1914, 1946).

Ware, Susan, *Still Missing: Amelia Earhart and the Search for Modern Feminism* (New York: W. W. Norton and Co, 1993).

Warner, Rex, *The Aerodrome* (Harmondsworth: Penguin, 1941).

Watt, Harry, *Don't Look at the Camera* (London: Elek, 1974).

Webster, Roger, 'Love on the Dole and the Aesthetic of Contradiction', in *The British Working-Class Novel in the Twentieth Century*, ed. Jeremy Hawthorn (London: Edward Arnold, 1984), pp. 49–61.

Weinberger, Barbara, *The Best Police in the World – an Oral History of English Policing* (Aldershot: Scholar Press, 1995).

Whitman, Willson, *Bread and Circuses: a Study of Federal Theatre* (New York: Oxford University Press, 1937).

Williams, Jenny, *More Lives Than One: a Biography of Hans Fallada* (London: Libris, 1998).

Williamson, Henry, *A Patriot's Progress* (with illustrations by William Kermode) (London: Geoffrey Bles, 1930).

Wilson, Nicola, *Home in British Working-Class Fiction* (Farnham: Ashgate, 2015).

Worley, Matthew, *Labour Inside the Gate – a History of the British Labour Party Between the Wars* (London: I. B. Tauris, 2000).

Websites

Arthur Lloyd History of Music Hall and Theatre website: <http://www.arthurlloyd.co.uk/ManchesterTheatres/RusholmeTheatreManchester.htm>.

Australian War memorial site: <https://www.awm.gov.au/findingaids/special/Souvenirs/ww2ctp.xml>.

The BBC Genome Project: <http://genome.ch.bbc.co.uk/>.

BFI Screen-Online: <http://www.screenonline.org.uk/>.

The Birth of Television archive: <http://www.birth-of-tv.org/birth/assetView. do?asset=1413260435_1147261168>.

The Changi POW Artwork of Des Bettany: <http://changipowart.com/ archives/703>.

Close Up North: Love on the Dole (Director: Lyn Webster Wilde; Halcyon Productions, BBC North, 28 minutes, 1/12/1994 (WGC/7/18/3); can be watched on YouTube: <https://www.youtube.com/watch?v=E25CcYw4s8M &nohtml5=False>.

Collins, Tony, 'Where's George? League's Forgotten Feature Film': <http:// tony-collins.squarespace.com/rugbyreloaded/2013/6/8/wheres-george-rugby-leagues-forgotten-feature-film> (originally published in *Forty-20* magazine in 2012).

Denman, James, and Paul McDonald, *Labour Market Trends: Unemployment Statistics from 1881 till the Present Day*, 1996: <www.ons.gov.uk/ons/rel/ lms/labour-market-trends--discontinued-/january-1996/unemployment-since-1881.pdf>.

George Mason University Federal Theatre Material Project site: <http://www. aladino.wrlc.org/gsdl/collect/ftpp/ftpp. shtml>.

Glasgow University Library Left Book Club titles: <http://www.gla.ac.uk/ services/specialcollections/collectionsa-z/leftbookclub/>.

Greenpark Images <http://greenparkimages.co.uk/history.html>.

Internet Movie Database: <http://www.imdb.com/?ref_=nv_home>.

Lost Hospitals of London site: <http://ezitis.myzen.co.uk/belmont.html>.

Manchester's Radical History website: <http://radicalmanchester.wordpress. com/2011/04/13/contraceptives-clinics-and-working-class-women-salford-manchester-mothers%E2%80%99-clinic/>.

Mullen, Chris, 'The Alphabet of Illustrators', *The Visual Telling of Stories*, <http://www.fulltable.com/vts/aoi/w/wragg/menuz.htm>.

New Zealand Office of Licensing and Classification History of Censorship page: <http://www.censor.org.nz/resources/history/1943.html>.

Reading 1900–1950 blog: <https://reading19001950.wordpress.com/>.

Rusholme and Victoria Park Archive site: <http://rusholmearchive. org/a-tour-of-wilmslow-road>.

Sagar, Keith, 'D.H. Lawrence: Dramatist' (2008): <http://www.keithsagar. co.uk/moderndrama/lawrencedramatist.pdf>.

Salford Blue plaque site: <http://www.blueplaqueplaces.co.uk/battle-of-bexley-square-red-plaque-in-salford-30214#.VUTQhv7wtiA>.

Saturday Night Theatre – a Tribute to BBC Radio Drama: <http://www. saturday-night-theatre.co.uk/broadcasts.php>.

Tameside blue plaque site: <http://www.tameside.gov.uk/blueplaque/ eliwhalley>.

Television Heaven website: <http://www.televisionheaven.co.uk/love_on_the_dole.htm>.

The Playwrights' Database: <http://www.doollee.com/PlaywrightsG/gow-ronald.html#14170>.

The Tolpuddle Martyrs' website: <http://www.tolpuddlemartyrs.org.uk/story>.

This is Lancashire site: <http://archive.thisislancashire.co.uk/2003/4/22/555294.html>.

TimeImage wikispace: <http://timeimage.wikispaces.com/Home>.

Timeline of the events of World War 2: <http://en.wikipedia.org/wiki/Timeline_of_World_War_II_(1941)#June_1941>.

Walter Greenwood interview (Kersal Flats local history channel): <https://www.youtube.com/watch?v=J1xr1UwLbQo>.

Wikipedia entry for 'Perm': <http://en.wikipedia.org/wiki/Perm_(hairstyle)>.

Working Class Movement Library website entry on Greenwood: <http://www.wcml.org.uk/contents/creativity-and-culture/drama-and-literature/walter-greenwood-and-love-on-the-dole-/>.

Wroe, Nicholas, interview with Edward Upward, *The Guardian*, 23 August 2003: <http://www.guardian.co.uk/books/2003/aug/23/featuresreviews.guardianreview10>.

Index

working class 1, 9, 44, 46, 48,
50–53, 55, 59, 60, 67, 73, 79, 89,
91, 96, 98, 101, 103, 104, 105, 107,
111, 116, 117, 119, 124, 127, 128n37,
131–38, 142–44, 147, 154, 156, 158,
160, 169, 173, 176, 178–79, 183,
186–88, 190, 192, 196, 203, 204,
206, 207, 211, 212, 215–17, 219,
227, 228, 229–30, 232–33, 235,
237, 251–55, 258–59, 265, 267–69,
276–77, 281
women 40–41, 63, 66–69, 71–74,
81–90, 98, 100, 101, 104, 123–26,
131–32, 156, 162–65

fortune-telling and séance
124–26, 128
writing by 16, 216, 221, 223n97,
224, 225, 259
Worley, Matthew 209
Worthen, John
'Towards a New Version of
D. H. Lawrence's *The Daughter
In Law*: Scholarly Edition or
Play Text?' 109n2
Wragg, Arthur 87n86, 155, 199,
211n69, 212–13, 215, 248
Jesus Wept 199n33
Psalms for Modern Life 199n33